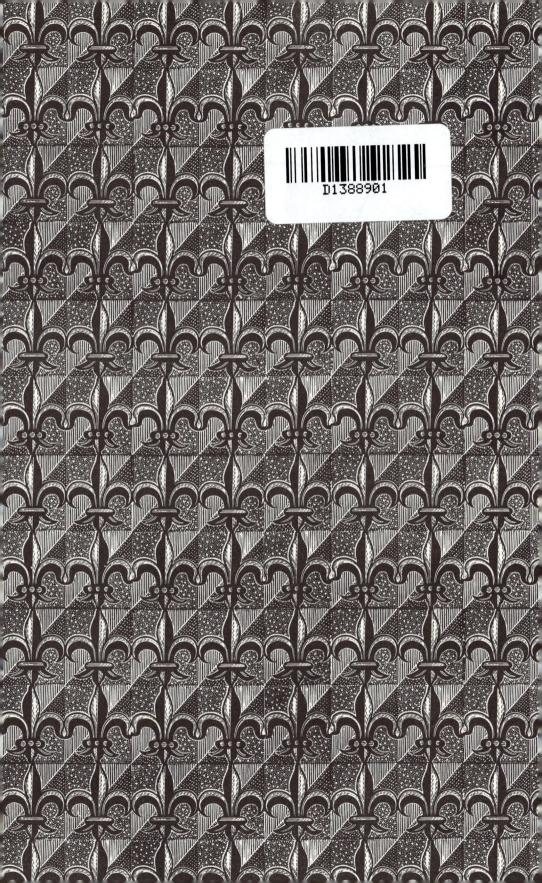
D1388901

A. J. P. Taylor

A. J. P. Taylor

A Biography

ADAM SISMAN

SINCLAIR-STEVENSON

First published in Great Britain in 1994
by Sinclair-Stevenson
an imprint of Reed Consumer Books Ltd
Michelin House, 81 Fulham Road, London SW3 6RB
and Auckland, Melbourne, Singapore and Toronto

Copyright © 1994 by Adam Sisman

The right of Adam Sisman to be identified as author
of this work has been asserted by him in accordance
with the Copyright, Design and Patent Act 1988.

The author and the publishers thank those listed below for copyright permission to reproduce the following: the estate of A. J. P. Taylor and David Higham Ltd for published and unpublished material; Penguin Books Ltd and the Librarian of the University of Bristol for material from the archives of Hamish Hamilton; the Delegates of the Oxford University Press for extracts from A. J. P. Taylor's published work and other material from their editorial files; Macmillan Publishers Ltd for material from their editorial files; the History of Parliament Trust; the BBC Written Archives Centre; the Trustees of the Liddell Hart Centre for Military Archives; the Clerk of the Records of the House of Lords acting on behalf of the Beaverbrook Trustees; the Humanities Research Center; the University of Sussex Library; the John Rylands University Library of Manchester; the *Guardian*; Wheaton College and the estate of the late Malcolm Muggeridge for material from his published and unpublished writings; the estate of the late Sir George Clark and the Delegates of the Oxford University Press for material from the Clark papers; the estate of the late Dylan Thomas and David Higham Ltd for material from the *Collected Letters of Dylan Thomas*; Mrs Jane Aiken Hodge and the estate of the late Norman Cameron for an extract from his poem 'The Dirty Little Accuser'. Every effort has been made to trace the copyright holders of quoted material and photographs. If, however, there are inadvertent omissions, these can be rectified in any future editions.

A CIP catalogue record for this book
is available at the British Library

ISBN 1 85619 2105

Typeset by Wilmaset Ltd, Birkenhead, Wirral
Printed and bound in Great Britain by
Mackays of Chatham plc, Chatham, Kent

To my father

Contents

Acknowledgements

My first thanks must go to Eva Taylor, for showing confidence in me initially and for her generosity, hospitality and encouragement throughout. She read the typescript as it was being written and offered comments, but never attempted to dictate what I should write. I am lucky that A.J.P. Taylor's widow is an historian in her own right, well aware that 'history is a version of events'. I should make it clear, however, that this is not her version, nor is it an official nor an authorised biography.

I owe a special debt to those others who read all or part of the typescript: Lord Dacre, Dr Richard Davenport-Hines, Martin Gilbert, Bruce Hunter, Pat and Mary Thompson, Katrina Whone and Professor Chris Wrigley. All of them have helped to make it a better book. It may be thought invidious to single out one person when I owe so much to so many, but I must give particular thanks to Kathleen Tillotson, who not only read the typescript but gave up much time to discuss it with me, chapter by chapter. She has patiently encouraged me to raise my standards, and often pointed out new lines of enquiry.

Many others read particular passages and gave me their comments: Dr Arthur and Joyce Adams, David Ayerst, E. J. Brown, Paul Ferris, Sheila Gregson, David Holloway, Robert Kee, Keith Kyle, Ruth McInroy, Dr Richard Overy, Geoffrey Rowntree, Clifford Smith, Dr Anthony Storr, David and Sylvia Worswick. I am very grateful to all of them. However, I have not always taken the advice I have been given, and I bear sole responsibility for what I have written.

One of the pleasures of writing this book was that it gave me the opportunity to meet so many interesting people. What surprised me was the hospitality and generosity shown to me by often busy and distinguished individuals, many of whom gave me more than one interview. I have been entertained to lunch, to tea, for drinks, in places ranging from El Vino's to the House of Lords dining-room. Some have welcomed me into their homes. I am grateful to them all, and only wish I had the space to express my thanks more graciously than in this list: Janet Adam Smith, Dr Paul Addison, Lord Annan, Ivon Asquith, Roy Avery, Dr Gerald Aylmer, The Right Hon. Kenneth Baker MP, Lord Beloff, Michael Beloff, Veronica Benjamin, Sir Isaiah Berlin, Lucia Biocca, Lord Blake, Katharine Bligh, Jane Bradly, Lord Briggs, Maxwell Bruce, Peter Burnstone, Dr James Campbell, Dr David Carlton, Sir Raymond Carr, Anne Chisholm, Professor Ian R. Christie, Professor Richard Cobb, Professor Robert Cole, Dr Chris Cook, Arthur Crook, Michael Davie, Hunter Davies, Len Deighton, Professor David Dilks, Professor Sir Kenneth Dover, Bob Doyle, Amelia Fell, Doris Fell, Michael Foot, Professor M. R. D. Foot, Margaret Forster, Professor Norman Gash, Sarah Gaskell, Suzie Gautier-Smith, Ann Giles, Professor Alfred Gollin, Richard Gott, John Grigg, Daisy Groves, Crystal Hale, Professor Colin and Christian Hardie, Dr Henry Hardy, Professor J. D. Hargreaves, Professor Cameron Hazlehurst, Sir Nicholas Henderson, Professor W. O. Henderson, Alastair Hetherington, Dr J. R. L. Highfield, Bevis Hillier, Della Hilton, Professor Sir Harry Hinsley, Professor E. J. Hobsbawm, Paul and Eunice Holliday, Alistair Horne, Anthony Howard, Professor Sir Michael Howard, Professor Gerald Howat, Sir David Hunt, Richard Ingrams, Professor Douglas Johnson, Paul Johnson, Professor James Joll, Mervyn Jones, Professor Denis Judd, Sir John Junor, Cynthia Kee, Janetta Kee, Betty Kemp, Terence Kilmartin, Professor Anthony King, Dr Peter Laslett, Professor Karl Leyser, Lord and Lady Longford, Professor William Roger Louis, Dr Peter Lowe, The Hon. Adrian Lyttelton, James MacGibbon, Dr Angus Macintyre, Dermott Manning, Professor David Marquand, Kathy Marten, Professor Arthur Marwick, Professor William H. McNeill, June Mendoza, Leonard Miall, Professor Karl Miller, Eddie Mirzoeff, Pamela Monkhouse, Roger Moore, Professor Kenneth O. Morgan, Jack Muggeridge, Eddie Mullins, J. P. H. Myers, Lord Justice O'Connor, Mary O'Neill, Alan Palmer, Dr Henry Pelling, John Prestwich, David Pryce-Jones, Giles Radice MP,

Agatha Ramm, Charles Ringrose, Professor Keith Robbins, Professor Adam Roberts, Sarah Roberts, Lord Rodgers, Professor John Roskell, Dr John Rosselli, Jennifer Rowntree, Dr A. L. Rowse, Stephen Sartin, Christopher Seton-Watson, Sir Maurice Shock, Susanna Shonfield, Dr Alan Sked, Lord Skidelsky, Sir Richard Southern, George Speaight, Sir Stephen and Lady Spender, J. I. M. Stewart, Lestor Steynor, Dr Eric Stone, Professor Norman Stone, Professor Paul Streeten, Ivan Sutton, Dr Leslie Sutton, Dr Helen Szamuely, Amelia Taylor, Dr Arnold Taylor, Daniel Taylor, Marjorie Taylor, Professor Howard Temperley, Llewelyn Thomas, Dr William E. S. Thomas, Brian Thompson, Bridget Thompson, Joy Thompson, Robin Thompson, Martina Thomson, Professor Richard H. Ullman, Professor John Vincent, Professor R. Vogel, Geoffrey Warr, Alan Watkins, Professor Donald Cameron Watt, Francis Wheen, David Wiseman, Professor J. Z. Young. If inadvertently I have left out anybody I apologise.

I am also grateful to those, too numerous to name, who replied to my advertisements in the *Times Literary Supplement*, the *London Review of Books*, the *New York Times Book Review*, and *Oxford Today*; and to the alumni of The Downs, Bootham and Oriel who responded to my circular letters.

The staff of various libraries and archives have lent me their professional help, and guided me when I was lost. If I have singled out a few individuals it does not mean that I am not grateful to the rest. My thanks, then, to the staff of the BBC Written Archives Centre, Caversham; the Bodleian Library; Bristol University Library; the British Library; the Brotherton Collection, Leeds; the History of Parliament; Kate Wheeler of the House of Lords Record Office; the Humanities Research Center, Austin, Texas, and Cathy Henderson in particular; King's College, London; the London Library; the London School of Economics Library; Jacquie Sen of the University of Manchester John Rylands Library; Elizabeth Inglis of the University of Sussex Library; and the Buswell Memorial Library of Wheaton College, Illinois. I am also grateful to the archivists of A.J.P. Taylor's schools and colleges: The Downs (Donald Boyd), Bootham (Clifford Smith); Oriel (Elizabeth Boardman); and Magdalen (Dr Janie Curtis). Andrew Auster, headmaster of The Downs, was very hospitable, but made me pay by asking me to deliver an impromptu speech about A.J.P. Taylor to an audience of school-children. Peter Foden, the Archivist of Oxford University Press, and John Handford, his equivalent at Macmillan, were both exceptionally helpful. Andrew Franklin of Hamish Hamilton and his secretary Jane patiently tolerated my time-consuming enquiries. Nicci Gerrard and Michael Ratcliffe at the *Observer* were unfailingly hospitable, allowing me to work under their feet for several days; my thanks to them both. The most unusual research I conducted was in the David Higham archives. These are situated partly in the Humanities Research Center; partly in a North London garage; and partly in the Higham offices – there I made some of my search in a small box-room located inside the ladies' lavatories. For this unique experience I thank Bruce Hunter; and for his help in many other ways.

Two teachers stimulated my interest in history and then encouraged me to believe that I should pursue my studies, albeit belatedly. I owe a great debt to both Keith Perry and Dr Colin Brooks.

I should like to thank George and Marjorie Misiewicz and Susanna Wadeson for practical assistance during the writing of the book. Vera Collingwood has expertly copied photographs, some of them in poor condition; she has also photographed some of the places where A.J.P. Taylor lived. She is a thorough professional, and I record my gratitude to her.

I am especially grateful to the Hélène Horoys Foundation, which twice made me generous grants; without its help this book could not have been written.

When I was an editor in various publishing houses I assumed that Christopher Sinclair-Stevenson's reputation as a prince among editors was exaggerated. I have been embarrassed to discover that it is fully deserved. I have made all the mistakes for which I used to curse my authors; but Christopher has sustained me throughout. I am lucky to have my first book published by him. I should also like to thank Neil Taylor and Emma Rhind-Tutt for their work on the typescript, and Rachel Peddie for her work on the proofs.

Lastly, I want to thank my wife, Robyn Sisman. She has not typed the manuscript, but she has done almost everything else to make it possible. Most of all she encouraged me to believe I could write this book, and gave me the steel to do so.

A. J. P. Taylor

Prologue: *North and South*

Somewhere south of Manchester, but north of Oxford, a line runs across England. Above the line is the England of the Industrial Revolution, of the 'dark satanic mills' formed in the eighteenth and especially in the nineteenth century. In the Midlands, and on each side of the Pennines sit great cities, attended by smaller industrial towns. The valleys are choked with mean and functional buildings, climbing the slopes so that even the Peaks are despoiled. Everywhere Nature is beaten down, obscured, defiled. The clear streams have been harnessed to serve the god of Production, and emerge soiled and tamed from the mills. Even the mountains have been conquered, by the railways and especially by the canals which ascend their slopes in astonishing sequences of locks. Clean and quiet now, these cities were until the beginning of this century the workshop of the world, the manufacturing heartland of a mighty empire, and the engine of the world's trade. The air tasted filthy; the sky was full of smoking chimneys.

Below that line is a different England. Apart from the capital itself, there are no cities of any great size, only a few ports. Even London has never been a manufacturing city like those of the north. Outside its sprawl lies a pastoral landscape, farmland studded with ancient market-towns. The hills are lower and less threatening; their slopes are decked with fields, not buildings. The rivers are cleaner, and when they were put to work it was to drive medieval flour or corn mills, not prostituted to serve the needs of industry. Before the coming of the motorways and the great power stations the air was pure.

The people, too, seem different and were more so than they are now. The people of the rural South lived in a society which until this century had changed only slowly. They were more settled and, if not necessarily contented, they tended to accept the way things were. Wealth was associated with land, putting a physical barrier between rich and poor. This was a conservative England, which worshipped in the Established Church on Sundays. Tradition was important, and in a place like Oxford that tradition might stretch back to the Middle Ages. Only in Wales and in the West Country, where a different sort of society prevailed, was this order seriously challenged.

The people of the industrial North were a new people. The cities themselves had sprung up and grown with astonishing speed. The rich were often newly so; their origins were the same as the poor they employed, and they tended to speak the same way; they shared many of the same habits. It was not hard to distinguish the new rich from the old. As for the poor, they led what now seem to us wretched lives in grim surroundings. Marx believed that these would be the vanguard of the revolutionary proletariat. Tradition counted for little in such a new society; and the religions men and women embraced were those that dispensed with priestly ritual, the nonconformist churches which spoke directly to men's consciences.

Cotton was king in Lancashire. The cotton industry created the towns in the first place; it was the cotton mills which dominated the skyline, and it was the cotton workers who inhabited the low houses which lined the streets. Early in the morning a tap on the window summoned them to work; their clogs could be heard clip-clopping down the cobbles.

Perhaps the greatest of these industrial cities was Manchester. In 1900 Manchester could hold up its head alongside London. Prosperous and vital, it was the centre of the world's trade in cotton, the unofficial capital of the industrial North-West. Merchant princes walked its streets. The city itself was full of fine Victorian buildings expressing confidence and pride in every soaring Gothic tower. Some of these housed a university which, the burghers determined, would rival the traditional centres of learning at Oxford and Cambridge. This was not the provinces; this was the quintessence of metropolitan life.

1: *Home Alone*

Alan John Percivale Taylor was born in Birkdale, about
twenty miles up the Lancashire coast from the Mersey
estuary, on 25 March 1906. Two months earlier there had
been a general election, and his mother, though confined by her
pregnancy to a bathchair, had waited for hours every day outside
the local newspaper offices to hear the results as they came in. 'I
witnessed the 1906 election from a privileged position,' Alan
would say later. His mother and father were intensely interested in
politics. Alan's father was active in the Liberal Party, speaking on
platforms and taking the chair at meetings. Many of his political
associates came to the house, and one of Alan's earliest memories
was shaking hands with the Liberal candidate for Southport, the
millionaire Austrian Baron de Forest.

The Liberal victory of 1906 was a landslide. The Liberals, under
the leadership of Sir Henry Campbell-Bannerman, obtained 377
seats, 220 more than their Unionist (Conservative) rivals who had
ruled the country since 1895. Many of the new Members of
Parliament were wealthy businessmen, like Alan's father; a good
many of them came from the industrial regions of England, as the
Taylors did; and a high proportion of them were nonconformists in
religion, like the Taylors. These men – they were all men – believed
in solid Victorian values, in the sanctity of contract and the
improving power of free trade. They were impatient with the
superstitions of the past, and they believed in Progress. The world
was steadily becoming a better place. They took it for granted that
all the causes they supported would be won in good time. Was not
their own prosperity itself evidence of the efficacy of their ideas?

Alan's father Percy was a Manchester cotton merchant, a

member of the 'Cottonocracy'. Every morning he would take the train into town, where he was the senior partner in the family firm. He wore a blue serge suit and a bowler hat, and as he set off to the station he would light the first of the day's Havana cigars.

The firm's headquarters were at Calcutta House, in Chepstow Street near the city centre. A uniformed commissionaire waited to open the door at the top of a broad flight of steps. Horsedrawn carts, labelled 'James Taylor and Sons' and piled high with cotton bales, drew up at the side. The name of the building hinted at the nature of the business, which was exporting cotton cloth lengths to India and China. When Alan was born the trade was thriving. Later in the century it would turn right around, cloth from India being exported back to England.

Alan's paternal grandfather, James Taylor, was a self-made man who had started life as a weaver. Tall and bluff, 'J.T.' spoke the Lancashire dialect. His father Edmund had arrived in the county from Scotland and had set up a store in Heywood, a town ten miles or so north of Manchester, marrying a local girl, Maria Ashworth. James was born in 1848, the year of revolutions. Appropriately he became a Radical in politics, and was later a keen member of the Preston Reform Club. Like many Victorian nonconformists, he was a teetotaller. But he remained a hard-bitten Lancashire cotton man; Percy's philanthropy filled him with mingled horror and sorrow. A pioneering motorist, he ordered anyone or anything in his way to 'Get out th' road'. Passengers were required to share the cost of the petrol.

J.T. was ambitious. In 1868 he married Amelia Lees, whom he tyrannised, inflicting twelve children on her between visits to brothels. Percy, the eldest son, was born in 1874. With money borrowed from his wife's Quaker family J.T. was able to set himself up as a cotton merchant. He joined the Manchester Cotton Exchange where, he claimed, he was the first man not to wear a top hat. Business was good; within six years the Taylors were able to move to a large house in Ashton on Ribble, the smart district of Preston.

In 1890, when he was sixteen, Percy joined the family firm, to be followed in due course by his younger brothers. One of young 'Mr Percy's' duties was to pay the mill-owners who came to town to collect their dues each Friday. They would spend all day in pubs, and Percy had to take their money round these, sometimes carrying thousands of pounds in cash. Later he would see the mill-owners drunk, their pockets crammed with banknotes, crawling down the side streets on all fours. In due course the Taylors bought their own mills, Oxhey Mill and Bute Mill in Preston, and Whalley Bank Mill in Blackburn. Percy liked this side of the business, though by then it was not so profitable. He preferred people to cotton, and mill-workers to mill-owners.

James Taylor and Sons continued to thrive. By the end of the century J.T. boasted of being a millionaire, and though this was probably an exaggeration, he was able to retire in considerable comfort at fifty. Thereafter Alan's father Percy ran the business with his brothers, never taking home less than £5000 per year and often more. Unlike his domineering father, Percy was a gentle, playful man. Even his features were more delicate. In most photographs he has a faraway look in his eyes. He was a keen amateur photographer, and used to entertain his friends and political associates with slide lectures.

In 1900 Percy came back from a chapel dance and told his brothers that he had met the girl he was going to marry. Alan's mother, Constance Sumner Thompson, was a handsome woman. She was twenty-two, four years younger than Percy, and came from a neighbouring family in Ashton. The Thompsons thought themselves superior to the Taylors, though they had much less money and though Connie's father William Henry Thompson had been born out of wedlock and was said to have walked into Preston with a pack on his back. He had a wholesale warehouse; unlike James Taylor he was a bad businessman and devoted his energies instead to his Sunday work as a Wesleyan lay preacher. Connie's mother Martha, on the other hand, had two brothers who were solicitors, at a time when to be a solicitor in that part of the world was enough to put you in high society. They spoke 'beautiful English'. They were not 'trade'.

Martha Thompson was a matriarch. She was a hard woman; when she was dying she told her children that she'd not been hard enough on them. She was a quicker thinker than her husband, and fought for her four daughters as well as her two sons to be properly educated. But education had its limits; she removed one of Connie's sisters from scripture classes at her Dame's school when they tried to instil the Creed. Martha imbued in her children a horror of drunkenness. Her favourite brother, a Radical journalist, had emigrated to Australia. Ten years later a policeman had come to the door to say that a man claiming to be him was in the local Poor Law hospital. He had struggled back to Preston, only to die a week later.

Connie's two brothers were at Preston Grammar School, the school Percy had attended. For all the strictness of their upbringing, the Thompsons were a close-knit family. 'Aren't we Thompsons wonderful?' read a telegram a Thompson boy received on passing his exams, and this was typical. They could be crushing about other people. Connie herself was abrupt. Percy lavished money on the two Thompson boys, and perhaps they resented him for it. Alan later said that when his uncle Harry – the darling of the Thompson family – wanted to become a solicitor Percy paid for his articles. Another account has it that Harry's brother John had to leave school to pay for them.

Connie accepted Percy's proposal of marriage. She was not in love, she later told Alan, but marriage to a wealthy man offered an escape from the tedium of her work as a schoolteacher. For their honeymoon they took ship to India, where James Taylor and Sons had several warehouses, and during six months abroad visited Delhi, Lucknow and Darjeeling as well as Calcutta. Percy's brother Jim ran the Calcutta end of the business. One evening he threw a glass of water over one of the Indian servants who had upset him; Connie threw one at him 'to see how he liked it'. On the voyage back Percy contracted typhoid fever, and the young couple were put ashore at Marseilles. Percy's father came to the rescue, the first and only time he ever left England.

Percy and Connie set up home in Birkdale. Their first home was in Cresent Road, a detached, red-brick building in a quiet, leafy neighbourhood. A few years later they leased a newly built house less than half a mile away in Barrett Road, a turning off the main road to the station. It was double-fronted, with leaded windows in bays on either side of two glazed doors enclosed in an elaborate wooden porch. Its size and detail suggested prosperity. Birkdale was a suburb of Southport, a pleasant seaside resort. In later life

Alan often said that he was amazed to come south to Oxford and find towns with no smoking factory chimneys. In fact there were no such chimneys in Birkdale.

Alan's descriptions of his mother are entirely negative: censorious, tight-lipped, snobbish. Photographs suggest a forceful, intelligent, impatient woman. She was a good golfer and dragged Percy off to be beaten on Saturday mornings, before despairing of his game. Yet inside 'there was a Madame Bovary struggling to get out'.[1] Even during her honeymoon she had formed a passionate attachment with a photographer, Tommy Hands, while on board ship for India, and when he later returned to England for a summer she was thrown into confusion. (He died in India a few years afterwards, depriving her of a romantic focus to her life for a while.) Like the rest of the family, she was devoted to her brother Harry, and like the rest of the family she lost no opportunity to criticise her good-natured husband.

In November 1902 Connie gave birth to a daughter, Constance Miriam. Percy doted on his little girl. He would sit beside her high chair, tasting the food to ensure it was not too hot before feeding it to her. When Miriam was only fifteen months old, she developed tubercular meningitis. After an illness lasting fourteen days she died. This tragedy was not made easier to bear by the fact that death in childhood was fairly common at the time; it was made worse by the fact that one parent blamed it on the other. Percy had a tubercular lung, and was forced to spend two winters in a sanatorium. It was believed that he had infected his daughter while tasting her food. This was probably unfounded. For Percy to have infected her he would have had to have open lesions on the lung, which would have made him cough uncontrollably. A much more likely culprit in those days was unpasteurised cow's milk.

Miriam's death hit Percy hard. His delight in other people's children only made his loss more poignant. When, much later, he found a girlfriend, she was as much a replacement for his lost daughter as his errant wife. Alan believed that his mother was less affected. 'Miriam's death merely increased her dislike for sex and childbearing.'[2] When a friend of hers died in childbirth, Connie told Alan that she had been killed by her husband. She may have been steeled by the fact that her own sister had died of tuberculosis.

Alan himself seems to have expunged any memory of his elder sister. He wrote in his autobiography that she died before he was born. In fact he was eighteen months old.

When Alan was born two years later he was therefore all the more special. Alan was small and supposed to be delicate; Connie worried about his health and consulted homeopathic doctors. Percy played with him, bathed him, and put him to bed at night, staying to tell him stories after the light was out. People said that his parents 'spoiled' him. He seems to have been a naughty child, competitive and full of energy. An uncle described him as a 'little devil'. Even as a small boy he was in the habit of arguing with adults. Because he was so precociously clever he could hold his own, which was especially annoying.

One person who did not spoil Alan was Connie's younger brother Harry. He was accustomed to his own way in everything; his brother John had allowed himself to be caned at school to spare him. Harry was dynamic and purposeful. When Alan was born he was twenty, a tall, slim young man with hair parted in the middle. He liked games, and was very good at them, though he had an unpleasant habit of jeering at losing opponents. He and John were still living at home when Connie married, and they were frequent visitors to the Taylor house. Harry ridiculed his cocky nephew, and argued him down.

While Alan was still an infant his parents had moved home once again. 'Bicknor' was in Crosby Road, a few streets away from the old house and closer to Birkdale station. It was a large detached building dating from 1887, solidly constructed with a fine stained glass window on the landing. A garden surrounded it on all sides, big enough for Connie to host a party there for the Liberal women of Southport, which Alan noisily interrupted in painted face and Red Indian suit. It was then the only house in Crosby Road with a telephone. It also had extensive attics, in which Percy built himself a darkroom, next to where the two maids slept. Besides these two the Taylors employed a gardener, a handyman and a charwoman, plus another girl who took Alan for walks. In the kitchen was a large bellboard which could summon the servants to any room of the house.

Alan was the only child in this substantial household. He had no friends his own age and he spent long periods alone. When adults came to the house he hurled himself at them, demanding that they read to him; indeed, he would kneel on a chair looking out of the window for anyone who might bring him a book. By the time he was four he had learned to read and write himself. A postscript added by Alan to one of his mother's letters written in 1910 shows an astonishingly fluent script for one so young.

Alan had battalions of soldiers ranged in formation on the floor of the attic, and extorted more soldiers from each new visitor. One little boy who came to the house knocked some of these over; Alan punched him. He left with his nose bleeding, and did not come back.

What company Alan had was mainly adult. The most important was one of the uniformed maids, Annie Clark, whom Alan called Nanna and whom he seems to have loved much more than his mother. He read to her, rather than vice versa. She called him Old Mr Ninety-Five because he was so precocious. Another maid, Jane, used to bath him occasionally when Percy was not available. Then of course there were his relations and, because Alan was the eldest male grandchild on either side of the family, he was much of his time in grown-up society. The Thompsons in particular were a close-knit family, spending a whole week together at Christmas. Alan's first Thompson cousin was Karin, born in 1910. He watched her being breast-fed, and afterwards his uncle John asked what he thought of the process. 'It was very interesting,' he replied. 'The baby was fed by a bulb which seemed to be attached to the body.'*

Karin's parents were ostracised by the rest of the family. Her mother, Kate, had married a Swedish lodger, and the Thompsons, particularly the two brothers, disapproved. Like many middle-class families they were sensitive about having to take in lodgers, and tried to increase the distance between them. Kate had let the side down.

Percy let the side down too when he told a dinner party that he had learned his carving skills from an uncle who was a butcher. Connie was embarrassed by the connection. Many of the people the

---

*On another occasion Alan told his aunt Madge: 'Of course I know where cows come from. But what I want to know is what the bull has to do with it.'

Taylors mixed with were wealthy. In his childhood Alan thought nothing of houses with lifts and billiard-rooms. Nevertheless he spent as much time as he could with the Blackwell family, who lived in Stanley Avenue, next to the infant school which Alan attended. The Blackwells were not rich, but they did possess one thing other families lacked: books. Alan referred to their daughter Elisabeth, who was then studying for a place at university, as 'the lady with the school in the attic'. Whenever he could he would call there for tea, and talk to the parents as much as to their two daughters, who were anyway much older than he. He argued with Mrs Blackwell about whether Jesus spoke Sanskrit or Aramaic. Joshua Blackwell, the father, would read him Beatrix Potter books; they bought each new one as it came out until they had a complete set.

Joshua was a socialist. He objected to people singing 'God Save The King' in the Congregationalist chapel which he attended along with the Taylors. Alan's parents often joined a group which gathered at the Blackwell house in the evening to talk politics around the fire. Alan would have to be entertained by Eunice Blackwell, six years his senior. They played a game called 'Prince's Quest', in which up to six different princes raced across a board in order to win a princess. Not surprisingly, this goal appealed to Alan more than to Eunice and she learnt to avoid 'scenes' by letting the little boy win.

Sometimes Joshua and Percy would take the two children for a walk among the sandhills, or they would go on bicycles. Beyond the sandhills the beach stretched a long way to the sea, so far that Southport pier was over a mile long. Southport was a very grand place. In the mornings Connie, clad in the Edwardian fashion with large hat pinned on and dress down to the ground bulging fore and aft, would take Alan by tram into central Southport, where she would drink coffee with her friends at Thom's Japanese tea-rooms in fashionable Lord Street. Lord Street was remarkable. Elegant and wide, it had trees in the middle and arcades down each side. Napoleon III had visited Southport in the 1860s. Much later Alan was to suggest, perhaps teasingly, that Lord Street had inspired Baron Haussmann's boulevards in Paris.

A humiliating incident from one of these excursions stuck in Alan's mind. His mother was engaged in a long conversation on a telephone in the tea-rooms; Alan tried to interrupt her, saying, 'Mummy, I have to go somewhere.' His mother went on talking, seemingly on and on. He repeated his demand, several times, until it was too late. He could hold on no longer; his trousers started to get wet and a little puddle formed. When his mother finished talking, she showed no concern for the little boy, but hurried him away so that nobody should witness his disgrace.[3]

What Alan liked most about Southport was Pleasureland, an amusement arcade full of animated penny-in-the-slot machines; and the pier, particularly the end where a Professor Powsey performed spectacular dives. Alan was impressed when Powsey dived in bound and surfaced free of ropes; but his *pièce de résistance* was to ride down into the sea on a bicycle set alight and blazing all around him. Such was Alan's first experience of professors.

Back in Birkdale, Alan attended a small private school kept by sisters, the Misses Filmer. It was in two houses, the junior school next to the Blackwells which Alan attended, and one for bigger children a few streets away. An Irish terrier called Paddy was trained to take messages between them. Miss Annie and Miss Kitty Filmer were gentle, upright ladies who stressed the importance of learning and hard work. Alan does not seem to have learned much there. While the class was being taught to read he would sit at the back with a book. He avoided other children; just like grown-ups, they were 'distant noises which did not interrupt my reading. Books were for me real life; people were an interruption.'[4]

He was four when he first read *Pilgrim's Progress* (though he skipped the boring bits). It became his favourite book, and he read it and re-read it until he knew chunks by heart; 'one of the greatest books in the world and the most subversive', as he described it many years later.[5] Alan called Joshua Blackwell 'Mr Greatheart'. Afterwards he read Lewis Carroll, J.M. Barrie, and Frances Hodgson Burnett, among other authors. What he particularly liked were historical novelists: Harrison Ainsworth, Charles Kingsley, Bulwer Lytton, G.A. Henty, 'the drabber and more factual the better'.[6] Henty's books set in the Thirty Years' War were his favourites, and with his toy soldiers he reproduced their battle plans on the attic floor, something he was later to do with maps and words in the pages of his own books.* He also read weekly adventure stories, including the serials in the *Boy's Own Paper*; comics like *Chips* and *Comic Cuts*; and more worthy publications like *The Rainbow*. His father used to read the adventures of Sexton Blake on the train and pass them on to Alan afterwards.

Alan's parents were not particularly intellectual. They preferred playing cards to reading, and they organised parties to play Racing Demon, the latest craze from America. Connie liked bridge, and bullied Percy into partnering her. Though they read political pamphlets they read no modern or even recent literature. Their favourite play was a farce. Alan remembered how they burned a work of which they disapproved, *The Guarded Flame* by W.B. Maxwell: it is the melodrama of a married woman who has an affair with her niece's lover, a man much younger than her invalid husband.

Alan went to the cinema in its early days, when it was regarded very much as a sensation. The programme was usually made up of 'shorts' — slapstick comics, stunts, cowboys and indians, etc. He did, however, see one of the first serious and therefore full-length films, D.W. Griffith's *Birth of a Nation*, later hailed as a masterpiece, though its attitudes make modern audiences uncomfortable. Occasionally the family would go into Manchester and see a show, or a pantomime at Christmas. He saw *Peter Pan* three Christmases running. Once he saw a performing bear in the street just outside the house.

On family holidays Alan was usually the only child in a large party of adults. At Borrowdale in the Lake District, for example, Alan was often left behind with Nanna while the others went off walking, sometimes for the whole day. When he did get out, the boy avenged himself on his uncle for all his teasing by throwing Harry's socks into a stream. Other people's socks have been going into the stream ever since, observed another historian seventy years later.[8] It was unusual for Alan to be an only child, more unusual in the Edwardian era than it would be today. Percy's six brothers

---

*'Long, long ago I read the works of Henty with more eagerness, more enjoyment and more application than I did those of any other history writer, perhaps even with more profit. I should not mind being acclaimed as the Henty *de nos jours*.'[7]

managed nineteen children between them; Connie's three had ten. But in 1913, when Alan was six years old, Connie became pregnant again. No one said anything to him about it. All he knew was that his mother began to spend more and more time in bed, and then he was sent to stay with the Blackwells for a few days. When he came back his mother appeared very ill, and she greeted him 'with what was for her unusual affection'.[9] Later he discovered that she had given birth to a stillborn child.

Connie was by this time thirty-five, and her health never recovered. She moved into a separate bedroom from her husband, not getting up until late in the morning and resting in the afternoon. (They were already in separate beds, a fact which shocked Connie's mother: 'A double bed is Percy's right.') It was given out that she had suffered 'eclampsia', and had been left with a damaged kidney. This seems an unlikely diagnosis. Eclampsia, a kind of epileptic convulsion of sudden onset, is a medical emergency, and at that time few women would have survived it. It is also extremely unlikely that a woman suffering renal damage could have lived another thirty years, as Connie did. More common is preeclampsia, an unpleasant condition but not one which normally results in permanent enfeeblement. Both eclampsia and preeclampsia almost always occur in the first pregnancy. For either to occur in the third by the same father – assuming that is what it was – is almost unknown.

Whatever had really happened, it seemed that Alan would never now have any brothers or sisters. The Taylors concluded that Birkdale was unhealthy, and decided to move. Perhaps they found their memories of the place too distressing. While they looked for a new home Connie decided to winter in Italy to speed her recovery. *En route* they stayed a few days in London, where Alan was taken to the House of Commons and saw Bonar Law, then leader of the Unionist Party, sitting on the Opposition front bench. From Paris they took the sleeper to Turin, Alan sharing a compartment with his father and Connie the adjoining one with Nanna. Like most children he found the experience very exciting. They went on to Alassio. After a few weeks Percy returned to England, leaving the others in Italy for several months before they too came back, via

Milan and Lugano. In Milan Alan saw Leonardo's *Last Supper*, the first picture that made any impression on him.

Back in England Percy and Connie settled in Buxton, a spa within an hour by train from Manchester, with fine Georgian buildings in yellow sandstone. Alan learned to swim in its thermal baths. It is the highest town in England, frequently cut off by winter snows. The cold climate was 'bracing', and therefore was supposed to be good for Percy's damaged lung as well as Alan's delicate chest. At any rate the air was clear of smoking chimneys. They rented a large semi-detached stone house on three floors, appropriately enough on the Manchester Road. It stood on a steep hill which curved down into the town centre. Vera Brittain was living in a nearby street.

Often Alan used to get out of bed early, collecting the newspaper from the doormat before his parents were up. One June morning a headline announced that an Austrian Archduke had been assassinated in Sarajevo. It seemed a long way off, and even when a general war broke out in early August it made little impact on Alan. Nor did it disrupt the Liberal consensus in the country. For one thing, men did not take it very seriously; they had grown used to peace, and had come to believe it was a natural state of affairs. The last time Britain had fought a battle on the mainland of Europe had been a century earlier at Waterloo, and the last time there had been a war between France and Germany had been the Franco-Prussian War nearly fifty years before. That war had been settled quickly; this one would be too. It would all be over by Christmas; then men could get back to the business of making Progress.

Percy soon began to have doubts. These were triggered by reading Shaw's *Common Sense about the War*.* He began to feel that Radicals like himself had been misled by the Government, by Lloyd George in particular. 'That man has been corrupted by power,' he told Alan. 'No-one will ever trust him again.' Soon he was reading pamphlets by anti-war writers like E.D. Morel and H.N. Brailsford, which Alan too lapped up. These men rejected the idea that either side was to blame; the thrust of their arguments was

---

*'A title more than usually impertinent', Alan remarked forty years later in *The Troublemakers*.[10]

that the War had been caused by secret diplomacy. Morel founded the Union of Democratic Control, with the aim of ensuring that such a war could never happen again. The UDC called for a negotiated peace and open or 'democratic' diplomacy afterwards. It wanted a 'scientific' settlement, with national boundaries adjusted on ethnic lines. The UDC attracted support from Ramsay MacDonald, the future Labour prime minister, and the Independent Labour Party (ILP), as well as intellectuals like Bertrand Russell. J.T. too opposed the War, as he had opposed the Boer War that went before it. 'Can't they see that every time they kills a German they kills a customer?' he moaned.

Alan now had to go back to school, after a break of eighteen months or so. For a little over a year he attended a small co-educational private school which took boys up to the age of eleven. It was run by the English wife of a Swiss, one Madame de la Motte. The children were often taken to play in the nearby woods. One of their games was called Cavaliers and Roundheads; Alan commanded the Roundheads. In his view 'the Cavaliers represented Privilege – long scented locks, silk garments, affected ways of speaking. The Roundheads were the party of the people – men of simple life, believing in equality and of course speaking in a Lancashire accent.'[11]

Out of school hours there was plenty of time for exploring the district. At weekends Alan and his parents often made long walks in the Derbyshire dales, starting out from Buxton by train and alighting at little local stations. Sometimes his grandfather would call and then they would speed about the countryside in his open car. Alan acquired a bicycle and, by ascending the hill above the house, found he could freewheel downhill a mile and a half. Another diversion was tobogganing. Further up Manchester Road was a hospital, where wounded Canadians from the front were brought to Buxton to convalesce. Alan used to salute the soldiers he came across in town. In the summer he watched them play baseball. In the very cold winter of 1916–17 the more mobile of them had blocked the road and turned it into a toboggan run. It was steep and icy, but though the run was dangerous Alan forced himself to go down it again and again.

Alan was less lonely in Buxton. Two of his cousins, Margery and

Nancy Taylor, came to live with him during the War, while their father was in India looking after the interests of James Taylor and Sons. He took them tobogganing, and made Margery laugh so hard she wet her pants. At home they played Ludo together. Alan also began to make friends at school. One of these lived on a farm outside Buxton, and Alan would cycle out to see him on summer evenings. Another was Eileen Mill, whose father ran the George Hotel at the foot of Manchester Road. They sometimes held hands on the way home from school, but what really excited Alan was the thought of visiting licensed premises. Alan's parents patronised 'temperance' hotels.

At the beginning of 1916 Alan went on to Buxton College, the local grammar school, though he was not yet ten, and eleven was the normal age for entry. He came top of the class in his first term, and was immediately moved up to the next, where he also came top, each time winning the form prize of a leather-bound book. Perhaps surprisingly, this does not seem to have made him unpopular. Buxton College was a 'rough' school, and like all schools during the War, it seems to have been made rougher by the departure of most of the younger masters for the Front. Alan's mother complained that he too was becoming 'rough'.

In January 1916 the Asquith government bowed to public pressure and imposed military conscription on unmarried men between the ages of eighteen and forty-one. Harry Thompson, now practising as a solicitor in the potteries and as always a frequent visitor to the Taylor house, was thirty. One day he arrived to see his sister Connie on his two-stroke motorcycle. 'Whatever happens, I'm not going,' he told her. He and his brother John were drafted into the Staffordshire Regiment, whereupon Harry refused to obey an order. After spells in the guardroom he was sentenced to two years' imprisonment. Connie threw herself into her brother's cause. She followed him around from prison to prison, staying in local hotels and sending in a constant supply of luxuries. Harry knew prisoners' rights and insisted on them; soon he had the prison governors eating out of his hand. Not everybody was so fortunate. Many of the conscientious objectors were beaten up by their warders, or kept in atrocious conditions. Some died as a result of their treatment; others went mad.[12]

One Sunday Alan was attending chapel with his mother and her sister when the preacher sneered at the 'shirkers'. 'Gather up your books and bibles,' ordered Connie, and they promptly left. That was the end of organised religion for her. From then on she was devoted to the cause of the conscientious objectors. For her, it was no longer a question of needing to win a war reluctantly entered into. Henceforth everything to do with the War was evil.

Everything included Buxton College, which had an Officers' Training Corps. The older boys trained in a field; trenches had been dug specially for the purpose. A 1915 photograph from *The Buxtonian* shows a line of boys in school uniform pointing gun-shaped sticks over the top of such a trench. This was not what Connie wanted for Alan. His name was down for Rugby, the public school most favoured by wealthy northerners. But Rugby too had an Officers' Training Corps; so instead she decided on Bootham in York, a Quaker school and therefore anti-war. There was one snag: Bootham did not take boys until they were thirteen. Anxious to avoid any taint of militarism, Connie found a Quaker preparatory school, The Downs, in the Malvern Hills. Alan had a friend who had gone on to boarding-school from Buxton College; when he returned in the holidays he had described the little boys sobbing after Lights Out. It did not sound promising to Alan. He did not want to go; nor did his father want him to. But his mother's mind was made up. Early in 1917 his parents took Alan to The Downs to begin his first term. 'In utter misery' he watched them drive away.

2: *Badger*

As an only child, Alan was accustomed to being alone and doing as he pleased. In his father's eyes he could do no wrong. He was used to a warm, comfortable home and everyday luxuries. Nanna pampered and adored him. All the more of a shock, then, to be dragged away into the Spartan existence of the boys' boarding-school. Alan hated the discomfort and the lack of privacy. He resented the regimentation, and his resentment fostered a spirit of rebellion.

The Downs was a new school, founded in 1900 by the headmaster, Herbert Jones. Although he was a Quaker and the school was run on Quaker lines, it was not a Quaker school in the sense of a school administered by the Society of Friends. It stood at the edge of the village of Colwall, on the western side of the Malverns. It was gradually expanding, but still small when Alan arrived, with only thirty-four boys in five classes. This gave it an intimate atmosphere, and meant that personalities loomed large. Jones himself was a former headmaster of the smart Quaker school, Leighton Park. A history of Leighton Park records that he was 'an excellent classroom teacher with firm but kindly discipline, but his powers were too limited to hold the school during an awkward period'.[1] Ill at ease with the staff, he seemed happiest teaching the boys intricate mnemonics to help them remember their Latin.

Though Jones was nominally in charge, his wife Ethel ruled the roost. 'Herbert! Will thee please come here!'* she bellowed at her husband across the lawn. 'Mrs Jones was a formidable figure. She had a high corsetted bust, swathed in red velvet, and hair piled

---

*It was Quaker practice to use 'thee' and 'thou' as forms of address.

high,' Alan wrote sixty-five years later. 'Character building was her obsession, and for her this meant punctuality and cleanliness. The price of these, she believed, was eternal vigilance, a quality in which she was by no means lacking. Her sharp eyes never dimmed. Everything and particularly the boys ran to the second, and every activity was meticulously observed.'[2]

A history of The Downs describes this 'martinet' as having 'an almost Germanic approach to everything, to people, to household duties, and to sickroom routine alike'.[3] She believed that boys left idle would get up to 'monkey tricks'. As a result every minute of the boys' day was regimented, or so it seemed. It began at 6.30 a.m.; they were given ten minutes to wash and dress. The baths were always cold* and the boys were meant to submerge themselves completely. Those who were not quick enough were forced to undress, change back into pyjamas and report to Mrs Jones. In the process they often missed breakfast. Those who did manage to get ready in time were lined up for inspection by Mrs Jones, who would make boys go back and wash off any trace of dirt.

There were lessons before breakfast at 7 a.m. On alternate days these were devoted to rote learning, either chunks out of the Bible or dates. Every boy had a date card, with all the sovereigns since the Norman Conquest at the top and important dates in English history at the bottom. After breakfast the boys had to make their beds, which were inspected three times during the process. Any one that failed to meet the required standard meant the unhappy boy had to begin again. If he passed, Mrs Jones or the matron uttered a strange cry which Alan first thought was 'Turnip and Co'. It turned out to be 'Turn Up and Go'.

Further inspections and timed chores followed throughout the day. Shoes were inspected at three stages during cleaning, and hands were inspected before each meal. The boys were timed when they changed for games and undressed for bed. Boys who failed to complete their tasks quickly enough might have to change their clothes up to three times, reporting each time to Mrs Jones. Talking

---

*The duty became a habit; Alan took cold baths every morning for the rest of his life.

after dark meant the boy had to get up and dress, then sit alone in
the darkened music-room for half an hour.

Meals were a further ordeal. The food itself was unappetising:
for breakfast lumpy porridge with treacle and wartime 'standard'
bread, made of maize or rye; for lunch cold meat, potatoes and
cabbage. Any lapse from good table-manners, such as spilling food
or neglecting a neighbour's empty plate, meant at the very least that
the offender was made to stand behind his chair for the rest of the
meal. A more severe punishment was 'plain fare', meaning bread
and water. Transgressors were liable to find themselves in 'The
Synagogue' or 'Sinner's Corner', the seats near Mr and Mrs Jones,
or, worse still, in 'Starvation Corner', right between them. One
such boy, having received no breakfast, in desperation piped up:
'Wilt thou have some toast, Herbert?' With what results history
does not record.

On Saturday evenings the weekend began with a compulsory
dose of Gregory Powder, the motto being 'Fear God, honour the
King, and keep your bowels open'. Any child who was ill was
assumed to be malingering, and was put on 'plain fare' until he
recovered. On Sunday mornings Quaker Meeting was held in the
gymnasium. The boys sat in silence facing the staff. Even here Mrs
Jones maintained her watch. Alan was completely unmoved by the
spirit but enjoyed the rare opportunity to let his mind wander. He
learned to sit silently without paying attention to what was going
on around him, a habit which sometimes disconcerted his com-
panions in later life.[4] Afterwards the boys wrote letters home. Jones
chalked up on the blackboard the subjects which were supposed to
form the body of their texts. Then he inspected the letters to make
sure they were long enough, upside down to allow the boys some
privacy. Alan's first letter home contained a despairing postscript:
'I hate this place. I hate this school. I cannot make my bed like a
parcel.'

He particularly disliked the hour designated by Mrs Jones for
'Stiff Reading'. The idea was that they should read some improving
work rather than a piece of fiction. Alan was the type of boy to read
serious books anyway, but he did not like being forced to do so. On
Sundays, stiff reading was confined to missionary stories and
practical good works. After Sunday lunch the boys made their way

to the gymnasium, where they lay down on red rugs while Mrs Jones read to them, children's classics such as *Robinson Crusoe* and *Lorna Doone*. In the evening there was a musical, non-denominational meeting, and then Jones read to the older boys, the Sherlock Holmes stories or Poe's *Tales of the Grotesque and Arabesque*. Other recreations included knitting for Armenian refugees or soldiers at the Front, a patriotic task Alan was to fulfil in both World Wars. There were walks on the Malverns and the occasional play to lift the boys' spirits.

Jones had a system for identifying the boys, which he adopted because there were so many of the same name. When Alan arrived at The Downs, for example, there were five Rowntrees in the school. Jones's method was to append a number to the surname. Thus Alan was Taylor One or 'Ta 1' to distinguish him from Taylor Two.

Alan was a pale, solemn boy who looked delicate, even unhealthy. But in the dormitories he soon became 'quite frisky', jumping up and down on his neighbours' beds and joining in pillow fights. He and a friend developed a secret vocabulary with its own nonsense terms. He had a subversive sense of humour. On Sunday evenings there was a service in the gymnasium which included hymns, unlike the morning Meeting, which was silent. One hymn began with the line: 'Blest be the tie that binds'; at this cue Alan fingered his tie, glanced cautiously round, and finally pulled out his tie and waved it. Jones frowned disapprovingly.

Alan quickly showed himself to be a brilliant pupil. He did this without seeming to be a 'swot', always an unpopular figure with other boys. He started in the lowest form and shot up through the classes, often, though not always, coming top. The other clever boys saw him as the one to beat, and their letters home are full of boasts such as 'I am first in form order with 72 per cent (5 per cent above Ta 1).' Clearly they expected their parents to be aware of young Alan's status. One quality that was obvious even then was his exceptionally retentive memory. His only problem, it seemed, was handwriting. Jones had a meticulous copperplate hand and placed considerable importance on good handwriting. Alan was naturally left-handed and had been made to write with the other hand. Perhaps as a result, his handwriting was more untidy than that of the other boys. Maybe too Alan's left-handedness contributed to his sense of being different, and being forced to 'correct' it increased his dislike of conformity. Some who have been through the experience report that it is enough to turn the victim into a lifelong rebel. Alan was aware of this theory as applied to others and typically pooh-poohed it in his own case.[5]

Like all schools The Downs had suffered an exodus of teachers to the War. Active young men disappeared to the Front, to be replaced by old men or conscientious objectors who were often not firm enough to maintain discipline. Before conscription came in Jones had made the situation worse by goading a master who was not a Friend into enlisting. The non-teaching staff, too, disappeared, to be replaced by a succession of Belgian exiles. Many of the duties Alan complained of, such as bed-making and shoe-cleaning, were in fact wartime exigencies. A more exotic duty was to be a 'Zep boy', putting up the Zeppelin blinds at night.

The War was not an easy time for Quakers. Some became conscientious objectors; some undertook active service in a non-combative role such as the Friends' Ambulance Unit; and some forsook their beliefs and enlisted. *Pax bello melior*, Jones taught the boys in class, but he tried to steer the school down a compromise course. He organised meetings of 'COs' at the school, hoping no doubt to find some teachers thereby, but he also put on entertainments for wounded servicemen, known as 'Saturday Pops'. One of these was a performance of *A Midsummer Night's Dream*, staged outside in brilliant sunshine. Alan was Puck; his performance was word perfect and generally reckoned to be outstanding. Later in life he was often described as 'puckish'. His performance as Maria in *Twelfth Night* was even more impressive, described as cheeky, pert and wicked, never bettered in the experience of one witness. The play was produced by Bryan Priestman, one of the younger masters with whom Alan had struck up a particular friendship, so much so that they were on Christian-name terms. In February 1917 Alan heard the matron tell Mrs Jones that there had been a revolution in Russia, whereupon he told Bryan momentously that it was a great day in the history of the world.

The Russian Revolution of 1917, particularly the Bolshevik Revolution in October, created a stir in England. The War had seemed deadlocked; now the new Russian Government proposed a peace conference, and when the Bolsheviks seized power they went one step further and made a unilateral peace with Germany and Austria. Those who had longed for an end to the slaughter – like Alan's parents – saw Lenin as a man of action, in contrast to their own Liberal leaders, with whom they had become increasingly disillusioned. The Bolsheviks argued that capitalism – and imperialism, being the highest stage of capitalism – had caused the War, and when they published the secret treaties between the Tsarist Government and the Western Powers, these appeared to confirm all the old suspicions which had led to the setting up of the Union of Democratic Control. For Connie the issue was clear: Lenin had ended the War; the Revolution would set Harry free. When one of Percy's brothers was killed in France in 1918 it must have increased his hostility to the War, too. But the Revolution meant more than just an end to the War. Lenin claimed to have discerned a new scientific law, the 'Materialist Conception of History'. The Bolsheviks had predicted the collapse of capitalism and the victory of the proletariat; they had triumphed. It seemed a self-fulfilling prophecy. What had happened in Russia would surely happen in England. Communism was The Future; it must mean Progress.

When Alan came home for Christmas in 1917 he noticed a change in his parents. They had become socialists, dedicated to the cause of the working class. For them, 'class war' did not mean more fighting, however; the most serious weapons they envisaged using were the strike and the ballot box.[6] At the time many on the Left looked no further than the election of a Labour government to bring on the millennium. Alan read their pamphlets and was converted. Unlike them, though, he did not envisage a bloodless revolution. 'Indeed it seemed to me rather pointless if blood did not flow. I remember my mother expressing her disbelief in some story of Bolshevik atrocities that she read in a newspaper. I thought the story did the Bolsheviks credit.'[7]

Like most Quaker schools The Downs emphasised the 'whole man'. Great store was put on 'hobbies', particularly nature study. One keen little boy collected 160 different wild flowers. This was not Alan's strong point:

I tried one variety after another, always in vain. I tried Aquarium.
My tadpoles died. I could not catch newts. My tank smelled. I tried
Astronomy and could never identify the stars. I tried Lichen, the
dreariest study known to man. Worst of all was the flower list . . . I
never got more than half a dozen – daisy, dandelion, buttercup and
after that what? My flowers had all withered by Monday and the
water in my jam jar stank. The whole affair was a nightmare to me.[8]

Other hobbies on offer at The Downs included fossil collecting,
pressed flowers, butterfly-mounting and carpentry. Alan did not
shine in any of these. More to his taste were the outings. The school
was perched in a 'bracing situation', 500 feet above sea-level on the
slopes of the Malvern Hills. From there one could ascend to the
British Camp, a remarkably preserved prehistoric hill fort, and
look down at fog below. Sometimes Jones would take the boys up
on the Hills in the snow, and there they could lark about, free at last
from the scrutiny of Mrs Jones. Or they would go swimming, boys
and masters alike naked, in a swimming pool belonging to a
neighbour. On one occasion George Cadbury, who with his
brother Richard had founded the famous chocolate firm, fetched
the boys in an open red charabanc to Wynds Point, his house at the
foot of the Beacon. In his address to them before providing a lavish
tea he agonised about his increasing wealth and his responsibility to
the community.

Alan was soon able to take walks on his own. His family doctor
had provided a certificate exempting him from football because of
his 'weak heart', and he was therefore free to roam while the others
were on the playing field. The same doctor also told him that one of
his lungs was in danger of collapse. The remedy was to spend as
much time as possible outside. 'Fresh air had always been a Downs
panacea,'[9] and during the summer classes were frequently held on
the lawn anyway. The treatment Alan now received had already
been tried on another boy called Buchanan, with apparently
successful results. During lessons Alan sat outside the classroom
window, wrapped up in rugs, overcoat and mittens. In very bad
weather his feet rested in a hay-box containing a hot-water bottle.
The master sat on the window-ledge, one eye on Alan and the other
on the four or five boys inside. Alan also ate his meals outside, with

another boy deputed to keep him company. At night the boys slept with the windows wide open; it was so cold in the dormitory that ice formed on the water jugs beside the bed. In his final term Alan slept out on the balcony underneath the awning. Before this, however, the school had been through two crises.

The epidemic of influenza which swept the world in late 1918 killed more people than the War that was just ending. One hundred and fifty thousand English men and women were to die of the 'flu that winter. Its arrival was anticipated by gruesome newspaper reports of what was happening elsewhere. In Manchester, for example, half the population contracted the disease, and the death rate was 7.9 per cent. Jones tried to isolate the school from contagion. In vain, and soon boys were collapsing all round. The matrons began to catch it, and then the staff; nurses arrived from outside, and themselves succumbed; and so on. The 'flu was a particularly dangerous and debilitating strain, affecting the brain. Many of the boys were thought to be near death. Jones himself took quinine constantly, and managed to resist the disease, but apart from himself only Mrs Jones's sister, one of the Belgian refugees, and one small boy escaped it. Eventually the earlier victims began to crawl about again; and after a while it became clear that everyone would pull through. Jones decided to close the school for a week. Alan's mother arrived and took him home to Buxton. One morning a few days later he was lying in bed when he heard sirens and church bells. It was the Armistice. The Great War was over at last.

The masters who had been away at the Front started to trickle back once the school re-opened. Most of them would not stay very long, but after what they had experienced they were in no mood to tolerate Mrs Jones's petty tyrannies. Discipline began to break down, and there were signs of insubordination from the masters in front of the boys. Eventually the entire staff demanded that Jones hand over the school to them. Jones resisted.

I said The Downs was my school, and Mrs Jones's, and we had built it up over nineteen years. It was the product of our life's work. If however I were foolish enough to hand the School over to them, there would be a dozen different schools, all superimposed and all

pulling different ways. It would indeed be a house divided against
itself. I was compelled to give them all a most emphatic NO.[10]

It was a brave stand, but Jones had lost his spirit for the fight. He
had already brought in Geoffrey Hoyland as a junior partner, and
now he prepared to relinquish control altogether. Hoyland's
impatience for change reflected a general unsettlement felt also in
other schools. It now manifested itself in the boys themselves.

Already during the War there had been a movement throughout
the country for pupils to have a greater say in the running of the
schools. No doubt it was the spirit of the times. Jones had been
pressed to institute boys' committees and boys' courts at The
Downs. He had resisted, but introduced instead a cabinet, known
for some reason as 'Bus', of half a dozen or so monitors. The whole
school met in solemn session at the beginning of each term and
elected these monitors by secret ballot. 'The elections began to be
lively affairs and personal feeling ran high; certain of last term's
government have made themselves unpopular owing to being too
"efficient", and a campaign would be set going against them by the
aggrieved party who would put forward rival candidates of their
own.'[11] A fundamental problem was the role of these representatives. Were they there to advise the headmaster on the running of
the school, as Alan maintained, or were they there to enforce
discipline, as the majority seemed to think? Were they delegates or
policemen? The issue was complicated by rivalry between the two
boarding houses, the new one presided over by Hoyland representing the Progressives, and by factions surrounding the two chocolate
magnates, Cadbury and Rowntree. To make things worse there
was an outbreak of stealing, much discussed at cabinet meetings.

In spring 1919 Alan, now thirteen, was among seven boys elected
to the cabinet. A Cadbury was Head Boy. Almost at once there was
an outbreak of mumps in the school, and most of the cabinet except
Alan were laid low. As they were completely isolated in the sick-
room and could communicate with the outside world only by
passing messages through the nurses or by furious faces at the
window, it was difficult for them to impose their authority. A party
soon grew up in the 'free' section of the school reacting against
orders from the 'occupied zone'. This was Alan's chance. He led a

rebellion, arguing that he could not act alone. The rebels organised a new meeting and fresh elections, and their candidates swept the board. The cabinet was now under Alan's control. It passed a succession of revolutionary proposals, including the abolition of 'plain fare' and corporal punishment. The school split into two factions. Feeling ran high. Angry letters passed to and fro between the sick-room and the world outside. Favours were worn; the rebels wore red. Red and green flags hung outside the windows of the dormitories. A poster war developed, and banners were carried. Soon skirmishes, often snowfights, took place between rival bands.

The Civil War, as it was known, lasted some weeks. Then it began to fizzle out. Exams approached; several of the rebels had gone down with mumps while members of the *ancien régime* gradually recovered, emerging from the sick-room full of wrath. Then the holidays intervened. When the school reassembled Jones asserted his authority once more. He told the meeting that certain boys, including Alan, should not be elected. The electorate followed his instructions. A 'coalition' cabinet took office. Alan sulked. 'If the other boys were too frightened to support me, why should I bother about them?'[12] He devoted himself instead to studying the proposed peace treaty.

Alan shared the view expressed by most Progressive opinion, that the Treaty of Versailles was a bad one. The peace-makers had redrawn the map of Europe, and redistributed the German colonies. Three imperial dynasties – Romanov, Habsburg and Hohenzollern – had ruled central and eastern Europe; now all were gone, to be replaced by modern, mostly democratic nation-states. The break-up of Austria-Hungary led to the emergence of several completely new nations. The guiding principle of the new order was the one advanced by the American President, Woodrow Wilson: 'national self-determination'. Wilson was determined to avoid any 'unscientific' anomalies such as Alsace-Lorraine. Once the peoples of Europe had reorganised themselves along national lines, it was felt, all disputes between states would wither away. A series of plebiscites were planned for the more ambiguous areas, to determine whether the inhabitants would prefer to be German or Pole, Austrian or Hungarian. But the victors were not keen to relinquish the spoils of war. The losers found their territory truncated. Nowhere exhibited these contradictory principles better than Czechoslovakia, the creation of Thomas Masaryk, a university professor. An uneasy amalgam of two separate peoples, the Czechs and the Slovaks, it was further destabilised by the presence within its borders of a large number of ethnic Germans. The Treaty of Versailles was iniquitous; grievances remained which could be resolved only by further territorial changes in the future.

Early in 1919 Alan's parents abandoned Buxton. From 1918 until he went to university in 1924, Alan's school holidays were spent mostly around Hawkshead in the Lake District. The Taylors moved there for months at a time; it became the place Alan loved more than anywhere else. He went for long bicycle rides down country lanes, swam in the lakes, and fished for pike with his father. Much later, when he tried to create a home for his children in the Isle of Wight, it was the memory of these holidays around Hawkshead which inspired him. Percy and Connie also bought a house in Preston, just around the corner from where they had both grown up and Connie's mother still lived. Like the house in Crosby Road, no. 17 Rose Terrace was a large red-brick building, with bays on either side of an imposing door surround.* Although presumably bought with Percy's money, the house was put in the name of Constance Sumner, possibly for inheritance reasons. John Thompson and his wife did the same.

The summer term of 1919 was Alan's last at The Downs. In May he won a scholarship to Bootham, earning a half-holiday for the whole school. In honour of Alan's achievement a daring party visited a nearby pub. He even played cricket against a rival preparatory school, and furthermore took three wickets, bowling underarm. To celebrate victory for The Downs the boys had sausages for tea. At the end of term there was a programme of concerts stretching over a fortnight. Alan was by this time proficient at the piano, and his swan-song was to play a number of Schumann solos.

After his release from prison in April 1919 Harry visited Alan at

---

*It is the only one of Alan's homes to have a blue plaque outside.

The Downs. When Alan described the conditions there, his uncle apparently declared that it sounded worse than prison. 'You have had a tougher war than I had.' Alan tells this story in his auto-biography to emphasise how miserable he was at The Downs. He calls the chapter about the school 'The Prison House'. Of course Harry had an easier war than most young men; Alan himself said that he had turned the prisons upside down.

Alan liked to make out that The Downs was a kind of latter-day Dotheboys Hall. It was certainly a peculiar school, with a strict regime. But one reason for the unusual methods of disciplining the boys was the Quaker reluctance to resort to corporal punishment. Most other prep schools at the time were pretty tough establishments, much tougher than The Downs. Three years after he left The Downs Alan felt relaxed enough to send a jokey letter to *Badger*, the school magazine, reporting on the progress of 'O.D.B.'s' at Bootham. If Mr and Mrs Jones had run such a terrible school, why should Alan have taken the trouble to go and see them at least twice afterwards, once a couple of years after he left and another time several years later, when he was at Oxford? Why should he have given The Downs such a poor report?

Perhaps the answer is that it made a good story.

3: 'The seed-time of life'

The summer of 1919 was idyllic. Alan's parents rented a large house in Hawkshead and he spent the whole summer holiday there. Percy bought a pony-and-trap, a romantic gesture when everybody else was going over to motor cars. A sign of this was the steamrollers to be found all over the country as old roads became tarmacked for the first time; the pony would rear up and bolt if she came across one. She could not drag a full trap up hills – a serious defect in the Lake District – and going downhill was dangerous when loaded. Nevertheless they managed to get about. Whenever the weather allowed, the family set off for a picnic.

The house was a former inn, with plenty of bedrooms. Percy and Connie, still in the first flush of revolutionary fervour, played host to young socialists, many of them former conscientious objectors just released from prison and sent on by Uncle Harry. Usually these young men came for two weeks' holiday, and often the Taylors would give them money to help with their studies. One of these, slightly older than the rest, in fact exactly the same age as Harry, was called Henry Sara.*

Henry was a fine figure of a man. Tall and well built, he had a handsome face topped by curly black hair. His mother was said to have been Spanish, which perhaps accounted for his Latin good looks. He had a commanding platform manner, honed by years of experience and aided by a resonant voice. The romantic effect was not spoilt by a wall-eye, supposedly the result of ill-treatment in prison. In conversation, he was persuasive and well informed. He had read all the Marxist classics, which he now introduced to Alan.

---

*Sara was pronounced with a long 'a', as in 'harem'.

Before the War he had been involved with the anarcho-syndicalist movement, and this had sharpened his political ideas. After the fighting began he had spoken eloquently at public meetings against the War in North London. In 1916 he had been arrested and conscripted into the Army, whereupon he had refused to obey orders or wear a uniform. After being maltreated in the barracks he had been sent to prison.

Connie fell in love with this socialist hero. For the rest of her life he was the object of her passionate devotion. She was forty-one; he was thirty-three. Alan thought that their relationship was platonic; it is impossible to be sure one way or the other. But like everybody else who shared their enthusiasms (and many who did not) Henry and Connie believed that revolution was just around the corner. It promised a new moral as well as a new social order. Together they would build a new world.

This was the beginning of a *ménage-à-trois* which shaped Alan's attitude to marriage. Wives would be unfaithful, emotionally if not physically; husbands would be supplanted by younger and more attractive men. Henry stayed all summer at Hawkshead, and was a frequent visitor to the Taylor household thereafter. He became, almost literally, a member of the family. Connie supported him financially, buying him suits and providing him with an allowance. She went off with Henry for weeks and even months at a time. She took him to the theatre in London, and they travelled abroad with Alan in tow. Alan was somewhat jealous of Sara, whom he nevertheless admired. Percy accepted the situation as he had done when Connie had become infatuated with Tommy Hands on their honeymoon.

He soon found a new interest of his own. One day Percy gave a lift home to one of his ILP friends in Preston, Syd Sharples. He was invited in to meet Syd's mother and his ten brothers and sisters; Syd's father, who had been a hairdresser, had died in the 'flu epidemic. Most of the children were already at work, going into the factories as soon as they reached the school-leaving age of thirteen. Percy asked if the two youngest girls would like to go to grammar school. He arranged to pay their fees, and thereafter was a frequent visitor to the house, bringing practical presents such as shoes as well as sweets and other goodies. One of the girls, then only ten or eleven, was Doris, known as Dolly because she was small; when she was a baby she had looked just like a little doll. She had flaming red hair – the result, it was believed, of being born on bonfire night. Percy and Dolly took to each other straight away. Perhaps she reminded him of the daughter he had lost. She called him 'Pa Taylor'; he called her 'Little Dolly'.

Percy was in some ways a child himself. When nephews and nieces came to the house he would stand on his head, so that the money ran out of his pocket for the children to pick up. His wife would go round making sure no one had picked up more than anyone else. This was typical of both. When rebuked by his wife, he would turn to others present with a helpless look in his eyes. But when Connie threatened to beat Alan, Percy stood up to her.

Alan went to Bootham in September 1919. Unlike The Downs, it was a proper Quaker school. It had about 140 pupils, of whom slightly fewer than half were Friends. There was silent worship every morning, the boys attended Quaker Meeting in the city on Sunday and Wednesday morning, and on Sunday evenings they received a brief address from the headmaster and longer talks from other worthy Friends. Bootham had been founded in 1823, as York Quarterly Meeting Friends' Boys' School. The Radical orator John Bright had been one of its early pupils, and there was a John Bright Memorial Library as well as a marble bust in the main entrance hall to remind visitors of the fact. Bright's words were inscribed on a bronze plaque in the library: 'A great love of books is like a personal introduction to the great and good men of all past time. If there be no seed-time there will certainly be no harvest, and youth of life is the seed-time of life.'

There was an annual prize for a Bright oration. Most of Alan's fellow-pupils chose to recite Bright's great speeches against the Crimean War; Alan, in revolt as usual, sought something to Bright's discredit and proposed to offer one of his speeches against the Factory Act. But these were not included in the volumes of his collected speeches, and Alan was then unfamiliar with Hansard. He therefore remained uncharacteristically silent.

Both Alan's flippancy and his radicalism can be seen as reactions to the Liberal philosophy of progress through social reform which prevailed at Bootham. *Membra sumus corporis magni** was the school motto. Joseph Rowntree's son, Seebohm Rowntree, sometimes lectured the boys on Sunday evenings about social problems and the need for 'good works'. Earnestness was drummed into them.

Bootham's name came from the medieval street leading north out of the city on which the school stood. Its frontage was a series of handsome Georgian brick buildings, some of them given by the founder of the chocolate firm, Joseph Rowntree; a distant relation, Arthur Rowntree, was now headmaster. There were various annexes straggling along the street, and on the other side of the road a new boarding-house named after the Quaker William Penn. Bootham was a public school, as formally defined; Arthur Rowntree had been admitted to the Headmasters' Conference in 1914. But it was not a 'proper' public school, in the sense in which people normally use the term. One of Alan's teachers described it as a 'republic'. The school stressed tolerance and reconciliation, in the Quaker tradition; there was no corporal punishment. This policy was severely tested in the years immediately after the War. As at The Downs, the temporary masters were elderly and timid, and they found it difficult to maintain discipline, particularly over the older boys. Some of them could not take the strain; one class exhausted three form masters in a single year. For a while the boys seemed uncontrollable. A new master, a Quaker, kept order only by banging a boy's head against the wall. When Alan arrived the school was still in turmoil; classes were rowdy, and bullying was rife. Alan preached anarchy in theory, but he was shocked by the consequences of a breakdown in order. A group of thirteen-year-olds decided that they would emulate public school prefects by taking it upon themselves to exercise discipline. No doubt because of his 'Bolshieness', Alan seemed a proper subject for punishment. They bent him over a desk and beat him with a cane. Alan's pride was hurt more than his bottom. He sought protection from older boys in return for doing their homework.

Alan rose quickly through the classes at Bootham. Because he was so bright he was one of the youngest in the form, and he looked

---

*'We are limbs of a great body.'

even younger because he was so short. In photographs he is almost always the smallest, and looks scruffier than most of the other boys. He acquired a reputation as an *enfant terrible*, who enjoyed provoking those in authority. Arthur Rowntree's daughter had married a son of General Smuts; it was slightly embarrassing for a liberal Quaker to be related to the Prime Minister of South Africa. Alan lost no opportunity to bring up this connection in debates. 'Alan's difficulty is not to swim against the tide,' Rowntree told Connie. 'His difficulty is to swim with it.'

The dormitory system at Bootham was unlike that of most other boarding-schools, where children are grouped according to age. Boys were allocated to a room when they arrived, and remained in it throughout their stay at the school. The rooms each slept half a dozen or so, who could be any age from thirteen to eighteen. The idea was to encourage boys to mix with those in other age-groups; another effect was to bring about strong loyalty within the dormitory and fierce rivalries between them. Alan was put in Room 24 of Penn House. When, in 1972, some alterations were being made to the building, ten volumes of 'Chronicles', running from 1921 to 1929, were found under the floorboards of the room. They form a scurrilous diary, written to be read out loud. Much of the first volume is in Alan's handwriting; clearly he was one of the initiators of a tradition which was secretly handed down through several generations. The Chronicles themselves are curious documents, full of schoolboy jokes and local references which make parts of them incomprehensible. Most of the entries are written in mocking tones; they are often parodies of adult documents of one kind or another. Because he was small and already inclined to be tubby, Alan's nickname was 'baby', and a typical entry is a spoof advertisement: 'Wanted. Nurse for four-month-old baby. If possible, rattle, cot and pram also. Nurse is not required to count baby's initials. Apply Taylor, Preston.'

There is a good deal more of this sort; Alan was clearly the butt of more or less good-natured teasing and his response was to play up to it. Thus he is described as 'petite and tres gros' [sic]; a mock book review concludes that the work in question 'could be understood by a babe (A.J.P.)' and 'proceeds from the sale of this paper towards buying a new rattle for Tailor' [sic]. Because he did not fit a conventional mould Alan became a 'character', known by his ridiculous initials, a clever fool who could say what he liked, indeed the more outrageous the better.

'A Soviet Government' was established in Room 24, and the Chronicles retitled 'Soviet Chronicles'. Like the government in Russia, the new government's priorities seem to have been military, and there are detailed accounts of fighting against other dormitories, with references to 'the A.J.P.T. brigade' signalling for help, or 'the opposing forces under A.J.P.T.' being put to flight. Alan seems to have been a doughty but not very effective fighter, as might be expected.

Alan's interest in politics extended further than the dormitory, of course. Following the lead of his parents he joined the Independent Labour Party in 1921. During the holidays he attended Sunday evening meetings of the Preston ILP, and even gave a talk on one occasion – probably an attack on parliamentary democracy. He also joined 'The Plebs League', whose object was 'to further the interests of independent working-class education'. Alan's mother was active in the National Council of Labour Colleges, an offshoot of The Plebs League, as was Henry Sara. The League issued a magazine, *The Plebs*, and 'Plebs Textbooks'; Alan dutifully swotted up on these as well as those recommended by his schoolmasters.

Alan's parents continued to march Left. Percy had extracted himself from the family business in 1920 with a share of the firm's capital, much to the consternation of J.T. The old man, now a widower, was furious at this betrayal. He broke off all relations with his son, and they did not speak again until 1933, when J.T. was on his deathbed. Even then they found it difficult to communicate. The settlement of £100,000 in cash left Percy a rich man. He started a wholesale confectionery business, and continued to run one of the cotton mills in Preston. But in his politics he preached fighting the bosses. He even joined a union, the gas workers' branch of the General and Municipal Workers' Union, though he had no connection with the gas works and, so Alan teased, did not even know where they were. Sometimes when he was speaking in public he was asked: 'How can you be a socialist and own a cotton mill?' Percy would reply: 'Well, you see, I'm in a system of capitalism . . .' The crowds seemed to accept this line of argument.

Connie was more Left still. According to Alan, she laundered money for the Communist Party. In 1924 she stood unsuccessfully as a Labour candidate in the Preston Municipal Election. A year later Connie was ill, so Percy contested the ward in her place, winning the seat. He remained a member of the town council on and off, representing various wards, until his death. Percy was very proud of Preston and used to talk in a proprietorial way of 'our water' and 'our juice' (meaning electricity). His policies in 1925 included building new swimming baths, enlarging Preston's boundaries, and replacing the town's cobblestone paving.

There was a strong feeling of comradeship within the Preston Labour Party in those days. The membership socialised together at dances and went on nature walks at weekends. Preston had the biggest single dock basin in the country, and when Russian ships put in their captains were invited to ILP meetings. The Party staged plays at its rooms in Glovers Court, and Alan directed a performance of *Masses and Man* by Ernst Toller, the rehearsals taking place at Rose Terrace. The Taylors made their home 'a refuge for all manner of persecuted and hunted people', including émigrés; according to the local paper, it was 'known as such all over Europe'.[1] Their house also attracted many visitors prominent in Left politics, including the wartime Labour leader, Arthur Henderson, and the editor of the *Daily Herald*, the future Labour leader George Lansbury, who became Percy's close friend. Another regular visitor was the Communist leader Harry Pollitt, who used to play solo whist with Alan.

This was the very aristocracy of the Left. Between them Percy, Connie and Sara knew almost everyone who mattered. It was still a relatively small world; while Labour remained a working-class movement, those few with money and education counted for a lot. Uncle Harry extended this network still further. His solicitor's practice had thrived, and by now he knew everybody who was anybody within the Labour movement. When Alan went to Oxford, for example, Harry was able to give him an introduction to G.D.H. Cole, the guru of left-wing academia. Alan once wrote that he was more or less born into socialism; if this was not strictly true, it could certainly be said that he grew up in the bosom of the Left.[2]

Thus when Alan wrote a letter to *The Communist*, published by the then recently formed Communist Party of Great Britain, attacking its editor, Raymond Postgate, it was not as if he were attacking a complete stranger. Postgate was a member of the Labour élite; his sister Margaret was married to G.D.H. Cole; he knew Lansbury, Harry and Henry Sara; quite likely, he had been a guest at the Taylor house. Postgate had urged Communists not to insert all writers and their works into the rigid compartments delineated by the Materialist Conception of History, and cited Dryden, Keats, Sterne and Wilde in support of his case. Alan's letter was a rebuke for this lapse from orthodoxy:

> He [Postgate] begins quite happily, but before we can get our bearings he has lured us into the morass of bourgeois thought. The Materialist Conception of History, I should imagine, deals in ideology, which surely expresses itself in literature; the logical conclusion from this, and I believe it to be true, is that literature 'dates'; that if we know the economic conditions of an epoch we know the kind of literature it produces, and vice versa. Postgate does not accept this, and therefore the whole superstructure of the Materialist Conception of History comes tumbling to the ground. Postgate's argument, in fact, if pressed to a logical conclusion, means that people are actuated not by their economic conditions – Oh! No! Nasty bread and cheese!! – but by their ideals, which happens, strange coincidence – to be exactly what the bourgeois would have us think – that he is in business for our good, not his own.

Alan acknowledged that the theme of any literary work may be sometimes unaffected by economic conditions, but maintained that 'in method of treating it and actual choice of subject the author is controlled by his economic circumstances'. He continued with an exhortation. 'Now do not, I beg you, ask why Keats wrote "Ode to a Nightingale". Although one may be in revolt against the economic circumstances, they are still the driving force.' Alan conceded that 'the desire for liberty' was a permanent characteristic in English literature. But 'even Postgate' – a typical Taylor rhetorical device, this – must admit that 'it has always taken on the form best suited to its economic circumstances'. The Materialist Conception of History was not of course an infallible rule which could never under any circumstances be broken. But it worked in nearly every case, and it was a much better guide than Postgate made out. Postgate had to admit, he said, that the Dryden passage he quoted was only a temporary lapse. 'I do not think that Postgate is quite a hopeless case, but he must be constantly on his guard against such outcroppings of his bourgeois upbringing. There is a passage about fearing the Greeks bearing gifts, and though I would not adopt that attitude to him, I would suggest that he adopt that attitude in dealing with his bourgeois culture.'[3]

Alan's political philosophy was outlined in a prize-winning school essay on 'Communism'. The content is pretty much standard Communist dogma, taken from the pages of *The Communist Manifesto* which he apparently knew 'backwards' and, no doubt, from the lips of Henry Sara. It is remarkable only in showing how rigidly a mind later so supple once thought – and in being one of the very few pieces he wrote with hardly a trace of humour. The Communist incentive, he wrote,

> is not an emotional one – they leave it to social reformers to go into hysterics over slum conditions; their position rather is based on historical methods and their chief mental weapon is the Materialist Conception of History . . . It has been shown by modern psychology that . . . the ideas and impulses which actuate his life are the result of previous experience, which experience is largely derived from his economic environment.

He traces the inevitability of the class struggle, dismisses the possibility of 'organic' growth and argues the necessity for a Dictatorship of the Proletariat to suppress the 'egoism' of the bourgeoisie. 'The Communists, far from conjuring up civil war artificially, strive to shorten its duration as much as possible' and 'to minimize the number of its victims'. The proletariat 'must end the domination of capital, make war impossible, transform the world into one co-operative commonwealth and bring about real human brotherhood and freedom.'

In 1921 Alan passed 'Matric' with distinction. He now joined the College Class with the other bright boys studying for university. The College was not really a class so much as a collection of individuals pursuing special and differing courses of work. A boy in

College Class was 'a man apart' from the rest of the school. Alan decided to enter for a history scholarship at Oxford. This was unusual; most of the other clever boys took science subjects and went to Cambridge. Those who wanted to study history generally went elsewhere to prepare for university entrance. Fifteen years earlier the historian G.N. Clark, for example, had gone on from Bootham to Manchester Grammar School in his last year to prepare for Oxford entrance. There was therefore only a handful of College boys reading history, and they were taught in tutorials by Leslie Gilbert.

Gilbert was unquestionably the most important schoolteacher in Alan's life. He was still a young man, not quite thirty, and had come into teaching late, having served in the Friends' Ambulance Unit during the War. Before the War he had read history at Manchester under the great medieval historian T.F. Tout, and emerged in 1913 with a First. Gilbert was a muscular Christian. Tout had followed him out of his viva and said: 'Mr Gilbert, if you don't do as well as you ought to have done, you can put it down to cricket.' Another of his passions was tennis; whenever a loud noise was heard outside, it was said jokingly that it must be one of Mr Gilbert's serves. Gilbert was a sincere Quaker; Alan, on the other hand, had lost what little faith in God he ever possessed. Bootham offers some magnificent views of the Minster, and it was looking through the classroom window at the great cathedral that Alan experienced the opposite of a religious revelation. A voice told him: 'There is no God.' From then on he was never again troubled by religious belief.[4]

In spite of this difference between them, Gilbert and Alan became lifelong friends. Years after Alan left Bootham they were still going on walking holidays together. Gilbert stimulated his pupils by constantly introducing them to new books and ideas, and engaging them in debate. He underpinned this by teaching the boys to express themselves in simple, taut, logical prose.

Under Gilbert's prompting Alan read innumerable historical works, beginning with the condensed edition of Gibbon and S.R. Gardiner's three-volume history of the English Civil War. Many of these were old-fashioned textbooks, among them the classics of narrative historical writing – Carlyle, Trevelyan and Macaulay, for example – now read more for their style than for their accuracy.

Interspersed with these were such intellectually challenging works as the philosopher-historian Benedetto Croce's *Theory and History of Historiography*: heavy going for an undergraduate, let alone a schoolboy. Alan also read H. G. Wells's *Outline of History* as it came out in serial form. An illustration of the various national symbols, 'the Tribal Gods for which men might die', left a permanent impression; he used this image to open his Ford Lectures, more than thirty years later. But perhaps just as significant in the long run was his wide reading in literature, biography and political theory. He learned much about the past from biographical works such as Strachey's *Eminent Victorians*, or from the novels of Trollope, Belloc or Disraeli. Marx too was an historian, of course; and political thinkers such as Swift, Burke, John Stuart Mill and Cobbett helped to shape his understanding of society's mechanisms, as did contemporary writers: Harold Laski, G.D.H. Cole and R.H. Tawney.

Strangely enough Alan learned historical method not from nineteenth-century textbooks, but from 'Natural History'. Bootham put great emphasis on the value of voluntary pursuits *per se*, particularly the work of the naturalist and the archaeologist, 'whose work is collection, observation, diary-keeping, dissection and the like'.[5] Alan was on the committee of the school Natural History Club from 1920 to 1924, and Chairman from 1922 to 1924. This may appear surprising, given his lack of interest in nature study at The Downs. But for him natural history meant archaeology, and archaeology meant church architecture. This was a great school speciality, since within the city walls there were no fewer than twenty-seven medieval churches, with an extraordinary number of magnificent ecclesiastical buildings, including the great Cistercian abbeys, not far away. The crowning glory was of course the Minster, which overlooked the school. The subject was encouraged by the frequent presence at the school of an authority on medieval church architecture, A. Neave Brayshaw, commonly known as 'Puddles'.

Brayshaw was a Quaker of independent means who had retired from a teaching job at Bootham twenty years earlier, while still in his early forties. He was a devout man, fond of little boys, and he devoted the remaining forty years of his life to voluntary work in

Quaker schools. He led expeditions of enthusiastic scholars to look at the parish churches of York itself and the nearby villages. Once a year he took a group of boys to France.

Alan was an enthusiastic pupil. Archaeology 'brought the past alive for me', and he gave more time to it than to all his other schoolwork. Indeed it became a lifelong interest. Puddles would explain the historical basis for the different architectural styles, encouraging the boys to take brass rubbings and keep notebook 'diaries', with sketches picking out details in colour, and carefully measured ground plans. Alan carried a tape measure and a set square for just this purpose. He spent the best part of a year on the Minster alone. The best 'diaries' were shown at a big exhibition held every Christmas. In his final year at Bootham Alan presented a particularly good one which was much praised. One of the cleverest pupils from Bootham's sister-school The Mount came to the open day and thought it much more learned than anything the girls could produce. His work won Alan the Old Scholars' Exhibition for Archaeology.

It was clear to all by now that Alan was a brilliant student. He was a prize-winning essayist. Other pupils were impressed above all by his scintillating intelligence, but also by his memory, his capacity for hard work and his wide reading; though some were repelled by what seemed to them intellectual arrogance. At Bootham the boys were encouraged to keep reading lists, and Alan's have survived for the years 1921–5. 'Somehow I read practically the whole of English literature,' he wrote in his autobiography, and it was hardly an exaggeration if the lists can be believed. In 1922, for example, he read 184 books, in 1923 219, and in 1924, the year he left Bootham and went to university, 244. Some of these books were not very substantial, adventure novels by Sax Rohmer and John Buchan, for example. But such frivolous titles were in a minority, and more than balanced by the works of Milton and Chaucer. The overall effect of these lists is awesome. In 1922, to take a year at random, he read Carlyle's *Past and Present* and *Heroes and Hero-worship*, eight Shaw plays, sixteen novels by Galsworthy, Rousseau's *The Social Contract*, Disraeli's *Sybil* and *Coningsby*, Gibbon's *Decline and Fall of the Roman Empire* (admittedly the abridged edition), Swinburne's poems, Marx's *The*

Eighteenth Brumaire of Louis Napoleon, seven Shakespeare plays, seven Ibsen plays, Melville's *Moby Dick*, Lord Acton's *Lectures on Modern History* and *The French Revolution*, More's *Utopia*, Tawney's *The Acquisitive Society*, G.D.H. Cole's *Social Theory*, Tacitus (in Latin), Nietzsche's *Thus Spake Zarathustra*, and Samuel Butler's *The Way of All Flesh*, *Erewhon*, and *Erewhon Revisited*. Plus another 127 books.

Boswell's *Life of Johnson* was his favourite, and later in life when asked to name the greatest of all Englishmen Alan usually settled on the great doctor, though often after a struggle with Cobbett, another author he encountered at Bootham. He acknowledged Cobbett, along with Bunyan and Shaw,* as influences on his style, though it is also possible to detect in his early writing traces of Lytton Strachey and G.K. Chesterton.

Another prize essay is much more personal than Alan's earlier polemic on Communism. It is a satire, claiming to be a translation from a document written by a foreign visitor to a small island in the northern seas, presumably Britain. The unknown writer describes the religion of these islanders, and their worship of various ideas – 'Nature', 'style', 'strength', 'convention' and 'self-interest' – which are portrayed as outlandish. By this ingenious conceit Alan is able to lampoon aspects of life at Bootham without ever shedding his disguise. The discussion on style, for example, describes a 'seance', at which one of the worshippers

> arises and reads something from a paper, preferably an account of the most trivial and uninteresting event in his life, while the other worshippers arrange themselves as comfortably as possible . . . If the priest conducts the service aright there should be at the end no sound until someone has walked round and roused the worshippers from their sleep; but if the account has been interesting enough to keep anyone awake the suffer[er] immediately leaps to his feet and screams, 'This essay was no fit subject for a literary society; it has got some point to it' or 'This essay was out of the ordinary and therefore had to use unusual words or thoughts, which is a serious

---

*Gilbert was a Shaw fan; a production of Shaw's *Arms and the Man* was performed at the school by Bootham and Mount staff in 1923.

fault; it should have been simple and orthodox, so that conscientious people might sleep without any uneasiness'.

'The true priests of the cult,' wrote Alan, 'are called "poets" . . . all of them go into ecstasies, for example, over the birds which keep them awake in the morning when they are trying to go to sleep.' These essays were read aloud, so that Alan gained extra value from his cracks at Bootham. It was all the sweeter that Arthur Rowntree was often in the chair at the Essay Society. The worshippers of the idol 'strength', he continued, 'devise a multitude of schemes whereby the devotee may be injured'; and so on. At the end the writer tries to reason with the island's inhabitants. Their adherence to convention, he argues, is 'a form of laziness . . . a kind of mental short-cut, whereby our ancestors did the thinking and we take the credit . . . each generation should do their own thinking and not obey ancestors, certainly no wiser and probably more ignorant than themselves'. (The reference is almost certainly to John Bright's remark that 'we stand on the shoulders of our ancestors, and we see further'.) But the idolators 'listened to me with quiet scorn or fled from me with vile abuse'.

This is a clever piece, well sustained. There is none of the doctrinaire woodenness which marred Alan's earlier essay on Communism. Yet it is even more clear that the writer sees himself as an outsider, exiled among ignorant barbarians, and this is a feature of a third prize-winning essay Alan read to the Society in October 1923, a playful piece entitled 'A Lunatic at Large'.* The lunatic is the writer, who wanders around London in a kind of fey whimsy, but he is twice interrupted in the middle of his narrative by his professor, who complains that he is acting the fool, and a conceited fool at that. ' "Why, of course," I returned, "what do you expect? I am incapable at footer and a cricket-ball terrifies me . . . so I must be conceited to keep up my self-respect. Only people who are really clever or really good at games can afford to be modest." ' A final thrust comes when the professor says that he doesn't mind the

---

A Lunatic at Large was the title of a popular novel published in 1899. Its sequel, *A Lunatic at Large Again*, was published in 1922.

cheap witticisms of little boys, whereupon the writer rebukes him for insolence.

In his essays Alan deployed a number of rhetorical tricks, such as affecting to be afraid of persecution, and he made good use of these in the Bootham Debating Society, which met once a fortnight. Alan spoke frequently in the debates. In the 1923 spring term there was a mock election to the York City Council. Alan was the Labour candidate's agent. While his candidate was speaking, a telegram purporting to be from Lenin arrived, arranged of course by Alan. Despite this *coup de théâtre* the Unionist candidate won the election.

Alan had a further opportunity to develop his platform technique at the annual debates with The Mount. They were for senior classes and staff. In March 1923 the debate was held at The Mount, and was preceded by half an hour's 'supper and sociability'. The boys and girls who were not speaking were partnered, each being given one half of a proverb, so that when the boys arrived, 'a joy for ever', for example, went round asking if anyone had seen 'a thing of beauty'. When even 'a rolling stone' had been found by 'gathers no moss', they sat down to eat, and at seven o'clock trooped up to the library for the debate itself. The motion was 'That the progress of civilisation has not tended to increase the happiness of mankind'. The proposer was Miss Kathleen Constable,* and the opposer A.J.P. Taylor.

Alan spoke almost without notes. This assembly, he remarked, 'perhaps because of its extreme youth', might not remember a time when there were no such things as votes for women. All the ladies in the company, he said, must be on his side, for it was to civilisation that they owed their emancipation. Civilisation provides romance, he went on, in the danger of being run over! The motion was defeated.

It was the year of Bootham's centenary, and the celebrations lasted all through the Whitsun week. There were articles in the press, and Arthur Rowntree was particularly pleased when a *Birmingham Mail* piece about Bootham was headed 'The Rugby of Quakerism'. The Mount put on a Pageant of Education, with

---

*Later to become the distinguished Dickens scholar, Kathleen Tillotson.

Kathleen Constable appearing as Virgil. On the Saturday evening a huge party was held in the garden of the Archbishop's Palace at Bishopthorpe, outside the city. Sadly, it poured.

Alan was still short and stocky; in 1923, when he was seventeen, he was not quite five foot five and weighed nine stone. He had grey eyes, and a pronounced chin with a distinct cleft. His fair hair was now swept straight back without a parting, and he sported racy tartan socks. A friend at The Mount described him as 'interesting looking'; though unfortunately he was also spotty. To boys of his age he seemed worldly and sophisticated. He was not popular. He was contemptuous of games and physical exercise, indeed of the whole school ethos. But there was also a gaiety about him. When looking out of the window one of the younger boys was astonished to see this 'elder statesman' stop, and for no apparent reason dance a jig on the path outside. Alan began to adopt some of the languid mannerisms common to those interested in modern literature and poetry in the early 1920s, though the effect was slightly spoilt by his northern accent. 'What energy that boy has!' he exclaimed drily, observing a contemporary kicking a football. He teased the devout: 'How's the inner light today?' He had no close friends until he 'fell in love' with his schoolfellow George Clazy.

George was if anything even cleverer than Alan. His father was a Church of Scotland minister, and George was an austere, almost ascetic Calvinist. His cold intellectualism was a challenge to Alan's rather disorganised jumble of Marxist ideas, and his physical beauty contrasted with Alan's cheerful unkemptness. 'At school we were together all the time, introducing each other to new books and drawing different conclusions from them.'[6] At home in the Easter holidays they wrote each other earnest letters of ten or twelve pages every day. They kept in touch after George departed Bootham for Edinburgh University at the end of the 1923 summer term, and went on walking holidays together in the vacations.

Alan now became a reeve, the Bootham equivalent of a prefect. As at The Downs, there was a measure of self-government in their appointment. The reeves were the subject of a vote by the Senior Classes 'which weighs largely with the headmaster in making the appointment'.[7] Reeves needed to be able to exercise control. They took 'prep' (homework) for two forms totalling thirty to forty younger boys, and sat at the head of the table and supervised meals. 'Everyone at Bootham regarded me very much as a joke, and the younger boys thought that I would be easy game. They soon learned better,' he wrote in his autobiography. 'After one set-to I had no further troubles.'[8] Alan was now a figure of some substance within the school, and even other boys his own age looked up to him. It was rumoured that he was a spokesman for the reeves, and that he was consulted by Arthur Rowntree himself. A reeve was entitled to his own study. Another boy who was reading history, Roger Moore, often used to come to Alan's study to talk about books, politics and school gossip. Once Alan showed Moore his private diary: 'You want to know what I'm thinking? There it is.' It was the day after Lenin's death, and Alan had written a whole page of tribute.

Alan always extracted as much as he could from the rules. Reeves could give boys leave from football, which was otherwise compulsory. Alan decided to apply this rule to himself. The headmaster protested that this was not how the rule should be interpreted. Like a barrack-room lawyer, Alan demanded to know where this was written down, and Rowntree had to concede that it was nowhere spelled out. Alan played no more football. He also gave himself permission to enter the city walls in the afternoon, which was generally forbidden.

That spring Alan went up to Oxford to sit the examination for a Brackenbury Scholarship to read history at Balliol. Afterwards he dined at high table with the tutors. He explained that he was a Communist, and produced his plans for the university in a workers' state: 'Blow it up after I have gone down.' Alan failed to win the scholarship. Leslie Gilbert, not perhaps an unbiased observer, believed Alan's erudition had 'scared the pants off the examiners'. There were three Brackenbury Scholarships awarded that year. Two were cut off in their thirties,* killed in the Second World War; the third was John Bowle, migratory professor and author of *Western Political Thought*.

---

*C.S.M. Brereton, killed in Singapore, 1942; T.W. Coghlin, killed in Sicily a year later. I am indebted to Mr T. H. Hughes-Davies for drawing my attention to the fate of the Brackenbury Scholars of 1924–7.

This blow, the first setback in his academic career, still rankled with Alan half a century later. He ascribed his failure to his father's wealth; he could afford to go to Oxford with or without a scholarship, while others might not be so fortunate, and Balliol had unfairly decided against him because of it. Perhaps this setback acted as a spur, urging him on to a First, which none of the Brackenbury Scholars of his year achieved. In March he tried for a scholarship at Oriel. He was ill and thought he had made a poor show of most of the papers. However, one of them contained a question about Gothic cathedrals. Alan was in his element. He failed to get a scholarship, but the college awarded him a special exhibition, worth £60 a year. All that hard work with Puddles had paid off.

Alan had one more term at Bootham. The next debate with The Mount was held in the John Bright Memorial Library; Alan proposed the motion 'That in the opinion of this House, Tradition, and the Dependence on Custom, is always harmful'. Miss Constable again joined the debate, quoting John Bright about standing on the shoulders of our ancestors and seeing further. Alan seized on this in his concluding speech, asserting that, rather than standing on their shoulders, people hid under the umbrellas of their ancestors, so as not to get wet. The motion was carried.

Alan began to take an interest in girls. Informal contacts with 'Mount Hags', or indeed other members of their sex, were not encouraged. Once, when a boy was found waving at girls, he was ordered to stand and wave a towel at the headmaster for an hour. Alan admired Kathleen Constable, and when she gave a talk at The Mount on 'Shakespeare's Theatre' he came along to listen. It was unusual for boys to come to such talks unprompted, and Alan entered the room in 'a rather determined sort of way'. After the Oxford entrance examinations were completed Bootham boys took special courses in local government, economics and other worthy topics, which included visits to slums and welfare institutions, as preparation for the wider world they were about to enter. Kathleen Constable came to do some preparatory work in economics at Bootham, and sat next to Alan in class. At the end of term the Rowntrees laid on the traditional 'Cocoa Works Party' for the two schools. It was a beautiful summer afternoon. Seeing

Kathleen Constable sitting with her brother, who was also at Bootham, Alan pounced. He sat down beside her and monopolised the conversation, ignoring Denis Constable completely. He told her that he had seen *Hedda Gabler* in Manchester with Mrs Patrick Campbell in the leading role, and proceeded to outline the plot. She refrained from mentioning that she was already familiar with the play.

It was time for Alan to leave Bootham. Looking back in his autobiography he acknowledged his debt to the school. 'The boys were sometimes intolerant, the masters never. They treated me as their intellectual equal. They argued. They never ordered. Quakers are often irritating: always looking for the common ground and reluctant to admit that it is sometimes necessary to fight, metaphorically or literally. Still, they are about the best thing the human race has produced.'[9]

The Society of Friends had a practical influence too. Almost by accident, when he went to The Downs Alan became part of the formidable Quaker network, which extended through Bootham to Oxford. There he came under the protective wing of G.N. Clark, himself an old Bootham and Manchester Grammar School boy. Forty years later Clark was to invite Alan to write the concluding volume in the Oxford History of England, perhaps the most influential of all his books. Here was a paradox indeed: Alan posed as a rebel and an outsider, but he dutifully followed his parents in politics and was at the heart of an alternative establishment of nonconformists. To find himself, he would need to rebel again.

4: 'Blow it up after I have gone down'

Oxford is a place apart. It reeks of antiquity; Alan's college, Oriel, celebrated its sixth centenary while Alan was up, and it is not the oldest. Oxford operates by unwritten conventions, and celebrates arcane rituals. Even its terminology is exclusive. The academic terms are known as Michaelmas (autumn), Hilary (spring) and Trinity (summer). Final examinations are known as 'Schools', and at the end of each term undergraduates face the ordeal of 'Collections'; they have to attend while tutors report publicly on their progress, or lack of it. The head of a college may be called Provost, President, Warden, Master, Rector, Principal, or Dean. As this suggests, the university's character comes from its colleges, which maintain their independence from the university. Each college has its own set of rules, written and unwritten, and separate traditions. The past intimidates the present; the clatter of centuries echoes in the quadrangles.

This is bewildering to the new arrival, particularly if he does not come from a traditional public school. In Alan's time such men were in a minority. Only a third of all Oxbridge undergraduates came from grammar schools, and only one in a hundred from working-class backgrounds.[1] At Balliol, for example, there were only three grammar-school boys among the 1924 intake, though it was thought of as one of the most progressive colleges. Oriel had no such reputation. Indeed the frontispiece to a well-known edition of *Jude the Obscure* had seemed to show a view of Oriel; it was rumoured that the college had contemplated taking out a libel action against Thomas Hardy. The Oriel of 1925, wrote one of Alan's contemporaries, took 'the manners and assumptions – not always admirable – of gentlemen's sons for granted. It was also taken for granted that, although there were plenty of menservants around to empty our slops and carry meals and coal-scuttles up to our rooms, we were essentially schoolboys still, and to be governed accordingly.'² Students were locked up at night to keep them out of mischief. Not only were most of the Oriel undergraduates in Alan's time public schoolboys, but many of them were from the same school: Charterhouse, the Provost's *alma mater*. When a council-school boy called Albert Smith arrived, an attempt was made at a Junior Common Room meeting to get up a protest at his admission, and he was widely ignored; until it was discovered that he was a good footballer, which soon made him one of the most popular men in the college.

Oriel is made up of a succession of quadrangles south of the High Street. The front gate faces the back of Christ Church, and inside the main quad the Hall porch is immediately opposite. The Hall itself has an imposing hammerbeam roof, and is hung with port-raits, including some of 'the Oriel fathers', the clerics who domin-ated the college in the mid-nineteenth century. Indeed it was only fifty years before Alan arrived that the rule obliging Fellows to take holy orders and forbidding them from marrying had been relaxed. Undergraduates who failed to attend chapel regularly were still punished by being 'gated'. Typically Alan found a way round this rule. He told the Dean that he could not in good conscience attend when he did not believe in God. The Dean conceded this point, but hoped that Alan would come to him and talk over his doubts. Alan answered that he had none.

From Alan's rooms on staircase VIII there was a distant prospect of Magdalen Tower. Later he moved to rooms on staircase IV, conveniently located for dining in Hall. There the Scholars and the Commoners were separated, and Alan was often conspicuous at the Scholars' table. Afterwards a group of five or six undergrad-uates would meet for intellectual conversation; Alan always had something to say about everything. The other Oriel undergraduates were not all upper-class athletes. Among Alan's contemporaries were James Meade, who would win the Nobel Prize for economics; Erwin Canham, a young American later for many years the distinguished editor of the *Christian Science Monitor*; Harold

Hobson and Desmond Shawe-Taylor, drama and music critics respectively of the *Sunday Times*; the poet Norman Cameron; and J.I.M. Stewart, who was to become an eminent scholar of English literature and to achieve another distinction as a writer of detective novels under his *alter ego* Michael Innes. Perhaps the most brilliant of all was Ronald Syme, a mature student from New Zealand who caused a sensation when it was announced that he had won not just one of the University's prizes for classics, but all four. Ironically he, as a Commoner, was marooned from all the clever talk at the Scholars' table.

Alan's work was curiously unsatisfying. To begin with, there were two terms of frustration before he crossed the hurdle of 'Pass Mods'. When he got on to history proper he found that it was not what he had hoped. The only lecture he attended which left any lasting impression, he later claimed, was the one in which Sir Charles Oman had demonstrated the use of the pike. Alan wanted to work on the recent past, the immediate background to the twentieth century or perhaps the run-up to the Revolution. Neither of his tutors supplied this. E.S. 'Stanley' Cohn taught medieval history, unfortunately in such a mannered and musical voice that every second word was inaudible, even when he was not diving under the sofa for a pencil or a box of matches; G.N. Clark had become bored with teaching and stopped anyway at 1688. Neither taught him anything about historical method or analysis. Such at least was Alan's memory of history at Oriel. Others remembered differently. Harold Hobson found Clark an exhilarating tutor, modest and cheerful, who bore his learning without ostentation. Most important of all, he taught his pupils to take nothing on trust. When you are faced with a statement or an alleged fact, he would say, you should always ask yourself, who says so? What authority is there for that statement? For unless the authority is sound the fact or the statement has no validity.[3]

Perhaps Alan was reluctant to acknowledge the influence of his tutor, who became a friend and who helped and supported Alan much later in his career. Clark may indeed have had a bigger role than Alan admitted in bringing him to Oriel in the first place. Clark was a Yorkshireman from a prosperous, middle-class, non-conformist background. From Bootham, he had gone on to

Manchester Grammar School, then won a Brackenbury Scholarship to Balliol. As undergraduates he and G.D.H. Cole had been prominent in the famous 1910 Oxford tram strike. He was elected to a prize Fellowship at All Souls in 1912, and after serving in the First World War he became a Fellow of Oriel. Active in Labour politics, he was invited to stand as a parliamentary candidate for Oxford in the 1920s. Later he became less radical; it was perhaps a sign of this that in 1936 he was received into the Church of England. According to Alan, he sought adoption as a Conservative candidate for the University. But he was a shy man, temperamentally unsuited to controversy. According to the *Dictionary of National Biography*, he retained the 'intellectual vigour and sturdy independence of his dissenting family background'.

Two years later Geoffrey Barraclough would follow Alan from Bootham to read history at Oriel, and he too would go on to a distinguished career as an historian. It was the Quaker conspiracy, the alternative old boy network. Alan avoided Barraclough; perhaps he was trying to escape from Bootham. There was a society for old Bootham/Mount scholars, 'The Cork and Water Club', but Alan avoided their meetings.

Indeed Alan hardly mixed with other undergraduates reading history. He had no thoughts of making a career in academic life. He was not invited to join the Stubbs Society, the élite from which future historians are supposed to be drawn. Once he was a successful historian Alan used to enjoy telling people that Clark had advised him against academic life, saying – perhaps rightly – that he was unsuited for it. As it was, 'history was not much more than a hobby for me'. It was interesting to him only as the story of the struggle for liberty and justice – what Ramsay MacDonald, in a different context, referred to as 'up and up and up and on and on and on'. Unable to take his preferred topic of the Chartists, Alan settled on the reign of Richard II as his special subject, which gave him the chance to study the Peasants' Revolt.[4]

There is a story that Alan took elocution lessons in Oxford to rid himself of his Northern accent. This may be no more than a malicious rumour, though in the early 1920s it would not have been unusual for an undergraduate to do so. Few educated people then spoke with regional accents; clever pupils tended to imitate the way their schoolteachers spoke. English tutors at Somerville offered a course in 'voice production', ostensibly to help the women speak verse but really a euphemism for eliminating accents. What is certain is that while at Oxford Alan lost any recognisable accent; his voice became stifled, rising often to a high pitch – ideal for the sardonic comment.

Oriel was a small, intimate college, much more self-contained than colleges are nowadays. It was, and is, the college of the Regius Professor of Modern History, though Alan claimed not to know the name of the incumbent while he was an undergraduate. Its tone was set by the Provost, the Reverend Lancelot Ridley Phelps, known by the undergraduates as 'the Phelper'. Phelps was then just over seventy. He was delightfully eccentric; he had a long white beard, and during the day he wore a black straw hat and an old-fashioned morning-coat. Stories of him are legion. A typical one has him listening to a sermon when the preacher asked: 'And what application, we may ask ourselves, does this Biblical incident have to our own times?' Phelps answered loudly from the congregation, 'None whatsoever, sir.'[5]

Phelps had been instrumental in getting Alan to Oriel, insisting against convention that an Exhibition be created for his benefit. They became friendly; Alan was often asked to lunch with him and afterwards they went for walks together. Phelps was a kind man, known for his interest in 'the social question'; he had been a member of the Royal Commission on the Poor Law and was on nodding terms with many of Oxford's tramps. Both he and Alan were known in their different social circles as 'characters'. Alan began to sport a bow-tie.

The Oxford that Alan came up to in 1924 is the Oxford described by Evelyn Waugh in *Decline and Fall* and *Brideshead Revisited*. Alan knew Waugh slightly, and he knew, at least by sight, most of the other famous undergraduates, such as Brian Howard or Harold Acton. Acton had come up to Oxford from Eton in 1922. He became the uncrowned king of the 'aesthetes', who eschewed the aggressive masculinity which, it seemed, had caused the War, and embraced instead a poetic dandyism. Acton and his mainly homosexual followers wore make-up, adopted exaggerated mannerisms and wore what seemed like outrageously effeminate clothes: silk shirts in pastel colours, white waistcoats, baggy trousers in silver or pink, and suede shoes. These were provocative to the 'hearties', the more athletic type of undergraduate. Clashes were frequent, so much so that even before they had come up to Oxford schoolboys like Tom Driberg had learned to dread what the hearties might do to them. In fact, the hearties were in the main unimaginative; their most usual form of persecution took the form it had always done: smashing up the offender's furniture and hurling his bed out of the window. 'Debagging' – removing the victim's trousers – was humiliating but less expensive. Another traditional punishment was 'sconcing', forcing the offender to drink a large measure of beer in one gulp, but this was normally imposed on other athletes at, for example, 'bump' suppers.

When Alan arrived in 1924 this Oxford was passing. The worst that happened to him was to be disturbed late at night by drunken public schoolboys trying to redeem him from Communism. But then Alan was neither one thing nor the other. Bootham was not a 'real' public school, like Rugby. Alan's family were wealthy, but they came from the North, and they were in 'trade'. His teetotal parents would be ridiculed by his fellows. He still had traces of a northern accent, and he held preposterous political notions. Worst of all he was serious, a bit of a prig. When he came up to Oxford Alan was more Arthur Potts* than Sebastian Flyte. The hearties disliked 'bores' at least as much as they disliked 'pansies'.

But as he got into the swing of things Alan began to loosen up. Like many undergraduates before and since, he tried on different identities until he found one that suited: swot, class warrior, hard drinker, womaniser, athlete, even fop. He regretted that knee-breeches were no longer in fashion, he told Harold Hobson, because he 'had a leg'. Hobson was impressed when Alan talked carelessly about the *Folies Bergère*, particularly by the knowledge he claimed of a Miss Carlyle.[6] Free from the supervision of his

---

*Paul Pennyfeather's undergraduate friend in *Decline and Fall*.

parents and blessed with a generous allowance, Alan began to develop a taste for cigars and good wine. He often sat up late at night drinking whisky with his friends. When Geoffrey Rowntree, a Quaker who had been with Alan at both The Downs and Bootham, visited him from Cambridge, they drank sherry in formal evening dress. Rowntree had never tasted it before.

On arriving at Oxford in those days undergraduates received notes from local tradesmen offering unlimited credit. Alan and his friends embarked on an opulent course of life. They hosted elaborate luncheon parties in their rooms and in the evenings flirted with the 'Georgeoisie', the aesthetes who frequented The George restaurant in the city or The Spread Eagle in Thame. They bought fashionable paintings and decorated their rooms with them, smoked expensive cigars or special cigarettes with gold butts, and wore hand-made clothes and expensive shoes.[7] Several of them experimented with 'up-to-neckers', roll-neck sweaters then very fashionable and daring because they suggested the wearer was homosexual.

Alan was later to write that during this 'Golden Age', this 'fantastic epoch', homosexuality was neither innocent nor wicked. 'It was merely, for a brief period, normal.'[8] He now became fond of 'Innes' (J.I.M.) Stewart, a small, good-looking Scot who came up to Oriel in 1925. Perhaps there was a homoerotic side to their friendship; several of Alan's acquaintances thought so, and Innes was certainly 'precious'. But this may not mean very much: homosexuality was fashionable. As Louis MacNeice found: 'in Oxford homosexuality and "intelligence", heterosexuality and brawn, were almost inextricably paired.'[9] Stewart's lasting influence was to encourage Alan's tendency to flippancy.[10]

It was in any case hard to keep up any kind of friendship with a woman at Oxford. One risked ridicule by even mentioning women undergraduates, who were fenced around with rules. Soon after she arrived at Somerville Alan wrote a facetious note to Kathleen Constable suggesting that they might have tea together at The Candied Friend, a popular undergraduate rendezvous. They did so, but both were embarrassed and nothing ensued. In his last year Alan became infatuated with a very different young woman, the much talked-about Morna Stuart,* but failed to press his suit. The Zuleika Dobson of the era was Elizabeth Harman, later Pakenham, later still Longford, but though she and Alan thereafter became warm friends they did not meet at this stage.

Despite their occasional affectations, Alan and his friends led what was in many ways an innocent existence. Almost every week he attended the Oxford Playhouse, where he saw plenty of Galsworthy, Chekhov, Ibsen, Strindberg and Shaw. Saturday nights were taken up with the Newlands Society, a play-reading group. Saturday and Sunday afternoons were spent touring the Oxfordshire countryside and eating enormous teas. For his nineteenth birthday Alan's father gave him a car of his own, a fish-tailed, open-topped Rover. This was unusual, though not quite as unusual as Alan later made out; at least three of his Oriel contemporaries owned cars: a Lancia, an Alvis and a Morgan. But Alan was certainly more privileged than the average undergraduate, even in a privileged college like Oriel.

Alan's car was unreliable but fast. It was fitted with an illegal device, a 'cut out' which by-passed the silencer. The result was a burst of speed, accompanied by a deafening roar from the engine. Alan used the cut out when overtaking; the effect on the other driver can be imagined.

Alan also developed a taste for 'mysteries'; his reading lists show the same prodigious volume but more frivolous content (perhaps because the earlier lists were scrutinised by his teachers). He became a devotee of Agatha Christie and P.G. Wodehouse, among others. Michael Innes's detective novels set in Oxford – published from 1936 on – are full of in-jokes he and Alan shared together as undergraduates. Alan's reading list for 1925 lists 167 books, including works by Galsworthy, Chesterton, Anatole France, J.M. Barrie, Shaw, Henry James, Hardy, Jane Austen, Max Beerbohm, Aldous Huxley, Wells, Saki, Osbert Sitwell, M.R. James, Turgenev, Trotsky, Sidney and Beatrice Webb, Arthur Schnitzler and Thomas Love Peacock.

Phelps encouraged the ethos of the 'scholar-athlete' at Oriel.

---

*Later the author of several novels, including *Night Rider* (1934) and *Till She Stoop* (1935).

Alan was not much good at football or tennis, but he did join the college Boat Club, and soon became No. 2 for the Second Torpid.* This was the most junior of the college boats, and Oriel was by no means the force on the river that it was later to become. The Boat Club minutes for 1924–5 record that the Second Torpid was only just able to find enough men for the crew, and then only by calling on some very inferior members of the Club. As it was, one of the crew possessed only nine fingers. Oriel Second Torpid finished thirty-fourth on the river.

The following year Alan was stroke, and Innes Stewart cox. The stroke is effectively captain of the boat, and it is he who sets the rhythm or the 'rating' for the others; it calls for technical ability and balance. At Torpids the Second 'Toggers' rowed through most nights, being 'bumped' only once and bumping Exeter II at the Free Ferry. The Boat Club records praised their 'dash'. In his autobiography and elsewhere, Alan states that following Torpids he was for a while in training with the First VIII in preparation for Eights Week, but the Boat Club records do not bear out this claim. Afterwards Alan resigned from the Boat Club. He was then entering his final year, so this may have been due more to pressure of work than lack of enthusiasm. The rowing obviously did Alan some good, for when he went to visit his old headmaster and his wife, Mr and Mrs Jones, who had retired to Sibford, 'it was very difficult to recognise the very robust undergraduate as the ailing little boy whom we had with us at Colwall'.[11]

Alan was more prominent within the college for his politics. He made no attempt to disguise his left-wing views, and as a result quickly became kown as the 'College Communist'. This led to a certain amount of persecution from the generally apolitical but anti-Communist public schoolboys. Other undergraduates suffered worse; one Communist at Merton had his books and furniture burnt time after time. 'People talk of a persecution complex,' he remarked to Alan. 'It is easy to have a persecution complex if you are a Communist at Merton.' In the end he went down without taking his degree. Alan learned to keep his political views to

---

*'Torpids', the bumping races run in Hilary Term, are traditionally not taken so seriously as those in the summer.

himself, at least within the college. He joined the Labour Club, then the largest political society within the University, as did several other Oriel contemporaries such as Harold Hobson and James Meade. The secretary of the Labour Club at the time was A.L. Rowse, elected a Fellow of All Souls at only twenty-one and already a cult figure in Oxford. Alan invited him to lunch at Oriel, and they became friendly. In his autobiography Alan says that he attended Labour Club meetings regularly and spoke often, yet other frequent attenders do not remember seeing him there.

It was an exciting time in politics. The first Labour Government had been formed in January 1924, after Labour had emerged from the election as the largest party but without an overall majority. The millennium would have to wait a little while longer, and now the Government was foundering over its friendly policy towards Soviet Russia. Another election was held in October, and a Conservative government took office, though Labour had in fact increased its share of the vote. Meanwhile a long-running dispute between the miners and the pit-owners threatened to escalate into a general strike. Young left-wingers like Alan hoped for a revolution.

In March 1925 a letter from him was published in *The Plebs*. It was in response to a piece by Alan's old antagonist Raymond Postgate, now chairman of the executive committee of the Plebs League. Postgate had deplored the division on the Italian Left, which he argued was preventing effective opposition to Mussolini as he tightened his Fascist grip on the country. Alan ignored Postgate's main argument; he objected to what he called Postgate's 'sneering reference to the Communist International, the great class-war organisation of the world'.[12]

That summer Alan had an opportunity to see the workers' paradise at first hand. Connie decided to go to Russia, and she took her usual retinue of Alan and Henry Sara. They went first to St Petersburg, newly renamed Leningrad, where they spent a week, and then on to Moscow for another five weeks, interrupted only by a brief trip to Nizhny-Novgorod, better known by its post-1932 name, Gorky. It was a good time to visit the Soviet Union. Lenin had died, and Stalin had yet to emerge as dictator. The country had recovered from the Civil War. The New Economic Policy had eased restrictions on agriculture and brought a temporary end to the famine. Meanwhile the Communists appeared to sympathetic eyes to be building a new kind of society, indeed a new kind of man. These were heroic days; the air was thick with reform. Connie and Henry had brought with them letters of introduction from important British Communists and trades union leaders, and they were received as honoured guests. Alan heard a speech by Zinoviev, President of the Communist International and a notorious figure in Britain because of a seditious letter he was supposed to have written which, it was thought, had contributed to the downfall of the first Labour government. He also met Kamenev, another member of the Central Committee; both Kamenev and Zinoviev were to be executed after the first of Stalin's 'show trials' in 1936. The visitors saw revolutionary theatre and *avant-garde* films. They witnessed athletic displays. They toured nursery schools, new hospitals and power stations under construction. It might not seem like much of a holiday, but Alan loved it, and it left him with a lifelong sympathy for the Russians themselves.

> All the people I met – school teachers, hospital workers, men and women in factories – still seemed full of revolutionary enthusiasm. The measures of enlightenment and emancipation that people talked about in the west were here being put into practice . . . If there was dictatorship and a secret police, no one noticed them. Conditions were primitive but the spirit was right.[13]

Alan had joined the Communist Party earlier that same year. The University branch was run by Tom Driberg – indeed, Driberg seemed to be the only other active member.* Meetings were held every two weeks or so in Driberg's elegant Christ Church rooms. Curtains were drawn, candles lit, and there was hot jazz on the gramophone. It was not very serious. Alan admits in his autobiography that he did nothing except make left-wing speeches at the Labour Club, an early example of 'entryism'. Even this may be

---

*In fact there were several other Communist undergraduates at the time, but none active in the University branch. Graham Greene and Claud Cockburn, for example, seemed to have lost interest, perhaps because their final examinations were looming; while P.R. Stephenson, an Australian Rhodes Scholar, regarded undergraduate politics as frivolous.

an exaggeration: a contemporary account has it that Driberg was 'for long a regular feature of the meetings' as the Labour Club's Communist Left Wing, but does not mention Alan.[14] Driberg was certainly busier, selling *Workers' Weekly* in Cowley – though this was partly a device to enable him to meet good-looking factory workers.

For some years the authorities had been trying to suppress the Left within the University. In 1921 the Vice-Chancellor, Lewis Farnell, had prevented Bertrand Russell from speaking to the Labour Club, indeed objected to the very idea of a University Labour Club, and declared that he would not have Bolsheviks in Oxford. His actions were condemned by the Union. In 1926 there was another flashpoint. The story is a murky one. The Conservative Government had authorised raids on the headquarters of the Communist Party, and it was subsequently discovered that two undergraduates, Ieuan Thomas of Merton and P.R. Stephenson of Queen's, were members. Why the others were not also identified is unclear. It was rumoured that Lord Birkenhead, a member of the Conservative Cabinet, had requested the heads of the two colleges to send them down, and had received a defiant response. Farnell's successor, Joseph Wells, was a friend of Birkenhead's. He pressed the two undergraduates to sign an undertaking preventing them from speaking their views in public or in private. A tremendous campaign was mounted in their support, and their cause was championed by A.D. Lindsay, the Master of Balliol. The Union passed a motion (later reversed) censuring the Vice-Chancellor for his actions.[15]

Meanwhile the negotiations between the miners and the pit-owners had broken down, and a chain reaction led to a declaration of a general strike, to begin at midnight on 3 May. It was no longer miner against owner, but organised labour against the Government, or as Alan saw it, class war. The issue divided the whole country. There was a rowdy meeting of the Oxford Union, which resulted in a large majority for the strike, and calls for undergraduates to lend active support to both sides. Provost Phelps sat in on one of several attempts to organise undergraduates to 'serve their country', in other words to serve as special constables or blacklegs. He got up at the end, after a patriotic speech by a military man, and declared that he had 'listened carefully to every word the general has said, and I have heard not a word of sense'.

G.N. Clark was one of a minority of dons sympathetic to the strike and prepared to speak in its support at Labour Party meetings. But the most prominent don on the side of the strikers was G.D.H. Cole, recently elected Reader in Economics at New College. Alan had received an introduction to Cole from his uncle Harry; Harry had met Cole through his wife, Joan Beauchamp, whom he had married in 1921. During the First World War, she and Cole had worked together as volunteers in the Fabian Research Department (later the Labour Research Department). Alan had been to tea with Cole and his wife Margaret, sister of Raymond Postgate, at their house in Holywell. Cole was an academic socialist, committed in principle, cautious in practice. He once said disapprovingly to Alan: 'All you like in politics is fighting.' Alan revered him none the less.

More typical was Kathleen Constable's tutor, Percy Simpson, who observed during a tutorial that 'a great many of our men have gone to serve the country: I'm sorry to say one or two have gone to support the other side'. Liberal-minded dons found themselves supporting both sides at once. Ernest Jacob and Roy Harrod, for example, felt obliged to leave Oxford halfway through the strike in answer to the Government's call for volunteers. At the same time each gave £10 to the strike fund. But most of the undergraduates, even some members of the Labour Club, were on the Government's side. They too thought that the revolution might be at hand; the difference was that they did not welcome it. One of the volunteers said to Alan: 'I wonder whether I shall ever come back.' An estimate has it that two-thirds of the undergraduate body took leave of absence during the period of the strike, and of those at least eighty per cent were doing 'national work'. Alan was in the minority. He went to see the Dean and asked leave to go and support the strikers. Very grudgingly, the Dean gave it. 'Other young men have gone down to do their duty. I suppose you can have leave to go down and do what you think is yours.'[16]

The Labour Club set up its HQ in G.D.H. Cole's house. From there another undergraduate, Hugh Gaitskell, organised a daily motor run to London. One of the volunteer drivers was W.H.

Auden, who was sent to collect G.N. Clark's car from Old
Marston. He had never been behind a wheel before, and it took him
a week to drive the two miles back into Oxford. The University
Strike Committee issued innumerable manifestos and leaflets, and
sent speakers out proselytising into the Oxfordshire villages. In the
city they organised a propaganda meeting which drew a large
number of unsympathetic undergraduates; the clash that followed
became known as 'The Battle of Hannington Hall'. The Communists, however, decided to go their own way. Comrades Driberg and
Taylor set off in Alan's car for London. There they planned to seek
guidance from the Communist Party of Great Britain. But the
offices at 16 King Street were shuttered and bolted, and they were
shooed away by the caretaker. Alan was anxious to mount the
barricades, and there seemed little chance of this in Oxford. He
decided to go back to Preston. Norman Cameron and Innes Stewart
motored up with him.

Percy was on the local strike committee. He advised Alan to offer
his services as a driver. There were very few people in the local
Labour movement who could drive or had a car, and of course
there were no trams or trains or buses running. With a TUC sticker
on his car, Alan became a courier, taking union officials about,
distributing strike pay and bulletins which Norman Cameron
produced, and collecting newsprint from Manchester as well as
returns of those on strike. The roads were empty; everything
stopped. Alan's routes took him through a succession of mining
villages, many of which had road blocks. The streets were full of
strikers hungry for news of how things were going, and often he
would give an impromptu speech at an open-air meeting. Alan
offered a lift to anyone he saw on the road. One passenger he picked
up started abusing the strikers; Alan stopped the car and told him
he could continue his journey on foot.

Percy enjoyed the strike. One evening a sinister figure with a
hook instead of a right hand called on him. They talked for a long
time in private; afterwards Percy set off for London. A few days
later he came home 'radiant', having heard that his name was on
the list of prominent members of the strike committees due to be
arrested. Percy believed that the Government had lost its nerve;
political upheaval was at hand. 'He packed an overnight bag and

waited hopefully for the knock on the door.'[17] Henry Sara too was active in the strike. One of the most famous pictures of the miners' leader, A.J. Cook, shows him speaking from the platform with Sara at his side.

The general council of the TUC called off the strike on 12 May. The first Alan knew of it was when his father came home visibly upset. 'We have been betrayed,' he said. Alan went back to Oxford that same afternoon, and during the next few days the strike-breakers drifted back. According to Alan, there was a surprising lack of bitterness, even a sense of comradeship, between the two sides. 'The middle-class blacklegs, performing manual labour for the first and only time in their lives, learnt to respect those who did it always.'[18]

The general strike was over, but the coal dispute lingered on. In its July issue the Bootham school magazine referred to the 'disastrous' effects of the coal stoppage. The strike had been smashed, the editorial asserted, by citizen volunteers and public opinion, but the continuing coal strike was infinitely more serious. It ended with the somewhat optimistic suggestion that all concerned should ponder the school motto. Alan was incensed, and dashed off a letter praising the 'noblest and most unselfish action from a great body of men that this generation has ever seen'. The blackleg forces had been breaking down, he insisted, until the working class was betrayed by the timidity of its leaders. He wanted it recorded 'for the future historian' that when the products of other public schools were hastening to enrol themselves as 'citizen volunteers', some old scholars were serving in the ranks of the working class. In a dig at Arthur Rowntree, he wrote that 'Bootham has of late years aspired more and more to become an ordinary Public School, with orthodox standards of gentility and a machine-made code of politics. That desire has, fortunately, never been attained . . .'[19]

Forty years later Alan's enthusiasm for the strikers had not dimmed. The response of union members in support of the miners had been 'fantastic'; it was an act of 'spontaneous generosity', even 'nobility'.[20] Another left-wing undergraduate – a friend of Alan's – thought that the strike had been a 'blessing' in many ways, despite its failure; 'a vision of what the future may be like – if we will it.'[21]

John Betjeman, one of Cole's more unlikely volunteers, considered it had been a 'lark'.

In his final year Alan moved out of college into lodgings. In Michaelmas term G.N. Clark began a sabbatical, and for a while Alan was taught by David Ayerst, only a year or two Alan's senior. Ayerst was *simpatico*. He had been chairman of the Labour Club during the strike, and like so many others, hovered on the brink of joining the Communist Party. He wrote to his mother that Alan was the only 'first-class man' among his pupils, 'a Communist who suffers from a slightly too rigid North Country fanaticism'.[22] Alan was also farmed out for a term to 'Sligger' Urquhart at Balliol, who stimulated his interest in nineteenth-century history and helped to undermine the whiggish ideas Alan had found in his textbooks. They studied the 1848 Revolutions, which Marx had used as a test-case for his theories of class struggle.

Alan had begun to lose faith in Communism. The Party had done nothing useful for the strike, he felt. Later he would write that the general strike marked the moment when class war ceased to shape the pattern of British industrial relations.[23] Perhaps it was the end of the class war for Alan also. When the Communist Party of the Soviet Union turned on Trotsky the following year the purge completed Alan's disillusionment: 'not that I necessarily agreed with him. I merely thought that a party that expelled Trotsky was not for me.' Though he still regarded himself as a Marxist, he allowed his membership of the Party to lapse when he left Oxford. 'I have remained left-wing, pro-Russian and anti-Communist ever since.'[24]

Sara too had become uneasy about what was happening in the Soviet Union. These qualms dated back almost to the Revolution. He had been disturbed by the suppression of the Kronstadt uprising in 1921, and after the Communist Party of Great Britain had come into being he had waited three years before reluctantly joining. Early in 1929 he began to associate with a tiny Trotskyist splinter group which became known as 'the British section of the Left Opposition'. He spoke at public meetings, on Clapham Common and elsewhere, criticising the Soviet leadership. In 1932 he was officially suspended from the Party.

In the Christmas holidays Alan borrowed Uncle Harry's open-top car for a tour of Cornwall; it was said to 'do 90 m.p.h. sideways'. When he returned it the Tonneau cover – the tarpaulin which protects the inside of the car when the hood is down – was missing. Harry was annoyed, and resolved that Alan should pay. He wrote to his nephew saying that he had bought him a Tonneau cover for his twenty-first.

Alan celebrated his twenty-first birthday in March 1927 with a dinner-party at The George. Among the guests were Innes Stewart, Norman Cameron and Tom Driberg. G.N. Clark was invited but did not attend. During the meal Driberg kept slipping out, but Alan thought nothing of it until a waiter approached him and asked for a word in private. He explained that he was a respectable married man – if Driberg kept coming out to him, he would have to go home. When Alan remonstrated with his friend, Driberg replied that he was only expressing his approval of the service. Driberg was by now prince of Oxford's *avant-garde*. In May he staged an unusual event in the Holywell Music Rooms; Driberg's poem, 'Homage to Beethoven', delivered by the poet himself through a megaphone, was accompanied by an orchestral piece, scored for, among more conventional instruments, typewriter keys and a flushing lavatory (offstage). It was the one concert Alan attended as an undergraduate.

Alan left Oxford that summer with a First. He had no idea of ever returning again to academic life. His initial plan, suggested by Uncle Harry soon after he had arrived in Oxford, was to become a barrister specialising in Left causes. This would provide dramatic opportunities as a defender of rebels. Alan had many of the qualities of an advocate: he was a natural extrovert, and a powerful speaker who enjoyed arguing against the odds. Accordingly he had eaten dinners in the Inner Temple for his last two years at Oxford. Then Harry suggested that instead he join his practice as an articled clerk, with a view to becoming his partner and taking over when Harry retired. One could champion the causes of the working class and still make plenty of money. A life of heroic comfort beckoned.

5: 'An uncouth fellow'

Alan had accepted Harry's offer only for want of anything better. While he was up at Oxford he had put off contemplation of the future. He still had no idea what he wanted to 'do'. Neither had most of his undergraduate friends. They despised those 'sub-men' who went on to safe jobs and established careers. But there seemed to be little alternative. Innes Stewart had been warned by his headmaster, the Rector of Edinburgh Academy: 'You know, Stewart, what happens to boys who don't know what they want to do in life. They become chartered accountants.'[1] A still more likely fate was to become a schoolteacher in a dreary preparatory school, like Betjeman and Waugh. 'It is surprising', Alan concluded, 'that we did not all follow Evelyn's example and walk out to sea with the intention of drowning ourselves.'[2]

So when Harry made his offer Alan had little hesitation in accepting. Harry had done well. He had made some useful contacts while in prison during the War, in particular with the Labour MP Josiah Wedgwood, who later became a Cabinet minister. Encouraged by these new friends, Harry decided to move his practice to London. One of his earliest cases was acting for George Lansbury and the other Poplar Councillors in their protest against what they saw as the inequality of the rates burden on rich and poor London boroughs. As has happened more recently, the councillors were made personally liable for unauthorised expenditure. Though the case was lost, and thirty councillors went to prison, 'Poplarism' became a national cause and triumphed in the end. In the process Harry had made his name. He became *the* lawyer for the Labour movement, with Ramsay MacDonald and H.G. Wells among his clients. He specialised in workmen's claims for compensation after industrial accidents – far more common then than now – which naturally brought him into very close contact with the trades unions (such close contact, in fact, that the firm eventually moved into Congress House). He also became official solicitor to the Communist Party – not very rewarding but good for his reputation, Alan remarked, without obvious irony[3] – and he defended the Communists arrested after the Zinoviev letter.

Harry Thompson was a tall man, energetic and dominant. He was said to employ only solicitors who had lost their membership of the Law Society, so that they could not quit and take their business with them. It was not to be expected that he and Alan could work together for long without a personality clash. Even before Alan started there was a row about a proposed partnership deed – reminiscent of the row between Percy and J.T. – which left Alan feeling that Harry had tried to cheat him and might do so again. Perhaps he took on Alan only to please his sister: she was delighted to have an excuse to spend more time with Henry Sara, who was by this time based in North London. She acquired a flat near Hampstead Heath and installed Alan there, with a house-keeper to keep an eye on him. After three years of independence in Oxford, Alan felt that he was once again his mother's 'prisoner'.[4] He was lonely in London, his loneliness relieved only when friends came to stay. He had no desire to mix with the 'Hampstead intellectuals' in the local Labour Party. Alan saw himself as a plain man, one whose people had not forgotten their humble origins. He felt out of place in cosmopolitan North London. Even Provost Phelps, who had always regarded Alan as a friend, felt that he was 'an uncouth fellow in many ways'.[5] The Oxford polish made him dull. His best friend Innes Stewart observed that he was 'inwardly as diffident and misdoubting as outwardly he was tough and arrogant'.[6]

Alan began working for the firm of W.H. Thompson as an articled clerk in October 1927. He realised straight away that it was a 'ghastly mistake'. For a start, he had not much to do, and what work there was bored him. As a consequence he spent most of his days reading novels. Harry had a hard, almost brutal side and he teased Alan relentlessly, as he had always done. It was no way to make a partnership, but it did help to make Alan tougher. More than Connie, much more than Percy or any of his teachers, Harry was the figure of authority against whom Alan directed his resentment. In doing so, he picked up some characteristics from his sharp-witted, impatient uncle.* Among Harry's formidable gifts were those of a showman. He wore blue shirts with soft collars and red ties, more like a poet than a solicitor. He had a strong sense of the dramatic, which helped in his profession. On one occasion, for example, he was called north to defend some union members who were trying to show Soviet propaganda films at a private meeting. The police were anxious to prevent the meeting, and used the flimsy pretext of the films being a 'fire hazard'. The lawyer from London arrived, and in the presence of the police officers, took out some matches and attempted to light a piece of film. The match burned to the end; the film failed to ignite. Harry tried again, with the same result. At the third attempt the police gave up: the meeting could go ahead.

Harry did try to help Alan. He gave him introductions, and put him up for the 1917 Club, a meeting-place for Bolshevik sympathisers above a bakery in Gerrard Street. He took Alan out to dinner, but even this was not a success because Harry remained an uncompromising teetotaller. Defiantly Alan insisted on having a bottle of wine, which he was forced to drink alone. At the end of the meal, Harry called for the bill but asked the waiter to 'give Mr Taylor a separate bill for the drink'. Harry was not a generous man. When his brother John went bankrupt, Harry lent him money on humiliating terms. During a game of bridge John asked his partner whether he could support him. 'He can't support himself,' was Harry's comment. One day when he was driving John and Sara in his car, he remarked: 'There are three overcoats in this car and they're all mine.' Alan was more like his uncle than his generous father; if Alan lent money to a friend, he charged interest.

Two such similar people could not work together for long. At Christmas Alan told his father he would have to leave. Percy feared Connie's reaction if he did so, and persuaded him to stay a while longer. Back in London Alan found a girlfriend, a Communist called Dora. They kissed — she took the initiative — the first time

---

*Though the habit of wearing bow ties came from his other maternal uncle, John.

Alan had kissed a girl since puberty. Despite this breakthrough, it was not a serious affair, but when Alan's mother heard of it she was 'desperate'. She agreed that Alan should break his articles and come back to Preston. His first job had lasted only six months.

This was not the only false start. Harry had introduced Alan to Gerald Barry, editor of the *Saturday Review*. At Barry's encouragement he wrote an 800-word review of John Forster's *Life of Dickens*, which had just been issued in a new edition. Alan contrasted it with Boswell's *Life of Johnson*, and stressed the immaturity of the Victorian age, exemplified by that 'precocious child', Dickens. The Victorians were 'without historical memories', the characteristic mark of childhood; they believed that they were, automatically, better than their fathers, whereas earlier writers, untainted by the idea of Progress and 'full of the classical traditions, were perpetually chastened by the knowledge that there had been better men than they were'.[7] Barry was pleased with the piece, but Alan failed to follow up; it would be six years before he wrote another.

Before he left London Alan attended Thomas Hardy's funeral service in Westminster Abbey. He had read that admission to the Abbey would be 'by card' at the North Transept door, and in all innocence proffered his visiting card; as few of the invited had turned up he was allowed in. He was ushered to a choir stall and sat directly behind the coffin. The behaviour of the pallbearers was entertaining. 'Galworthy was the only one who knew the drill and behaved impeccably. Shaw spent his time looking around and waving to his friends. Baldwin also did not show much attention, MacDonald was not in touch with the service though he behaved with more decorum than Baldwin did.'[8] Also in the procession Alan recognised Gosse and Barrie, Kipling and Housman. The rearguard was composed of the Vice-Chancellors of Oxford and Cambridge Universities: singular mourners, Alan remarked, of Jude's creator.[9]

Then Alan was back at home, with nothing to do. Percy and Connie were more apart than ever; Connie was often away for months at a time. Percy was preoccupied with Little Dolly, now nineteen. When Connie was away, Dolly and her sister Hilda often came to stay with him, and he took them on excursions to Wales and to Stratford. On Sunday mornings Percy and Dolly went to the swimming-pool at Lytham. He was not entirely honest about their friendship. When Connie taxed him about being away so long, for example, he told her that he had been teaching a little girl to swim.[10] When he wanted to visit Dolly, he pretended to be going to a meeting. Sometimes he left the house late at night, after Connie had gone to bed, to go round to Dolly's house; they would sit up talking or he would read her stories until the early hours of the morning. Their relationship was impossible to categorise, partly because they both believed that it was 'soppy' to be sentimental, to talk about your feelings. He doted on her, called her 'love' and lavished presents on her; she thought he was the nicest, kindest man she had ever known. During the War he had contracted a duodenal ulcer, which dogged him all his life and added to the trouble he already suffered from his tubercular lung and chronic bronchitis. When his ulcer was particularly painful she gave him a hot water bottle and talked to him while sitting on the floor by his bed. She sat on his knee to shave him.

Connie remained ignorant of their relationship for many years. 'When she did find out she was indignant: there was nothing intellectual in it.'[11] Perhaps with good reason, Connie was jealous of Dolly and was rude to her when she came to the house. Dolly was frightened of this dragon, who seemed to her like a 'schoolmarm' — which of course was just what she had been. Alan sided entirely with his father, though he recognised that Percy was a 'dodger'. He provided an alibi for Percy; they would set off together 'for a walk' and then part once they were out of sight of the house, allowing Percy to see Dolly without fear of recrimination from his wife. Alan's attitude to them was ambiguous; he told Dolly much later that he had always regarded her as his stepmother, but he also thought that Percy was 'a new father to her, and she was the daughter he had lost. Neither of them ever understood that they were in love, and neither of them wanted it any different.'[12]

From his father Alan learned deviousness. Being trapped with a quick-witted and sharp-tongued wife, Percy escaped into a world of 'romancing'. He had a gift for inventing stories, which delighted Alan but infuriated Connie. 'She was always trying to trap him into the prosaic world of reality and never succeeded.'[13] He was increasingly deaf, which helped him to escape; though like many deaf people, he heard well enough when he wanted. But his deafness made it hard for him to keep up with the conversation, and his deliberate Lancashire ways irritated Connie. It tended to confirm the family opinion that she had married beneath her.

Though now living in London, Sara was still a frequent visitor to the house. He played cards with Percy and the two Sharples girls. According to Alan, he and Percy got on well, though Dolly thought he was a 'scrounger'. The Thompson brothers, on the other hand, despised Sara; they could not bring themselves to call him by his first name, so they called him 'comrade' instead. This was not a sarcastic reference to his political activities, for they too were both left-wing; it was a social difference. Innes Stewart called him The Armed Worker or Connie's 'Tame Man'.

Alan decided to go back to Oxford. It seems that he had no particular plan. He tried to get his exhibition restored and, not surprisingly, received no response. G.N. Clark said that if he wanted to become an historian he should learn German. The Regius Professor, H.W.C. 'Fluffy' Davis, recommended Alan to his old friend A.F. Pribram in Vienna. Pribram replied that he would be happy to see the young man. Here at last was a prospect of something definite to do. Alan went straight out to Vienna by sleeper, and Pribram agreed to take him on as a research student, starting in September. Alan was 'entranced with the prospect'; though later he confessed to not having read any of the books Pribram lent him to read over the summer. But he was 'bewitched' by Vienna, which was a place of pilgrimage for left-wingers in the 1920s. New ideas were emerging from the rubble of the Habsburg Empire, in psychology, in art, in philosophy and in politics. 'Red Vienna' seemed a paradise, a model socialist city.

His immediate future settled, Alan returned to Oxford, an unofficial postgraduate student. He drifted along until the end of the Trinity term reading novels and casually studying the foreign policy of the nineteenth-century Radicals for a prize essay which he failed to win. Then he went off to the West Country for a short holiday with his parents. It was not a success. His mother was 'more than usually intolerable in bad weather'; she 'went into tantrums because it rained and my father just couldn't think what to do with her'. He wrote to his Oriel friend Charles Gott that there could be little fun with 'this bitch' about.* It seems that Alan was having some kind of romantic adventure, because he went on:

> The Sussex expedition was attended with all success – she is indeed a fascinating young woman and I shall certainly have the good time with her some time. But the more wuzzy I go, the less I am interested in marriage – I regard myself as quite safe from it. But we both went gug-gug and I daresay that if she hadn't been a little unwell we should both have gone nunc-nunc too.[15]

There is unfortunately nothing to reveal whether the fascinating young woman was Dora or somebody else, or whether nunc-nunc was achieved on any other occasion.

Innes Stewart had just come down from Oxford with a First, and since he had even less idea what to do with his life, decided to accompany Alan to Vienna. George Clazy came with them for a few weeks before returning to Edinburgh. The pound was so overvalued at the time that they were virtually unconscious of any financial impediment, particularly in the defeated countries of the Central Powers. They decided to make it a sort of Grand Tour, taking a few weeks *en route* and stopping at Berlin, Dresden and Prague on the way. Prague seemed backward by comparison with the much more civilised German cities.[16]

Alan had already been to Germany in the summer before he went up to Oxford, when his mother and Henry Sara had taken him with his Bootham friend Moore on a trip which included Berlin, Dresden, Frankfurt, Weimar and Bonn. In the Ruhr they had been shocked to see French occupying troops, some of them black; frustrated in its attempts to extract the reparations agreed at the Treaty of Versailles, the French Government had decided the previous year to march into Germany and take what was due to France in kind. This was an offence against Progressive opinion everywhere. E.D. Morel had taken the lead in the campaign against the French occupation with his pamphlet *The Horror on the Rhine*. Though the French had now departed and the country seemed to be

---

*At the time Alan used 'bitch' as a general term for women. Nearly half a century later he again used this same term to describe his mother.[14]

recovering from economic crisis, there remained a sense of grievance in Germany, a view that somehow she had been unjustly
treated in the post-War settlement: one shared by many foreigners,
particularly those on the Left who had opposed the War in the first
place. Maynard Keynes' *The Economic Consequences of the Peace*,
published at the end of 1919, had delivered a devastating blow,
intellectual and moral, to the credibility of the peace settlement.
Keynes had condemned the Treaty of Versailles as a 'Carthaginian
Peace', arguing that the reparations would impoverish Germany
and thus the rest of Europe. By the time Alan arrived in Vienna ten
years later there was in England a yearning for reconciliation with
Germany.

These feelings – that Germany had been unjustly treated, of
revulsion against the War – had their impact on historical studies
too. There was a lively and sometimes impassioned debate about
'War Guilt' (*Kriegsschuldfrage*), a phrase which had been incorporated into the Treaty of Versailles and used to justify the
large reparations extorted from the defeated countries.* Most
Progressive-minded people felt uncomfortable with this concept;
they dismissed the notion that Germany had been the aggressor as
simplistic. At the same time there was an urgent need to explain
how such a disaster could have occurred. The Union of Democratic
Control had put the blame on secret diplomacy; and historians
argued that if archives were opened its true causes would be
revealed. Governments began to publish volumes of diplomatic
documents, each aimed at establishing their country's innocence. It
was a good time to be a diplomatic historian.

Pribram himself was at the centre of these currents. A Viennese
Jew who had been born in England, he had made use of his dual
heritage, and of the fact that the Austrian state archives had been
opened after the downfall of the Habsburg monarchy, to become
an expert on pre-War diplomacy. His books included *Austrian
Foreign Policy 1908–1918* (1923) and *The Secret Treaties of
Austria-Hungary, 1879–1914* (1920). He was working on another
book, *England and the International Policies of the Great Powers,
1871–1914*, and editing *Österreich-Ungarns Aussenpolitik, 1908–*

---

*France had been made to pay reparations after the Franco-Prussian War.

1914, the Austro-Hungarian diplomatic documents. Like most forward-thinking people, Pribram disliked the idea of War Guilt.

Pribram was then nearly seventy. He was a courteous, generous man, witty and charming, and exceptionally widely read in four or five languages. Friends from artistic as well as academic circles were attracted to his house on the Billrothstrasse, the most eminent of them all, perhaps, being Sigmund Freud; Pribram and Freud went for walks and regularly played cards together. His best friend was Ludo Hartmann, the Austrian Ambassador in Berlin. Alan was one of his many foreign students, among them several Americans; one of these, William L. Langer, was later to become an eminent historian. As European representative for the Rockefeller Foundation Pribram was responsible for sending Frederich Hayek, the godfather of modern conservative economics, on a scholarship to the United States.

Alan and Innes found lodgings in the city centre, just behind the Opera. They shared a large room – 'about the size of a tennis court', wrote Innes to Charles Gott, but he was probably exaggerating – which they had for twelve pounds a month, including five meals a day. They went skating at the skating-rink next door, and learned to ride the Austrian way, bouncing up and down rather than rising and falling as riders do in England. They frequented the Opera, where Alan saw the whole Ring cycle; he liked to sit reading the libretto in the fifth gallery. This was the beginning of a lifelong interest for Alan, whose only previous experience of music had been Driberg's production in the Holywell Music Rooms; in his second year Alan had a season ticket for the Vienna Philharmonic. But these were mere distractions for the two young men; their preoccupations were learning German, and sex. Indeed the two were interrelated, at least according to the theory of an American who impressed them by claiming to learn the language while seducing the wives and daughters of the men to whom he had letters of introduction. Alan and Innes tried to follow suit, Alan finding a 'sleeping dictionary' who allowed him to take off her clothes, but only the top half. Both had a session with a prostitute, which they did not much enjoy, followed rapidly by a medical check-up. In fact Alan and Innes were shy of women, and innocent about sex. In Germany they had seen a darning mushroom and speculated that it might be some form of contraceptive. According to Alan, Innes blushed furiously when spoken to by a girl. They consoled themselves in masturbation.

Alan's letters from Vienna are full of references to 'boyish fun'. He and Innes teased each other; Innes called him 'Comrade Toggles, the well-known Preston proletarian'; Alan wrote that at least he didn't *smell*. They played leapfrog at two o'clock in the morning in The Ring. Alan sent a long, rambling letter to a university friend who had taken up teaching, purporting to be from a broken-down cleric resident abroad and desirous of placing a natural son in a cheap school, enclosing a photograph, actually of himself but purporting to be 'my own dear boy, my precious John Thomas'. Alan and Innes both read *Ulysses*, then banned in England, as soon as they arrived; Alan wrote a letter to his family recommending it as a highly moral work. He told Charles Gott that he found himself 'remarkably like L. Bloom, its dirty hero: he had a sense of scientific curiosity quite in my own line'.[17]

As for the German, Alan set out to learn it methodically. He read German historical works with a dictionary by his side, looking up every word that he did not understand. At school he had read Zola's *Germinal* to learn French in the same way. He taught himself to write the German *Schrift* so that he could read it in the archives. He also found a local teacher to help him with his pronunciation, and she suggested he should meet one of her pupils, a nineteen-year-old girl who was keen to learn English. This was Else Sieberg, Alan's first serious girlfriend. Soon they were meeting every lunchtime, and Alan often took her out in the evening. They began to talk about marriage. Then one night they ran into some of Else's relations in a restaurant. Respectable girls did not go out to eat with men unchaperoned, particularly with a foreigner. She was forbidden to see him again.

After three months in Vienna Alan and Innes were joined by friends from England: Charles Gott, Geoffrey Rowntree and an artist, Peter Mann. Mann painted the upper half of his unadorned girlfriend, and exhibited the work in their digs, much to the disapproval of their landlady. The new arrivals stayed until the summer; Stewart went home in the spring. Alan did not attend Pribram's seminars, and after the first term was not even registered as a student at the university. His first impression of the university had been 'very low – the students are grubby'. He spent his days working in the *Staatsarchiv* and would join 'the boys' in the evening, unless he was meeting Else. Occasionally he would attend a lecture, though these 'are all about the sort of thing I used to do at Bootham'.[18] Pribram's were the exception: he was famed for his brilliant impromptu lecturing, which served as a model for Alan when he later became a lecturer himself. Alan's original idea for his research topic had been to tie in to his previous work on nineteenth-century English Radicals; he would study their links with Viennese radicals before the 1848 Revolutions. Pribram thought this unrealistic, and sent him off to the Chancellery to study Anglo-Austrian relations between 1848 and 1866. Many of the documents in the archive were in French or English, which helped. Pribram had given him no training in historical method:

> I had never seen a diplomatic document before and simply plunged in at the deep end . . . I did not know the difference between an official despatch and a private letter. I had no idea how to weigh the reliability of historical evidence. I did not even know that I must note the number of each document, an ignorance which caused me much unnecessary labour.[19]

Maybe if he had paid more attention to G.N. Clark he might have found the going easier.

One thing Pribram did teach Alan, however, was never to believe something merely because it had been written down. All documents are suspect, particularly those written some time after the event. All witnesses to history give biased accounts, whether deliberately or not, and the historian must make allowance for this.

Once he had spent a while in the archives Alan narrowed the focus of his research into a study of the diplomacy surrounding the Italian problem in 1848–9, 'an international crisis that never quite came off'. It would entail later work in the French and British archives to turn it into a thesis, but not the Italian; to work in a Fascist country was out of the question.[20] When he had been at it for a while, he announced to Pribram his determination to write a history of the Habsburg monarchy. 'Well, yes,' said Pribram. 'You are right; it has never been done. You only need to know seventeen languages and live ten times as long as mortal man.'

Alan was by no means yet fixed on a career as a professional historian. Indeed he vaguely considered becoming a foreign correspondent, making use of his newly acquired German.

Curiously, Alan seems to have taken little interest in Viennese politics, then dangerously polarised, with rising tension between right- and left-wing paramilitary groups. Harry had given him a letter of introduction from Ramsay MacDonald – the once and future Labour prime minister – to Otto Bauer, the leader of the socialist Left. Alan called on Bauer and they had a brief talk, but that was that. Alan was more excited when an Austrian policeman confiscated his passport, which was returned with its validities for the British Empire and Morocco cancelled. At last he was being taken seriously as a subversive. It seems that the British Government was concerned about Communists stirring up unrest in the colonies, a concern which persisted at least until the 1950s; but the immediate reasons for the action remain obscure. Alan kicked up a stink through Harry, who complained to Hugh Dalton, the relevant minister. He speculated that someone in Oxford had reported him as a suspicious character. If indeed he was regarded as a security risk, this lasted for a disappointingly short time; when his passport came up for renewal four years later the validities were restored. His reaction to the Great Crash in 1929 is not recorded, but probably it confirmed to him, as it did to other left-wingers, that capitalism was doomed. While he waited for the end, however, he continued to draw an allowance from his father, now supplemented by a Rockefeller Research Fellowship which he had gained thanks to Pribram.

Alan went home for Christmas 1929, and again in the summer of 1930. He and his family went to the Shaw Festival in Malvern, where Alan again recognised the great man, this time sitting next to his equally famous namesake, aircraftman Shaw, also known as T.E. Lawrence. His mother was furious when she spotted Sara outside their hotel talking to a girl he had picked up, and there followed 'a terrific row, with my father and me more or less literally ducking under the table'.[21] This was not the first time Connie's jealousy had been aroused; in 1924 Sara had had an affair with a

married woman while on board ship to Russia with Connie and
Alan.

A new career presented itself to Alan that summer. The second
Labour Government had just taken office, and George Lansbury
was First Commissioner of Works. There were plans to increase the
number of inspectors of ancient monuments; Lansbury remembered that the son of his friend Percy was interested in medieval
architecture. Perhaps he would like to become an inspector? Alan
convinced himself that he would. 'The job would be interesting and
yet totally remote from real life which was exactly what I
wanted.'[22] He kept up a vague interest until the following summer,
when he was told that because of the slump the planned expansion
of the department would not now take place. It was a fortunate
escape. One of the assistant inspectors appointed sometime after
was named A.J. Taylor.*

Alan was still in England, on holiday in the New Forest, when he
heard of George Clazy's death. Clazy had fallen in love with a girl
and threatened to commit suicide unless she married him. When
she refused, he gassed himself. It was a sad ending, but somehow
appropriate for such a severe character. To Geoffrey Rowntree,
who was with him at the time, Alan seemed very sorry but not
heartbroken; though in his autobiography he described Clazy's
death as 'a terrible loss to me'.[23] Rowntree returned to Vienna with
Alan and together they travelled down to Trieste, following the
Adriatic coast to Split. Then he went back to England, leaving Alan
alone for his second year in Vienna.

Alan was not alone for long. Pribram introduced him to Ian
Morrow, a translator who taught him the techniques of his trade.
He also met Margaret Adams, a lapsed Catholic from an upper-
middle-class Anglo-Indian background, in Vienna studying
German and taking piano lessons. Margaret was a year older than

---

*Arnold Joseph Taylor, later Commander of the British Empire and Fellow of the
British Academy, became Assistant Inspector of Ancient Monuments in 1935. A
distinguished career in public service culminated in his being elected President of
the Society of Antiquaries in 1975. Another narrow escape involved a different A.J.
Taylor, who began reading history as an undergraduate at Manchester University
in the year after Alan's departure; eventually he became Professor of Modern
History at Leeds.

Alan, but fortunately two inches shorter than his five-foot-six; she was an attractive woman, with blue eyes and long brown hair. She was not intellectual, Alan wrote, 'but then no intellectual woman attracted me sexually'.[24] But she was intelligent enough to read the manuscripts of his books and make helpful comments. She was certainly 'artistic', one of those who is drawn to creative people; friends found her warm and considerate. Before she returned to England Margaret and Alan sailed up the Danube for a romantic weekend. They spent the night together, but 'nothing was achieved as often happened with me'.[25] Once he returned to London Alan mentioned his difficulties with intercourse to Geoffrey Rowntree, who recommended him to F.H. Dodd, a Quaker physician who practised a conversational style of analysis, relying heavily on the interpretation of dreams. Alan persisted for only one or two interviews. Other friends of his were being psychoanalysed in Vienna itself. His flatmate there, for example, a painter called Basil Rocke, was being analysed by Wilhelm Stekel, an imaginative and prolific physician who before the War had been a member of Freud's inner circle and who had himself been treated by Freud for impotence.[26] Alan too had a talk with Stekel, but was discouraged from going any further when Stekel announced that he was Faust and Alan Hamlet.[27] Thirty years later Alan told a colleague of Viennese extraction that psychoanalysis had no bearing whatsoever on the way Englishmen felt, thought or behaved.

Alan soon solved his problem in any case. When he came back to England at the end of his two years in Vienna, he and Margaret spent five days together touring the Thames Valley in a borrowed baby Austin. 'Margaret had been to a gynaecologist who had relieved her of her virginity and given her some instruction. After some days of fumbling efforts we finally achieved success at the Shillingford Bridge Hotel.'[28]

While he was still in Vienna Alan received a telegram from Ernest Jacob, head of the history department at Manchester University, offering him a job as an assistant lecturer. This was a complete surprise. Pribram had been invited to give the Ford Lectures in Oxford; unfortunately he felt that his English was not good enough to give them in his usual spontaneous style, and he had fallen back on reading from notes. One night in All Souls he had talked to

Ernest Jacob, who mentioned that he urgently needed someone to teach modern history. Pribram, perhaps grateful to Alan who had helped him with the translation of his lectures, recommended his young pupil, and Jacob had not hesitated. The next morning he sent his wire to Alan.

Alan had found something to 'do'. He had no real idea what lecturing at a provincial university involved. It might not be much better than teaching at a dingy prep school. But it was enough 'until some more exciting prospect presented itself. I certainly did not intend to remain a university teacher for life, particularly as the beginning of the Great Depression suggested that the revolution might arrive after all.'[29]

6: 'Who whom?'

Manchester University sits astride the Oxford Road. In one direction the road leads north into town, towards the centre of the city which was once the very heart of the British Empire; the other points south, towards the Cheshire countryside and eventually to that very different city of Oxford. In one direction, chimneys; in the other, spires. There had been much traffic along that road: young Oxford graduates like Alan coming north to start their first job, and older men, their reputations made, going back again. The university itself faced both ways; the teaching staff acknowledged their paymasters, yet many of them yearned to return whence they had come. The Mancunians were understandably infuriated by the attitude that Manchester was a good jumping-off point; but still their clever men looked south. In the case of the historians this was curious, because for most of its first half-century the Manchester History School was, in the opinion of many, the finest history department of any university in Britain, finer even than those at Oxford or Cambridge. Its patriarch was T.F. Tout, a powerful figure, in his time one of the leading scholars in Europe, who had come to Manchester in 1890. Tout's school emphasised first-hand research and the use of original documents; when he retired in the mid-1920s, it had established no fewer than five professorial chairs. By the time Alan arrived these had been cut back to three for reasons of economy.[1]

Though the trade which sustained it was in decline, Manchester was still a great city. It was a place of noise and bustle and dirt. The chimneys still smoked, polluting the air and begriming the Victorian buildings; large smuts came in if you opened a window. Clanking trams converged on the city centre, where they waited in long lines. Cart-horses dragged along cotton bales on drays. This was a city jealous of London, proud of its distinct identity, eager to demonstrate its civic achievements. Opposite the Midland Hotel they were building an impressive new library, to be opened in 1934 by the King. Its university was matched by a first-rate orchestra, the Hallé, and a newspaper which was arguably the best in the country, the *Manchester Guardian*. It was still possible – just – to argue 'what Manchester thinks today, England thinks tomorrow'.

Alan began his career as an academic in October 1930. He was the youngest of the teaching staff; some of the others seemed like relics. Donald Atkinson, for example, was professor of ancient history. His marriage to an assistant lecturer had coincided with the publication of a piece of research on Etruscan pottery which he had published in a limited-circulation learned journal. The wedding had been announced in the local press, so that when he next walked into the lecture theatre he was greeted with congratulations and the stamping of feet. After the noise had died down, he peered over his glasses and thanked the students: 'I should like to make it clear that I could not possibly have achieved what was done without the help of others.'

Jacob was a kindly man, impulsive but somewhat reticent; 'a curious look of indignant embarrassment would come into his face when those of whom he could not approve were mentioned'.[2] Like Tout and his successor Powicke, he was a medievalist. Readers of his essays on ecclesiastical history could sometimes feel they were caught up in an animated bibliography. Despite his impulsiveness, punctuality was not his forte; when his volume on the fifteenth century in the Oxford History of England, first announced in 1935, finally appeared in 1961, one reviewer commented that it would probably have been a better book if it had been written twenty years earlier. Alan stood out in this company; dynamic, impatient, enthusiastic, he seemed the very antithesis of some of his older colleagues.

The history department was in the new Arts Building, constructed only four years earlier in the Neo-Classical style, complete with pillars, mouldings and friezes. In appearance it was (and is) similar to some of the Oxford women's colleges. Alan's room, which he shared with Ted Hughes, another lecturer in modern history, had a high ceiling and a parquet floor; it was entered through a heavy hardwood door capped with a half-moon fanlight. One corner was cut by a chimney breast, and inside an egg and dart surround there was a coal fire. Alan's duties were to lead a weekly tutorial group of half a dozen or so Honours students, and to give lectures for the two courses on European history. He was to cover modern European history in ninety-six lectures, forty-eight from 1494 to 1815, and another forty-eight from 1815 to 1914. Vague recollections from Henty helped him to cope with the Thirty Years' War. The last part was the hardest, because the Oxford history school had stopped at 1871 and there were no standard textbooks to crib. The few books on the subject which had been published agreed that the Germans had been badly treated after the War, and therefore, by reverse logic, that they were not responsible for it. This fitted with everything Alan had been taught to believe. 'I thus prepared for my students a Union of Democratic Control version of events in which the Great War was all the fault of the Entente Powers.'3*

He also had to lecture to commerce students in the evenings; one of these was his cousin Karin. Later Alan came to resent that he had done so much lecturing in his first year, before a professor of modern history was appointed; he said it was two men's jobs, not one. All the same, the university functioned only from Monday to Thursday; when afterwards he moved out of the city he so arranged things that he needed to be there for no more than two and a half days each week. And he enjoyed lecturing; in 1931 he began speaking to branches of the Historical Association, something he was to continue doing for more than half a century. As he was fresh from Vienna, it was appropriate that his first talk, given in Preston, should be on Metternich.

Pre-War undergraduates taking Honours were in the minority; far more were doing simply a General or Pass course. A high proportion of those taking history Honours were women: in 1930, for example, thirty-one of an intake of fifty. It was a small enough department for all the Honours students to be on personal terms with the staff, and Alan was particularly informal, encouraging

---

*i.e. Great Britain and France.

students to use his first name, though among themselves they referred to him as 'A.J.P.' Many undergraduates reading other subjects attended Alan's lectures, swelling the turnout to more than a hundred at a time; often the large Arts Theatre was packed. Alan peered along the ranks of note-takers in the hope of finding a pretty girl; later he lamented that 'Manchester has everything except beauty'. He had started by reading his notes, but after a while he began to give lectures extempore. Though he refined it over the years, his method remained essentially the same. At the beginning he marched in and started speaking straight away, creating a sense of urgency and purpose. Instead of standing behind the lectern he would pace up and down, very near the front row, projecting his voice to an imaginary listener at the back. He had hardly any notes, or so it seemed; just the odd quotation on file cards which from time to time he would fish out of his pocket and read. Alan learned to time his lectures to the dot, so that the bell for the next lesson would ring as he was delivering his last sentence. The effect was startling. Soon he was in total command of his audiences. He could pack a hall with undergraduates even at nine in the morning.

Alan's lecturing technique later became a legend. His Bootham record shows that he had a flair for public speaking even as a schoolboy, and that he had already learned some rhetorical tricks. A generation before, the great Tout had disdained to prepare carefully wrought lectures; he had made sure of just enough for his purpose and then had let himself go.[4] Alan followed Tout's precedent. His lectures were full of self-confidence and verve. On the one hand, Alan seemed to have a marvellous grasp of everything he was talking about; on the other, he brought a fresh and independent approach to otherwise tired old themes. The undergraduates enjoyed listening to this young man, so different from some of the other lecturers.

Alan was back on home ground. All the values he championed were here. Why should he ever leave? Yet almost immediately he began trying to return to Oxford. When G.N. Clark became Chichele Professor of Economic History in 1931, Alan applied for Clark's old job at Oriel, but he did not receive even an acknowledgement of his application. Then Alan applied for a post at Corpus, where the President, Sir Richard Livingstone, remarked, 'I hear you have strong political views.' 'No, President,' Alan replied, 'extreme views, weakly held.' He did not get the job. Perhaps he had made too many enemies as a bumptious undergraduate. During a lunch in 1935 his old tutor, Stanley Cohn, who had by this time moved on to Brasenose, was heard to remark of Alan: 'I'll see him dead before he gets into Oxford.'

In his autobiography, written nearly half a century later, Alan claimed that he tried only 'casually and reluctantly' to get back to Oxford, and then only because Jacob and Namier were 'for ever on at me' to do so.[5] But it seems unlikely that Jacob would encourage a man to leave whom he had appointed only the year before; Namier had not even arrived in Manchester when Alan applied to Oriel. However 'casual' the applications, it is hard to believe that Alan had such a low opinion of himself as to have no expectation of success. Innes Stewart, for a while his closest friend, assumed that he had always intended to get back to Oxford, although it would be difficult 'as he had no impulse to lower any flag he might be sailing under'.[6]

In reality, Alan was embarrassed about wanting what any other ambitious young historian might have wanted, because it conflicted with his stance as a committed Northerner. This was not an easy corner to escape from. Provincial sentiment ran deep, and Alan's arrival back in Manchester had been celebrated as a return to the fold. When Alan had won his Rockefeller Research Fellowship, the notice announcing the fact in the *Preston Herald* was headed 'Well done, Preston!' A profile in the same paper when Alan was made a full lecturer in 1936 gives a flavour of this chippy parochial pride; headed 'A Brilliant Prestonian', it predicted that he would probably be made a professor in two or three years' time. (In fact, he was offered a chair at Manchester in 1953, and refused it.) While an undergraduate at Oriel, the newspaper added scathingly, Alan had decided that 'instead of acquiring the Oxford accent, he would pursue knowledge, and, if possible, wisdom and understanding'. He was an industrious apprentice, the article continued triumphantly, who adopted as his motto 'Work on, work on, and spend not time fooling'.[7]

Alan was now twenty-four. He moved into lodgings near the university, and drove his new open-top car back to his parents' house in Preston at weekends. Percy had a slightly sardonic attitude to his clever son; whenever anybody asked him about Alan, Percy said that he was at the University of Heidelberg. Percy was just as busy as ever with Labour Party business, though in 1931 he was defeated in the ward which he had served as Councillor since 1926. It was a black year for what remained of the Party, after the defection of its leaders to form the National Government, and a crushing defeat at the subsequent general election which reduced the number of its MPs to only fifty-two; the Conservatives and their allies won 521 seats. Bitterness at this 'betrayal' coloured Alan's views for much of the 1930s. Labour, now led by Percy's old friend George Lansbury, seemed likely to be in permanent opposition. The Party lost ground on the Left as well as on the Right. The economic crisis which had caused the split in Labour's ranks looked to many like the last stand of capitalism, and added to the allure of revolutionary politics.

Percy was re-elected on to the town council as representative for another ward the following year. He was still seeing Dolly, though now that she was older their friendship had become strained. He did not attend her twenty-first party in 1930, but like a parent turned up at three o'clock in the morning to carry the girls home in his car. Dolly felt she had to get away; she went on a Mediterranean cruise, and aboard ship met a man her own age from the other side of the Pennines. When they married a couple of years later, Percy gave her away.

Alan was restless at home. He played table tennis on the expanding oak dining table, and went riding on Blackpool Sands. To some extent he was still dominated by his mother; he trailed after her, he wrote in his autobiography: 'I was tied to her apron strings and took a long time to cut loose from them. Even then I did it only by tying on to somebody else's.'[8] Margaret was in Vienna, studying the piano at Alan's insistence; he believed that every woman should have a career. She came back to England at Christmas and they spent some time together in Manchester; then he went out to Vienna in the spring. Alan was reluctant to commit himself, finding reasons not to marry her: she was Roman Catholic, she was not intellectual, they were not suited to each other. In the summer he moved down to London to complete his research on the

Italian problem; Margaret was there too and it seemed they must marry or break. Alan decided they should marry. Having screwed up his courage to propose, he found another man paying court to his prospective bride. 'I said the most wild and provocative things in order to drive him from the room. I well remember the feeling of desperation as I uttered one absurd and outrageous statement after another and found him still obtusely there, until I was reduced to personal offensiveness.' Eventually the rival retired, leaving the field clear for Alan; and his proposal was accepted.[9]

On the appointed day he turned up at Marylebone Town Hall, with Geoffrey Rowntree in attendance. Margaret was waiting, and together they walked through to the register office. The ceremony began; at the last moment, when Alan was asked to solemnly declare his commitment to Margaret, he answered 'No', turned on his heel, and strode out.

Rowntree was shocked, and he followed Alan in silence to the 1917 Club. When they arrived all Alan would say was that he had decided a few moments before not to go through with it. Margaret was understandably distressed, and departed for a short holiday in Russia. When she came back, Alan tried again. This time the wedding passed off without incident.

Perhaps Alan had been concerned at how his parents would react to his marriage; at any rate, they were upset when they heard about it afterwards. They were hurt not to have been invited to their only child's wedding, nor even to have been informed beforehand. They disapproved of Margaret because of her Catholic background, and they disapproved of marrying in a register office. They did not at first give the young couple a wedding present; Alan complained about this to his father, and Percy made amends with a set of silver fish knives and forks. Alan took his new bride to Preston for a couple of days to try and heal the breach; this attempt was only partly successful. According to Alan, Connie complained that he had inflicted on her 'a severe psychological shock and thereafter walked with a heavy limp. She never forgave Margaret for not being a left-wing intellectual.'[10]

Though Alan made fun of his mother's affliction, she was becoming more and more of an invalid, confined to bed for much of the day. Whether she suffered lasting renal damage as a result of her stillborn child it is impossible to say, though it is considered unlikely. Perhaps her illness was psychosomatic.

The newlyweds were well set up. On top of his salary of £300 as an assistant lecturer, Alan had some shares and Margaret had a private income, making a total of £900 a year.* Alan often quoted Johnson's remark that 'There are few ways in which a man can be more innocently employed than in getting money.' He liked to play the stock-market, and by 1940 he had accumulated capital of more than £8000. They were able to live quite comfortably, running a motor car and employing a daily woman. They did not have to wash the dishes or make the beds. Alan and Margaret found a furnished flat in Didsbury, a suburb to the south of Manchester. It was the top floor of a large eighteenth-century house called The Limes, which also contained several other flats; on the floor below was a leather-jacketed Communist scientist from the Shirley Institute and his wife, George and Dolly Eltenton,† and on the ground floor were Malcolm and Kitty Muggeridge. The Muggeridges and the Taylors quickly became intimate friends. Malcolm was a leader-writer on the *Manchester Guardian* and a friend of the editor Ted Scott, son of the great C.P. Scott. Kitty was a beauty, niece of Beatrice Webb, the diligent Fabian. When the Taylors moved in to the top flat of The Limes, the Muggeridges had just decided on a trial separation. Kitty was going to London to pursue a career as an actress. Alan and Margaret accompanied Malcolm to see her off at the station; next day she came back.

Alan and Malcolm both had modern ideas about marriage. Alan, for example, believed in sharing the chores, which meant that he cooked breakfast. More obscurely, he held that married couples should take separate holidays, and should sleep in separate beds: 'they put the individual above the marriage'.[12] But this was not the only reason for sleeping alone. It seems that the women in his life

---

*Namier's annual salary on his appointment as a professor in 1931 was £1000; male unemployment benefit was reduced that year from 17/- to 15/3d a week.
†It was George Eltenton who brought about the downfall of the American nuclear physicist J. Robert Oppenheimer. During the War Eltenton, by then working in California, asked a friend of Oppenheimer's to persuade him to pass nuclear secrets to the Russians. Oppenheimer's reaction was seen as ambiguous, and his less than frank subsequent behaviour led to his being excluded from further secret work.[11]

disliked his habit of sleeping with his legs stretched straight out in bed, one he had adopted as a boy in the belief that it would help him to grow. When, at nearly seventy, he regularly shared a bed with a woman, 'the emotional effect was shattering'.[13]

Alan believed that couples should pool their income and share their expenditure, recording both meticulous accounts. In these matters, of course, he was following the example of his parents. Malcolm believed in open marriage, or what was then called free love.[14] What Margaret and Kitty believed is not recorded.

In 1934 Muggeridge published a novel, *Picture Palace*, so obviously depicting the real people around him that it had to be suppressed. The central character, Pettygrew, is a journalist on a newspaper, and is modelled on Muggeridge himself, as the newspaper is modelled on the *Manchester Guardian*.* Pettygrew's friend, Rattray, a lecturer at 'Accringthorpe University' who in many ways resembles Alan, is in love with Pettygrew's wife, Gertrude. Pettygrew claims to be delighted.

> You understand the basis of our marriage. Jealousy is inconceivable. We're both promiscuous, as you know . . . Our view is that marriage should be a source of happiness, not a routine, a discipline. We have never interfered with each other's freedom.[16]

He encourages Rattray to sleep with Gertrude: 'it'll strengthen the bond between us'. Gertrude is repelled, but she is portrayed as having no power of independent choice; she succumbs to Rattray, and then leaves Pettygrew and Accringthorpe for London. At the end of the novel they are reconciled; Pettygrew realises that he has imposed his abstract, unnatural ideas on her and repents.

Did Alan, then, have an affair with Kitty Muggeridge? In Alan's eyes Kitty was 'ravishing', 'staggeringly beautiful'. Thirty years later Alan described how 'in those days Malcolm used to make out that his was a "permissive" marriage and acted on this doctrine,

---

*Ironically, it was this, rather than any personal libel, which caused the book to be withdrawn. Muggeridge had suggested that the newspaper depended for its survival on the much racier, more popular, *Manchester Evening News* – he compared it to someone living off the immoral earnings of his daughter – and on these grounds the editor, W.P. Crozier, applied for an injunction.[15]

though Kitty got great unhappiness from it'.[17] Many of the scenes described in the novel had real-life parallels, for example the daily walks that Rattray and Pettygrew shared. But all one can infer is that the possibility occurred to Muggeridge.

About this time Alan took Muggeridge to meet his parents, and many years later Muggeridge described the impression they made on him:

> I remember him [Alan's father] well – a stocky, well-built man, ready on request to stand on his head, and often accompanied by a charming young girl called Dolly Sharples. Alan's mother, on the other hand, was a tall, cadaverous-looking lady, formerly a teacher, who balanced out Dolly with a Trotskyite, Henry Sara, whom she idolised and supported all her life, thus delivering him from the tiresome necessity of earning a living. Alan took me to see his mother when she was doing a course at one of those starving places where the well-to-do nibble Ryvita and dream of becoming slim and beautiful; actually only acquiring, as poor Mrs Taylor did, bad breath and a kind of gaunt despair.
>
> It is not difficult to detect these two strains in him [Alan]. From his father comes his shrewdness, his joviality and his care about money; from his mother, the unattached fanaticism floating about inside him, so that he goes on doggedly cherishing a vision of triumphant workers bringing to pass an earthly paradise . . .[18]

One afternoon in the summer of 1931 Ernest Jacob invited Alan to come into the common room and meet his new professor. Sitting there was a large man with a tightly rolled umbrella; when he spoke, it was in a thick, middle-European accent. Lewis Namier was a Polish Jew, from a Galician landowning family, who had been disinherited by his father. He had come to England in 1907, read history at Balliol, and had fought in the Royal Fusiliers before being transferred to intelligence work. After the War he had been a temporary lecturer at Balliol for a few years. In the early 1920s he was analysed in Vienna by Theodore Reik,* one of Freud's pupils,

---

*Curiously, there was a feud between Reik and Stekel, Alan's analyst. Reik was not medically qualified, as Stekel believed an analyst should be. Reik was prosecuted for treating a patient without qualifications; Freud supported him and the case collapsed.

and he had made a close study of Freud's works. Like Alan, he had an intense interest in central Europe; unlike Alan, he scorned ideology. Marx was his *bête noire*, though according to Isaiah Berlin, Namier was somewhat similar to Marx:

> He too was an intellectually formidable, at times aggressive, politically minded intellectual – and his hatred of doctrine was held with a doctrinaire tenacity. Like Marx, he was vain, proud, contemptuous, intolerant, quick to give and take offence, master of his craft, confident of his own powers, not without a strain of pathos and self-pity. Like Marx he hated all forms of weakness, sentimentality, idealistic liberalism; most of all he hated servility. Like Marx, he fascinated his interlocutors and oppressed them too . . . those who met him were divided into some who looked on him as a man of genius and a dazzling talker and others who fled from him as an appalling bore.[19]

Namier despised sloppy thinking, which he described as wobbling with the brain.[20] His reviews of works which failed to come up to his high standards could be devastating. His own writing, based on meticulous scholarship and employing a new methodology – 'structural analysis' – represented an intellectual revolution in historical study. His books on England in the latter half of the eighteenth century demolished the 'Whig interpretation' which had hitherto been the consensus. To Namier, attempts to account for human behaviour by invoking the power of ideas were absurd. Ideas were mere interpretations by the mind of deep-seated drives and motives which it was too cowardly, or too conventional, to face.[21]

It was a review of one of these books, *England in the Age of the American Revolution*, which had prompted Jacob to offer the Chair of Modern History to Namier.[22] Namier thus became Alan's boss. Alan always denied that he was Namier's pupil, though he acknowledged Namier as one of his two 'masters' (the other was Lord Beaverbrook).[23] He pointed out that he had arrived at the university a year earlier, and that once Namier became his colleague he depended on Alan for advice about how it worked. Indeed, Namier was semi-detached from Manchester and all too obviously hankered to return to Oxford; he continued to live in

London, something the city fathers considered slightly disloyal, and when he came up to teach stayed only a few nights each week in lodgings out on Alderley Edge. Namier was remote from the undergraduates, and he displayed little enthusiasm for administration. 'What have the others got to do with their time?' he asked.[24] Alan deputised for him on university committees, arousing the indignation of some of the other professors. But intellectually there was no doubt who was the senior. Namier was nearly twenty years older than Alan; his learning and his experience of the world were correspondingly wider, and his thinking more developed. When Jacob introduced them Namier had already published many important essays and two profoundly influential books. Sir Isaiah Berlin has written of Namier's 'immediate intellectual and moral impact'.[25] Namier was too powerful and subtle a thinker to ignore; and furthermore he was at the height of his powers in the 1930s.

Namier was a passionate historian. Everything he wrote was personal, and he delivered his points with a kind of controlled ferocity. The mixture of corruption, hypocrisy and oppression by which the Habsburg Empire was governed was in his mind associated with his father's way of life.[26] His hostility to Germany was inspired by the threat that German power presented to Europe in general and to Jews in particular. Even his obsession with the English landed classes has been linked, not unreasonably, with his own disinheritance. For Namier, therefore, history was not a subject in isolation, but part of a continuum which also took in his journalism and his political activities, Zionism in particular.

Namier's writing combined careful argument with emotional punch. He wrote clear, even beautiful English prose – though it was not of course his first language – with a precision which matched the clarity and the penetration of his thinking. This was illuminated by startling, often poetic metaphors.

Alan could not but be stimulated by this extraordinary man. He became a tougher, more rigorous thinker. Many of Namier's arguments challenged assumptions inherent in Alan's upbringing. Alan began a process of re-shaping his intellectual and moral universe, discarding ideas he had inherited from his parents. He adopted many of Namier's views, and even some of his habits. Most important of all, perhaps, Namier taught Alan that history *matters*. In the early 1930s Alan was by no means committed to academic life; he had drifted into it almost by accident, and for a while he contemplated the alternative of a career in journalism. He later admitted that but for Namier he might not have persisted with history.[27] 'Talking to him was an inspiration, always bringing out the best in me and giving me confidence . . . Many a time when writing a review or a chapter of a book I have thought, "This is no good. I can't go on with it," and then, "Lewis will be disappointed with me if I don't."' If Alan was too independent a spirit to be, as Malcolm Muggeridge called him, Namier's 'acolyte', even this was no contradiction; because for Namier, iconoclasm was the mark of a great historian.[28] Perhaps the best way to sum up Namier's effect on Alan is to employ Newman's words about his first master, Whately: 'He had not only taught me to think, but to think for myself.'

They made a strange pair, this large, clumsy, middle-European and the short, whimsical Northerner. But they became intimate friends. Being alone in Machester (his wife had left him in 1920), Namier was a frequent visitor to the Taylor household; he told Berlin that some of his happiest hours had been spent there.[29] For his part Alan found Namier lovable, despite his intellectual severity; 'To me he was a man of great fun and irresponsibility.'[30] One summer afternoon, for example, he walked with the Taylors and the Muggeridges to a stream where Alan liked to bathe. The two married couples stripped off and jumped in. Namier could not resist joining them and removed his trousers, declaring, 'There are still young people in the world and I am one of them.' Afterwards they all ran around to dry themselves. On another occasion, when dining with the Taylors and the Muggeridges, he started to attack Beatrice Webb, whom he despised. Kitty Muggeridge said how right he was, because Auntie Bo was a dreadful creature. When Namier realised his *faux pas*, he was embarrassed and tried to backtrack, saying that Beatrice Webb was a very intelligent and interesting person.[31] He dropped another brick at a Manchester party, a lively occasion at which the men and women were exchanging clothes; the idea was to find a member of the opposite sex of approximately the same shape. Namier approached a slim and elegant young woman, who was not amused at the prospect.[32]

Alan described his demeanour at parties as that of a patient friendly elephant.[33]

It was not a relationship of equals. Namier described Alan, incorrectly, as 'my assistant'; Alan deferred to his professor. In part this was because he was Namier's protégé. Namier recommended Alan to the *Manchester Guardian*, and he repeatedly pushed Alan at his publisher, Harold Macmillan. 'I consider Taylor one of the coming men on pre-War diplomatic history, and, as such, I think he is worth the attention of publishers,' read a typical letter from Namier to Macmillan.[34] Namier was the editor of a new series for Macmillan called 'Studies in Modern History'; he proposed to include in it Alan's thesis on the Italian problem, and invited Harold Macmillan up to Manchester to meet him. The future prime minister duly came, and discussed the book with Alan; he proposed publication on a commission basis, with Alan paying a subsidy of £50 towards the cost of production. Initially Alan seemed willing to contemplate this course; but then he withdrew. Namier wrote to Macmillan regretting that Alan had been unable to accept 'your very handsome and generous offer – you have done all you could to make things easy for him'.[35] Alan had decided to publish the book instead with Manchester University Press. A Tout Memorial Publication Fund had been established in 1926; this enabled the University Press to publish the work without a contribution from the author. As a result Alan never took his degree. Doctorates were then thought to be a little *infra dig* in England,* favoured by Americans or Germans, and Alan never bothered to pay the necessary fee to claim the title 'Dr'.† Forty years on, this cavalier attitude still caused resentment in the Manchester Senior Common Room; 'That man owes us eighteen guineas,' the assistant bursar remarked whenever Alan's name came up.

The Italian Problem in European Diplomacy, 1847–1849 was published in 1934. It is an intricate study of a single issue; but there is a much broader underlying argument. The policy of European nations, Alan held, is based on a series of assumptions with which

---

*'I only wish you would not allow anyone to call me by that foolish title "Dr",' wrote Namier to the Editor of the *Manchester Guardian* in 1946, 'which I do *not* possess, having deliberately and carefully avoided that infliction.'[36]
†He had taken his Oxford M.A. in 1932.

statesmen have lived since their earliest years and which they regard as so axiomatic as hardly to be worth stating. It is the interaction of the differing national principles which in the long run determines the history of Europe.[37] The book is as detailed and heavy with footnotes, some occupying more than half the page, as one would expect from a thesis; but unexpectedly the detail is leavened by bold metaphors and a strong narrative, as well as some cheeky asides. Despite these, the book was respectfully reviewed in the academic journals. One approving review which may have given Alan particular pleasure appeared in the pages of *Bootham*, and was signed 'L.H.G.' – Leslie Gilbert.[38]

Namier's influence is obvious, and his unfailing patience and wisdom are acknowledged in the foreword.[39] Absent is any Marxist interpretation, such as one might expect from an historian with Alan's views. 'Somehow I never managed to bring Marxism into my historical work,' Alan wrote in his autobiography. 'Like Johnson's friend Edwards,* I too have tried to be a Marxist but common sense kept breaking in.'[40] This absence becomes more noticeable still in Alan's next book, *Germany's First Bid for Colonies*. 'Both show an ingenuity in the interpretation of documents,' wrote James Joll thirty years later, 'and in suggesting that the obvious motives for action may not necessarily be the true ones.'[41] Indeed Alan had an intuitive flair for documentary work. He had a remarkable ability to empathise with those he was writing about; to see beyond the letters and memoranda into their minds and hearts. He was a shrewd 'guesser'. Namier envied his 'green fingers', his ability to get things right by instinct.†[43]

Alan had his differences with Namier, of course. Namier was in rebellion against heroic history, the idea of history as the activities of the great; Alan was more romantic, and in this sense more traditional. Namier was interested in Henry Fox, as the epitome of

---

*'I have tried too to be a philosopher; but, I don't know how, cheerfulness was always breaking in.' Boswell's *Life of Johnson*, 17 April 1778. This is two jokes in one; Alan always enjoyed baiting his philosopher colleagues.
†'The men who succeed in this world are not those whose heads are stuffed with facts, but those with a native shrewdness and an ability to get things right by instinct. The gardener with "green fingers" does better than the man whose shelves are crammed with horticultural books.'[42]

a certain class; Alan in his son, Charles James Fox, as the champion of liberty.[44] Namier gave his name to a form of microscopic analysis which Alan never attempted to copy. And Namier was from a landowning family; he despised the masses. After he made some particularly slighting reference to the working class, Alan was stung to reply: 'When you speak like that you are talking about my own forebears and the class to which I emotionally belong.' Namier could not understand, Alan wrote in his autobiography, that 'I was devoted to the class I sprang from'.[45] This may seem odd, even ludicrous talk from one whose father and grandfather were rich enough to be the equivalent of modern millionaires. Alan, some might feel, was a gilded youth. But this is to apply a later standard to an earlier, more innocent age. In the 1930s many young left-wingers from privileged backgrounds identified with the proletariat; Eric Blair, the old Etonian, actually tried to turn himself into George Orwell, the working man. Alan and his friend Malcolm Muggeridge saw nothing incongruous about referring to themselves as 'intellectual workers'.

In later life Alan described himself as upper middle class.[46] But that was not the end of the story. Alan was well aware that his grandfathers had ascended from obscurity; it would be easy to sink back. James Taylor and Sons, the source of the family wealth, had gone into a steep decline after Percy's withdrawal, and eventually the firm had to be sold. One of Alan's paternal cousins became a bus driver; as Alan put it, 'clogs to clogs in three generations'. While Alan's father dissipated his fortune, Alan built up his capital. It became a point of principle for him not to use his savings, to live from the interest alone.

The Didsbury ménage did not last long. Muggeridge was saddened when his friend Ted Scott drowned, after his sailing dinghy capsized on Windermere. Scott had been Muggeridge's patron on the paper; now that W.P. Crozier was in the editor's chair he was less in favour. Like most left-wing intellectuals, Muggeridge was fascinated by Soviet Russia, and he decided to go and see what was happening there for himself. Within a month of Scott's death, it had been agreed that Muggeridge should take six months' leave to go to Russia; he would act as deputy correspondent and send occasional

contributions to the *Manchester Guardian*. This was not such a
friendly act as Alan later described. Crozier made it clear that he
was not committed to taking Muggeridge back on to the editorial
staff when he returned.[47]

It was the period when Western sympathisers arrived at Soviet
ports by the boatload, and embarked on the return journey with
their heads stuffed with propaganda. The slump at home quickened
the tide. Bernard Shaw, Sidney* and Beatrice Webb (who had only
just returned when the Muggeridges set out), Lady Astor, André
Gide, G.D.H. Cole and his wife, Raymond Postgate and countless
others, all went to see the new civilisation and came back with their
doubts, if any, silenced. Almost without exception, they were
astonishingly gullible; Professor Julian Huxley, for example, had
no difficulty in believing that 'Stalin himself sometimes comes
down to the Moscow goods sidings to help'.[48] Margaret Cole knew
of the existence of the OGPU, the Soviet secret police, but thought
of them as 'kindly souls who came to our rescue and found us seats
on crowded trains'.[49] They believed what they wanted to believe;
they saw what they wanted to see. Russia was, they liked to think,
their own creation: a state brought into being by an abstract
principle, a 'scientific' society. They were fed exaggerated statistics
about the progress of the Russian economy; and contrasted this
unfavourably with the apparent crisis of capitalism in the West. It is
perhaps all too easy now to mock these well-meaning pilgrims.
'How deeply the Left craved to give the benefit of all the doubts to
Moscow!' Michael Foot would write half a century later. 'No one
who did not live through that period can appreciate how overwhelming that craving was.'[50]

Muggeridge shared in the general enthusiasm. He was not sure
about Communism itself, but he was certain that what he was
about to witness was 'the birth of a new kind of civilisation. The
essential thing is the new values it embodies; and these, once
enunciated, cannot come to nothing.'[51] Perhaps he was thinking of
the sexual liberation held out as an added attraction of a visit to the

---

*Created Baron Passfield in 1929; his wife preferred to remain Mrs Webb.

USSR; as he later put it, 'in each male heart a vision, never to be realised, of a *comsomolka* with a red kerchief over jet black hair, with dark glistening eyes and flushed cheeks, dancing a revolutionary dance'.[52]

Alan apparently warned Muggeridge that he would not like Russia; Malcolm, he says, brushed such warnings aside.[53] Alan was right. Soon after Muggeridge arrived, he wrote to Crozier that 'things are pretty grim here . . . In some parts of the country famine conditions already prevail, and even in Moscow the majority are not getting nearly enough to eat.' In the North Caucasus 'seventy peasants were shot for hoarding grain, and to store more than 100 pounds of grain is punishable by the death penalty'.[54] He began to file articles which described the terrible condition of the Russian people, and his letters to Crozier became impassioned: 'For my part, I believe that every scrap of support and encouragement given by, for instance, the *M.G.*, to the illusions and hopes, understandable enough, about what is going on here, is a crime, and, in a purely journalistic sense, a mistake, since the regime is bound within a year or so to be utterly discredited.'[55]

This was not what Crozier wanted to hear, nor perhaps what *Manchester Guardian* readers wanted to read. 'Truth like everything else should be economised,' C.P. Scott had taught.[56] Crozier informed Muggeridge that there would be no job for him on the *Manchester Guardian* when he returned. He began to cut Muggeridge's pieces to take out the 'comment'; 'if we denounce we are in unpleasant company'.[57] Muggeridge was furious when he saw, belatedly, how the stuffing had been removed from what he had written: 'I realise that you don't want to know what is going on in Russia or let your readers know . . . I feel utterly disgusted . . . The hypocrisy of it all, the salesmanship, the Kingsley-Martin-Bernard-Shaw-Sidney-and-Beatrice-Webb slop that frothed around that dark tyranny and famine made me sick.'[58]

Alan shared Crozier's distaste for Muggeridge's new line, and in a long, handwritten latter to Muggeridge he tried to 'put you right about Russia'. What he wrote is worth quoting at length, because it reveals how his politics remained those of the schoolboy class warrior:

You'll realise that I'm not hitting you, because I love you – as man to man – more than anyone else I know, but your ideas: rather like the wrestling match of Birkin and whatever his name was in *Women in Love*, though with no sexual significance . . .

As Margaret remarks the essential argument between us was already clear enough before you left England – do you remember how indignant you got when I opposed your advocacy of Communism on moral grounds, because it was 'better'. Well, that is still what is wrong with your attitude – you can't see clearly enough the ruthlessness and the necessity of the class war: it seems to surprise you that, for example, there should be espionage in Russia, as though there wasn't any in England from 1914 to 1918. But first, may I try to make the general position clear, because the details fit into this. There are two, very obvious main themes we must treat apart – the workers and the peasantry and just because Russia is a workers' state we must start with them. You say that everything you care for is crushed in Russia as in England – well, here are some things that make the Russian workers in a better position (remember that I am completely excluding the agricultural position). In Russia no one can live by owning – that is absolutely true, undeniable: no landlords, no capitalists and that alone is to my mind worth unending sacrifices: it is the vital and essential thing you ignore and which apparently means nothing to you. In Russia things (however wastefully) are produced for use and not (however efficiently) for profit: that's why Russia shall go up and we shall go down . . . Then the Russian worker has a control over his work – through the factory-committees – which no worker ever had before: he can criticise, he can control the management: what he says, goes.

Then, even from your own moral point of view, look at the fight against illiteracy (no tyrannical government dare educate its people); look at the new schools; look at the (very wasteful, badly-built – but still there) new houses; the clinics – with no air of charity about them: the marriage laws which have destroyed the horrible Christian family and made people, for the first time, free in their personal relations. Then think of the fact that a new generation is growing up free from Christianity – that's something, that's worthwhile: you will reply that they are getting Marxism instead, but as that is (a) this-worldly instead of other-worldly (b) in accordance with the facts, I don't mind . . .

You'll say this is all idealistic claptrap, which bears no relationship to the sufferings and privations of the present, which brings me to the peasantry. For the present position is due to the failure of agriculture.

Even you don't attempt to deny that industrially the Five Year Plan has (on the whole or taken generally) succeeded, even though you attempt to belittle it . . . The peasant failure is because of the isolated position of Russia. If the whole world had gone Communist in 1919 the workers everywhere would have been in an invincible position: they would have been able to win over the peasantry with the products of industrial Europe and also kill them (economically) with the cheaper foodstuffs from the large-scale capitalist farms (owned by the Workers' State) in America and Australia. But as only Russia went Communist, a weak, young working class was left face to face with a backward, individualistic peasantry. It had to buy food from this peasantry and it couldn't get the money back again from the peasantry by offering cheap machine-made goods, because Russian industry was too backward. As a result the more culpable peasants hoarded money and became, in a small way, capitalists. By 1928, there was a danger that the urban socialism would be swamped by a new capitalism, coming from the kulaks and that had to be fought, even at the cost of famine. The collective farms weren't started because they would be immediately more efficient, but because – for the Workers' State to survive – the kulaks and indeed the individualistic peasantry had to be destroyed. There's the problem and that's what you ought to have understood before you began to write about the peasantry because the famine issue is, in a sense, irrelevant . . .

Your general impression of window-dressing and hypocrisy seems to me so utterly irrelevant. It's as if you dismissed the General Strike of 1926 as a fraud, as negligible, because the leaders were incompetent, drunken sods. But the General Strike was a fact and, despite the hypocrisy and cowardice, it showed that there was such a thing in England as working-class solidarity. In a greater degree, because it is in power, it is a fact too in Russia and that's why I hate your disparagements, your contempt for Russia. Attack the leaders if you like, attack their policy: but have the grace and good sense to recognise that – as in England there is a solid workers' movement which is going forward, despite up and downs – so in Russia there is a workers' movement in power, which is holding on somehow – on forced rations – until we, the workers of the rest of the world, come to rescue it. Why do you think your attacks on Russia are welcomed in the capitalist press? Because when you attack Russia, you weaken the working-class movement everywhere. I can't believe you want to be on the side of the owners, the Christians – well, you are now: if you can't praise the Workers' State, well for god's sake leave it alone and come away.

The assumed abhorrence of Christianity makes ironic reading in view of Muggeridge's later religiocity.

> You'll never know Russia [Alan continued] until you go to ordinary workers' clubs, rest-homes and so on. My aunt Joan* spends four months on a collective farm every summer, just as a worker, and the result is that she comes home more enthusiastic every summer. But really I've known lots of chaps who have become converted by living among the workers and you certainly never will find out about Russia until you do the same. If you do think of staying on, I do hope it will not be as a journalist, but as a teacher of English or something like that. You see when I talked about the old revolutionaries, I didn't mean the people at the top, but the old party members all through the country, not a single one of whom you have obviously ever met.
>
> At the same time, I'm glad if Russia has helped to empty you of chauvinist hopes and slogans – there's no room for them in the workers' movement. You say that you can't get out of the shit by shouting and I agree – but I believe we can get out of the shit by all the workers acting together. Come away from Russia, where you are weakening the working-class movement, and back to England, where you can help it avoid the mistakes the Russians have made. After all, if they have failed, we must succeed. You say you like to prick Crozier's and the cunt's† little balloons: but don't you see that your present articles help to blow them up . . .
>
> I wrote to Kit and told her not to bother about the money – as long as you pay me interest once a year.[59]

After such a finger-wagging, Muggeridge might have smiled at this last sentence. Even at the peak of his fervour for the working-class movement, Alan did not lose sight of the principles of good housekeeping.

Muggeridge poured out his bitterness in a brilliant satirical novel.‡ *Winter in Moscow* (1934) depicts a cruel and soulless

---

*Joan Beauchamp, Harry Thompson's wife; on May Day each year she got the chauffeur to raise the Red Flag outside their house.
†Possibly a reference to Kitty's aunt.
‡Thirty years later Alan wrote that it was probably the best book ever written about Soviet Russia, just as the Webbs' book *Soviet Russia: A New Civilisation?* (1935) – later reprinted without the question-mark – was probably the most preposterous.[60]

tyranny; but most of all it is a novel about journalism, and telling lies by omission or by euphemism. The refrain 'impossible to make an omelette without breaking eggs', initially innocuous, is repeated and repeated until it takes on an appalling significance. Lenin had said that the only interesting question in life was 'Who whom?' Who exploits whom? Who puts whom to death?

In his preface,[61] Muggeridge tells how he 'took a great dislike to the Dictatorship of the Proletariat, and, even more, to its imbecilic foreign admirers'. Muggeridge was very upset by what he had seen, and upset too by the suggestion which came back from the *Manchester Guardian* that henceforward he send his pieces to the *Morning Post*, an extreme right-wing paper.[62] Though the suggestion was no doubt made sarcastically, he decided he had nothing to lose. When Muggeridge's articles started to appear there Alan was shocked; he wrote telling Muggeridge of the 'terrible grief and pain' he had caused. We all have to do some pretty unpleasant things to raise money, Alan said snidely, and suggested that when Muggeridge paid him the interest on the money Alan had lent him he pay back some of the principal as well.[63]

It seems that Alan's faith in the Soviet Union was unshaken by the Moscow treason trials, which had already begun while Muggeridge was there – a trial is described in *Winter in Moscow* – and which reached their zenith in the mid-1930s. Alan appears to have accepted the guilt of those accused, even the ones whom he had encountered on his visit ten years before.[64] In a review of a biography of Robespierre, he remarked that 'a revolution cannot be judged by the ordinary standards of academic morality'.[65]

Alan's blindness to the truth of the Russian purges contrasted oddly with his nonconformist instinct for justice. Writing about the Dreyfus case, for example, he remarked that 'the difference between free and unfree countries is that in the free country there are always men who will champion the unpopular cause at whatever cost. It is this stage army of the good, with its slightly ridiculous reappearances, which alone keeps our liberties alive.'[66]

Ironically, Alan was in the process of breaking his links with the local Communists in Manchester; he warned the theatre director Joan Littlewood against them. His own stance became increasingly anti-Communist but pro-Russian. He was strongly opposed to rearmament under the National Government, which he thought might ally itself with Germany against Soviet Russia* – the very opposite of what happened, as it turned out. He demanded an Anglo-Russian alliance – something advocated also by Namier – without which, he declared, 'our enemy is here'. A visit to Austria and Germany in the summer of 1932 had convinced him that war between Germany and France was imminent. He would oppose British entry into this war, as his parents had opposed British participation in the last one. In 1933 he joined an anti-war group that became known as the Manchester Peace Council, and soon he was their main spokesman, going out in the evening once or twice a week to speak to church groups, trades union branches, any members of the loose coalition of progressive opinion which wanted to prevent another war. In 1934 he was one of thirty speakers, among them Aneurin Bevan and Arthur Greenwood, who addressed a crowd of almost three thousand in Manchester's Platts Fields protesting against Fascism and the Incitement to Disaffection Bill. Alan claimed that the Bill was a war measure, a deliberate preparation for the next European war. 'Are we going to allow ourselves to be slaughtered,' he asked, 'or are we going to refuse to fight for capitalism and raise instead the standard of Socialist England?'[68] In the 1935 *Bootham School Register* he listed his hobby as 'expert and constant anti-war speaker'.

By this time Alan was no longer living in Manchester. From the moment he had started working at the university he had wanted to live in the country. Initially he considered the Lake District, his childhood playground, but this seemed too far away to be practical. Then he and Margaret found a cottage at the top of a steep hill in Higher Disley, on the edge of the Derbyshire Peak District. He bought it for £500 and they moved out there in the spring of 1933.

---

*This idea did not seem as unlikely then as it might do now. British troops had fought the Red Army after the end of the First World War, and only the threat of a general strike had prevented British intervention on the Polish side in the Russo-Polish War. As a result the slogans 'Hands off Russia' and 'No more War' had become equated. Throughout the inter-War period the Soviets suspected the Western powers of planning another war of intervention, and made much of this in their propaganda.[67]

Alan was happy there; towards the end of his life he was to say, somewhat melodramatically, that it was the only place where he had ever been happy.

7: *Top of the World*

Three Gates was not a comfortable house; formed mostly out of old agricultural buildings, it was long and wedge-shaped, only one room thick; as a result it was cold and damp, despite massive central heating radiators driven by a solid-fuel boiler. It had no electricity when Alan and Margaret arrived. Perched on the top of the ridge and facing north it was dreadfully exposed, and in winter the snows often cut them off from the valley. The summer up there was six weeks shorter at each end than down below. What made it special was the view. A lane divided the house from the terraced garden, beyond which fields sloped down sharply. From the house you could see straight across to Kinder Scout, the most dramatic of the Peaks; a few yards down the lane was open country. For someone who loved walking, as Alan did, it was a 'dream house'.[1]

They soon set about making it more comfortable. Electricity was installed; and each spring they limewashed the outside walls in pink. Though it seemed isolated, the house was only twelve miles from the university; Alan enjoyed the journey in his open cars. He liked to drive fast, and was not insulted to be called a demon driver. He always kept the top down; though with no heater it was very uncomfortable in cold weather. Because pre-War cars had no demisters he often had to push up the windscreen, making it colder still. He cut quite a figure in check cloth cap and goggles, wrapped in a rug, with a hot-water bottle on his lap – irresistibly reminiscent to some of Mr Toad. There were far fewer cars then on the roads, of course; most of the people the Taylors knew used public transport. To appease his conscience for his position of privilege Alan filled up his cars with Soviet petrol.

Car commuters like Alan were then a novelty, known locally as 'neet and mornin' buggers'. Disley was still very much a village, and Disleyites regarded Alan with awe. They referred to him as 'Professor' Taylor to distinguish him from Jimmy Taylor, a lecturer in industrial chemistry at Bolton Technical College, who lived nearby. Alan was regarded as a dangerous man who had acquired Continental tastes – drinking beer at mealtimes and, worse still, eating cabbage cooked in beer, an outlandish and unpatriotic German habit, which caused the cook to tender her resignation. Fortunately Margaret was an excellent cook. 'She's Cordon Bleu, you know,' Alan would boast.

At weekends there were plenty of visitors, and usually at least one long walk, bad weather notwithstanding. Strictly speaking they were trespassing much of the time and they had to keep a low profile, sometimes literally; the landowners barred walkers from their moorland because they said it ruined the shooting. At the time there was widespread resentment in the North-West of England that the public were, at least officially, confined to the crowded and built-up lowland, resulting in frequent acts of defiance. The most famous of these was in 1932, when students organised a mass trespass on Kinder Scout; there was a battle with the gamekeepers trying to keep them off, and when some of the students were arrested Alan spoke up in their defence. The controversy led to the setting up of the Ramblers' Association, which campaigned for access to such land. Alan's friend Paddy Monkhouse, who had been a prime mover in the mass trespass, became a member of the new Peak District Planning Board, a precursor of the National Parks.

In hot weather Alan's walks were punctuated by swims in the high waters of the rivers that ran out of the Peaks, and nude sunbathing. The 1930s were the great years of naturism; taking off your clothes was tantamount to shedding your bourgeois inhibitions. Though neither of the Taylors was slim, they were, according to Muggeridge, 'assertive about their nakedness'.[2] Alan had acquired the habit of swimming and sunbathing naked as a schoolboy and as an undergraduate; it was something he enjoyed all his life. As a bonus there was the pleasure of watching naked women running around to dry themselves.

The move out of Manchester was symbolic. Three Gates was a

proper home, where a young married couple might start a family. Alan began to put down roots; literally as well as metaphorically, for he threw himself into gardening with gusto, producing exotic vegetables with the help of cloches and manure. Alan was Mr McGregor as well as Mr Toad; his green fingers useful in the garden as well as in the archive. He became reluctant to go into the university; and when visitors arrived at the house he greeted them in shorts and gardening gloves. He was proud of his vegetables, and liked it when G.N. Clark's wife called him a peasant. This was not an insult; Clark himself had the manner of a countryman. Here was another echo of *Picture Palace*; Rattray, the university lecturer, lived in a cottage in the country and took a great interest in his garden.[3] Alan grew no flowers, however (though Margaret did). For him gardening was always a practical activity, producing food for his family.

Alan was carefree. He was happy in Higher Disley; he was happy, it seems, with Margaret; he was happy in his work. He was hitting his stride; he had begun to make a name for himself as a diplomatic historian, and from November 1934 onwards he was a regular reviewer for the *Manchester Guardian*. He began with a life of Robespierre, which Namier passed to him, apparently because he could not be bothered to review it himself. Namier passed him more books, and soon they were sent to him direct from the paper. From 1935 onwards he was reviewing twenty-five to thirty books a year, signing the reviews with his initials; he started to keep an album of press-cuttings. Alan was often seen in the *Manchester Guardian* offices in the 1930s; apart from reviews he wrote the odd obituary, and from early 1938 he was also writing leader-page articles. A.P. Wadsworth, a leader-writer since 1932, became his best friend in Manchester.

'The very first time I met A.P.W.,' Alan wrote on Wadsworth's retirement twenty years later,

> he was pushing a pram very fast on the rough path beside the Mersey. We tore along, lamenting the feebleness of the British Government and foretelling with cheerful gloom the coming woes of the world. At the same time AP steered the pram past every obstacle and made the occupant feel that she, too, was making a valued contribution to the

discussion. That is the image of the man that lives in my mind. The
zest, the eagerness for new ideas, and the readiness to meet them with
ideas equally new of his own – these qualities stand out at once.
Underneath is a rock-like steadiness of judgement and a deep,
unfailing humanity.[4]

Wadsworth was a small, plump, soft-spoken, twinkling man,
fifteen years Alan's senior. He had joined the *Manchester Guardian*
in 1917, and worked as Labour correspondent and leader-writer
before becoming Assistant Editor in 1940. Wadsworth had an
eager interest in social and economic history, and in 1931 he was
the co-author of *The Cotton Trade and Industrial Lancashire*, a
work described by the *D.N.B.* as a 'masterpiece . . . He saw the life
of his day with a historian's perspective.'[5] Alan never considered
Wadsworth anything less than his equal. For Alan, Wadsworth was
an economic historian of great distinction,[6] and he listened respectfully to Wadsworth's advice on academic affairs. Like Alan,
Wadsworth was aggressively 'Lancashire'. He was said to dislike
Namier, perhaps because Namier made no secret of preferring
London (or Oxford) to Manchester.

Though the Taylors had moved out of the city, they still enjoyed
what it had to offer. They often went to the cinema; Alan was keen
on comic films, especially those of W.C. Fields, Buster Keaton, the
Marx Brothers and Charlie Chaplin. They also enjoyed the
Manchester theatre – especially Noël Coward – and Alan liked the
music-hall in Stockport, where he saw such artists as George Robey
and Clapham & Dwyer. He affected to be unmoved by more
highbrow entertainments. When they visited his Oxford friend
Norman Cameron at his house in London, Alan claimed to feel like
a fish out of water in the company of the poets he met there –
Robert Graves, Cecil Day Lewis and Louis MacNeice among them.
Much of this philistinism was a pose, of course; one he had
practised even at Bootham.

The Taylors' chief pleasure in Manchester was music, however.
Alan had a subscription to the Hallé from the time he arrived at the
university, picking up where he left off with the Vienna Philhar-

monic. Margaret started the Manchester Chamber Concerts Society to encourage chamber music, and with Alan's help she organised a first-class programme of concerts at the Central Library Concert Hall. As a couple they moved in Manchester high society, among the city merchants who patronised the arts and dominated local politics. Here was a contrast with Namier, who never found himself in Manchester society.

Another source of happiness was his teaching. Alan taught a weekly tutorial group of half a dozen or so, each of whom had to write an essay every fortnight. These seminars, which lasted four hours, began with the undergraduates reading their essays out loud, followed by open discussion, in which Alan, copious notes at his elbow, made sure that the readers were never allowed to get away with anything inaccurate or dubious. He had a habit of plucking at his left thumb, making a slight clicking noise with his tongue as he talked.

Alan was popular with his students, who enjoyed his sense of humour and the free exchange of opinion in his tutorial groups. Some of them were invited to visit his home at weekends. They would make their way out there by bus, climb the hill and be greeted by Alan from the garden as they walked up the lane. Once inside, they would be given tankards of beer from the barrel Alan kept on tap in the kitchen – something which offended his teetotal mother – and entertained with recordings of Mozart operas or symphonies. 'If Hitler only listened to Mozart rather than Wagner,' Alan remarked on one occasion, 'then we wouldn't be having so much trouble with him.' The records were played on a remarkable gramophone with an enormous papier-mâché horn; it had thorn needles, which needed to be clipped from time to time with special scissors. Since the 78 r.p.m. records lasted only a few minutes anyway, this process meant little extra interruption.

After something to eat there would always be a walk across the moors, with Alan and Margaret – much admired by Alan's male students – leading the way. Throughout there would be talk, usually about politics and particularly the international situation, to which Alan could never remain indifferent. One of the student visitors was David Wiseman, a Communist prominent in university politics. Another was Maurice Oldfield, later to become head of

MI6. Oldfield was best man at Wiseman's wedding on 2 September 1939, the day before Britain declared war on Germany; among the telegrams that it was his duty to read out was one sending 'Revolutionary Greetings' from Gerald Wolfson, who would become parliamentary correspondent of the *Daily Worker*.

Other visitors included fellow academics, *Guardian* journalists, and artistic friends, musicians and poets. One of these was introduced by Norman Cameron. In April 1935 the young Dylan Thomas needed somewhere to stay, and the Taylors agreed to have him for a week or two. In the event, he stayed a month. Dylan was twenty-one, eight years younger than Alan, and already being talked about as a genius. He was a difficult guest. He drank very heavily whenever he had the chance, and his behaviour was 'poetic'. His patron Norman Cameron wrote a poem, 'The Dirty Little Accuser', which sums up how his many hosts felt about him:

> Who invited him in? What was he doing here,
> That insolent ruffian, that crapulous lout?
> When he quitted a sofa, he left behind him a smear.
> My wife says he even tried to paw her about.

In Alan's autobiography, published nearly fifty years later, he wrote that he disliked Dylan intensely. He ridiculed Dylan's poetry.[7] But much would happen in the meantime. When Dylan came to stay in 1935, he and Alan read Rabelais together and laughed at his bawdiness. It was Alan who had invited Dylan to Disley, after all. Alan was able to make Dylan work for his keep, painting the outside of the cottage. He and Margaret rationed Dylan's drinking and, since Dylan had no money, he was unable to go to the local pub until he discovered a group of left-wingers halfway down the hill who were prepared to stand him drinks. Chief of these was a Mr Bloomfield, whose Joycean name delighted the young poet. On at least one occasion Dylan, being the worse for wear and afraid of Alan's wrath after a night in The Ploughboy, begged a bed from Bloomfield, paying his way with an autographed copy of his *Eighteen Poems*.

Another visitor was a governess who had worked for Alan's aunt Sarah and who had kept in touch with the family after she had left.

She came out to Higher Disley with her new husband, a German Nazi: Alan refused to shake hands with him. More welcome was Alan's father, who dropped in with his two nieces whom he was taking to Craven Arms for a few days' holiday; and Percy's brother Harold, who had been thrown out of the family firm by J.T. and was living in Moss Side digs with his children – his wife had left him – in very reduced circumstances. Alan often picked them up and they would drive out to Disley for tea and a walk. In 1936, however, Alan asked Harold to stop coming. Margaret was going to have a baby, and Alan was frightened of infection, remembering what had happened to his sister Miriam. He insisted that Margaret was kept in clinical purdah. A healthy baby boy was born the following April, and named Giles – his second name Lewis, after Namier. The Taylors engaged a Norland Nanny to begin with, and following her an Austrian refugee lived with them and looked after the child. Alan took extraordinary pleasure in his little son, as his own father had done.

By this time Alan had become a well-known figure in Manchester Left circles. He spent four years on the local Trades Council, just like his father in Preston, and he often spoke at the discussion groups of the local Left Book Club held at the Burlington Café, opposite the university. After the 1935 general election he was sufficiently esteemed to be asked to stand as Labour candidate for Macclesfield, the constituency which embraced Disley. He was wise to decline. Labour failed to take the seat at a by-election in 1939, and failed again even in the big swing to Labour of 1945. Later he would tell Hugh Dalton that 'all men are mad who devote themselves to the pursuit of Power when they could be fishing or painting pictures, or sitting in the sun'.[8]

Alan's political views in the early 1930s, though perhaps muddled, were consistent with those of many other left-wingers. Mistrust of the National Government – originating in the idea that Labour had been intrigued out of office by a capitalist conspiracy – influenced his attitudes to foreign policy. The 1930s are difficult years to decipher. The political maps show all the same names, but in different places. Some of the most vigorous British opposition to Nazi Germany between 1933 and 1939 comes from the Communists, while Labour and Conservative leaders alike preach appeasement. Progressive opinion advocates non-intervention in foreign disputes, except in Spain, where non-intervention is condemned as a sham. There is a National Government at the beginning of the decade, and a Coalition Government at the end; but the new members of the Cabinet of 1940 are those who were shut out of the Cabinet of 1931. In the early 1930s the Labour Party is pacifist, the Conservative-dominated National Government internationalist; in 1939 left-wingers and diehard imperialists speak for England in unison. 'No one was consistent in the 1930s,' Alan later concluded; he himself was no exception.[9] In the early 1930s he attacked the National Government as warmongers; in the late 1930s, as appeasers.

The historian should never forget, Alan was fond of saying, that events now long in the past were once far in the future.* Of nothing is this more true than of the Second World War. From a post-War perspective it is easy to say that conflict with Hitler was inevitable, and attempts to appease him futile. But this is not how it appeared in the early 1930s. Many Englishmen sympathised with Germany's grievances, and thought the settlement reached at the Treaty of Versailles punitive and unjust. Alan, and many others like him, thought that if these wrongs could be righted, the German people would have no need for Fascism. Thus when Hitler started to press for a redressal of the Peace terms, he was pushing at an open door. Underlying all of this was a profound longing for peace. Peace councils, Peace Pledge Union, *Peace News*, the Peace Ballot, Peace with Honour – the 1930s were full of peace. The horror of the First World War had taken more than ten years to sink in; an outpouring of memoirs, novels and films at the beginning of the decade accentuated the revulsion already felt. There was a half-baked idea that arms, not people, cause wars, and if only arms could be got rid of, or at least regulated, everything could be settled amicably. A great Disarmament conference was organised in Geneva, with a former British Foreign Secretary in the chair; he sat there for more than two years.

Nations were more likely to disarm if they felt secure. At the end

---

*He was paraphrasing F.W. Maitland: 'It is hard to think away out of our minds a history which has long lain in a remote past but which once lay in the future.'[10]

of the First World War an American President, Woodrow Wilson, had proposed a new world order, and settlement of disputes by international regulation. 'International anarchy', which many took to be the underlying cause of the Great War, would be no more. This is what people had hoped for when they fought 'The War to end Wars'. A new organisation, the League of Nations, would enforce 'collective security',* using the weapon of sanctions; these were harmless enough, as they never had any effect. In the last resort armed force might be righteously employed – what Alan called 'perpetual war for the sake of perpetual peace'. In fact the United States never joined the League. The international order was threatened by revolutionary Powers – the Fascist countries and Japan – with dreams of empire and aggressive intentions towards their neighbours. Meanwhile France and Great Britain, the old European Powers, accustomed to settling disputes by trials of strength, attempted to conform to this new system. With one hand they offered a carrot to appease the aggressors, but they kept a stick in the other in case the carrot proved insufficient.

Left-wingers like Alan sneered at the League as an 'International Burglars' Union'. They saw no reason to defend the international order which they were themselves trying to overthrow. If Great Britain would not ally itself with Russia against the Fascists, then she should keep out of continental disputes altogether. Many Communists, locked into their Marxist ideology, believed that Fascism was a last gasp of a collapsing capitalist system and would disappear of its own accord. Although of course he was opposed to Fascism in principle, Alan saw no need to resist Germany and Italy by force. Nor did most other Englishmen in the early 1930s.

The international order was challenged when Mussolini announced his intention to attack Abyssinia (Ethiopia) and to make it an Italian colony. The League of Nations applied 'sanctions' on everything except oil: the only thing the Italians really needed. Mussolini ignored the League and sent an expeditionary force to Abyssinia. Alan was intensely interested in these

---

*A term coined by Dr Beneš, President of Czechoslovakia; he was a victim of its failure.

developments, but he was not yet prepared to abandon his non-interventionist principles. At a crowded meeting in the Downing Street Cooperative Hall in Ardwick, Alan opposed the imposition of sanctions on Italy, much against the majority feeling of the audience.

When an Anglo-French plan was revealed for partitioning Abyssinia, providing part of it as a new Italian colony, there was an outcry, 'the greatest explosion over foreign affairs for many years, perhaps the greatest since the campaign against the "Bulgarian horrors" in 1876'.[11] Alan addressed another crowded meeting at the university. It was a matter of great moment, he said, that the reputation of Great Britain as a country prepared to see just treatment for small nations should be maintained. He believed it was an imperialist plot: 'it is no accident that the one bit of Italian [occupied] territory to be surrendered to Abyssinia is Assab; because Assab, a fortified port, would be a great menace to Aden . . . This Government has pursued a policy of buying Italy off in order to pursue its own imperialist aims.'[12] The meeting condemned the Hoare-Laval plan by a majority of 234 votes to two.

The plan was withdrawn, and Mussolini completed his conquest of Abyssinia. A few months later Hitler was to send German troops into the demilitarised Rhineland. And in July, Spanish generals rebelled against the republican government, precipitating Spain into civil war. The rebels were assisted by Germany and Italy, the government by the Soviet Union; soon the war was seen as a wider struggle between Fascism and Democracy. For the generation of the 1930s, Alan wrote later, the Spanish Civil War was the emotional experience of a lifetime. 'It has rightly been said that no foreign question since the French revolution has so divided intelligent British opinion or, one may add, so excited it.'[13] Here was an opportunity for intellectuals in otherwise peaceful countries to play their part in the struggle against Fascism – sometimes literally, by joining one of the International Brigades, but more commonly by sending aid to and arguing the cause for the Spanish government. But to join the 'fight against Fascism', even from a distance, meant abandoning non-interventionist principles. And to support 'Arms for Spain' undermined still further the principle of disarmament.

Alan now made a complete *volte-face*; he started to argue that rearmament was necessary, even under the National Government. This was of course heresy to his colleagues on the Manchester Peace Council. But Alan's ideas were undergoing an overhaul. The great question of the time for all diplomatic historians was to explain the disaster of the First World War. Alan had made this the focus of his research and, with Namier's encouragement, started teaching European Diplomatic History 1890–1909 as a special subject. A German Jewish refugee sold him a complete set of the German diplomatic documents, *Die Grosse Politik der Europäischen Kabinette*; as Alan worked through them his Union of Democratic Control interpretation dissolved. It was not secret diplomacy which had caused the war, he concluded, but German expansionism. This was a disturbing finding in the light of developments in Europe. What could happen before could happen again. In the late 1930s many left-wingers were reluctantly deciding that it was necessary to resist Fascism, but Alan had gone one step further; he now felt that it was Germany, rather than Fascism, which threatened Europe. The menace from Germany grew in Alan's thoughts; while the appeal of the Revolution diminished. By 1938 he could write sarcastically about the Soviet Union as a 'socialist paradise' which imprisoned Austrian socialists. In another review he recalled 'the far-off days when socialism had the character of an inspired religion and to join was to experience all the ecstasies of conversion'.[14]

Namier was anti-German as a result of being a Pole: anti-Fascist as a result of being a Jew. He was an implacable opponent of Nazi Germany and did his utmost to warn people in England of the dangers lying ahead. He was delighted by 'the night of the long knives', in which Hitler's old associate Röhm and his Brownshirts were massacred by the SS. When Alan met his boss at Disley station one morning, Namier could not wait to tell him the good news. As the train pulled in he leaned out of the window, brandishing his newspaper, and shouted: 'The swine are killing each other. The swine are killing each other.'

Alan's next two books were both published in Namier's series. The first was a translation from the German, by Alan and his

Vienna friend Bill McElwee,* of Heinrich Friedjung's *The Struggle for Supremacy in Germany, 1859–1866*; Alan wrote an introduction to the English edition (1935). The second was another monograph, *Germany's First Bid for Colonies, 1884–1885: A Move in Bismarck's European Policy* (1938). In it he argued that Germany's attempt to establish an overseas empire in the mid-1880s, far from being the result of ineluctable historical forces, was a short-term manoeuvre by Bismarck designed to pick a quarrel with Britain. For Alan this was an historical joke, a delicious irony; indeed one reviewer rebuked his display of 'undergraduate levity', while another praised his 'pleasantly ironical style'. This ingenious argument showed how much Alan had changed from the young enthusiast for the Materialist Conception of History; indeed, for the reviewer in *International Affairs*, the moral of the book was that the student of world politics should draw rather less on Marx and rather more on Machiavelli. Alan himself intended the book to take a jab at fashionable theories of economic imperialism.[15] Colonies were an expense, not a profit – an insight which crops up again and again in Alan's work.[16]

In a complete reversal of the standard Left position, he argued that well-meaning British statesmen had unwittingly encouraged German aggression by pandering to German complaints:

> The average Englishman was ashamed of the British Empire and believed (quite wrongly) that it had been acquired in some wicked fashion . . . This sense of sin placed British governments at a disadvantage in their dealing with Germany; they were convinced of the justice of German grievances even before the grievances were expressed† . . . there they stood, ears anxiously cocked for the next German complaint.[17]

These words of course had an uncomfortable resonance in the late 1930s. The book could not have been more topical; only a few

---

*W. L. McElwee, after a false start as a lecturer at Liverpool University, became senior history master at Stowe. Among his pupils were Robert Kee and Noel Annan.

†The London Library edition of *Germany's First Bid for Colonies* has the words 'then as now' written in the margin at this point.

weeks before publication Hitler had declared to the Reichstag that
the German demand for the network of colonies confiscated after
the First World War would be pressed with ever-increasing vigour.
Its very title alluded to the fact that Hitler was once again demanding a German 'place in the sun', though like Bismarck he was never,
it seemed, seriously interested in territorial gains outside the
European mainland. The blurb for *Germany's First Bid For Colonies* ended with the suggestion that it was particularly apposite in
view of recent events; reviewers certainly saw it that way,* and
unusually for an academic book it was covered by the Sunday
papers. One of these reviewers was Llewellyn Woodward, an
Oxford don who had been an external examiner at Manchester in
the early 1930s; he had written a book on the Anglo-German naval
race before the First World War,[19] which Alan had reviewed
favourably in the *Manchester Guardian*. Woodward had been an
anti-appeaser from the moment Hitler came to power. He had been
one of the first historians to make critical comparisons of the
official publications of pre-War documents, as a result of which he
had cast doubt on the impartiality of the German series. *Die Grosse
Politik* had selected and arranged the German diplomatic documents in such a way as to spread the guilt for the War among all the
great powers, and had been insufficiently criticised as such. The
tendency was to blame diplomatic intrigues; on the contrary,
thought Woodward, the real cause of the War of 1914 was the
'barbarian standard of value' prevalent in the German governing
class. Diplomatic historians had played a part in letting Germany
off the hook; Alan was an honourable exception.[20] Woodward
wrote supporting Alan's application for a tutorship at Magdalen in
1938.

This was Alan's third attempt to get back to Oxford. He did not
expect to be any more successful this time than he had been before.
But Woodward's recommendation carried weight; he was regarded
as the authority on modern diplomatic history, and was an Oxford
'insider', known as 'the Abbé' because he had thought of taking
holy orders in youth. Alan was invited to dine at Magdalen, and
after an unpromising evening he was surprised to receive a letter

---

*'No volume could be more apposite . . .'.[18]

from the President announcing that he had been elected a Fellow of
the college.

The Taylors prepared to come south. Before they did so another
international crisis exploded, this time over Czechoslovakia. The
Nazi regime demanded territorial concessions from Czechoslovakia to include the Sudeten Germans within the Reich; the
proposed settlement would strip Czechoslovakia of much of her
industrial and mineral wealth, and undermine her defences. Britain
and France were her reluctant champions. Alan, who had just come
back from a holiday in France, was convinced that the French
would not fight, but he was convinced also that Hitler was bluffing.
He took the line 'Stand up to Hitler' at meetings of the Manchester
Peace Council, perhaps not the best forum for such a message. And
it may not have helped his argument that he had so recently
preached the opposite case. At any rate his listeners, and maybe the
British people as a whole, were not prepared to go to war for
Czechoslovakia.* The Prime Minister, Neville Chamberlain, flew
with his French counterpart Daladier to meet Hitler and Mussolini
at Munich, and there agreed to almost all the German demands.
When he arrived back in England he announced 'peace with
honour'; some, including Alan, thought it was the opposite. Feelings on both sides ran high. The meetings Alan addressed on the
subject were very rough; he was interrupted by hecklers shouting
'you want war', 'you mean war', 'we don't want war', and had to sit
down before he had finished.[22] Both The Times and the New
Statesman and Nation, two publications not normally in agreement, came out in support of the Government's appeasement
policy. Namier was desperate; not to understand that Hitler meant
everything he said – that Mein Kampf was to be taken literally –
that Hitler had a plan for a war of conquest – was self-deception
worthy of Germans and Jews, he told Isaiah Berlin.[23] Standing in
front of his students in the lecture theatre, he recited Eliot's 'The
Hollow Men' in a passionate denunciation of the Chamberlain
Government. A Popular Front was formed to oppose the Govern-

---

*'Public opinion in short tends to want the glory without the suffering and the prize
without the pain. It is not prepared to translate the threats of diplomacy into action
and yet it is angry when the diplomats do not threaten.'[21]

ment's foreign policy, embracing Tory anti-appeasers as well as left-wing anti-Fascists. Favourable comments about Churchill – for so long the bogey of all progressive opinion – started to appear in Alan's writings.[24] When Duff Cooper, First Lord of the Admiralty, resigned in protest against the Munich agreement, Alan wrote him a fan letter:

> May I express my appreciation that in this hour of national humiliation there has still been found one Englishman not faithless to honour and principle and to the traditions of our once great name? If England is in the future to have a history, your name will be mentioned with respect and admiration.[25]*

By this time Alan had arrived in Oxford. The city was in the grip of a by-election campaign, which had become a virtual referendum on Munich. The Master of Balliol, A.D. Lindsay, was the opposition candidate, supported by the Popular Front (among his supporters were Harold Macmillan, MP, and an undergraduate named Edward Heath); the Government candidate was Quintin Hogg, later Lord Hailsham.† One of Alan's new colleagues, the philosopher J.L. Austin, came up with a rallying-call for the opposition: 'A vote for Hogg is a vote for Hitler.' The university was split down the middle; the Chancellor, its theoretical ruler, was none other than Lord Halifax, the Foreign Secretary, the man Alan later described as the 'prince of appeasers'. Magdalen was as divided as the rest of Oxford; among its dons were several important supporters of the Government's policy.

At the beginning of each academic year the Fellows of Magdalen have a dinner to celebrate the restoration of the President and thirty-three Fellows whom James II had tried to displace in favour of Roman Catholics. The 1938 Restoration Dinner – the two hundred and fiftieth anniversary – took place on 25 October, two days before the by-election.‡ Geoffrey Dawson, the editor of

---

*In 1962 Alan's former pupil Martin Gilbert found this in some boxes of Duff Cooper letters which had been shunted along a Foreign Office corridor. Gilbert sent it to Alan, thinking it might amuse his old tutor. 'Your latest discoveries make me think that you are carrying your researches too far,' Alan replied.[26]
†Later still Quintin Hogg and then Lord Hailsham again.
‡Hogg was returned, though his majority was halved.

The Times, was a guest. It is a tradition that after the dinner new Fellows stand up to give an inaugural speech. These are not formal orations – often the port has been passed a few times and the speakers are incoherent. If intelligible, the speeches are intended to be amusing. When his turn came Alan made a powerful speech denouncing appeasement. Oxford was a fairy-tale environment, he said, while outside the storm-clouds were gathering. He concluded by saying he was sure that when the crisis came the dons of Magdalen would resist Hitler as steadfastly as their predecessors had resisted James II. Some of his listeners were restless. What was this man doing, taking advantage of tradition to make a political point? He was embarrassing their distinguished guest. It was a poor start.

8: *The War of the Words*

Late in 1938 Kathleen Constable, now married to Geoffrey Tillotson, was walking across Magdalen Bridge when she recognised Alan. They had not seen each other for more than ten years. She too had made a career in academic life – mainly in London, but was teaching two days a week at Somerville and St Hilda's. 'So you're in the same racket?' she asked Alan, as they arranged to have tea in his rooms. She congratulated Alan on his good fortune in becoming a Fellow of an Oxford college. Many would consider that one was better off as an Oxford or Cambridge Fellow than as a Professor at a provincial university. There was free food, sometimes free drink, and cheap lodging, often in magnificent surroundings.

Magdalen was very rich. Herbert Warren, who became President of the college in 1885, had set out to attract aristocratic and wealthy undergraduates and consequently their endowments. When Alan arrived at Magdalen, it was socially one of the most prestigious, a rival to Christ Church, the grandest of them all. The Prince of Wales, the future Edward VIII, had been an undergraduate there before the First World War.* Magdalen's reputation as a repository for aristocratic but not necessarily academic students had begun to change in the late 1920s, when a group of ambitious young dons led by the philosopher T.D. 'Harry' Weldon had set out to transform the college by choosing pupils on merit and raising the standard of the teaching staff. By 1939 Magdalen had become an intellectual power-house; among the Fellows were C.S. Lewis, C.T.

---

*When he became King, *Isis* printed the headline 'Magdalen Man makes Good'.

Onions, editor of the *Oxford English Dictionary*, the philosopher
J.L. Austin, and the scientists Peter Medawar and J.Z. Young.

The Taylors needed somewhere to live. They had their eyes on
Holywell Ford, a large nineteenth-century house built on the site of
an old mill in the quasi-medieval William Morris style, owned by
the college. Though only just outside the college walls, it might
have been deep in the country, there being no other buildings
nearby. The stream flowed underneath the house and poured into a
pool below a terrace, the haunt of an otter. A path called Addison's
Walk, the favourite route of the eighteenth-century journalist, led
from the house along the river to the college. Holywell Ford was the
only building on an island between two branches of the River
Cherwell. It was a situation romantic enough to stir the heart, and
there was a large garden suitable for growing vegetables.

Holywell Ford was not available until the beginning of the 1939
academic year, but after that it was promised to the Taylors.
Meanwhile they rented a furnished house in Marston Road during
the term and spent the vacations away from Oxford. Three Gates
was still theirs, so they went back to Higher Disley for Christmas; it
was so cold that the cylinder head on Alan's car cracked. (They
finally sold the house in the New Year, for £800.) For the spring
vacation they left Giles with his new nanny and spent a month
travelling around French North Africa. Alan was so taken with
Morocco that he wrote an enthusiastic piece for the *Manchester
Guardian*, describing it as 'one of the greatest works of civilisation
of our time'.[1] When the summer came the whole family set out for
Savoy in Alan's car, a huge open-top Ford Pilot. They stayed a
month in a little house at Yvoire on the shores of Lake Geneva,
about fifteen miles from the Swiss border, and then moved up to
Montriond in the mountains. They had rented a chalet, where they
meant to stay until October, and invited friends to come and join
them.

Alan had a book to write. In April he had proposed to Harold
Macmillan a 'not too learned' history of Austria in the nineteenth
century; Macmillan consulted Namier, who was confident that
Alan could produce a good book on the subject: 'Without undue
conceit I know that he will turn to me to advise and help him
anyway, and I shall gladly do so as he is a very good friend of mine.'

Macmillan wanted to publish the book within Namier's series, and offered terms, which Alan rejected: 'as the book I had in mind was of a more popular character I am afraid I must decline and wait to renew our connection when I have something more serious to offer'. Perhaps he was irked by Macmillan's remark that Namier's 'supervision' would be 'most valuable and helpful'. Macmillan wrote suggesting there had been some misunderstanding; and again Alan rebuffed him. 'The book I have in mind is not a work of scholarship, but one from which I should make some money.' Although there is a handwritten note on this last letter saying that 'no reply is, I think, necessary', it seems that Macmillan decided to pursue the matter, for a few days later he made the journey up to Magdalen and dined at High Table with Alan. Before the meal they had been a successful pair at bowls. 'It did not occur to me that there was much to him,' Alan wrote in his autobiography. Macmillan told him that publishing new books, other than novels, was a luxury for them, a luxury of which his brother Daniel disapproved; 'financially we should do better to stick to Kipling and our other classics'.[2] Nevertheless, the visit was successful, because a week later Alan accepted Macmillan's revised offer – an advance of £75 against a 15 per cent royalty, rising to 20 per cent, a distinct improvement on the original proposal of a flat 10 per cent royalty.[3]

Out in Savoy, Alan worked at his book every morning. By mid-July, he had already produced 20,000 words. He told Muggeridge that he had written it too quickly: 'It's a bit flaccid, but that's my weakness, I go slapdash at a thing until I get it done and it doesn't work so well with writing as with lecturing.'[4] By the end of August, he had practically completed the first draft, though he did not send the manuscript to Macmillan until the following July. In the meantime he had the chance to read the book Muggeridge had recently completed on the decade just ending; and its cynical style influenced Alan's final version. This was his first 'real book', the first book he had written for a non-specialist readership. He succeeded triumphantly. The book remains in print fifty years after its first publication.

The Habsburg Monarchy, 1815–1918[5] charts the decline and eventual disappearance of the only European Great Power based solely on a dynasty. The Habsburg Empire included at one time or other the modern states of Austria, Hungary, Czechoslovakia, Belgium, large parts of modern Romania, Italy and Poland, and much of what was until recently Yugoslavia. It had disintegrated in 1918; but some form of 'Danubian confederation' and the restoration of the Habsburgs, absurd as that might now seem, was frequently advocated both before and during the Second World War as a solution to the problems of the Balkans. Alan had no doubt that the Empire was an anachronism, no longer viable in a nationalist era. A parallel theme of the book is the conflict between the 'master races' – Germans, Italians, Magyars and Poles – and the subject peoples of the empire, primarily Slavs. Alan's sympathies were firmly with the latter, and in his journalism he championed the Slav states which emerged when the Empire collapsed, particularly Czechoslovakia and Yugoslavia. But in the book he 'tried to sympathise with those whose traditional supremacy was being challenged as much as those on whom the supremacy was being exercised, and I have not pretended that the victory of the new nationalities was more than a reversal of the previous order'. He might well have pointed to Czechoslovakia, where several million ethnic Germans (the number is disputed) found themselves unwilling citizens of the new state, founded in 1918. But then the breakup of the Habsburg Empire was bound to have been messy; there was no conceivable settlement in Central Europe which would not involve injustice to some of those living there. 'The story has no moral, except the broad moral that people can live happily, either as individuals or in communities, only on the basis of mutual tolerance and respect; but this moral is not a contribution to practical politics.'[6]

Reviewers enjoyed the book. Oscar Jaszi, writing in the *Journal of Modern History*, thought that

> few foreigners have understood the complication of this problem as well as the author . . . He belongs to that rare class of historians who are able to supplement the factual evidence with a high grade of psychological insight and artistic imagination . . . What we read in his book is not dead history but an often thrilling analysis of personalities and mass psychological insights.[7]

The book abounds in pungent descriptions, wrote Robert J. Kerner in the *American Historical Review*, 'even if at times there is a touch of the facetious or even the flippant concealed within'.[8] F.M. Powicke thought that he was a master of his subject, and praised him as a lucid, witty and epigrammatic writer: 'He writes well and has his subject under firm control . . . He is, in short, a very intelligent man who knows what he is writing about.'[9] The least complimentary review came from his old tutor, A.F. Pribram, then living in Kew Gardens, an exile from the Nazi Reich. Alan had risen to his challenge to write a history of Austria (although not a complete history); indeed he had quoted his tutor's discouraging words* at the beginning of his preface. Pribram deplored the lack of attention to foreign policy; remedying this defect was one of the principal changes Alan made when he came to revise the book after the War. Even so, the review was generally favourable.[10]

The reviewers' emphasis on style was appropriate; Alan took pains to write simply and clearly. Writing history is like W.C. Fields juggling, he wrote later – it looks easy until you try to do it.[11] Alan himself praised those, like Namier and Churchill, who knew how to use the language; and scorned those who did not. Reviewing a work by William L. Langer, another of Pribram's old students, he wrote: 'The style of this book is most difficult. It reads as if it had been written in German and then translated by a Frenchman who learned his English from the Hollywood talkies.'[12]

It was not enough just to be comprehensible. Alan felt that the historian had a duty to entertain the reader, or at least to keep him reading. Wadsworth had taught him that a piece in the *Manchester Guardian* was no good unless people read it on the way to work. Readers should get the same pleasure from reading history as they do from reading novels, Alan thought, and he took as much trouble with his style as with his scholarship.[13] Critics sometimes said that he tried too hard. Alan admitted that 'the most important works of history often seem to the general reader rather dull and technical, while the popular successes usually merit the censure of the historian. It is no easy task to be both interesting and accurate.'[14]

The Habsburg Monarchy is dedicated to Namier with 'gratitude,

---

*See pages 78–79.

affection and esteem'. Many of the ideas in the book came from him. In his Preface Alan acknowledged the debt he owed to Namier, though later he repudiated this.[15] In talking to his students he spoke of Namier's work almost as if it were the Holy Writ. Indeed, it sometimes seemed as if Namier were the *only* authority he accepted without qualification. He was no less enthusiastic in print. Reviewing Namier's *In the Margins of History*, he wrote: 'No readers of these hard gems of wisdom will ever ask again what is the use of history – or historians.'[16]

One of the scientists at Magdalen asked Alan why anyone should study history: 'How predictive is it?' 'Well, people like to hear a good story, you know,' Alan answered, tongue-in-cheek. While they were walking back to the college from Holywell Ford an undergraduate asked Alan much the same question. 'What's it for?' 'There's only one reason,' Alan replied: 'because it's such fun. It's fascinating.' He had enunciated this view more fully in a 1938 piece:

> The only danger to history today is that historians are sometimes too modest and try to find excuses for their task. It is safer, as well as sounder, to be confident. Men write history for the same reason that they write poetry, study the properties of numbers, or play football – for the joy of creation; men read history for the same reason that they listen to music or watch cricket – for the joy of appreciation. Once abandon that firm ground, once plead that history has a "message" or that history has a "social responsibility" (to produce good Marxists or good Imperialists or good citizens) and there is no logical escape from the censor and the Index, the OGPU and the Gestapo.[17]

Alan liked to undermine accepted ideas or beliefs by pretending not to understand them. One evening in France the subject of the Ascension of Christ came up at dinner. Alan said he couldn't think why Jesus had to go away when all his disciples thought he was such a good thing. On being given a conventional explanation, Alan said, 'Oh, I see. You mean sort of "We don't want to lose you but we think you ought to go."'[18]

The holiday in Savoy was cut short by the worsening international situation. The outbreak of war took Alan by surprise; in May he had written to Muggeridge that 'one of the few things one

learns from history is that chaps can only behave in a given way . . .
For that reason I don't think we'll have a war. Hitler wins bloodless
victories and doesn't know any other way – so he would never start
a war.'[19] In a sense, of course, Alan was right. When the Nazi-
Soviet non-aggression pact was signed in August 1939, many on
the Left were full of fear and confusion. Some lost their belief in a
Communist utopia overnight. Alan, on the other hand, took the
news cheerfully. 'This ruled out a German attack on Russia and
therefore in my opinion the likelihood of any war.'[20] On 1
September German troops invaded Poland. Alan decided to run for
home. As the Taylors drove across France they saw French troops
mobilising, and they arrived at the coast on 3 September, the day
Britain and France declared war. Alan was in such a panic that he
abandoned their car at Dieppe.*

Once across the channel they found refuge for the night in a
Seaford hotel. All England was in turmoil, the trains packed with
evacuees. The Taylors made their way to Bickmarsh near Bidford-
on-Avon, where Margaret's mother and stepfather had a large farm
on the ridge of the Cotswold escarpment. They stayed there a
month, until the beginning of the Michaelmas term when they were
at last able to move into Holywell Ford.

The first months of the War were an anti-climax. Englishmen
had anticipated saturation bombing from day one; instead there
was a 'Phoney War' which lasted until the spring of 1940. While
Poland was quickly overrun and a ferocious war was being fought
at sea, the Western Front was quiet. Several weeks after the opening
of hostilities an undergraduate who had been with the Taylors in
France said in amazement: 'It's all as if nothing had happened.'
Alan replied: 'Well, it hasn't, has it?'[21]

The Taylors spent Christmas 1939 in Preston with Alan's parents. Afterwards Percy contracted pneumonia, when he insisted on
going out in bad weather. He died in February, less than a month
before Sebastian, his second grandchild, was born. Alan travelled
up to Preston for the funeral; Percy was buried in the local
cemetery, a Red Flag emblazoned with hammer and sickle wrapped
around the coffin. 'Percy Taylor believed man to be naturally

---

*He went back a few days later to collect it.

good,' read his obituary in the *Preston Herald*: 'if men behaved anti-socially it was because circumstances, particularly the environment of a capitalist civilisation, had perverted them. He believed an earthly paradise a distinct possibility, but he had no belief at all in paradises after this life.'[22] Percy had been a generous man, giving or lending money to everyone; when his desk was opened up after his death, a shower of IOUs spilled out. His fortune of £100,000 had dwindled to a little more than £9000 in twenty years.*

Alan was now responsible for his mother. She had degenerated into a helpless invalid, not expected to live much longer. Alan had her brought down to Oxford in an ambulance, and placed her in a nursing-home. When her brother Harry and one of his nieces came up to Oxford to see her they found she was being neglected; a hot-water bottle had burnt through her flesh to the bone. There was an unpleasant scene between Alan and his uncle, and Connie was moved out of the home into a house in North Oxford with two nurses to look after her. She lived on another six years, causing Alan expense which he resented: 'She's living on my patrimony,' he said.

Many of Alan's friends and relations found him mean. He would not allow visitors to pick fruit from his trees, for example; 'We only eat windfalls in this house.' At Christmas time he sold the mistletoe from the garden. A young married couple staying with the Taylors were amused to find they were expected to share bathwater, and not more than a few inches deep at that. When Lord David Cecil spilt some of his wine during a dinner at Holywell Ford, Alan was noticeably annoyed about the waste. He is supposed to have sold a photograph of one of his children to the manufacturers of the hot drink Bournvita, and signed a certificate affirming – quite falsely – that the child had been brought up on it. This last story has become a family legend, and may be apocryphal; reputations have a tendency to generate their own supporting evidence. But one incident from this time suggests more than mere parsimony. Alan and Geoffrey Rowntree, friends since their schooldays at The

---

*Though perhaps he had transferred some of it to Connie, for when she died six years later she left over £17,000.

Downs, had been in the habit of exchanging generous presents; Alan used to send Rowntree lists of books he would like to receive. When a birthday present failed to arrive one year, Alan wrote his old friend an explosive letter. This was not the first such lapse, he wrote, but as Rowntree had taken no notice of his earlier complaints, Alan wanted nothing more to do with him. Rowntree was astonished. He replied that he thought Alan was being very melodramatic; but if that was what Alan wanted, he could bear it. They never spoke to each other again.

Visitors remember Holywell Ford when the Taylors lived there as a busy, jolly place. There always seemed to be people staying and children running around. Apart from the immediate family, the Taylors took in refugees from Central Europe – as Alan's parents had done – as well as paying guests. At any one time there might be five or six strangers living with them. As in Higher Disley, groups of undergraduates came to listen to records played on Alan's enormous gramophone. There were plenty of parties, and meals on the terrace when the weather was kind. Margaret liked to patronise 'artistic' people, and filled the house with poets, painters and musicians at weekends – a wag described her as a sort of middle-class Ottoline Morrell. Peter Pears and Benjamin Britten came to Holywell Ford, as did Cecil Day Lewis. The most entertaining dons – Isaiah Berlin, Nevill Coghill, and A.L. Rowse, for example – were often found there. It seemed very sophisticated and bohemian. To at least one of Alan's students, Margaret appeared to affect a cultural chic, always interested in the latest this or that. Alan called the house 'a nest of singing birds* . . . You can't move a foot in this dovecote without fluttering a poet,' he told a journalist who came to interview him for the *Oxford Mail*. He depicted himself as a philistine, tolerating these invasions with good humour. Students would be invited to Margaret's parties to keep him company; 'Come over here if you want to escape from my wife's mint tea,' he would say. The *Oxford Mail* printed an autobiographical sketch:

---

*'Sir, we are a nest of singing birds' – Samuel Johnson, quoted by Boswell, on Pembroke College.

> Humble, retired, academic, shunning the light, pursuing an inde-
> pendent course. No time for public life, too taken up with my garden,
> growing vegetables for six people, teaching young men, writing
> books on modern history, beating my children soundly, maintaining
> an unequal struggle against them for existence.[23]

Undergraduates came to Holywell Ford for their tutorials. The bursar had told Alan that he could not offer him rooms for teaching in college because these were needed for the possible evacuation from London of the Judicial Committee of the Privy Council. Teaching at home was much more fun in any case. Sometimes pupils would arrive at Holywell Ford to find Alan finishing a game of backgammon with Giles. Tutorials were punctuated by children appearing at the door – sent scampering away by a bellow of 'Out!' – or falling in the mill-race. The mill-stream passed underneath Alan's study, and he fantasised about installing a trapdoor which could be operated whenever a student was too boring. He was a stimulating tutor, but an exacting one; Alan's students found that regurgitating the conventional wisdom was not enough. 'Why?' he would ask, when a student had been sure of being on firm ground. Alan's predecessor had been J.M. Thompson, a cleric who had lost his faith and become an expert on the French Revolution; when Alan arrived he announced to the pupils he inherited: 'I think you are going to have to try somewhat harder than you have been.'

Alan's tutorials followed the normal Oxford routine. The student, wearing a gown, began by reading an essay on a topic set at the last tutorial; Alan sat with eyes half-closed, stroking a Siamese cat on his lap and often smoking a pipe. Sometimes he would use the stem of his pipe to worry a prominent wart on his forehead. He seemed not to be listening, though if something in the essay particularly irritated him he might utter a shriek of pain. Once the essay was finished he would come to life, discussing the topics raised in the essay and suggesting new angles not mentioned by the student. He liked being argued with, but not being contradicted – 'Don't you bandy dates with me.' When Karl Leyser, himself later a Magdalen don and professor of medieval history, politely corrected a mistake Alan had made, Alan leapt to his feet and grabbed a volume of *Die Grosse Politik* from the shelf, brandishing it like a weapon to defend his argument. He was very emotional, almost weeping.

Alan's study at Holywell Ford was lined with volumes of documents, enabling him to go to a reference almost immediately. He was particularly good at teaching his pupils how to deal with 'gobbets' – those short quotes on which pupils were supposed to discourse in their examination papers. Alan taught his students how to get every last ounce of significance from a document, teasing out the points. He was intolerant of pupils who failed to meet his high standards, particularly the aristocratic ones. One such, the heir to a dukedom and acknowledged as a 'dummy', aroused Alan's particular wrath. Alan told his tutorial partner that the young nobleman had no manners, treating his tutors as if they had come through the servants' entrance. The other student thought that Alan was imagining things.

Few Oxford undergraduates shared Alan's left-wing views. One of his very few Communist pupils, perhaps the only one, was John Biggs-Davison, who later became a right-wing Tory MP.

Robert Kee was a favourite pupil. He had been among the visitors who had come to stay at the chalet in Montriond. Kee was extremely handsome, admired by both sexes in Oxford, and he was reputed to have had a great number of affairs. One day Alan picked up the extension telephone in his study and overhead Kee tell Margaret that it was impossible for him to go to the theatre with her. 'All became clear to me.' He realised why Margaret had seemed so listless; why she lurked outside his study when one of Kee's tutorials was imminent; why she was so keen for Kee to attend their parties. In Savoy she had been unsettled, and Alan had felt that she was growing increasingly impatient with him and their infant son. When Kee had arrived she contrived to spend much time alone with him, and on family walks the two of them had marched ahead so that they were soon out of sight. At the the time Alan had thought nothing of it.

Once they were back in Oxford, Margaret's infatuation with Kee had become more intense. She fell helplessly in love. She harassed Kee in his lodgings. Once she 'thrust herself physically on him';

they undressed and went to bed together, but failed to go through with it. When Kee joined the RAF, she followed him to his camp, and was sometimes away from Holywell Ford for days. She confided in Alan's friends. 'I'm really an awfully bad cow,' she told A.L. Rowse. She telephoned Nevill Coghill to tell him about her 'pash'; it seemed to him as though the telephone had turned into a kind of lobster, clawing at his ear.

Perhaps it was not surprising that a passionate woman in her mid-thirties should feel attracted to such a glamorous undergraduate. Her pregnancy may even have accentuated these feelings. Certainly her infatuation continued, apparently unabated, after the baby was born. Maybe she felt lonely in her separate bed. Oxford was a dreary place during the War, with few young men about and very little going on. Petrol rationing made travel difficult. The university was still organised as if all the dons were bachelors, as indeed they had been within living memory.* Alan often dined in college, where women were not admitted and the worst wartime hardship was the reduction from four courses to three; Margaret spent evening after evening alone.

Alan wrote a note to Kee saying that he appreciated the situation and hoped that it would not disturb their friendship. Otherwise they kept silent about it. He pleaded with Margaret to 'make an end of Robert Kee', but it seems that she would not listen. To others, he expressed the wish that they would consummate the affair and lance the boil. It was a 'humiliating, contemptible' situation. In fact few of Alan's colleagues or pupils had any idea what was going on. If Kee 'behaved faultlessly', that did not make it any less painful – indeed, it was doubly humiliating to see his wife prostrating herself before a much younger man who did not encourage her advances. For Alan, there was an extra burden in the thought that 'this was the Henry Sara affair on a worse level'. He was that much more reluctant to acquiesce because he felt that his father had done so. He resented being cuckolded on his father's behalf as well as his own. But he felt there was nothing he could do. 'I became barren and indifferent to life, displaying a zest that I rarely felt. I was

---

*The celibacy rule for Fellows had been abolished by the Royal Commission of 1877.

scarred for good. It was like losing an arm or a leg. There was no chance of my being a complete man again.'[24]

Kee was embarrassed by Margaret's behaviour. He confessed later that at the time he had no idea how much it had hurt Alan. Alan presented himself as disenchanted, ungullible. In contrast to Margaret, he appeared to be cynical about love, often equating it with sex. 'She must have her greens,' he would say. But once Kee left Oxford in 1940 to join the RAF, the Taylor marriage seemed to settle down. They remained tender to each other. Alan talked ruefully and longingly about their earlier happiness, and appeared to be still very much in love with Margaret. It hurt him when Margaret went into deep mourning — in spite of the clothes rationing then in force — after hearing that Kee's plane had been shot down. (Kee survived, and was soon writing letters from a prisoner-of-war camp in Germany.) Alan and Margaret would have two further children, Amelia, born in 1944, and Sophia, born the following year.

Alan was very much the dominant male in this household, and nobody was allowed to disturb his routine. He went to bed promptly at 10.15 p.m., even when guests were present. At night when Alan and Margaret were settled in their twin beds, he would read aloud to her; in this way they worked through Gibbon's *Decline and Fall of the Roman Empire* and the Authorised Version of the Bible. In the mornings he got up early and worked. At around 7.30 a.m. he would set off round Addison's Walk; often he met C.S. Lewis and together they would plunge, naked, into the Cherwell for a swim. At breakfast he doled out lumpy porridge to the children, unadulterated with sugar or milk — visitors found it inedible.

Alan was finishing *The Habsburg Monarchy*, and just writing about the Hungarian aristocrat Karolyi, when the door bell rang. 'There stood a man with a limp and a cleft palate: none other than Michael Karolyi himself.'[25] Karolyi seemed to have stepped straight out of history. He had been Prime Minister and then President of Hungary just after the First World War, and had begun the long overdue process of land reform by redistributing his own vast estates. In 1919 a coup had driven him into exile; now he was living in Oxford. He took his present hardship cheerfully, and claimed never to regret the loss of his immense fortune. Like Percy, he applauded the Revolution which would strip him of his wealth. Karolyi introduced Alan to other Central European refugees living in Oxford. Alan adored him, indeed he almost hero-worshipped him.

Alan had been thirty-three when the War began. He was in no hurry to volunteer for one of the Armed Forces, and the university soon obliged by certifying his work as being of national import-ance, thus providing him with exemption from military service throughout the War. In his autobiography he wrote that he was not ashamed of this, claiming that he would have made a poor soldier.[26] Indeed many Oxford dons seemed to feel that the War was none of their business. But not all: one Oxford historian failed the eyesight test three times in succession and gained admittance to the Army only by bribing the recruiting sergeant. By March 1940 ten Magdalen Fellows had been granted leave of absence for approved war service, and three years later their number had risen to eighteen, two of whom had been mentioned in dispatches. By October 1943, 243 Magdalen undergraduates had gone out of residence temporarily to join the Armed Forces or to undertake some other form of national service.[27] The college student body shrank from 144 undergraduates in Michaelmas Term 1939 to 96 a year later.

A curious statement in his autobiography suggests that Alan may have been more sensitive than he revealed about not playing a more active role in the great struggle against Fascism. He says that only one undergraduate, John Biggs-Davison, went off to fight straight away. In fact dozens of Magdalen undergraduates volunteered in 1939, some of whom were later killed. C.S. Lewis wrote to one that autumn, mentioning the empty rooms with the names of the recently departed undergraduates still on the doors. Alan cannot have been unaware of this exodus: why did he deny it?

Far from joining the Forces, Alan contemplated 'the duty of war resistance' when Russia attacked Finland and for a while it seemed possible that Britain and France might go to Finland's aid. It may seem extraordinary that he was prepared to resist Britain's struggle with Germany – whatever that meant in practice – for the sake of solidarity with the Soviet Union. But all the Left was in disarray. Britons remembered the First World War; and thought that the Second would be the same. Repugnance against the slaughter on the Western Front was still very strong. As late as 1941 many – Bernard Shaw, Vera Brittain and Kingsley Martin amongst them – argued for a compromise peace; Communists denounced another 'imperialist war'. Ironically, it was the Communist Party which helped to convert Alan into a Churchillian warmonger. When the Communist-dominated university Labour Club opposed support for Finland and was disaffiliated by the Party, Alan agreed to speak to a breakaway Democratic Socialist society.* 'I was as much against Communists at home as I was on the side of Soviet Russia abroad and so could not well refuse.'[28]

The problem resolved itself in March 1940, when a peace was signed between Russia and Finland, after Finnish resistance had proved unexpectedly strong. Alan was able to join the Local Defence Volunteers, later known as the Home Guard. He was in a company commanded by Frank Pakenham, later Lord Longford, which included as well as 'townees' several dons, among them C.S. Lewis and J.L. Austin. This academic line-up made it possible for the sergeant to issue the command 'Dons, fall out.' It was not a force strong enough to deter the enemy. They had rifles, but only one clip of ammunition between them, which was accidentally expended by a veteran of the First World War. In the process he injured his commander in the foot and J.L. Austin in the rear.†

Alan saw his gardening as a more practical form of war work. He would dig for victory. Food, particularly fresh food, was scarce in the War, but Alan kept the family supplied with plenty of vegetables and fruit, and so many eggs from his hens and ducks that he was forced, no doubt reluctantly, to give most of them away. It was hard labour: the garden was a large one and the soil was heavy. At first undergraduates helped him, but when the supply dried up he

---

*After some hesitation, G.D.H. Cole became President. Roy Jenkins and Anthony Crosland were among its undergraduate supporters.
†Another account has it that the second chef at Christ Church shot Pakenham in the bottom.

did it all himself. At Christmastime Margaret's stepfather sent a turkey from Bickmarsh Hall.

A succession of 'PGs' (paying guests) at Holywell Ford meant that Alan could draw plenty of rations. He also drew rations for the children. On one occasion he went to collect their arrears of orange juice, amounting to twelve bottles. When asked how his children could get through so much juice, he replied, 'Don't be silly. I don't want it for them. I want to put it in my gin.'

Alan's most obvious contribution to the War effort was his lecturing. The Government recruited an army of propagandists from the ranks of the progressive intelligentsia to fill posts in the Ministry of Information, the Political Warfare Executive, the BBC, the Crown Film Unit, the Army Bureau of Current Affairs, and other similar organisations. Like hundreds of other writers, scientists, and intellectuals – among them J.B. Priestley, George Orwell, Ritchie Calder, Harold Laski, Julian Huxley and Cyril Joad – Alan would talk Hitler into submission.[29]*

Very early in the War Alan had become involved in education for the Forces, going out in the evening several times a week to lecture on European history to audiences of servicemen ranging in number from three to 500. This had the advantage of providing him with unlimited petrol, and even an army car with a smart woman chauffeur when he got tired of driving. In the summer of 1940 he volunteered as a speaker for the Ministry of Information (MoI), and soon he was giving talks to civilians in Aylesbury, Banbury, Oxford, Reading, Wolverton and throughout the southern region. The idea of these talks was to boost morale; Alan went into shops and offices, secured a ten-minute break, and addressed the staff on the War and what it meant.† Alan liked to see himself as a latter-day Bolshevik.

In September 1940 there was an exodus of evacuees from

---

*'I regard wartime propaganda with complete scepticism except as a means of keeping intellectuals out of mischief.'[30]
†His favourite audience in fifty years of lecturing was during the War, he said much later, composed of girls from the Portsmouth Woolworths.

London to escape the Blitz. Thousands arrived in Oxford, where the arrangements for them were far from adequate. They were housed in public buildings of various kinds; many of them crammed into the Majestic Cinema, where they slept between the seats. Some were sent on to Wolverhampton, only to return when they were refused accommodation there.[31] The Oxford Communists exploited their misery, preaching peace. Alan took the initiative to organise concerts and speakers, any form of distraction until the evacuees could be found proper homes.

The local MoI committees were voluntary bodies, often left-wing in composition; frequently they upset the established authorities. In October 1940 Quintin Hogg, the MP for Oxford, complained in the House of Commons about one of Alan's speeches. He asked the Minister of Information 'whether his attention has been drawn to a public speech in Oxford by Mr A.J.P. Taylor, a member of the local Information Committee appointed by the Minister of Information, to the effect that a withdrawal from Egypt would not be major disaster; and whether he is prepared to take steps to prevent members of committees from committing themselves to irresponsible statements of this nature without consulting the Ministry?' It was an 'irresponsible and ridiculous statement', Hogg went on, which had caused 'very grave public disquiet' in Oxford.[32] The Minister of Information was Duff Cooper.

Later in the War Alan taught history to those civil officers who had been recruited to administer Italy and Germany once these had been defeated. He was still of course lecturing at the university, where the number of his listeners was swelled by officer cadets taking six-month courses. Alan's Oxford lectures were no less impressive than those in Manchester. He would be informally dressed, that is to say in a corduroy suit with a bow-tie. He liked to encourage the idea that he had come unprepared; 'Now, what am I going to say this morning?' he asked one undergraduate who walked with him from a tutorial as Alan was on his way to give a lecture. He told Isaiah Berlin that he decided the first half of the lecture while walking round Addison's Walk beforehand; the second half, according to Alan, was pure ham.

The Hall at Magdalen would be full; indeed later in the War the crush was such that he had to relocate to the Examination Schools, where the largest lecture-hall in the university was to be found. As the bells sounded in Magdalen Tower, Alan walked down the central aisle, pointedly removed the lectern placed on the dais, and leaned back on the top table. He cast a rapid glance over the assembled throng and then began speaking. The voice was strong, clear, measured, flat – no obvious rhetorical tricks, no notes, hardly a gesture, and rarely a pause. When he came to the climax there would be a great surge of sound. The lectures were studded with anecdotes, and the occasional familiar prejudice – 'The Germans have all the ghastly virtues. Clean streets!' – or brilliant aside – 'The chief requirement for anyone accepting ministerial office is the constitution of an ox.' He ended just as the bells rang out once more. At this signal, he announced the topic for the next lecture and strode out.

Alan tried to get on to the staff of the Political Intelligence Department (PID), where Namier had worked in the First World War. It had been evacuated from Chatham House in London and conveniently relocated to Balliol. The Foreign Office asked for a summary of statements on British war aims and, as all the experts on the staff were busy working on their respective countries, Alan volunteered to write it.* 'I read all the ministerial statements both before the War and after its outbreak, reaching the conclusion, now obvious enough, that the British Government had no war aims nor indeed any idea what they were doing.' He had completed quite a long piece when an order came down from the Foreign Office: all discussion of British war aims was undesirable and premature. Therefore not only should any further work on them be stopped, but the existing summary destroyed.[33]

In May 1940 the 'Phoney War' came abruptly to an end, and the real War began. The Germans attacked France; only six weeks later they had accepted the French surrender. Chamberlain resigned, and a new National Government was formed, with Churchill as Prime Minister and Labour in coalition. For Alan, this was the best of all possible outcomes. He was even pleased to be free of the

---

*In his autobiography he says he was 'grudgingly given unpaid work'.

French 'entanglement'. 'The summer of 1940, with the threat of invasion and the RAF battling the Luftwaffe in the sky, was a romantic adventure. Even if the Germans came, someone should remain to lead the ultimate liberation and I wanted my sons, if not myself, to be among them.'[34] When invasion threatened, Alan argued from the analogy of the Napoleonic wars that it was a bluff to cover the real German intention of an attack on Egypt. He later took this mistaken deduction as a warning against trying to learn from history.

The Battle of Britain reached a climax in late August. Just after eight o'clock on the evening of 7 September, the Home Guard stood to arms, having received the signal that invasion was imminent. The scare lasted only a few days. As soon as it was clear that the danger was over, Alan resigned from the Home Guard.

Margaret's war work involved making shells from eight to twelve each morning. She also organised fund-raising concerts at Holywell Ford and in Oxford Town Hall. Though the music was of a high standard, her financial arrangements were not, and she was hauled before the local Labour Party committee when one of her concerts proved to have lost money. She was given a brutal ride, and she sat there with head bowed, suffering; she even offered to make up the deficit herself. Some of the piano recitals were given by Natasha Litvin, and in April 1941 she came to Holywell Ford as a paying guest with her new husband, the poet Stephen Spender. They were creative, sociable people – the kind of guests Margaret enjoyed. Alan was working at his garden allotment one June morning when Spender came back to the house waving a newspaper. 'Hitler's invaded Russia,' he announced. Alan threw down his spade and exclaimed: 'He couldn't have been such a fool!'

This was a moment long anticipated. Some who identified with the Soviet Union had feared there might now be a compromise peace between Britain and Germany. Their fears were soon allayed. Churchill had decided his policy in advance, and that same day he broadcast to the nation proclaiming the alliance of England and Russia – 'the greatest act of statesmanship of this century', as Alan was later to describe it.[35]

Russia's entry into the War, however involuntary, caused a revolution on the Left. Alan's aunt Joan, for example, who had hitherto opposed the 'capitalist war', now began to support it wholeheartedly, making shells like Margaret. Alan's position was somewhat different. Having been increasingly critical of the lack of freedom in the Soviet Union in the late 1930s, henceforth he suppressed his misgivings. But his new attitude stemmed from *realpolitik* not ideology. Germany was a permanent menace to the peace of Europe, he had decided, and Anglo-Soviet accord was the only way to counter this threat. Anglo-Russian estrangement was 'the most profound cause of the present war'.[36] After the War he wanted a 'strong and enduring alliance between this country and Russia, to sit on the heads of the Germans'.[37]

Indeed the transformation of the Soviet Union into Britain's main fighting ally affected everyone, whatever their political ideas. Overnight the Communist Party became part of the Establishment; the 'Internationale' was played on the BBC. Russia's fate was identified with Britain's; solidarity with the Soviet Union was equated with patriotism. As the German armies drove ever further forward into Russia, there was a sense that Britain was not contributing enough. 'Russia bleeds while Britain blancoes' read a contemporary graffito – a reference to the whitening rubbed into the military equipment before drill parades, a symbol of pointless activity. The Communists campaigned for an expeditionary force to take the pressure off the Soviet armies: 'Second Front Now'.

Despite his support for Russia, Alan offended the Oxford Communists by explaining the practical obstacles to a Second Front in one of his MoI talks. They applied pressure for his dismissal as speaker; Alan relished the paradox of being persecuted from this quarter. In March he had begun broadcasting on the Forces Service of the BBC for a programme called 'Your Questions Answered', but his broadcasts were unexpectedly discontinued in June; he sought an assurance from his producer, Trevor Blewitt, that a Communist claim that he had been barred from the BBC was untrue.[38] Blewitt's reply is not in the BBC files, so it is difficult to confirm or deny Alan's suspicions. He did not broadcast again for more than a year.

In March 1942 Alan, at Namier's prompting, wrote to *Time and Tide* praising Rebecca West's book about Yugoslavia, *Black Lamb and Grey Falcon*, which had been reviewed the previous week by

Wickham Steed. As a result of Alan's comments she visited him at Holywell Ford, and they became friends. The proprietor of *Time and Tide*, Lady Rhondda, was enthusiastic for the lesser nationalities of Europe; she thought that Alan was very much the man for her. For a brief period he became a regular contributor to the weekly. Later that year, though, he antagonised her by referring contemptuously to the Baltic 'states'.[39] 'Russian policy has a single object, security, and she regards the frontiers of 1941 as essential to this object' — these frontiers implied the absorption into the Soviet Union of much of pre-War Poland, as well as Latvia, Lithuania and Estonia.* 'The Peoples of Europe can enjoy freedom only under the joint protection of England and Russia,' he continued, 'and just as we postulate a group of friendly states in Western Europe with similar social systems to our own, so does Russia in Eastern Europe.'[41] There were protests, particularly from Polish exiles. The editor felt obliged to print a note explaining that she 'profoundly disagreed' with her reviewer; and when Alan replied to his critics in the next issue, there was an equally long editorial piece refuting his arguments. Alan appealed to Namier for support, but Namier said that he had had enough trouble over borderlands after the First World War and did not want to become involved again. Lady Rhondda was not pleased; Alan wrote only a couple more reviews for *Time and Tide*.

Dylan Thomas turned up again at Christmas, this time with his wife Caitlin. They were all invited to a party at J.Z. Young's house in Holywell. Caitlin danced with Young. Swinging her leg high, she kicked some of Phyllis Young's ornaments off the mantelpiece. Mrs Young burst into tears and rushed upstairs. Her husband shouted: 'Never mind. Go on dancing.' Whereupon Caitlin swung her other leg and knocked off the remaining ornaments. Dylan sulked in the corner, as he always did when he thought Caitlin was getting out of hand. A homosexual pupil of Alan's who was also present decided he was in love with Nevill Coghill, and he went round the house

---

*Eighteen months afterwards he wrote that the Baltic countries could enjoy a secure national existence 'only within the framework of the Soviet Union'.[40]

roaring 'I want Nevill'. Then he fell drunkenly asleep in the kitchen; Alan and John Young had to carry him back to the college.[42]

Alan's talks for the MoI had become commentaries on what was happening in the world. 'People liked hearing about the War and I liked telling them. Also it taught me to look at war as history in the making and so prepared me to write a history of the War many years later.'[43] His work for the MoI warned him not to place too much reliance on archival sources. After each lecture he was supposed to hand in reports; Alan always exaggerated the number of people attending and manufactured evidence of public opinion to support causes he favoured, such as the opening of a Second Front. 'Home Intelligence was in fact propaganda in reverse. We were trying to instil some common sense into the mandarins of Senate House.'[44] In his autobiography he commented that researchers now study these reports to ascertain the state of public opinion: 'I do not think they should attach much weight to mine.'[45]*

On 8 February 1943 Alan gave a MoI talk at the Oxford Union on 'Russia's Part in Europe'. The Russians, he said, 'had given a demonstration of foresight and efficiency which had astonished the world and which made it clear that the social system which could produce such miracles was a government second to none in its capacity as ruler of a great empire. Every claim which the Soviet Government had made had proved itself justified . . .' He predicted even greater success for the Russian armies in the future. Those who want to defeat Germany, he went on, must accept Russia as the predominant land Power on the continent. 'For any civilised man the perpetual prayer should be that Russia may establish a predomination over Europe and maintain it. In no other way can civilisation be secured. It is madness to suppose that the Russians, if they once destroy Germany, can be tricked of their power by some elaborate juggling.'[46]

This was one of the last MoI talks Alan gave. He had already upset the Communist Party. Then another remark in one of his

---

*'I know how history is made,' he would say later.

commentaries, that the Tunisian campaign had developed disappointingly after its stirring opening, was taken to be a crack at the expense of the inexperienced American troops. Alan's status as a MoI speaker was abruptly terminated. He made as much as he could of this drama. 'I won't go quietly,' he told one of his students, and gained some revenge by giving an interview to the local paper headed 'My Waterloo'; he covered the accompanying portrait with a sticker which read 'Banned by the Ministry of Information'.[47]

All this lecturing about the War had turned Alan into something of a pundit. He joined a group organised by Frank Pakenham to discuss the future of the world. One evening the Pakenhams came to dinner at Holywell Ford. Alan, emulating Wellington, brought out an atlas and put his forefinger down on the map. 'This is where the War will be decided,' he announced portentously. The others were surprised to find him pointing at Vigo, a town in Northern Spain.

Through Frank Pakenham Alan met Gerald Berners. Lord Berners was a flamboyant homosexual, who lived in peacetime with his boyfriend Robert Heber-Percy in Faringdon House, a stately home about twenty miles from Oxford. There he pursued the life of an aesthete, painting, composing, making music and writing wistful novels. Alan himself appears in one of these, *Far from the Madding War*, as Mr Jericho, tutor of modern history at 'All Saints College', who invents an 'important military device'. An ebullient personality, Mr Jericho is described as a great ranconteur and embellisher of college gossip, as arriving and departing suddenly, and as quick in speech and gesture. 'He would suddenly whip off his spectacles, polish them with his handkerchief, replace them, and stare through them with greater intensity than before. The gesture was accomplished in one rapid movement.'[48] Emmeline, the book's heroine, spends the War gradually unpicking a fifteenth-century tapestry in response to being told that war means destruction.

When Faringdon House was commandeered for use by the American Army, Berners took up residence in a suite of elegant rooms in St Giles'. He came to eat with the Taylors at Holywell Ford every week, or took Alan and Margaret to dine at The George. On one occasion he arrived unexpectedly to tea, which forced

Margaret to conceal the underclothes she had been mending under the nearest cushion. At weekends they often drove out to Faringdon House, where Heber-Percy ran the Home Farm. Alan remembered nothing of their conversations 'except that we laughed all the time'.[49]

In May 1943 Alan was asked by the Political Warfare Executive (PWE) to help prepare a handbook on Hungary for the British troops who, it was thought, would one day occupy the country. He took leave from Magdalen, and moved to London, where he worked on the handbook at PWE's headquarters in Bush House. Though said to be tremendously readable, his section of the book was rejected as tendentious; Alan believed the Foreign Office found it too left-wing. He was noticeably upset by this rejection, but he was persuaded to undertake another task for PWE, this time writing a chapter on Weimar for a similar handbook being prepared about Germany. He took the line that Nazi Germany, far from being an aberration, was a development of tendencies already present beforehand. Once again, his contribution was rejected.

Twenty years later Alan was sceptical about the value of such propaganda. He wrote of PWE that it did no harm, 'providing a useful distraction for politically-minded Englishmen and planners who might otherwise have been a great nuisance'.[50]

Alan was also in demand from foreign governments. He became an unofficial adviser to the Czech government-in-exile, having established a warm friendship with Hubert Ripka, a member of the exiled Czech government, who kept him supplied with whisky and cigars; through Ripka he had come to know Beneš himself. Alan became one of Beneš's intellectual confidants,

> which meant in practice his telling me secrets which had been common talk for weeks . . . Conversation always took the same form. Beneš would ask, "How do you see the situation now?" and, as I cleared my throat to reply, would go on, "One moment, I will put certain points before you. Firstly . . ." He would then expound uninterruptedly until the time came for me to leave.[51]

Alan believed that a strong Czechoslovakia was crucial for the containment of Germany. The minority German population concentrated in Sudetenland near the German border were the 'problem' which had brought about the Munich crisis: if necessary, the Sudeten Germans should be expelled. Bohemia was 'the gateway to Eastern Europe', 'the keystone on which the entire Nazi domination of Europe depends ... Unless Czechoslovakia is remade with complete political and economic independence Germany will have won the War.'[52] Czechoslovakia combined the best of East and West, he thought: 'In Prague two worlds meet, the Slav world and the world of Western civilisation ... the Czechoslovaks are destined to resemble in Russian eyes the British and in British eyes the Russian ... In British and Russian relations with Czechoslovakia lies the key to the new European order.' Czechoslovakia would be a 'mediator' in the post-War world.[53] These words were part of a speech given at the Czechoslovak Institute in 1943 to celebrate twenty-five years of Czechoslovakia's existence. Jan Masaryk, the Czech Foreign Minister and son of Thomas Masaryk, a university professor who became the founder of Czechoslovakia, was in the chair; for Alan, Thomas Masaryk had been 'the greatest man of our age, a man who honoured us by being our contemporary'.[54] Masaryk had striven to prevent the estrangement of England and [Tsarist] Russia; Alan commented that 'Anglo-Russian co-operation came too late to save Czechoslovakia'.[55]

In February 1944 Alan gave a talk to the Oxford Masaryk Society on 'The Study and Teaching of History as a Cause of the Present War'. There was a mixed audience of undergraduates and dons, so crowded that some listeners had to sit on the floor. Alan spoke without notes. His argument was an extension of the one Woodward had championed. Historians, particularly liberal, well-meaning diplomatic historians, had committed a grave disservice by explaining away Germany's guilt for the First World War. Through their books and their teaching they had misled readers and students and helped to produce a climate of appeasement. The teaching of history in England was all wrong – in favour of the Germans because they were Protestants, and against the French because they were either Catholics or atheists. If the teaching of history in England had been sound, he said, we would have realised the German danger and done something in time. Hitler had done us a favour, however. If Hitler had not come along, Weimar Germany would have done much the same thing and all Europe would have been under German domination by now. But Hitler had performed two valuable services: first, he had made England go to war for the sake of another country; and second, he had made England accept Russia as an ally. So good old Hitler!

Alan was also taken up by the Yugloslavs. In 1944 a large car arrived at Holywell Ford, bearing a man in a Soviet-style uniform under a greatcoat. This was General Velebit, Marshal Tito's representative in England. Alan was known to be sympathetic to Yugoslavia: would he help with their propaganda? He would. In December, briefed by Slovene refugees, he wrote a piece for the *New Statesman and Nation* arguing that Trieste belonged to Yugoslavia. 'Here the Slav world and the world of Western democracy overlap and combine. In short we can be more confident of the future of the Anglo-Soviet alliance when we have learned to think of Trieste as Trst.'[56]

Alan foresaw a post-War Europe 'partitioned' between the Slav countries, dominated by the Soviet Union, and the Western countries, dominated by Britain. He believed that an alliance between the two Great Powers at either end of Europe was necessary to resist the inevitable German revival. 'In the near future, say the next twenty years, the Soviet Union is our natural ally,' he wrote in April 1945; the alliance would be

> specifically directed against a renewal of German aggression . . . As to America, we shall always have a sentimental friendship even though America is ceasing to be a predominantly Anglo-Saxon country, but you can only have an alliance with a country which is prepared to act and has weapons to do it with . . . we had better hesitate before we again rely on the moral indignation of the middle West.[57]

In 1945 Alan was certainly not alone in having an exaggerated sense of British power. The exhilaration of imminent victory was deceptive; the illusion was sustained by the series of Great Power conferences in which Churchill appeared to play an equal role with Stalin and Roosevelt (and Truman). At the end of the War British prestige stood higher than ever before; in the eyes of all Europe,

Britain symbolised defiant resistance to German hegemony. During the War Britain had been a haven for the governments of almost all the countries which had been overrun; these would presumably now be restored. British politicians had dispensed favour to one group and withheld it from another, with the casual authority of indulgent parents. It seemed certain that Britain would play a leading role in European reconstruction.

Kingsley Martin, editor of the *New Statesman and Nation*, was a frequent visitor to Oxford during the War; he and Alan came to know each other well. Kind, stingy, vain, serious, Martin loved talking and listening to those he judged to be well-informed; so much so that his colleagues believed him to be 'the prey of the last speaker'.[58] Interested in psychoanalysis, he was, perhaps, the personification of the bleeding-heart liberal, tortured by personal guilt, agonising over the sufferings of others. Nine years older than Alan, the son of a Congregationalist parson, Martin had served in the Friends' Ambulance Unit during the First World War, before reading history at Magdalene College, Cambridge. He spent three years as an assistant lecturer in Harold Laski's Department of Political Science in the mid-1920s, before becoming a political leader-writer on the *Manchester Guardian*. At the beginning of 1931 he had been appointed editor of the *New Statesman and Nation*, a job which he held for thirty years. Under his direction, or lack of direction, it became an enormously important and successful journal, the conscience of the intellectual Left. Kingsley Martin in his heyday was the Left incarnate, wrote Muggeridge: 'each press day he was crucified for the sins and deficiencies of mankind, each Monday he rose again to bring out another issue'.[59]

Kingsley Martin's intellectual roots were similar to Alan's, but unlike Alan he had not broken free from them. Throughout the 1930s he had tried to reconcile pacifism and anti-Fascism, which led him to support the Munich agreement, a mistake of which he was later ashamed. In 1940 he had favoured a compromise peace with Germany. Martin's partner in life, Dorothy Woodman, as a fellow traveller, suffered no such doubts; she did what the Party told her to do, thought what the Party told her to think. Active in the Union of Democratic Control, she turned it into a Communist front organisation, thereby destroying it as an independent force. Alan regarded her with suspicion.

Trevor Blewitt had taken over responsibility for talks on Foreign Affairs in the BBC Home Talks department, and he approached Alan again in 1944. 'How admirable your willingness still to contemplate the trouble I should cause you!' Alan replied. 'Of course I should like to see you and even to smell again the dust of the microphone . . .'[60] Alan suggested various possible topics for talks.

> I should like to give a talk on nationality in the margin, perhaps taking Trieste as a good illustrative case . . . I should like above all to give a talk on the two key countries, Yugoslavia and Czechoslovakia, as the essential links between England and Russia, geographical and still more spiritual links – Slav countries with a Western culture, both democratic and yet not anti-Bolshevik.[61]

Soon Alan was back on the airwaves, even making an appearance on 'The Brains Trust'. Late in 1944 he took part in a panel – with Kingsley Martin, the diplomat Lord Vansittart, and Barbara Ward, then assistant editor of *The Economist* – discussing over three broadcasts the future of Germany.[62] Alan was in the chair, and took a hard line. 'The German people have forfeited, for a very long time, the right to be a great people, and . . . in our lifetime they must put up with the fact that they shall not possess any of the things which a great power possesses.' Alan enjoyed debating with the other panellists, he told Wadsworth. 'Vansittart is inarticulate, but charming. Barbara Ward is, for a woman, very clever, with the sort of charm which a clever woman has. That is, she has everything except what a woman ought to have. But Kingsley Martin – I always forget, until I see him, how intolerable he is – vain, ignorant, dreadful.'[63]

The broadcasts were a success. The BBC were so pleased by the first two debates, Alan informed Wadsworth, that 'they are thinking of making the four of us a regular feature on foreign affairs'.[64]

Not everyone liked them, however, and a critical letter appeared in the *New Statesman and Nation*, questioning whether any other people would have done more than the Germans to resist Nazi oppression. Alan defended himself vigorously in the next issue, contrasting the German record with the British opposition to the War against the American colonies, the Crimean War, the Boer War, to the 'policy of oppression' in Ireland. 'Where was the German Gladstone? How many Germans opposed Bismarck's campaign against the Poles?' This letter provoked a hot response from C.A. Smith, who referred to Alan's '*mélange* of assertions, leading questions and omissions'. Alan stuck to his guns – 'no one would doubt that many, perhaps most, Germans dislike the ruthlessness and barbarity of Nazi rule when applied to themselves; but these same lovers of liberty support a line of action in foreign affairs which can only be attained by Nazi methods.' Smith hit back: Alan's conclusion was 'bunk'. He referred to 'Mr Taylor's reckless mixture of truths, half-truths and untruths' and his 'tendentious selection of facts'; 'if it is a sample of the 'history' now taught at Magdalen College, Oxford, there are other people besides the Germans in need of re-education'.[65] Alan was livid. He sent a letter to Kingsley Martin, headed 'without prejudice', demanding a printed expression of regret and a statement that he enjoyed a deservedly high reputation as an historian. He insisted that a piece he had written on Trieste was held up until he had 'received some redress'.[66]

Martin urged Alan to reconsider:

> Here is a controversy in which you and other people have been hitting hard. Two letters attacking your view of history appear, one of them ending with a personal remark. You then say in fact: I refuse to continue this discussion on its merits; withdraw into a dignified silence under protection of the law, and require the N.S. & N. to make a formal apology, which everyone will know is forced on them. In the future (if you persist) the attitude I and other editors would have to adopt is that this is a man who hits hard in controversy himself, but takes libel actions if he thinks his opponents unnecessarily offensive. This attitude would make it difficult for us to continue our pleasant personal and business relationship. Perhaps

more important, the public would judge that you are a touchy, irascible sort of person who 'can't take it'.

This wise letter must have mollified Alan, because the next day Martin wrote again to thank Alan for 'your reasonable attitude this morning'; adding 'I am not sure if you realise how "provocative" you in fact are'.[67]

But though Alan dropped his threat of libel action, he returned to his original theme in a private letter to Martin.

> The basic issue is whether the German Left were good Europeans – ready to live and let live in Europe. I say the historical record is against them . . . they cannot be relied upon to protect us from a new war . . . In fact, anyone who is in favour of a united Germany is led by an inevitable and fatal logic to desire first a peaceful and then a warlike German mastery of Europe.[68]

He made this point more succinctly at the beginning of a piece on German unity: 'What is wrong with Germany is that there is too much of it.'[69]

Alan had just completed a book which brought together all his thoughts on Germany. His friend Denis Brogan had suggested that he use the chapter on Weimar which had been rejected by PWE as the basis of a book, and Alan began corresponding with Hamish Hamilton, a publisher with whom Brogan was connected. His new book, he told Hamilton, would be 'a general summary of German history for the layman . . . like Rowse's recent book on English history,* but less eulogistic. In fact a *1066 and All That* in German terms.'[70] By May 1944 he was 'pouring out words', and by the end of September he had finished. The book was 'as hot as can be', he told Blewitt; 'a good thing it doesn't have to pass your censorship.'[71] Hamilton liked the book – 'I am further delighted to observe that you seem to dislike Germans almost as much as I do!'[72]

Alan was not sorry to be changing publishers. The link with Harold Macmillan had been broken when Macmillan had with-

---

*Presumably *The Spirit of English History* (Cape, 1943).

drawn from publishing business on becoming a minister early in 1940. Henceforward Alan was in the hands of the more aloof elder brother, Daniel. There was a series of small irritants – they continued to send his correspondence to Disley, they got his initial wrong on the reprinted jacket – but his main complaint was about sales. Once Hamilton had accepted his new book, Alan wrote to Macmillan commenting on a royalty statement which showed only fourteen sales of *The Habsburg Monarchy* in the previous year; 'I could have sold more copies than that myself.' He informed them that he had just completed a history of modern Germany; 'but in view of the disappointments I have had with *The Habsburg Monarchy*, I have offered it to a publisher who is interested in selling books'.[73]

The Course of German History is vivid, exciting, openly partisan.* It is an indictment, Alan the prosecuting counsel. The history of Germany is a history of extremes, he begins. It is a nation which has learned through long centuries of bitterness and disappointment to admire only force and follow only authority. In their struggle with the Slav peoples of Central and Eastern Europe, the method of the Germans has always been the same, from Charlemagne to Hitler – extermination. The attack on Russia on 22 June 1941 was the climax, the logical conclusion of German history. Hitler was no aberration; the entire German people were guilty of the Nazi crimes. German liberalism had prostituted itself to the worship of power. Indeed, 'the failure of the "good" Germans, not the ranting of the "bad" ones, was the real crime of Germany against European civilisation'.[75]

Some of the central ideas in *The Course of German History* had been anticipated by Namier, in a series of essays about Germany which he published in 1941. Hitler was the most representative German who ever lived, Namier wrote, and he argued, like Alan, that the German danger would have been still more formidable without the Nazi menace.[76] These essays were reprinted in *Con-*

---

*"No civilised nation has such a record of atrocity . . . It is much easier for the historian to ignore these hard facts. If he shows sympathy for the German cause, blurs the record, and stands above the battle, he will soon win a reputation for scholarly impartiality. I am not an impartial historian; I prefer the truth.'[74]

flicts, a volume which Alan repeatedly urged on his undergraduate pupils.

Namier gave Alan's book qualified praise: 'Still his combination of ruggedness and impressionable vivacity renders him also impatient of the careful labour of perfecting and polishing – he discovers precious stones by the handful, and puts them half-cut into circulation.'[77] Namier might have been more effusive had he not intended to write a similar book himself.[78]

The Course of German History is full of telling metaphors and brilliant paradoxes. 'German history reached its turning-point and failed to turn'; 'Bismarck's Reich was designed to give Germany stability and peace; but ultimately it doomed Germany to upheaval and war'; 'Bismarck, the greatest of all political Germans, was for Germany the greatest of disasters'; 'Greater Germany had taken her Prussian conquerors captive'; 'Captain Brüning was half-way between General Ludendorff and Corporal Hitler, with the weaknesses of both, the advantages of neither'; and so on. An American reviewer, Sigmund Neumann, described it as 'an impatient book, vivid and tempestuous, pointed and pugnacious, concise and overzealous, severe and sarcastic, ambitious and angry'.[79]

Later Alan was to describe *The Course of German History* as his 'unfavourite' book.[80] Admirers of Alan's work who find the Germanophobe line hard to stomach point to its wartime origins. It is a *pièce d'occasion*, they say. But it was the wrong piece for the occasion, at least for PWE. Many of the reviewers who praised the book at the time it was published would qualify their opinion once the passions of the War had receded. Alan himself disliked the book for different reasons; the epigrammatic, paradoxical style was, he later thought, 'too clever by half'.[81] His hostility to Germany did not diminish after the War. Germany remained a threat to the other nations of Europe, he argued, and he resisted the idea that the Nazi period was exceptional. Everything Alan wrote about Germany from the mid-1930s onwards is consistent.

Hamish Hamilton lived up to Alan's expectations. *The Course of German History* sold out soon after publication. Six months later it had sold 6000 copies; while Macmillan had taken five years to sell fewer than 2000 of *The Habsburg Monarchy*. The comparison was unfair, of course; it had not been easy to sell (or even to print) books during the War, whereas *The Course of German History* was published in the summer of 1945, a particularly opportune moment. Translation rights were sold in several languages; and an American publisher brought out an edition. Alan wrote a description of himself for the Americans:

> Born at Southport, Lancs. (a discreditable item, this) in 1906; normal education; since 1938 Fellow and Tutor of Magdalen College, Oxford; lived two years in Vienna and ran over the continent in the normal aimless way. I contribute a good deal in the way of articles and leaders to the *Manchester Guardian*; and at the moment the BBC is using me as one of their regular commentators on World Affairs – but I don't know how long this will last. During the war I was sent around by the Ministry of Information giving war commentaries, but was sacked in 1943 as a result of Communist complaints that I was anti-Russian. I used to write also for *Time and Tide* and for *The Spectator*, but have been turned down off both on the ground that I am too pro-Russian; the *New Statesman* puts it the other way round and refuses my work on the ground that I am anti-German. This will all appear nonsense to an American public. The only sensible political remark, perhaps, would be to say that I believe the only solution of the German problem to be the Anglo-Soviet alliance.[82]

Alan found time for many small acts of kindness during the War. He wrote light-hearted letters to his pupils serving in the Forces, and he was a regular visitor to Nicholas Henderson, a friend of Robert Kee's who was hospitalised in Oxford in 1943–4. Despite Margaret's infatuation he also kept up a correspondence with Kee himself, now a prisoner in Germany. Kee's letters were full of mysterious references to seemingly non-existent aunts; light dawned when a stranger called and explained that these were in fact code-words, intercepted by the censor before the letters reached Holywell Ford. At his prompting Alan inserted code-words into his own letters, for Kee to pass on to his colleagues in the camp. But perhaps the aunts were real after all, because Kee at his end was equally puzzled by the unnecessary detail of academic politics which began to appear in Alan's letters.[83]

In April 1944 Wadsworth, who had just taken over as editor of the *Manchester Guardian*, asked Alan to produce the odd long leader: 'and not too fierce, please'.[84] By this stage of the War Wadsworth was so short of staff that he had to write a leader every night, sometimes two. For the next eighteen months or so Alan produced regular leaders to order for Wadsworth. 'Please tell me anything you would like – and of course if anything won't do. I am not an experienced journalist and I know it; but I would do anything for the *M.G.* . . . I am always absolutely at your command.'[85]

Notwithstanding what he wrote to Wadsworth, Alan was by this time a skilled journalist. Once he had made up his mind what to say, he did not hesitate; words poured forth. Often he would work out his thoughts in conversation; then he would swing his chair away from the person he had been talking to and begin typing. Alan's leaders show his perennial preoccupations: the need to disarm Germany after the War; the reasonableness of Russian aims; and the community of essential interests between Great Britain and the Soviet Union. He repeatedly stressed the need to allay Russian suspicions through patience and understanding. He had no doubt that Britain was a Great Power, one of the three (sometimes four, when France was included) which should dominate the post-War world. His leaders reflected this assumption, advocating strong and independent British policies on the Straits, Egypt, Persia and elsewhere around the world. On 4 June 1945 he wrote a leader arguing that Britain must abandon her traditional policy of isolation from Europe.

> We must lead in Europe or ourselves be led; we cannot stand aside. The Balance of Power in Europe has ceased to exist and can never be restored. Germany is the only first-class Power on the Continent west of the Soviet frontiers, and will remain so potentially despite the magnitude of her defeat. Were the three Great Powers, none of whom belongs to the European continent, to withdraw from Europe, Germany would again dominate Europe within a few years . . .[86]

Late in 1944 Alan went up to Manchester for a few days. Afterwards he wrote enthusiastically to Wadsworth: 'Words cannot express how much I enjoyed myself in Manchester. If the North is in your blood, you can't get it out.'[87]

On VE Day Alan and his son Giles bicycled out to Blenheim Palace, the home of the evacuated British Council, where Alan's university friend John Betjeman showed them round the servants' quarters. That night they had champagne in the Hall and danced round a bonfire outside in the meadow.

While the War was continuing, domestic politics had been to a large extent suspended. Alan certainly had no desire to oppose a coalition government led by Churchill. After the War was over, he had said in 1943, he would like 'a nice quiet revolution to put an end to economic problems';[88] but he was prepared to wait. A fortnight after the end of the War in Europe Labour announced it was withdrawing from the coalition, and a general election was called for 5 July 1945. Frank Pakenham was standing for Oxford; he used to come to Holywell Ford, Alan told his pupils, to change out of his smart clothes into a suit he kept there which he thought more appropriate to a Labour candidate. Alan threw himself into a hectic round of campaigning, speaking on behalf of Pakenham and his wife Elizabeth, the Labour candidate for Cheltenham, as well as Aidan Crawley, the candidate for North Buckinghamshire. Often he would go on to the platform before the candidate arrived, and always he would speak in favour of an Anglo-Soviet alliance. The result of the election did not become clear for some weeks, until all the returns from the Forces overseas had come in; Labour had won a large overall majority, and Churchill resigned on 26 July. Alan was full of hope for the future; he believed that fundamental change was in the offing.

As the War was coming to an end Alan telephoned a Labour friend, David Worswick, to tell him that he planned to dabble in university politics. The Institute of Higher Learning in Madrid had decided to donate some Spanish books to Oxford. In Alan's eyes this was Falangist propaganda. He asked Worswick to rustle up some friends and come along wearing gowns to Congregation, the university's legislative assembly, where as usual there were only half a dozen dons present. When the topic was raised, Alan made a tremendous speech and demanded 'scrutinium', a vote. Instructed by Alan, the interlopers chanted in unison 'non placet', and the books were rejected. Decisions at Congregation were irreversible; as a result of this embarrassment many hard words were exchanged in Oxford. Immediately afterwards the Hebdomadal Council promoted legislation requiring a week's written notice of any opposition. It was characteristic of Alan to use a traditional means to a radical end.[89]

Alan was involved in college politics too. In 1942 the office of President of Magdalen had become vacant when the old President died. For a while the Vice-President, Alan's fellow-historian Bruce McFarlane, had run the college, and he had hopes of becoming the new President. Alan, however, supported an external candidate, the scientist Sir Henry Tizard. Tizard was successful by only one vote; McFarlane was not pleased. Alan became Secretary to the Tutorial Board, known colloquially as Senior Tutor. He sat on most of the college committees, knitting scarves for the Forces to fill the time during meetings. Members of the bursarial committee were entitled to payment in the form of one nutmeg a year, a privilege suspended during the national emergency. Now that the War was over, Alan claimed the six nutmegs he was owed as back-pay. For raising such a triviality he was firmly rebuked.

9: 'The ideal life for a man'

Towards the end of the War the Taylors rented a room in London. It was in Percy Street, at the foot of Charlotte Street, on the northern fringes of Soho. Margaret furnished the room and made it comfortable. Alan was often in town, broadcasting for the BBC or meeting his Central European friends, and it was useful to have a base. Sometimes Margaret accompanied him; they often spent an evening together at the theatre or the cinema. One night, when they returned to the room after eating out, Margaret told Alan that Robert Kee would be dropping by; he had been released from prisoner-of-war camp and was back in England. For months Margaret had been excited at the prospect of his return. When Kee arrived, she offered him use of the room. Alan felt betrayed; he realised that Margaret had been preparing it for Kee all along.

Kee took over the room at Percy Street, and Alan found lodgings elsewhere. For a short while Kee was at a loose end and spent much of his time in their company; Margaret's passion for him burned as bright as before. Then he found a girlfriend, Janetta, a friend of Ralph and Frances Partridge. He introduced her to the Taylors, and she came with him to Holywell Ford; the four of them took a short holiday together. Margaret appeared to welcome Janetta, lending her clothes and talking intensely. She seemed over-anxious to please, often on the verge of tears. At times she played the part of a helpless, pathetic woman, while Alan portrayed himself as a solid pipe-and-slippers man, interested only in practical matters.

Kee soon wearied of Margaret's attentions: 'That poor woman gives me the shudders,' he moaned. 'Time and again Margaret tried to take Robert unawares and I was her unwitting tool,' Alan wrote in his autobiography. 'Robert complained to me. He complained to others and Margaret's infatuation became the common talk of Oxford – or so I thought. I felt humiliated and resentful. My last spark of affection for Margaret was extinguished.'[1] Alan had worked hard at trying to save the marriage while Kee was away. Now he felt that all his work was in vain. One night Alan and Margaret saw *Brief Encounter*, a film about two married people who have an unconsummated love affair. Alan was so upset that he could not speak afterwards. He identified the lovers with Margaret and Robert Kee: 'It was, I think, the bitterest moment of my troubled life.'

Alan was convinced that history was repeating itself: 'perhaps my father suffered the same fate and maybe I was unconsciously following his example.' Like his father, he felt no hostility towards the other man; his resentment was directed against his faithless wife. Percy had been on good terms with Henry Sara, who came to the cremation when Alan's mother died in April 1946; it was the last time he and Alan were to meet. A few years later Sara married.

Perhaps it hurt Alan particularly that Margaret thought of Kee as a returning war hero. He certainly seemed sensitive on this point. Several years later one undergraduate noticed a certain tension between Alan and the Regius Professor, V.H. Galbraith, caused by Alan's suspicion that he was being 'got at' for remaining in Oxford throughout the War. 'Let's see, Taylor,' remarked Galbraith genially at a meeting of the university history society, 'you were too young for one war and too old for the other, weren't you?'

Alan felt isolated in Oxford. In Manchester he had been a big fish, in the mainstream of politics and social life; in Oxford he was out of the current. He wrote in his autobiography that he never made a single intimate friend there, though many of his former colleagues remember him with affection. His isolation was partly circumstantial. Because he taught at Holywell Ford, he had less cause than other dons to come into college. In his undergraduate days he had formed the habit of eating a simple lunch of bread and cheese alone in his room, which cut him off from his colleagues. No doubt the unhappiness of his marriage and his resulting sense of humiliation discouraged his social life. Other Oxford historians disliked his brashness and were suspicious of his journalism. It was perhaps not surprising, therefore, that Alan was defeated when he tried to gain a place on the Faculty Board, the authority which administers the teaching of history throughout the university. He did not much mind; like Namier, he regarded administration as a trivial distraction from more serious work. Later he was often criticised for not playing a bigger part in Faculty affairs. The teaching of history at Oxford has traditionally been dominated by medievalists, and indeed 'modern history' is still defined as beginning in the fifteenth century. Alan and those who thought like him – mostly younger colleagues, many of whom had returned from active service – wanted to stimulate the study of 'contemporary history'. Together with Alan Bullock, a like-minded historian who had worked for the BBC during the War, he started the Recent History Group, a society of Faculty members and research students which met three or four times a term in the evenings and invited speakers, often from outside the university. Talks were followed by half an hour or so of discussion. The Group was successful in directing the attention of Oxford historians towards the more recent past, and its format was subsequently imitated by other similar societies.

In October 1946 Tizard ceased to be President of Magdalen. He had been tempted by an offer to become the Government's scientific adviser on defence; friends assured him that he could accept this post and continue as President. But when Tizard raised the matter with the governing body of the college, McFarlane interrupted before he could explain his intention to stay. This is very grave news, he said without hesitation; we now have forty days to look for a new President. Tizard had been outmanoeuvred; weary of college intrigue, he resigned.

As one of Tizard's supporters, Alan had played a prominent role in the administration of the college. Now he found himself out of sympathy and out of favour with the new President, the art historian T.S.R. 'Tom' Boase. Boase's sensibilities were very different from Alan's; he enjoyed high society and elegant living. Boase was known by undergraduates as 'the shopwalker'; his habitual Savile Row suits contrasted with Alan's corduroy.

Powicke resigned as Regius Professor of Modern History the

following year. Alan lobbied hard for Namier to succeed him. The post was in the gift of the Crown, which acted on the recommendation of the Prime Minister. Attlee asked J.C. Masterman, the Provost of Worcester, to recommend a new name. Masterman took soundings among the Oxford historians. Almost all the young wanted Namier, but their elders were reluctant. He was too difficult, too serious, too Jewish. Alan's advocacy of such a man – irresistible on paper, intolerable at High Table – did him few favours with his colleagues. 'I succeeded in making myself disliked by the respectable. I did not succeed in making Lewis Namier Regius Professor.'[2]

Alan's enthusiasm for the Soviet Union meant that he was out of step with the *Manchester Guardian*. Towards the end of 1945 he took offence at an extraordinary article by Bertrand Russell which appeared to him to be advocating a preventive war against Russia.* 'Don't blame me if I can't join your anti-Bolshevik crusade which is making a third world war certain,' he wrote bitterly to Wadsworth. 'Or perhaps . . . you think we should take advantage of the atomic bomb and knock the Russians off their perches now.'[3] Wadsworth did not respond to such goading, and he and Alan remained on good terms personally. They addressed each other as 'Dear AP' and 'Dear AJP'; and Alan signed his letters 'love, Alan'. But Alan's next leader, which argued that Russian foreign policy was essentially defensive and advocated maintenance of the Anglo-Russian alliance, was the last he wrote for the *Manchester Guardian*.

The Cold War has been 'the greatest disaster in our lifetime', Alan wrote later; it 'has devastated my life'.[4] Perhaps this seems melodramatic; Alan escaped the persecution suffered by many who found themselves ideologically misaligned. But the Cold War certainly blasted his hopes for a better world. Immediately after the War, it was Great Britain that seemed the Soviet Union's arch-enemy, the United States on the sidelines. Britain was the imperial

---

*Russell advocated the threat of a preventive war to compel the Soviet Union to accept the internationalisation of atomic energy – another example of 'perpetual war for the sake of perpetual peace'.

power, the oppressor of the coloured peoples; Russia the trouble-maker, stirring up sedition in the colonies. Alan's twin loyalties were stretched. Later, of course, Britain dropped out of the reckoning, and America became Russia's main opponent. Alan refused to recognise an ideological war between East and West, between Democracy and Communism. He believed that the Western Powers were trying to 'roll back' the Soviet Union from the positions it had won through much sacrifice in Eastern Europe, to reduce Russia to the state of a second-rate power.[5]

Alan outlined why he disagreed with Wadsworth: 'I am sure that it is much more important to keep hammering away at the ideal of full employment and a rising standard of living throughout Europe than either to lecture the Russians about their lack of democracy or to fuss about the Security Council and the technical question of the maintenance of order – if people have enough to eat and decent prospects, the machinery of international relations will soon get right.'[6] In September Alan grumbled to Wadsworth that he had become fond of the phrase 'iron curtain'. 'This was invented,' Alan told Wadsworth, 'not by Churchill, but by Count Schwerin von Krosigk, Foreign Minister in the Dönitz government, in his only public utterance. Anti-Bolshevism makes strange bedfellows; but I can't believe you can really want to take your foreign policy from Dönitz and his associates.'

'Isn't it an "iron curtain"?' replied Wadsworth. 'You try to get behind it, my lad, and you'll see . . . Do you still hanker for a tour of the barbarians?'[7] For the past two years Alan had been pressing the *Manchester Guardian* to send him to Central Europe as a special correspondent as soon as the War ended. In 1946 he went for three weeks to Czechoslovakia, where he was treated as a visiting dignitary. He spent several hours with Beneš, now reinstated as president. Beneš took Alan to the window, and showed him the view of Prague. 'Is it not beautiful?' he asked. 'The only undamaged city in Central Europe, and all my doing.'

The image stuck. Beneš's cynicism – all he had done was to surrender to superior force – appealed to Alan's temperament. But like most jokes, it contained a truth. The Czechs had been betrayed by the Great Powers; they had been overrun by the Nazis. The experience had been extremely unpleasant, but not calamitous.

Their cities had not been razed, their people* had not been butchered (except, of course, the Jews) – unlike, for example, the Poles, who had fought the Germans with the backing of a guarantee from Britain and France. This insight lodged in Alan's mind, to re-emerge in his book *The Origins of the Second World War* fifteen years later.

Alan was not used to travelling by air, and he had left a note for Margaret in case he was killed, 'saying that she should not repine and it was better for me to be out of the way while the memory of happier days was still fresh with us. Maybe an air accident would have been all for the best but it did not happen.'[8]

Dylan and Caitlin Thomas turned up again early in 1946. They had been forced to leave their London flat, and Dylan had broken his arm trying to climb back in through a window. In the garden a few yards upstream from Holywell Ford was a little one-room summer-house, known as 'The Studio', which the Taylors offered as a refuge. This was to be the Thomases' home until the following April, when Dylan managed to get a grant to send them to Italy for the summer. Being only one room, it was not suitable for a family, so the two Thomas children lodged in the main house. Dylan and Caitlin joined them there at mealtimes.

The summerhouse was cold and damp, and it was hard for Dylan to find space to write; after a while Margaret bought him a gypsy caravan to work in. The Thomases were unconventional guests; Dylan was known to make free with his hosts' property. One day he decided to chop up a rocking-chair from Holywell Ford to feed the fire. Margaret came across its remains on the path to the Studio; she looked at them in astonishment. On another occasion Dylan was invited to a Taylor dinner party; among the other guests were the dons Lord David Cecil and Hugh Trevor-Roper, who has written an account of what ensued. 'The poet appeared at the dinner table already drunk and unable to speak. He promptly overturned a full decanter of claret – good claret too – drenching the fastidious Lord David. That dinner party was not a success.'[9]

---

*See p. 298–9.

Dylan was constantly short of money, though he still spent extravagantly, relying on others to pick up the bill. Returning by taxi from London late one night, he woke the Taylors to pay the fare. Dylan tried to borrow money from Alan, as he tried to borrow money from everybody, but Alan was unforthcoming. With Margaret, however, he was more successful. She became his most consistent patron; he later acknowledged his 'almost national debt' to her.[10] She tried to help him sort out his tax affairs. She supplied him with a steady stream of cash, books, clothes and other necessities, she paid for his children's schooling, and she provided him with accommodation in which he lived free or at a low rent for the rest of his life. But the more she gave him, the more he wanted. He wrote her begging letters full of fear, ladling on the 'descriptive stuff' because he knew that was what she liked.[11] She soon exhausted the income her capital provided. When her mother had died she had inherited enough money to buy some paintings: a Graham Sutherland, an Utrillo, a Boudin, an unfinished Sickert, a Degas, a Renoir and a Toulouse-Lautrec lithograph of Oscar Wilde. She now began to take these down from the walls and sell them, together with other valuables like her piano, in order to be able to keep Dylan. Alan seemed not to notice, and Dylan and Margaret laughed at him behind his back.

But Alan did notice. He loathed 'spongers'. He could not stop Margaret doing what she liked with her money, but he resented getting bills for the barrels of beer Dylan had ordered to be delivered and put down to Alan's account at Morrell's. When Dylan's name came up in conversation with Kathleen Tillotson, whom Alan had not seen since before the War, his face darkened; 'he is a very wicked man'.

Margaret was delighted to have a poet living at the end of the garden. She showed him her own poetry, which he pretended to take seriously. He wrote detailed critiques of her poems – one which has survived is twelve pages long. He encouraged her to think that they would write a film script together. In the evenings they went out drinking. Alan felt she was making a fool of herself, and neglecting her duties as a wife and mother. Once again he felt humiliated when he heard that Dylan had been boasting in the pubs around Oxford about his success in extracting money from Margaret. Dylan was a recognisable celebrity, and when people saw him with Margaret they gossiped. Alan's manner to her became cold. Visitors to Holywell Ford heard Alan say that he was good around the house, and look pointedly at Margaret.

It was hard for Margaret. She was impractical about money, which often formed the basis of their quarrels; and she was uneasy in the role of a don's wife. She could be bright and assertive at dinner parties, often the only woman to keep up in the otherwise male conversation; on other occasions she could be completely silent. Caitlin Thomas observed that the life of the university seemed rather fascinating from the outside, like being in a monastery: 'the ideal life for a man'.[12] One evening Alan took Dylan in to dine at High Table, a privilege not available to women.

Margaret aspired to be the leader of a salon. She gave literary parties for Dylan, at which Alan often felt out of place. The Thomases fed her taste for Bohemia, so lacking in provincial Oxford society. And she was fascinated by Dylan himself. She was not alone in this: many found him marvellous company, and forgave his foibles. He had a curious quality of vulnerability and helplessness that made people want to protect him, even when he behaved badly. The writer and publisher Dan Davin, for example, remembered affectionately how, after Dylan had stayed the night, 'I was surprised to observe that he was wearing a shirt I recognised as mine'.[13] Margaret was sure Dylan was a genius; as such excused from normal social rules. She felt a responsibility to provide for him, indeed an importance in doing so. She fussed over him, getting him out of bed in the morning and packing him off to work. Her marriage had been soured by the Robert Kee episode. Dylan represented a romantic focus for her life.

Dylan exploited Margaret's affection in every way possible. At the same time he and Caitlin appeared to resent Margaret's *largesse*. Caitlin was a proud, sometimes jealous person, not one to hide her feelings. She resented it when Dylan disappeared for days and she was forced to borrow from Margaret: all the more so when Margaret reminded her that Dylan was a genius. She exploded when it seemed to her that Margaret was copying her 'very individual' style of dress.[14]

Dylan belittled Margaret, saying she got on his nerves. In a letter to Caitlin he referred to her as 'maudlin Magdalen Maggie'.[15] It seemed not to matter how rude he was to her or how badly he behaved. One Sunday the Thomases were due to lunch at Holywell Ford, and Margaret had gone to a great deal of trouble – rationing was still in force – to obtain and prepare a hare. Dylan had been drinking, and sulkily refused to come to the table to eat. 'But, Dylan, darling, you must – I've gone to so much trouble,' Margaret protested. Very reluctantly, Dylan consented: 'All right, then, I'll eat the hare of the bitch that dogs me.'

In April 1947 the Taylors were invited to Yugoslavia, a reward for Alan's efforts on behalf of the Yugoslav claim to Trieste. The Thomases were off to Italy for the summer. Just before they left Alan remarked to Caitlin that Margaret was often unbalanced because she imagined she was in love with Robert Kee. Caitlin told Alan that Margaret now fancied herself in love with Dylan. 'My heart sank at the thought of one obsession succeeding another indefinitely. My mother's obsession with Henry Sara seemed staid by comparison.'[16]

Alan enjoyed himself in Yugoslavia; 'it was what Communism ought to be'.[17] His visit rekindled the idealism he had experienced during his trip to Russia in 1925. On his return he wrote to Wadsworth that it had been 'fascinating . . . I haven't the skill to convey either the excitement or the friendliness.'[18] Two enthusiastic *Manchester Guardian* pieces followed. 'The spirit throughout the country is like a vast Boy Scout camp . . . Almost all the leading men, whether Communists or not, are former schoolteachers, mostly from secondary schools. The effect is rather as though the Left Book Club suddenly took over both the central and local government of this country.'

In Zagreb Alan allowed his enthusiasm to speak too freely when he predicted, accurately as it turned out, that before long the Yugoslavs would quarrel with the Russians. A Soviet English-language broadcast alluded to the visit paid by a 'Professor Taylor', who had allegedly disseminated anti-Soviet doctrines in the manner of 'Goebbels and Churchill'; fortunately, it went on, the 'justifiably indignant' people of Yugoslavia were well able to distinguish him as 'an agent of imperialism'. Alan commented to Wadsworth that 'the whole thing is excessively delightful'.[19]

In 1948, after Tito's break with the Russians, Alan returned to this theme:

> Tito is a warning to me always to have the courage of one's convictions and to believe one's own judgement rather than that of others. I ought to have gone on record twelve months ago that the Yugoslavs were too independent to fit in with the rule of Moscow. I am now ashamed that I complained to the Jugs at being attacked from Moscow radio: it seems that I was saying all the things for which Tito has been condemned. My guess is that Tito will hold out for some time. His demonstration of national independence will make him popular with the Serbs; and his agitation for Trieste and in Carinthia has always given him a hold over the Slovenes. Thus he is back in the position of King Alexander, ruling against the Croats (who are in part Catholic and in part loyal to Moscow); the Albanians (who will presumably go with Albania); and the Macedonians (whom the Bulgarians will now stir up). Alexander kept this regime going for years; and indeed it is the only sensible one for Yugoslavia. If Tito can hold the Macedonians, then he is safe . . . a daring western policy would offer Trieste to Tito and would certainly give him economic assistance on generous terms. After all, if Yugoslavia becomes independent of Russia, Italy no longer matters. The comical thing is that the Cominform charges are mostly true. Tito *is* a Turkish grandee; the party *has* no internal discussion; there *has* been no collectivisation and so on. All the same he symbolises the triumph of nationalism over Communist solidarity.'[20]

Alan recognised that Yugoslavia was a federation of peoples, not a national state, but he believed that Tito had found an 'idea', the mission which eluded the Habsburgs.

> In a curious roundabout way, 'federal, democratic Yugoslavia' – the official name of Tito's state – is an attempt to realise the international dream which was supposed to lie behind the old Austrian Empire, the Habsburg Monarchy: to discover for the peoples of central and eastern Europe a political order which would be neither German nor Russian, but something in between. Tito, in fact, is the heir of the Habsburgs; and the conflict between Tito and Stalin is a new version of the old conflict between Habsburg and Romanov.[21]

There was an irony in Alan's enthusiasm for Yugoslavia, for he had just completed a revised edition of *The Habsburg Monarchy*; one of the principal changes he made was to remove the 'liberal illusion' that a compromise was possible between the national principle and a supra-national dynastic state. Once launched, the national principle had to work itself out to its conclusion. He had discussed the national problem in Yugoslavia in a letter to Wadsworth in 1945.

> In my opinion the Tito regime . . . is much worse than people realise here and the Czech government much better . . . the Czechs have got the national balance right and Tito has got it wrong – any system which tries to run Yugoslavia against the Serbs, who are the only state-conscious people, must be totalitarian, though I'll admit that the Serbs have no very clean record of democracy.[22]

In 1945 the Yugoslavs had published Alan's pamphlet on Trieste, then a 'free city'. It was very much a live political issue, its status undecided;* Truman had sent a telegram to Churchill urging him to resist Tito's designs on the city. When Alan gave a talk on the BBC Home Service which appeared to push the Yugoslav case for Trieste, the Ministry of Information contacted the Controller of Talks, R.A. Rendall. 'Some concern has been expressed,' Rendall told George Barnes, the Assistant Controller, 'that a man with known views on the Yugoslav question should be speaking on this subject when it was about to be decided upon . . . It is . . . obviously important that we should not allow Taylor to use the occasion to press his own viewpoint.' The Political Intelligence Department (PID) reported that 'Taylor at a dinner party the night before had expressed himself unwisely as regards the use he might make of his broadcasting to favour the Yugoslav cause'.[23] Alan came into the BBC to explain. 'He would have preferred that his Trieste pamphlet which expressed entirely his own views, and was not touched by the Yugoslav government, should have been published independently, but it was only in this way that he was able to get paper,' minuted the Controller of Talks. 'I said we should have to take care that the Trieste difficulty did not recur, from which he did not dissent.'[24]

---

*Trieste was handed back to Italy in 1954.

Alan took his work for the BBC very seriously. In March 1946 he asked them to reconsider his fee of fifteen guineas for 'World Affairs':

> It is, I suppose, the most important political talk of the week and a simple mistake could have all sorts of international consequences . . . Moreover these talks often land me in a notoriety which for an academic person like myself is most unwelcome. Since you invite me to talk fairly often, I suppose that I have succeeded in giving satisfaction; and I feel myself that I am getting more experienced. I think therefore the time has come when my fee should be reconsidered; though of course I am willing – as a public duty – to continue at my present fee trying to serve you.[25]

In May Blewitt came to the conclusion that Alan should not be used again in the 'World Affairs' series. There had been much discussion about Alan's microphone manner, and Blewitt set down his concerns in an internal memorandum. 'His admirable qualities are vitiated by a certain cynicism, which is out of place in an objective and ultimately educational series for the ordinary listener . . . it is apparent in his tone of voice at the microphone quite as much as in the "tone" of the script.'[26] When Alan realised that he had been dropped he wrote to complain: 'I don't expect the BBC to invite me [to speak] if they don't like what I say; but I think that, since I have worked regularly in the series and aroused interest in some listeners, I deserve the courtesy of some explanation instead of being ignored as though I had committed some crime.'[27]

Alan was soon back on the radio, this time with four broadcasts on the Third Programme, as part of a series on foreign policy. Previous speakers had included E.H. Carr and Arnold Toynbee. Alan used his talks to attack free trade and to argue for a Socialist reconstruction of Europe. America, he believed, would soon fall victim to an economic catastrophe; while the Soviet economic system went from strength to strength. 'American strategy and policy are not concerned with our security; they are only concerned to use this island (like Japan on the other side of the world) as an aircraft carrier from which to discharge atomic bombs, and the Americans appreciate quite well that all the cities of England and Japan will be destroyed in this process.' The 'only possible policy' by which Britain could remain prosperous and a Great Power was an Anglo-Russian alliance. 'The advantages of co-operation between Russia and England are so obvious and . . . the dangers of association with America so blatant that I am amazed that even the fog of a century of suspicion, thickened up by the smoke of ill-informed anti-Marxism, is enough to keep England and Russia apart.'[28]

Alan's talks on foreign policy caused uproar. An indignant MP called them 'nauseous and contemptible', and read out chunks in Parliament; replying, the Lord President of the Council, Herbert Morrison, described them as 'anti-American, anti-British and not particularly competent'.[29] Perhaps the reference in Alan's first talk to 'not saying anything that will make a Member of Parliament of limited intelligence ask questions in the House of Commons' was responsible. The next speaker in the BBC series was the journalist and historian R.C.K. Ensor, and he joined in the condemnation of his predecessor. 'What I disapproved in him was not merely the substance of his talks, but the manner. The substance to my thinking consisted too largely of shallow half-truths, more danger-ous than plain untruths because more specious, yet not a bit more trustworthy to build on. But I also, if I may say so without needless discourtesy, objected profoundly to his jaunty cocksure manner.'[30] It was an extraordinary attack to make in the context of a talk that was supposed to be about modern diplomacy; but it represented how a good many of Alan's colleagues had come to feel about him.

'I daresay it did not occur to you or to others who were looking after this programme that I had feelings to be hurt,' Alan wrote afterwards to Harman Grisewood, the Assistant Director of Talks: 'but I have.' After a calming letter in reply Alan wrote again to say that he was not mollified; he still thought personal abuse on air a bad thing, 'but a useful precedent for me'.[31]

The Third Programme had already accepted an idea of Alan's for a series on nineteenth-century prime ministers, to be delivered by various historians. There was difficulty drawing up a list of speakers; as Alan pointed out to Blewitt, 'You are dealing with academic persons, not with journalists; and they need months of preparation even to write the simplest article. To the academic mind a month is too short notice; besides, they fear any kind of public appearance.'[32] Alan offered to give all six talks; as it turned out he was required to give only two of them. One of his subjects was Lord Salisbury, the Tory grandee, whom one might expect to be a butt of Alan's ridicule. Not a bit of it: Salisbury was a 'great man', 'the greatest advocate of Anglo-Russian co-operation'.[33]

After the series had finished Grisewood wrote referring to complaints about the series. Alan responded pugnaciously:

> I am sorry you did not like the prime ministers. I thought most of the talks were excellent . . . But perhaps the BBC dislikes talks which arouse too much interest. So far as I could tell, the criticism came from those who would have liked to do the talks themselves; and even some who declined to take part in them and then objected to others doing so.[34]

The same day he wrote to George Barnes, who had become Head of the new Third Programme: 'I think I am now permanently out of favour with the talks department. Praise from the Radio critic of the *New Statesman* has been my ruin.' Barnes replied harshly. A fool can be provocative, he said, referring to the *New Statesman* review. 'These talks did not make me alter my opinion that a lecture, however skilfully potted, will never obtain the interest of the critical listener in history.' In an internal memorandum to Grisewood he concluded that Alan had not begun to tackle the question of history in broadcasting; Grisewood agreed that 'Taylor is second-rate'.[35] With views like these it is perhaps not surprising that the BBC was slow to respond when Alan began to lecture on television.

After this exchange Alan's broadcasts on the Home Service dried up to a trickle; nothing in the next six months and then only four book reviews in the next so many years. Two talks he proposed, one on *The Times* and Anglo-German estrangement and the other on the origins of the recent War, were rejected by Barnes. When he was finally commissioned to do a book review by a new producer, Peter Laslett (himself an historian), Alan wrote to clear the air:

> While I enjoy working for the BBC, I expect a certain reciprocity. I am, of course, responsible for the things I say; but the Corporation is responsible for putting me on the air, and I deeply resent the attitude

of senior officials who first welcome my scripts with enthusiasm, and then, when there are complaints, blame me for the trouble that I have caused them. The least that one deserves is to be told frankly when a script is unsatisfactory and not to be flung out without a word of explanation, as I was discarded overnight from 'World Affairs'.

At all events, I hope that our relations will prove satisfactory to both of us and that the Corporation will display a more adult attitude than it has done in the past.[36]

After this exchange, Alan settled into an attitude of facetious resignation. Replying to another producer's comments on his script, Alan wrote that 'concealed in it there is no doubt some dreadful sentence which will again get me banished to outer darkness'.[37] Earlier he had the satisfaction of being able to review a book of Third Programme talks 'introduced' by Grisewood. 'Could the editor of a collection of learned articles write more pompously?' he asked. He mocked 'the spirit of earnestness' that 'broods over Broadcasting House, and most particularly over the Third Programme'.[38]

Dylan had no sooner arrived in Italy than he wrote to Margaret asking her to find him a house 'in or near Oxford, so that we can see each other again. I want so much to come back to Oxford. Oh, anywhere a house. I am lost without one. I am as domestic as a slipper, I want somewhere of my own, I'm old enough now, I want a house to shout, sleep, and work in. Please help; though I deserve nothing.' In May he wrote that they would stay in Italy until July, 'and then to lovely unfound house in Oxfordshire, the house built around the desk you bought me? Oh I *do* hope so.' A week or so later Margaret sent him a telegram to say that she had found South Leigh Manor, on the Oxford side of Witney, about five miles from Oxford. Dylan wired back, 'House sounds lovely. Please take it,' and then wrote, 'I rely on you, your help, your letters, so, so much.'[39]

In fact South Leigh was not a manor but a farmhouse, and it was not lovely; it had no electricity, no gas, cold water only, and an outside lavatory. Nevertheless it had cost more than £2000; Alan had agreed to buy the house on condition that Margaret stopped giving Dylan money.[40] Dylan was supposed to pay rent of £1 a week, though as it turned out he rarely did so.* Arriving back in England in mid-August, he was soon installed at South Leigh. He collected the gypsy caravan from Holywell Ford and took it over there, where he used it to work. Not much work was done: in the three years after the War he wrote only one poem.[42]

Dylan and Caitlin were a tempestuous couple. Their frequent rows often became fights, in which Caitlin, 'a very physical person' as Margaret described her, was well able to hold her own with her small and sometimes drunken husband. Once Caitlin was so furious with Dylan that she tipped over the caravan with him inside. This seemingly uninhibited couple had a cathartic effect on other people's marriages; as one friend said, if you got too close you were 'emotionally clobbered'; perhaps physically too.

Margaret tried to honour her agreement with Alan not to give Dylan any more money. Dylan complained to one of his cronies: 'My lady patron no longer pays, at least not in money; a night at the opera, yes, ballets and cocktails whenever, but not one more crisp crunchy note can I dig from her breast.'[43] But she could not stay away from Dylan, and went out to South Leigh whenever possible. Alan often arrived back in Oxford from London to find Margaret gone. According to Cordelia Locke, a friend of Dylan's, Margaret was 'besotted'; she slept on the floor of South Leigh with the dog. A letter from Dylan to Caitlin, who had taken the children to stay with her mother, describes Margaret staying at South Leigh all weekend, 'duckeying and weeping'. Alan came out on his bicycle, and there were 'SCENES' on the road; 'the bitch was red-eyed all evening'.[44]

Alan wrote to Dylan that he was destroying their marriage. He recognised a familiar pattern; a middle-aged husband supplanted by a younger man who sang for his supper. The parallel with Sara extended even to Alan's hand-me-down suits which Dylan wore. Margaret's feelings for Dylan were totally different from those she

---

*Dylan's earnings in 1947–8 were estimated for Income Tax purposes at the then considerable sum of £2482. Alan's income for 1948 as Fellow and Tutor of Magdalen was £1350.[41]

had for Alan – indeed Dylan personified what Alan lacked. Dylan was warm, Alan cool; Dylan lyrical, Alan prosaic; Dylan Bacchanalian, Alan methodical and disciplined. Margaret thought that Dylan was a bad boy whose behaviour had to be tolerated for the sake of his genius. By acting as his patron, she would allow that genius to flower.

Caitlin apparently found a letter from Margaret to Dylan which said that 'to sleep with you would be like sleeping with a god';[45] though whether they actually had an affair remains open to doubt. A story which still circulates in Oxford has Alan returning unexpectedly to Holywell Ford to find Dylan and Margaret *in flagrante* on the kitchen table;* but this may be no more than college gossip. According to Caitlin, Margaret planned an elopement while they were living at South Leigh. She wrote to Dylan to say that she would be waiting for him on a certain day at Paddington Station with a packed suitcase. Dylan failed to keep the appointment.[46] 'I'm always the one that's left out,' Margaret complained.

In a way Margaret was as romantic about Caitlin as she was about Dylan. Margaret often kept house for them while Dylan and Caitlin went out pubbing together. When Dylan came back from America Margaret met him at Southampton, and on the way back to London he told her about his new girlfriend, the 'marvellous fuck' he had found there. Margaret's reaction was to tell Caitlin about it, which only made Caitlin dislike her more. And when the girlfriend arrived in England and Dylan took her away for a weekend, Margaret telephoned all the hotels in Brighton to track them down.

In March 1949 Margaret succumbed once again. Dylan had decided that he could find his Muse again only in Laugharne, the coastal village in Wales were he and Caitlin had lived intermittently in the late 1930s and early 1940s, and where his parents now dwelt. He persuaded Margaret that she should buy him a house there, though she had to sell two-thirds of her capital to do so. For Alan this was the last straw. 'I might have stood for anything else, but breaking one's word over money went against my deepest principle – the sanctity of contract.'[47]

---

*The college is even said to have preserved the table as a memento.

Alan was no longer just indifferent to Margaret; he was resentful. He recognised a parallel in the life of the architect Sir Edwin
Lutyens – perhaps a revealing comparison. Lutyens was often away
from home, and even when at home often returned to his drawing-
board after dinner and worked until after midnight. His wife Lady
Emily fell hopelessly in love with Jiddu Krishnamurti, an Indian
boy who was believed to be the new Lord Maitreya, or World
Teacher. As Lady Emily admitted, her husband, her home, her
children faded into the background; Krishnamurti became her
entire life, and the next ten years were spent trying to sublimate a
human love. Gradually Emily came to think of Krishnamurti more
as a son than a lover, but she continued to neglect her husband,
indeed to long for Krishnamurti to tell her to leave all and follow
him. Moreover, her intimacy with Indians and her dislike of the Raj
undermined Lutyens' career in India, where he built many of his
most famous buildings.[48] 'Lutyens stuck to her, made her follies
easy and endured his unhappiness for many years,' Alan wrote in
his autobiography. 'Should I follow his example or should I break
away? I went over the problem for many years without finding an
answer.'[49]

Harry Thompson had died in 1947, a year after his sister Connie.
His practice had grown steadily; on his death the firm had a staff of
seventy. Control then passed to his two sons, and the business
continued to expand until it employed more than 500 people. Alan
must sometimes have reflected that had he stayed on with his uncle
he might well have become a millionaire.

Alan remained very interested in money. His correspondence
with the BBC, for example, was full of petty disputes about
payment. He objected when he heard that other speakers were paid
more for appearing on the same programme; and always insisted
on first-class return fares from Oxford as expenses, resisting any
suggestion that these were unnecessary when he was in London for
other reasons. Stories about his avarice began to circulate in the
college; on one occasion he was said to have pulled a wad of notes
out of his pocket and brandished it in front of a student with the
words 'that's what I like'. In 1948 he wrote to Wadsworth about

reviewing a biography of Bismarck. 'Of course I ought really to write a life of Bismarck myself, but the effort to make money on the side to keep four children going distracts me from serious work.'[50]

Alan's pleasure at his new publishers did not prevent him from striking a hard bargain. He reclaimed the rights in *The Habsburg Monarchy* from Macmillan, who, 'furious at my desertion', had declined to bring out a new edition, and offered them instead to Hamish Hamilton. When the latter proposed a lower royalty, Alan bridled. 'I think you are the most wonderful publisher that any author could have . . . I have complete confidence in you. At the same time, when it comes to settling a contract, I expect you to look after your interests and I do my best to look after mine. If you don't like this attitude, you must keep clear of writers who are born in the North of England.'[51]

Alan had several such sharp exchanges with Hamilton, but they never became acrimonious; these were two businesslike people who respected each other's position. Alan particularly liked the fact that Hamilton appeared keen to *sell* his books. He felt he was in good hands. 'If ever you want a testimony to your brilliance as a publisher (which I should think most unlikely), you know where to come for it,' he wrote to Hamilton in 1949.[52]

The new edition of *The Habsburg Monarchy* received mixed reviews. A piece by C.A. Macartney in *History* summed up the case for the prosecution.

> Mr Taylor's merits as an historian are considerable . . . His weaknesses, which unfortunately have grown perceptibly since *The Habsburg Monarchy* was first issued, include cock-sureness and a complete intolerance of those of whom he disapproves, whether living or dead. Everybody has to be scored off, and, with very few exceptions, almost everyone who figures in his pages is a villain, an imposter or, more frequently still, a fool.[53]

'I like being called the Evelyn Waugh of modern historians,' Alan commented to Hamilton, referring to one of the more flattering reviews, 'but I wonder whether Evelyn Waugh is equally pleased.'[54] A dozen years later another reviewer, Sebastian Haffner, would make the same comparison.[55]

In 1948 Alan asked Roger Machell, who had become his editor, 'Please break the news to Hamilton that I propose to offer him a volume of essays – nothing, I believe, is more dreaded by a publisher.'[56] Dreaded or not, Hamilton rose to the fly, and Alan's first volume of essays, *From Napoleon to Stalin*, was published in 1950. He dedicated it to Wadsworth. The book was a bit of a rag-bag, as Alan freely admitted to Machell; 'I think I'd better invent a theme and put it into an extended introduction which the reviewers (an expert speaks) could then copy.'[57]

The reviewers reacted badly to such cynicism. Elizabeth Wiske-mann, for example, writing in *The Spectator*, found it disappoint-ing that Alan had not bothered to revise the contents, most of which had originally appeared as book reviews. Even the *Manchester Guardian* was critical: 'Read as a collection the essays suggest a constant trailing of the coat, and the piling up of audacious opinion produces the effect of a firework display that has gone on too long.'[58]

Alan encouraged Namier to move with him to Hamish Hamil-ton, and in the same year wrote to tell Hamilton that Macmillan had turned down Namier's proposed volume of essays 'with the offensive arrogance which marks the dealings of that distinguished firm'. Alan had been astonished to learn, he told Hamilton, that it had taken Macmillan twenty years to dispose of two thousand copies of Namier's *The Structure of Politics at the Accession of George III*, 'the most important work of English history published in our lifetime'.[59] Hamilton became Namier's publisher. In 1948, Alan persuaded Magdalen that Namier should be the inaugural Waynflete Lecturer. Alan had become Namier's patron; their roles had reversed.

For a serious piece like a paper in the *English Historical Review* Alan would do two drafts. 'See, I can be dull as well,' he would say; 'look at all these footnotes.' But in fact there were very few such articles. In Alan's otherwise prolific career he wrote no more than half a dozen or so pieces for learned journals based an original research (as opposed to review articles). Most of his scholarship went into his books. He was working on a new volume, which would take a decade to complete.

> It is a very strange thing [he had written in 1942] that the story of the Struggle for Mastery in Europe has never been attempted. German historians cannot do it, because to them the struggle (that is the resistance to German domination) seems merely wrong-headed; American historians cannot do it, because they do not realise what was at stake. It would be a superb opportunity for an English historian, if one could be found with real standards of scholarship and understanding.[60]

One could be found. Alan had been working on such a book since he had finished *The Habsburg Monarchy* in 1941, and had completed 100,000 words when he put it aside to write *The Course of German History*. 'It will not be ready for years,' he warned Hamish Hamilton, 'hardly before the atomic bomb blows us all up . . .'[61] He worked almost exclusively from the published documents, but even so it was a formidable undertaking, requiring him to read, besides the British volumes, the French, German, Russian and Italian. He did not read Russian easily, but fortunately some of the documents were available in translation.

In the preface to the 1951 edition of *The Course of German History*, he set out more clearly what he was trying to achieve:

> There can hardly be a more urgent topic than the relations of the Great Powers since 1848;* yet none so neglected or perverted. There is no Professor in European History in either Oxford or Cambridge; and the principal work on the period is still a book written solely on the basis of German sources by a German Professor who retained his chair and prestige throughout the Nazi dictatorship. The Germans still enjoy the advantages which sprang from being the first to publish their diplomatic documents in however tendentious a form. The most famous American authority on the First World War insisted not long ago that the views which he had formed by studying the German sources had not been changed by the publication of British, French, and other texts. Sooner or later we shall have to escape from the German version of the events of the last hundred

---

*Originally he had planned it to start no earlier than 1878.

years. I myself am halfway through a history of the relations of the
Great Powers between the revolutions of 1848 and the collapse of
the European system in 1918. If I can ever snatch leisure from the
time-consuming life of a College tutor and complete it, this present
book will appear more sensible.[62]

Alan was encouraged in his great work by Woodward, the historian who had played a part in bringing Alan to Oxford. He read an
early draft of the book and made helpful comments. Woodward
was haunted by a fear of a new 'war guilt' controversy, which
would shift the blame from where it belonged and lead in time to a
third German war. He thought of Alan as an ally. In 1947,
however, a review appeared in the *Times Literary Supplement*
criticising the first volumes in the series *Documents on British
Foreign Policy, 1919–1939*, which had been edited jointly by
Woodward and Rohan Butler; in particular, it deplored the
absence of private letters or minutes, often more significant than
the formal documents themselves. 'The volume appears to have the
deliberate purpose of vindicating the British foreign service.'[63] Like
all the book reviews in the *Times Literary Supplement*, this article
was unsigned and therefore anonymous. Woodward was furious,
and he harassed Stanley Morison, the editor of the *Times Literary
Supplement*, so much, Alan believed – a belief not shared by
Morison's biographer – as to cause Morison's resignation. In the
process Woodward discovered the name of the reviewer: Alan
Taylor.

There was an eager interest in diplomatic documents after the
Second World War as there had been after the First. There was not
the same mystery about what had caused the War – everybody
agreed that Hitler was to blame – but there was considerable
interest in discovering the extent of British and French appeasement, and the reasons for the failure of the Western Powers to reach
a defensive alliance with the Soviet Union. Nor was there the same
competitive element in publishing the documents,* since the captured German documents were being published under Allied con-

---

*At least not between the European Powers; but the United States and the Soviet
Union, Alan wrote in 1948, 'fling at each other fragments from the German
archives'.[64]

trols – but it remained important to set the record straight, all the more so if you believed, as Alan did, that historians themselves bore a responsibility for the Second World War because they had failed adequately to explain the First. Alan reviewed most of the volumes of diplomatic documents – British, French and German – as they were published; after he stopped reviewing them in the *Times Literary Supplement* he persuaded Wadsworth and later Martin to pass them to him for review, and they made good copy for the left-leaning press, as they were generally embarrassing to the Tories. He also reviewed the memoirs of the generals and statesmen which proliferated after 1945. As a result of all this reading and reviewing he began to think afresh about the origins of the War.

Namier had been reading the same books, and in 1948 produced *Diplomatic Prelude*, a masterly work which summarised what was known of the diplomacy immediately preceding the War. He succeeded in constructing a convincing and authoritative narrative from fragmentary and disparate sources, often of dubious provenance. In the process Namier showed what could be done with contemporary history. Alan described *Diplomatic Prelude* as a 'showpiece of the historian's art . . . a sentence often says as much as many pages by another writer';[65] elsewhere he described Namier as the greatest living historian.[66] Namier's *The Structure of Politics at the Accession of George III* could no more be ignored in a discussion of modern history, Alan declared, than *The Origin of Species* could be ignored in a discussion of biology.[67]

Namier was still able to show Alan the way forward. In 1950, for example, Namier published *Europe in Decay: A Study in Disintegration, 1936–1940*, reprinted book reviews which developed some of the ideas in *Diplomatic Prelude*. 'The official "Conservative" leaders of 1938–1939', he wrote, 'were mostly ex- or semi-Liberals of middle-class Nonconformist extraction, whose Liberalism had gone rancid . . .' The following year Alan broadcast a review of a collection of foreign policy documents, edited by James Joll. 'The opponents of collective security and advocates of a straight deal with Germany at the time of Munich were mostly Radicals gone sour from Neville Chamberlain downwards.'[68] Who can doubt Namier's influence on Alan, extending even to the metaphors in which he expressed his ideas?

In his consideration of *Diplomatic Prelude* Alan was already moving away from the assumption that Hitler had planned a war in the West. 'Certainly, Hitler aimed at German domination of Europe; but he, too, went about this in a most blundering way and, as Namier shows, was quite taken aback at the end when he found that, against all expectation, England and France were really going to war.'[69] 'Hitler intervened only on a sudden impulse, without plan or preparation,' Alan wrote the following year. He dismissed the Hossbach Memorandum, a junior officer's account of Hitler's address to his generals in 1937, which had been produced by the prosecution at the Nuremberg Trials in an attempt to prove a Nazi conspiracy to commit 'crimes against peace'. 'This is evidence that he [Hitler] was a violent and unscrupulous man; it is not evidence that he had any concrete projects, and his prophecy of events* bears little relation to what actually happened.'[70]

Appeasement was by now a dirty word. In 1940 three left-wing journalists, Frank Owen, Michael Foot and Peter Howard, had produced *Guilty Men*, a book which accused Chamberlain, Baldwin and others associated with the policy of appeasement of sharing responsibility for the War. This became the new orthodoxy, and the appeasers were vilified; Baldwin, for example, was said by a Conservative MP to need the gates outside his house to protect him against the just indignation of the mob. Alan recognised the hypocrisy in singling out 'the appeasers'. He reconsidered the subject in 'Munich Ten Years After', a piece for the *New Statesman and Nation*.

> One must be just, even to the English 'men of Munich' . . . they felt the moral strength of the German case. For twenty years, English writers, particularly on the Left, had denounced the injustice of the Versailles settlement . . . English and American historians, of irrep-

---

*Hitler foresaw civil strife in France, crippling the French Army, and war in the Mediterranean between Britain, France and Italy. He argued that Germany would need to attack Austria and Czechoslovakia simultaneously.

roachable liberalism, had declared that Germany was no more
responsible than any other power for the war of 1914. Who among
us can claim innocence?

He rejected the analogy some people made between what happened
then and appeasement of Russia now; this was

> twaddling scraps of history . . . the greater the readiness to conciliate
> Hitler ten years ago, the more determined the resolve to resist the
> Russians now* . . . In any case appeasement or resistance was not
> the fundamental issue of Munich. The fundamental issue was
> whether England (or more generally the Western Powers) could
> work with Russia . . .[71]

Another historian whom Alan praised very highly was Hugh
Trevor-Roper. Trevor-Roper, though eight years younger than
Alan, was already a well-known Oxford figure. Witty and irreverent, he shared Alan's impatience with the old men of Oxford. Both
wrote clearly (and, in Trevor-Roper's case, elegantly); both were
unafraid to write for the press and broadcast on the BBC; both were
good conversationalists. Though Trevor-Roper was on the Right
and Alan on the Left, neither was a conventional Party man. They
enjoyed each other's company, and quickly became friends. In
1948, Alan wrote of Trevor-Roper's *The Last Days of Hitler* that it
'develops its story with all the brilliance of a symphony conducted
by a great master'.[72] He praised the book again and again.[73] In a
special supplement of the *Times Literary Supplement* in 1954, he
hailed it as a masterpiece. He praised Trevor-Roper for being
anxious – 'as every great historian must be' – to reach a wide
audience. Every rational man must wish, Alan concluded, that he
had written Mr Trevor-Roper's book.[74]

'No historian achieves the highest excellence,' Alan believed,
'whose work cannot be read for pleasure as well as profit.'[75] He
was very much opposed to the 'scientific' view of history, 'the

---

*He may have been thinking of Lord Dunglass, later, as Sir Alec Douglas-Home,
leader of the Conservative Party and Prime Minister, 1963–4; an appeaser before
the War, he was now advocating a very firm line against Russia.

modern delusion that if only we know enough facts we shall arrive at the answer'.[76] On the contrary, 'the real task of the historian is to throw overboard all facts but the essential'.[77] The great German historian Ranke had believed that reconstructing the past was like constructing a brick wall; if only enough facts could be collected, the edifice would be complete. The tendency of the Germanic school of history was to write more and more about less and less. Alan derided other historians for producing works that did no more than précis the sources.[78]

Alan was by now writing book reviews more and more frequently, until he reached a rate of one a week, which he maintained throughout the 1950s. The reviews appeared in the *Manchester Guardian* and the *New Statesman and Nation*, the *Times Literary Supplement* and *English Historical Review*; and occasionally in American magazines like the *New Republic*. Often he would review the same book twice in different journals; his editors seemed not to mind, though perhaps the authors and their publishers did. The pick of the reviews were published, along with other short pieces, in volumes of essays, of which *From Napoleon to Stalin* was the first: five in all, and these were then quarried for two paperback volumes of 'greatest hits'.

The reviews reveal a continuing and passionate concern about Germany; between 30 January and 24 May 1946, for example, he reviewed seven successive books on the subject. Over and over again he hammered out the same messages: Hitler had not been an aberration, German liberalism had failed, Germany must be kept disarmed, an Anglo-Russian alliance was vital to contain Germany. Commenting on American proposals for the economic regeneration of Europe, he wrote that 'if the Ruhr is rebuilt, the second German War will have been fought in vain'.[79] 'I suppose I am the only person in the British Isles who still regards the Germans as the greatest danger for the future and the nation most likely to cause a third world war,' he wrote in 1949; though he diluted this assertion with a joke: 'The great historical service of the Germans was to make a united Europe, peaceful and planned, an impossibility for a long time to come . . .'[80]

His hostility to Germany was permanent. In 1950 he published a review which echoed the argument he had made seven years before to the Masaryk Society. It would be a great mistake to regret Hitler's victory in 1938, he wrote.

> He differed from the generals and diplomats in method, not aim; indeed, since he was incapable of systematic thought, he had no aim except to take advantage of the moment. The old-stylers were infinitely more dangerous to the rest of Europe, since they were more skilful in method and clear as to their intentions. They meant to establish Germany as the dominant power of Europe; and they would have done it except for Hitler's pursuit of theatrical violence. We should therefore be very grateful that Hitler broke loose in 1938.[81]

'I have always been as soft on Russia as I was hard on Germany,' Alan admitted in 1972.[82] After the War he wanted Britain to maintain friendly relations with the Soviet Union. He argued that the new Communist regimes in Central Europe, 'with all their dogmatism and violence and intolerance, will be an improvement on the old police states'.[83] And when Stephen Spender attacked Russian policy, Alan objected. 'How can you criticise our allies, who won the War for us and sacrificed I don't know how many million lives?'

A sense of obligation to the Soviet Union for its preponderant role in defeating Nazi Germany was common to many Britons at the end of the War. This was matched by a corresponding resentment of the United States. No doubt jealousy, conscious or unconscious, played a part. Those who had been born when British superiority was taken for granted were not likely to welcome its new status as the world's largest debtor nation.* And like most recipients of charity, the British resented their benefactors. For more than a year the British people had stood alone against Germany; their reward was rationing and 'austerity'.

Most intellectuals sneered at the United States. Before the War, the attitude that America was an immature civilisation was so

---

*Even in the 1930s, British payment of American loans incurred during the First World War led to resentment – "we have paid enough" – especially when Germany reneged on its reparations to Britain. The costs of the Second World War vastly increased this burden, and were still being paid off in the 1960s.

common among educated Englishmen as to excite no comment when expressed.[84] C.S. Lewis's remark was typical: 'The so-called Renaissance produced three disasters: the invention of gunpowder, the invention of printing and the discovery of America.'[85] Violent crime perpetrated by gangsters such as Dillinger and Capone appeared to bear out the notion that Americans were still cowboys in suits. Left-wingers in particular viewed the USA as 'the great beast' – though they were impressed by Roosevelt's New Deal. There was very little contact between America and Europe, and most Englishmen's idea of the United States was through the medium of Hollywood. America's self-imposed isolation from Europe, until 1941, made it seem like a vast backyard.

The War itself created new strains. Resentment of the United States, Britain's closest ally, was common to both Right and Left. The Right felt that America was 'lording it over everything', and trying to dismantle or even take over the Empire; the Left was suspicious of American capitalism. Alan later wrote that Britain was the 'poor relation' in American eyes. Despite the fact that the British behaved in a spirit of 'unreserved co-operation' during the War, there was 'never a true pooling of resources'.[86]

This prejudice against America persisted, particularly in older people. Macmillan's patronising Greeks and Romans analogy was typical. When Keith Kyle was appointed US correspondent for *The Economist*, Harold Nicolson warned him 'there is one thing you will miss in America – that is the adult mind'. Anti-Communist hysteria in America in the late 1940s only heightened the distaste. Left-wingers were horrified by McCarthyism, which seemed in its way as bad as what had happened in the Soviet Union during the 1930s. Alan was not alone in seeing the United States as a greater threat to world peace than the Soviet Union. Graham Greene – a contemporary of Alan's at Oxford and a fellow-Communist in the 1920s (albeit for a very short time) – has remarked that he would rather end his days in the Gulag than in California.[87] Like Greene, Alan retained a sympathy for the Communist dream, even if the reality disappointed.

G.D.H. Cole emerged from a taxi drawn up outside Balliol having just returned from lecturing in Chicago, and was asked what America was like. 'Just as I always knew it would be – hateful.' Alan was no less dismissive. Reviewing an American textbook, he wrote: 'Like most American writing for university audiences, he presents secondary-school material in an adult way – altogether a parable of that curious nation.'[88] In 1945 he told a radio audience that 'nobody in Europe believes in the American way of life, that is, in private enterprise: or rather, those who believe in it are a defeated party, which seems to have no more future than the Jacobites in England after 1688.'[89]

Alan himself was still a prisoner of quasi-Marxist ideology. He was sure that an unplanned economy led to chaos, and repeatedly predicted an economic crisis in the capitalist countries, particularly America, 'altogether dwarfing the crisis of the nineteen-thirties'. Russia, on the other hand, would come right of its own accord: 'Once Russia feels secure, really secure in the international field, then the demand for political liberty in Russia will, it seems to me, become overwhelming . . .'[90]

Alan believed that Russian policy was defensive, aimed simply at peace and prosperity. He wanted a 'business partnership' with the Soviet Union.[91] He welcomed the economic proposals for the socialist reconstruction of Europe put forward by the Russians at the Warsaw Conference, contrasting these with the 'wild guesses' of the Marshall Plan.[92] 'I have no sympathy with anti-Russian hysteria and think we should judge Soviet affairs with the same critical, but friendly, detachment with which we judge American affairs.'[93]

'English people don't like the idea that the continent of Europe, still less their own island, has to be the centre of conflict between Russian Communism and the American "way of life",' he said in a 1947 broadcast. 'Many English people would like England to represent the "third force"'[94] – an idea much talked about at the time, and not just on the Left. The year before he had broadcast a similar message: 'If we really are a Great Power, we are strong enough to be friendly with both [Russia and America] without choosing sides.'[95]

Events taking place in Eastern Europe made it difficult to maintain such an even-handed approach. Soviet-backed Communists tightened their grip on the countries liberated by the Red Army.

In Czechoslovakia Beneš had run a coalition government which had included Communists since elections in May 1946. In February 1948, the coalition broke apart, when non-Communist ministers, led by Ripka, resigned. For a week or so Czechoslovakia seemed on the brink of civil war. Then Beneš, fearing disaster for his country, accepted a Communist-controlled government, though Jan Masaryk remained Foreign Minister. Two weeks later Masaryk's body was found below a window in a courtyard of his own Ministry. The elections which followed ushered in a Communist dictatorship. Beneš resigned and died three months later.

Alan had anticipated a crisis after conversations with Beneš and Ripka when he stopped in Prague on the way back from holiday in Yugoslavia the previous year. He railed at the BBC: 'If your organisation was at all enterprising, you'd put me on air to talk about the Czech crisis . . . I've expected it since the autumn and probably know more about it than anyone else you are likely to get.'[96]

If Alan was shocked at these events he showed no sign of it. But a change in his thinking about Central Europe is detectable. Three months after the Czech crisis, he wrote to Wadsworth about a piece he planned for the centenary of the Slav Congress on 2 June: 'My Slav piece will be anti-Russian for a change – its theme whether east-central Europe could not manage without either Germany or Russia.'[97]

In April 1948 Alan saw Muggeridge, who taxed him with being a fellow-traveller. Alan replied that he recognised the impracticality of the position of the Socialist who believed in working with the Communists, but that even so he preferred this position to working with anti-Communists. Muggeridge said this seemed to him 'quite insane'. He wrote in his diary that Alan seemed slightly disconcerted; and Muggeridge noted enviously that he was 'very well dug into the economic system which he wants to destroy'.[98]

That August Alan attended a conference in Wroclaw, Poland. Until the end of the War Wroclaw had been part of German Silesia, known as Breslau; now the Poles had pushed the German border west, just as their own eastern border had been pushed west by the

Russians. Indeed Wroclaw was the new home for the University of Lvov, a city formerly Polish and now part of Russia. It was therefore a particularly appropriate situation for a Cold War conference. The so-called 'Congress of the Intellectuals' was not going to be a spontaneous affair; the 'delegates' would hear a series of prepared speeches, reiterating the same theme in an inexhaustible process of mass hypnosis and reaching a climax in a unanimous resolution against American Fascism. As Alan pointed out in a piece written just after the conference, uniformity and unanimity were essentials of Communist culture; and it was important to the organisers that nobody broke ranks.[99]

Unfortunately for them the British 'delegates' had been carelessly selected. All those attending sought reconciliation between East and West, but not all were fellow-travellers, like Hewlett Johnson, the 'Red Dean' of Canterbury, or Professor Hyman Levy, who dismissed as 'fantastic' the claim that the issue of intellectual freedom was of any importance. Among the British at the Congress were J.D. Bernal, Ritchie Calder, J.B.S. Haldane, Julian Huxley and Christopher Hill. Picasso was another 'delegate'. Messages of goodwill came from Shaw and Einstein.

The Congress opened on a belligerent note. The Soviet writer Alexander Fadeyev, one of the five presidents of the Congress, made a brutal speech, denouncing the 'reptilian Fascists' in the West who were plotting a new war. The Soviet Union had defeated Nazi Germany single-handed, he declared. American imperialism was to blame for all the evils of the world. His denunciation extended to the 'reactionary aggressive' elements in American culture. American films were 'trite'; American detective stories 'trashy'; American swing music 'a form of contemporary St Vitus' Dance'. 'You can see the dollar sign on all this disgusting filth,' he announced. Fadeyev's reptilian listeners particularly resented his attack on Western writers; T.S. Eliot, Henry Miller, Eugene O'Neill, John Dos Passos, even Sartre and Malraux were likened to 'hyenas' and 'jackals'. It was agreed within the British group that someone ought to respond to these slanders.

Alan got up to reply the following morning. The organisers had wanted him to submit his speech for approval beforehand, but Alan explained that he never worked from a prepared text. As a result his words were broadcast by simultaneous translation throughout the Congress, and relayed through loudspeakers in the streets of Wroclaw and Warsaw. Alan began by recalling that the Soviet Union had entered the War only after being attacked by Germany, just as the United States had done so only after being attacked by Japan. Britain and France, on the other hand, had gone to War freely on behalf of Poland, and Britain had sacrificed much to help the Soviet Union. Yugoslavia, not mentioned by Fadeyev, had lost two million men in a struggle as heroic as any. Some people in England, and more in America, now said that the Soviet Union and Nazi Germany were indistinguishable. As intellectuals, he said, we should refute such assertions. It was equally the business of intellectuals to reject, instead of repeating, wild slogans about American Fascism. Alan said he had come to the conference to look for ways of peaceful co-operation. Instead Fadeyev had produced only lies and hatred, and turned the conference into a piece of war-mongering. Alan declared that he hated all authoritarian influence, whether from Wall Street or the Kremlin. It was the duty of intellectuals to criticise the Great Powers, particularly the government of one's own country. He ended with a plea for intellectual honesty, tolerance, love and the pursuit of truth.[100]

Alan's words astonished the Slav delegates, who were quite unprepared for any departure from the Party line. Many were privately delighted. One of those present was a representative of the Czech Ministry of Information; her eyes filled with tears as she listened to Alan. Thirty-five years later she wrote to tell Alan his speech had been unforgettable; to her he was a hero.[101]

He was also very popular with the British attending the Congress. One usually enthusiastic fellow-traveller summed up the general feeling: 'Of course I did not agree with all that Mr Taylor said, but *by God, it needed saying.*' The organisers of the Congress were not so pleased. They tried to orchestrate a general resolution on which all those attending could agree. When it was clear that many of the British, French and American delegates would refuse to put their names to any motion which denounced American imperialism as the sole threat to world peace, it was watered down into a verbose jumble of generalisations. Even then Alan and a few others refused to sign; while some, including Kingsley Martin, signed but also issued a separate statement. A letter was sent from Wroclaw to the *New Statesman and Nation* signed by those who felt unable to accept the resolution there passed as the whole truth: among them Alan himself, the artist Felix Topolski, the novelists Richard Hughes and Olaf Stapledon, the journalist Edward Crankshaw and the young publisher, George Weidenfeld.[102]

Alan's defiance at Wroclaw made him famous in the West, particularly when the story was written up in the *New York Times*. 'Professor Allan Taylor' had made a 'particularly forthright' speech, the *Times* correspondent reported; moreover, he had been 'the first of the Western delegates to pick up the Russian challenge'.[103] There were pieces in British newspapers too, for example a leader in the *Daily Telegraph* praising Alan. It was written by Malcolm Muggeridge, who in his diary expressed the wish that it would embarrass Alan in front of his left-wing friends and associates.[104] In a long piece for the *New Statesman and Nation* about the Congress, Kingsley Martin remarked that Alan was quite consistent. 'In England he attacks British policy; in the Eastern Zone he attacks Soviet policy.'[105]

Alan returned from the Congress via Paris. There he called on a young woman whom he had first noticed the year before, in the audience at one of his lectures; in her honour he began his address 'Lady and gentlemen'. She had come to Holywell Ford to consult him about the possibility of doing a thesis in Russian history. Her name was Eve Crosland. Alan had been trying to impress her for some time; he had given up trying to win back Margaret. In April he had asked Hamish Hamilton whether a special page could be tipped in substituting Eve's name for Namier's on a single copy of the new edition of *The Habsburg Monarchy*: 'as you can guess I want to give someone a present'.[106] He had wined and dined her, and showered her with presents. Now he appeared before her in Paris as the champion of intellectual freedom.

Martin's piece had depicted Alan at the rostrum 'like a British bull terrier challenged to a fight by a Russian wolf'. He continued: 'Mr Taylor has a large wart in the middle of his forehead. I had the illusion while he was speaking that this had swollen and looked like an instrument of offence. The bull terrier looked like a British unicorn.'[107] This 'devil's horn' had been there for years; undergraduates had watched fascinated as Alan fiddled with it during tutorials. Now Alan, suddenly self-conscious, had it cauterised.

Mary Evelyn Raven Crosland was a tall, slim, athletic-looking woman. She was the youngest of three Crosland children, her elder brother being the Oxford don and future Labour Foreign Secretary Tony Crosland. She had taken a degree in history from Westfield College, which had been evacuated to Oxford during the War, and had afterwards done a year's postgraduate research in international and diplomatic history before teaching at a girls' school in North London. In 1947 she joined the London office of the *Manchester Guardian* as a journalist; in her letter of application she had referred to her 'passionate interest in current affairs (especially international and colonial)'. It was a clever family; her mother was a lecturer in Old French, also at Westfield College, and her father, who had died when she was still a child, a Deputy Under Secretary at the War Office, Churchill's chief economic adviser at the Cairo Conference in 1921. Eve's mother Jessie wanted the children to excel at anything they undertook, but could not believe there were others as useful as dons and civil servants.[108] Naturally Eve was flattered by the attentions of such an eminent academic as A.J.P. Taylor. She had always seemed a bit of a bluestocking; one Oxford contemporary was amused to find her doing something as frivolous as working on a newspaper, especially since a woman reporter in the late 1940s inevitably found herself covering 'soft' stories about women's lunches, and the like. Others remarked that she was highly strung. After her first interview at the *Manchester Guardian* the London editor wrote that 'she dresses plainly but well, talks fluently but has not yet acquired social ease'.[109]

Alan's friendship with Eve grew warmer as his marriage cooled. When Kingsley Martin asked him to address the Union of Democratic Control, Alan replied that of course he would, though he got in a crack: 'Its record on Germany is, I suppose, the worst in the country. It was even founded as a pro-German institution . . . Be sure to send an invitation to the M.G. and that talented young journalist Eve Crosland can come and write me up.'[110] In November 1948, after an evening with Muggeridge, he wrote to explain that 'were it not for the children, Margaret and I would no longer be living together'.[111] Early in 1949 he tried to arrange with Wadsworth for Eve to accompany him on a trip to Yugoslavia which he had planned with John Betjeman and the artist John Piper. 'She's often been a great help to me in the past, as she knows Russian and is an amateur diplomatic historian; she would make life much easier for us three impractical men.'[112] Wadsworth appeared to see through this rather flimsy deception; he liked Margaret and indicated to colleagues that he disapproved. Eve for her part was unsure whether she should go with Alan to Yugoslavia. She asked her boss, the London editor John Beavan, who ducked the issue by recommending her to ask 'a woman of the world'. Eve consulted Mary Stocks, the Principal of Westfield College; the Principal told her never to miss an opportunity. But the trip was cancelled anyway.

Alan took Eve instead to the Empress Josephine's house in Malmaison, fifteen kilometres west of Paris, which had become a museum to Napoleon. Perhaps Alan identified himself with the little dictator. Though she gave out that she was sexually experienced, Eve kept Alan at arm's length until he began to give up hope. Then she telephoned him in Oxford one day to say she longed to hear his voice. Alan rushed down to London and they spent a weekend together in Brighton, just as Dylan had done with his American girlfriend.

Robert Kee was now living in a large house in Sussex Place with his girlfriend Janetta, soon to become his wife. Alan used the upstairs as a place to meet Eve, who continued to live at home with her mother in Highgate, until she moved out into her own flat in October 1949. Alan began to introduce her to his friends. In December, for example, he took 'his girl' to tea with Muggeridge, who thought her 'pretty dumb, but better looking than before'.[113] Tony Crosland was annoyed when he heard about them. Though he was not very close to his younger sister, he felt protective of her. 'What is the college doing about Alan and Eve?' he asked indignantly.

Not long after the Wroclaw Congress Alan complained to Muggeridge about a broadcast which suggested that Soviet behaviour was a revival of the spirit of old Russia, that Russian policy remained essentially the same, whether Tsarist or Bolshevik.

> Surely it is made far worse by their being Marxists. That's the decisive thing; and it's surely dangerous to suggest that non-Russian Marxists might be easier to get along with. I'd say that, tiresome as Russians are, they are no worse than anyone else, except civilised western man; but that it is impossible to hope for honesty or compromise from a Communist. It is curious that you, a non-Socialist, should attribute Soviet vice to national character and that I should put it down to their perfectionist religion. But at bottom you have a regret for religion, and I have not.[114]

'Alan now very anti-Communist', Muggeridge noted in his diary after Alan had been to tea.[115] Reviewing a French book on 1848, Alan described the Marxist essays in it as propaganda, displacing honesty and scientific enquiry for automatic phrases recited in the manner of the medieval church.[116] He used the same metaphor elsewhere; 'Communism is a great secular religion . . . It is a great mistake to suppose that these fanatical religions can be beaten by tolerance and sympathy.'[117] Communism was 'a disease of the mind . . . there has been no peril like it since the days of militant Islam.'[118] Reviewing E.H. Carr's *Studies in Revolution*, Alan deplored the lack of moral condemnation of Communism: 'to write about evil with detachment is to be on the side of evil'.[119] He began to refer to the Communist and Russian 'oppressors' of Eastern Europe.[120] In 1950 he attended a *New Statesman* lunch with Ilya Ehrenburg, 'a violent dispute from start to finish so far as I was concerned', he reported to Wadsworth. 'These Bolshie emissaries really are poisonous – enough to turn me from being a fellow-traveller!'[121]

He advocated a 'business deal' with the Russians, not so much an agreement as a truce. More trade between the Soviet Union and the West would not only lessen tension but undermine Communism. 'Democracy will show itself even more fertile and constructive; and Communism will be shown for the barren thing it is'.[122] 'I care for intellectual freedom very deeply,' he avowed in 1951, 'and can think of nothing else which can make existence tolerable.'[123] 'The liberal intellectual must have no loyalties except to the spirit of free enquiry,' he said in a radio broadcast: 'once you begin to consider the claims of society, intellectual integrity is at an end.'[124]

But despite his mistrust of Communism, he believed the real problem in world affairs was not the Soviet Union but the overwhelming power of the USA and its inability to know what to do with it.[125] In 1949 the Yugoslavs had broken with the Soviet Union, while remaining Communist. He was especially pleased when a Yugoslav pamphlet, referring to his speech at Wroclaw, described him as 'an English reactionary'.[126] Now he returned the compliment; the best policy for Britain was that 'we should be America's Tito'.[127]

Alan's intellectual roots were never far from the surface. In 1949, for example, he celebrated the three-hundredth anniversary of the execution of Charles I with 'The Man of Blood', a piece for the *New Statesman and Nation*. 'Only those nurtured in the tradition of Radical dissent,' he wrote, 'can say: "This was the day of our victory!" '[128] This was the schoolboy who had captained the Roundheads against the Cavaliers speaking. Perhaps the most accurate summary of his politics came in a piece about de Tocqueville: 'Above all, he who loves liberty must have faith in the people. Otherwise he will, like Tocqueville, withdraw from public life and despair of the future'.[129] All rulers, he seemed to say, were suspect; only 'the people' could be trusted.

It would be a mistake to depict Alan's views as consistent, or even as moving consistently in one direction. In truth, he blew hot and cold about Marxism and the Soviet Union, for example, and what he wrote in one place might not be what he would write in another. In particular, his journalism was often distinct from his historical work. When writing a piece of popular polemic, his heart tended to rule; when writing scholarly history, his head. Often his historical enquiry would lead to conclusions which contradicted his prejudices. This is perhaps not so surprising or unusual, but in Alan it was more obvious than in most academics.

Late in 1949 Alan offered his services to the fledgling BBC Television Talks department. 'I wondered whether you ever had an opening for a lively talker on current affairs in television. As you know, I can do very nicely in impromptu discussion; and if you are ever thinking of this sort of thing, I'd be grateful if you'd think of me. I realise it is a new trade, but I'm not too old to learn it.'[130] His approach was welcomed. The Controller of Television, Norman Collins, was planning a series of television discussions, which began in May 1950. Alan appeared in the third of the series, broadcast in August, and by October, when the sixth programme was broadcast and it became weekly, he was one of a settled team which also included the MPs Michael Foot and Robert Boothby, and the 'rustic philosopher', W.J. 'Bill' Brown. 'The regular team', wrote one of the thoughtful pioneers of television, 'seemed, in combination, to provide a remarkable effervescence of wit, commonsense, intellectual honesty and political passion. Week after week matters in the news were discussed by intelligent men who seemed to be thinking independently, not merely mouthing the clichés of routine party politics.'[131]

'In the News' owed much of its character to the fact that it was presented and directed by two freelancers, Edgar Lustgarten* and John Irwin. The panel would gather at Lustgarten's flat in Albany for an early evening drink and a preliminary discussion of topics selected at the last possible moment. At 6.30, the team strolled down to the Ecu de France, a nearby restaurant, where they continued their talk over a relaxed meal in a private room downstairs. Then around 7.30 a pair of elderly Rolls-Royces arrived to ferry them to the Lime Grove studios. When the cameras had been set, and the lighting and sound adjusted, the team had another break, usually spent in The British Prince pub at the end of Lime Grove. They went on air about 10.00 p.m., for thirty minutes' live argument which was all the more spirited for the convivial build-up. Afterwards the team repaired to John Irwin's flat in Holland Park, where they listened to a sound recording of their discussion over a nightcap. Then the cars took them home.

'In the News' quickly became one of the most popular and

---

*Alan first met Lustgarten when they appeared together on the radio programme 'Your Questions Answered' in 1945.

successful programmes on television.[132]* Because there was then only one television channel, and limited hours of transmission, individual programmes were more prominent than they would become, even though the number of viewers was of course far fewer than it is today. The novelty of television ensured that those who appeared on it were the subject of intense public interest. 'In the News' would run for years, and the panellists who made up the team became national celebrities. The programme itself became news, its discussions reported in the newspapers. Alan became, in the words of the newspaper headlines, the 'TV Don'.

In July 1950 he had another skirmish with the BBC. Since the end of the War Alan had been a frequent speaker on the Overseas Service, broadcasting four or five times as often as he did on the Home Service even when he was in favour – once a fortnight by 1950. The talk that caused the trouble was for a regular series in the 'London Calling Europe' programme called 'As I See It'. The Korean War had just started. Alan condemned the United Nations intervention; for him this was another version of the old League of Nations principle: 'perpetual war for the sake of perpetual peace'. He advocated 'appeasement'; Great Britain should try to stop the fighting. The BBC refused to allow the broadcast to go out, arguing that his talk could have been misunderstood by a foreign audience which might have taken it as representing BBC policy.[133] Alan was good-humoured about this rejection, but subsequently made a fuss when it was proposed to pay him a smaller fee. He insisted on fulfilment of his contract. 'If I had been asked to give a talk in line with official policy, I should have declined; I have never done such a thing in my life . . . I don't complain of not broadcasting; these things happen from time to time.'[134]

The following day a letter from Alan condemning the war in Korea was published in *The Times*. He remarked that 'appeasement is still one of the noblest words in the language, in spite of its abuse twelve years ago; and appeasement should at all times be the object of an enlightened diplomacy.'

---

*It drew an audience of about 50 per cent of the viewing public, or 8.3 per cent of the total British population, i.e. the viewing public was then calculated as 16.6 per cent of the population.

In August the Taylors moved to London; Alan had been given a sabbatical year, which he planned to spend working in the Public Record Office in Chancery Lane. Their new home was in Park Village East, on the edge of Regent's Park, but Alan was to stay only a short while. By January 1951 he was asking Wadsworth to pass him messages through Eve; in May he and Margaret were divorced. Three weeks later he and Eve married in Kensington Register Office, with Boothby and Phil Zec, editor of the *Sunday Pictorial*, as witnesses. Boothby complimented Alan on his young bride; 'you've really done well for yourself this time'. Tony Crosland did not attend.* Alan's old *Manchester Guardian* friend, Paddy Monkhouse, also recently remarried, sent a congratulatory telegram from Manchester. Alan's reply suggested that Margaret was having some form of psychiatric care; but 'Eve is a good girl and will see me through'.

---

*Four days after the wedding Alan, perhaps encouraged by his new wife, wrote to Crosland from Eve's flat. He had heard from Boothby about Crosland's excessive drinking, and urged the young politician to lay off the drink altogether. Alan was apparently 'shaken' by Crosland's curt reply, to the effect that how much he drank was none of Alan's business.[135]

10: *In the News*

Alan and Eve travelled to Italy for their honeymoon; staying first in Alassio, and when this proved too hot and crowded, retreating across the French border, where they called on Michael Karolyi, once again living in exile, this time from a Communist regime. Then they made their way back across France to Etretat, where Alan had holidayed with Margaret and the boys four years before. Alan was gloomy. He was going back to Oxford after a year's absence, and he realised that the children would no longer be there.

They returned to Holywell Ford, which they found almost empty; Margaret had taken most of the furniture to London. It was a huge house, and now there were just the two of them to share it – except for Alan's cat Colette, which Eve disliked. She complained to Alan that she found the house cold and damp. She had given up her job with the *Manchester Guardian*, and despite Alan's efforts to push her into a career with the local press, nothing substantial materialised. She had almost no social life in Oxford. After she had been there six months she complained to Alan that not a single person had dropped in on her; Alan asked her pointedly how many people she had dropped in on. Eve was a good amateur pianist, an LRAM; Alan arranged for her to play piano duets with his colleague James Joll, but he did not like it when he thought they were getting on too well. When Alan and his new wife attended the Show of Argent, a function at which all the college silver was displayed, nobody acknowledged them, and they stood apart from the crowd. Noticing this, the Dean of Divinity made a point of welcoming Eve. She never came to the college again.

Part of the problem was Eve's shyness. But Margaret's shadow

loomed large. Family friends felt uncomfortable about this much
younger woman who, it appeared, had usurped Margaret's place.
Alan and his new wife were ostracised, or so it seemed to them; one
friend of Alan's whom he had known for quarter of a century
stopped speaking to him altogether – though this may have been
because Alan had criticised one of his books in the *Manchester
Guardian*. Divorce was still socially unacceptable in the Oxford of
1951; it was disapproved of by many who tolerated adultery or
homosexuality, and remarriage made things yet worse. 'At least I
am his wife and not his mistress,' Eve pleaded.

In 1952 Alan was due for re-election as a Fellow of the college.
Normally these re-elections are a formality, and proceed unopposed. When Alan's name came up, Godfrey Driver, an eminent
Semitic philologist who was also a devout Christian, opposed
Alan's re-election on grounds of immorality. Alan, he said, was a
'fornicator'. He also denounced Alan for writing for the newspapers, a sin almost as grave. Harry Weldon said that he had never
heard such a disgraceful attack on a colleague. When it came to the
vote, only the elderly lexicographer Onions – also a Christian –
supported Driver, and Alan was re-elected; but the affair left a
wound. Alan was hurt that more of his colleagues did not come
forward afterwards to express their sympathy or regret. Privately,
many of them hoped he would leave of his own accord.

'I have just failed to be elected a Professor (not that I applied for it),'
Alan wrote to Anna Kallin, his Third Programme producer, 'and
aren't I glad!'[1] The post was that of Professor of Modern History,
commonly known in Oxford as the 'Third Chair'.* Woodward was
the departing incumbent, and his influence may have counted
against Alan. The other outstanding candidate was Hugh Trevor-
Roper; and he had a powerful lobbyist in the person of his old
tutor, J.C. Masterman, now Provost of Worcester – the home of the
'Third Chair'. But the electoral panel was dominated by medievalists of the old school, who believed that historians should edit only

---

*The other two being the Regius Chair of Modern History and the Montague
Burton Chair of International Relations.

chronicles and for whom anything after AD 1500 counted as journalism. Taylor and Trevor-Roper were too popular for them. The Chair was offered instead to a compromise candidate, one who had not even applied and who expressed surprise at his appointment. Alan dismissed him as a 'nonentity'; 'in considering me they had scraped the bottom of the barrel, and now they've gone outside the barrel altogether'.

'Mad Maggs has bought a house in Laugharne for her and her horrors,'[2] Dylan wrote to a friend in 1951, a month after Margaret and Alan divorced. He and Caitlin had been living for the past couple of years in the house Margaret had bought for them in Laugharne, and now that Margaret was free it seems that she contemplated joining them. She rented a house there for a while, but then returned to London. Margaret was increasingly concerned to prevent Dylan from going back to America, where the money and the women were easier. Later that year she bought a house for Dylan in London, in a 'desperate hope' that he could find his bread-and-butter work in England. Caitlin had refused to spend another winter in Laugharne, so the whole family moved down to Delancey Street in Camden Town, bringing even the gypsy caravan, which they kept in the garden. Dylan wrote to one of his friends that they were moving 'to a house an insane woman has bought us'.[3]

There were plenty of pubs nearby, and Dylan took advantage of these. Camden Town drinkers became accustomed to the sight of him, and also of Margaret, searching for him from pub to pub. She seemed infatuated.

The lure of America proved too strong to resist, and Dylan set off there again early in 1952; Caitlin insisted on accompanying him. As usual they spent faster than he earned, and while they were away Llewelyn Thomas suffered the humiliation of being turned away from school because his father had not paid the fees. When Dylan returned from the second trip to America in June he was in poor health, tired and bloated from too much drinking.

Margaret was now very short of money. She had run up an overdraft of nearly £1000, and relied heavily on Alan's support. 'My husband . . . was placed in serious financial difficulties through no fault of his own,' she wrote later.[4] She concealed from him the real price she had paid for the house in Laugharne because she feared Alan's wrath; even twenty-five years later she was prepared to take legal action to prevent its being disclosed, as the truth 'would cause great upset within my family'.* When Dylan continued not paying rent on the Boat House, she talked about having to sell it; Caitlin referred contemptuously to the 'whims of our patroness'.[5] Dylan had found another rich woman to milk, Marged Howard-Stepney, and Margaret offered first to lease and then to sell the Boat House to her. Unfortunately Miss Howard-Stepney died before this transaction could be completed. The financial pressure on Dylan mounted.

Dylan went to America again in the summer of 1953, where he discussed a collaboration with Stravinsky. When he came back to Wales he was a sick man, now suffering black-outs. But he decided to return yet again to America in October, and Margaret was part of a small party that saw him off to the airport from Victoria Air Terminal. He never returned. News came from New York that he was in a coma, brought about by a combination of drink and medically administered drugs. Caitlin sent him a telegram saying 'Wait for me', and set off for the airport; Margaret was so moved that she cried. Dylan died on 9 November without recovering consciousness.

In January 1951 Alan had begun writing for the *Sunday Pictorial*. This was something new for him. The *Sunday Pictorial* was a paper for the masses, requiring lively and dogmatic journalism. Though this column lasted only a year, it was followed by a similar slot on the *Daily Herald*, which became known as 'I Say What I Please'. Now that he was a television star he was in demand as a pundit; his column on the *Sunday Pictorial* had the by-line 'A million people see and hear this man on Friday nights'. Alan's articles were short

---

*After the serialisation of Paul Ferris' biography of Dylan Thomas appeared in *The Observer* in 1977, Margaret sent a letter from her solicitors claiming the house cost only £2500, not £3000 as she herself had informed the Dylan Thomas Trustees. She asked for this to be corrected in the book.

polemics, their titles often finishing in an exclamation or a question mark, such as 'Stop This Sham!' Alan enjoyed 'writing for the proles', being known to the masses on television. His image was that of a provocative, independent champion of the people, denouncing bureaucrats and intellectuals. Soon he was writing a column almost every week. Some felt that such hack work was beneath the dignity of an Oxford academic. Kingsley Martin wrote to Alan deploring a piece he had written entitled 'Scrap These Stupid Drink Laws!' Alan replied politely but firmly:

> Of course the problem of writing for the *Sunday Pic* has exercised my mind. But I ask myself: ought I to be content with teaching ten or fifteen undergraduates at Magdalen, or even with writing for the fairly limited readers of the *New Statesman* and the *Manchester Guardian*? If Phil [Zec] gives me the chance of addressing five million people, ought I to take fright at the shade of Joad and turn it down? It is a difficult job that takes me a long time to learn; and I daresay I shall make lots of mistakes before I get better. But I surely ought to try. For my own part, I'm content if once every two months or so I can get in a piece advocating a more independent foreign policy and appeasement with Russia, but especially with China.
>
> I've written some lousy articles for the *Sunday Pic*, but curiously enough I don't think my article on the drink laws one of them. I'm quite unashamed of it. I sincerely think we should have the same liquor laws that they have in France – drink available to all at all times. I'd like to see a persistent campaign by the Left to prove that Socialists stand for liberty in personal matters – more drinking, more gambling, easier divorce, no identity cards, no passports, and so on . . .
>
> As for my academic reputation, it has gone down the drain long ago; and it has done me more harm to write for the *New Statesman* than the *Sunday Pic*, simply because academic people read the one and not the other . . .
>
> You say that serious papers will want me less. But no serious paper wants me at all as a political writer. I haven't written a leader for the *Manchester Guardian* since 1945; and I would not like to reckon when I last wrote anything for the first half of the *New Statesman* . . .[6]

Alan offered to make a bargain with Martin; if he could honestly say that Alan's reviewing for the *New Statesman* was losing its quality, he would either change his style in the *Sunday Pictorial* or end his contract with the paper. Alan denied that journalism corrupted his standards of scholarship; on the contrary, it improved his historical work, by teaching him to write faster and more simply.

Some of Alan's more purist colleagues thought his academic work amounted to little more than journalism anyway. Alan had tackled such criticism in his piece on *Diplomatic Prelude*: 'Most English historians disapprove of contemporary history and think that it is not history at all – they regard it as a form of journalism . . . The first aim of the journalist is to interest; of the historian it is to instruct – of course the good journalist and the good historian try to do both.'[7]

One reason why Alan wrote for the newspapers was to make money. He was supporting two families, three if the Thomases were included. Like most *New Statesman* contributors, he grumbled about the low rates of pay, arguing that the weekly supported working-class pay claims: 'If railwaymen, why not reviewers?'[8] Kingsley Martin was notoriously parsimonious. He felt that writing for the *New Statesman* should be a pleasure, even a privilege. His belief was that the better-off contributors need receive no more than a nominal amount; only the poorer contributors should get the market rate. Even some of his most distinguished contributors were paid by the inch; it was a standing joke that when a newly printed issue arrived, the Editor would sit in his office using a ruler to measure how much the contributors should earn.

Martin was jealous of Alan's television success. 'You only do it for the money,' he said accusingly to Alan. 'No,' Alan replied, 'I do it because I'm good at it,' though he admitted he liked the money too. Alan wondered whether his television success might not help the sales of his books. 'I suppose that you couldn't exploit my television fame by using a photograph of me in some way for publicity with my new book of essays,' he wrote to Machell. 'I suppose that viewers are not readers.'[9]

Alan's radio broadcasts on the Home Service had dwindled to an occasional appearance on 'Any Questions'. His work for the Overseas Service, on the other hand, continued, reaching a peak in the early 1950s, when his former pupil, Keith Kyle, became the producer of the 'London Commentary' programme, broadcast daily on the North American Service. Alan became extremely skilled at these five-minute talks, which went out live. Contributors were supposed to come in to the BBC half-an-hour before the broadcast so that their scripts could be approved and, if necessary, modified. Alan came in half-an-hour beforehand to *write* his script, handing it to Kyle for approval only a few minutes before going on air. He accepted any changes suggested by Kyle without demur. Though at first Kyle was alarmed by this procedure, Alan's professionalism soon reassured him. Alan wrote without hesitation, nothing crossed out. After a while he cut down the writing time to fifteen minutes.

'In the News' became a victim of its own success. Many of the discussions were about politics, and the political parties resented the prominence given to panellists who were on the fringes of their parties, or not politicians at all. The new Director of Television, George Barnes, came under political pressure to vary the team; representatives of the main bodies of opinion within the two parties should be used.* By the end of 1951 he was asking the Conservative Chief Whip, Patrick Buchan-Hepburn, to suggest names of Conservative MPs who might take part in the series. He insisted that the regular team could be used no more than once per calendar month, and often vetoed proposed speakers. The producers protested in vain against the dilution of their most effective team; but Lustgarten and Irwin had little clout. The popularity of the programme steadily diminished.

The following August Alan wrote to tell Kingsley Martin that 'the party machines have again been in operation and have as good as driven me off television. And as I have also parted from the *Sunday Pic*,† I am virtually unemployed. I am forced to write a book.'[10]

By November 1952 Alan was fed up. He was taking part in a

---

*The parties had agreed that broadcasting appearances should be rationed 6:5:1, in approximate proportion to their seats in Parliament.
†After a change of editor.

discussion with three other panellists who were all MPs, none but himself part of the original team. When one of the Tory MPs referred, somewhat confusingly, to 'you Leftish organisations', Alan interrupted: 'I am no organisation. I represent absolutely nobody, I'm glad to say, but myself, nobody nominates me, though many people try to prevent my appearance.' The discussion turned to the subject of the Rent Restriction Acts. Alan took no part in the debate, besides saying that he differed fundamentally on the issue from the Labour MP, the future Prime Minister James Callaghan. The argument became increasingly heated, with Callaghan interrupting and taunting one of the Tory MPs. Then Alan intervened. Horrified at the purely political statements being made, he denounced the politicians on the panel: 'When I was invited to take part in this programme, I thought that four individuals were to sit round the table and express their individual points of view, but this is too much like totalitarianism – except instead of there being one official party, there are two. No one seems to be allowed an individual belief.' The others were behaving like party 'automata'. He announced that he would take no further part in the discussion, and turned away from the table, his features frozen in a pout. Callaghan tapped him on the shoulder, but Alan kept stubbornly tight-lipped and silent for the three or four minutes of the programme that remained. The others continued their discussion as before. When the broadcast ended, the BBC switchboards were 'swamped' with telephone calls from viewers.

'The Sulky Don' made good copy for the press, better still when he was 'rested' after the next programme. 'I'm sacked,' he told reporters. The BBC Board of Management may have found it easier to reach this decision after reading reports of a talk Alan had given in Slough, where he had denounced the BBC as an 'evil monopoly' which held back technical development. In his *Daily Herald* column he said that television should be fun, 'but we shall never get the sort of television we want so long as it is a monopoly, run by people who think they know better than we do'.[11]

In fact Alan had been himself agitating for some time for changes to 'In the News'. In May 1952 he had written to Barnes to say that he should like to have a talk, partly to work off some grouses, partly to air some ideas. Despite my seeming irresponsibility, I worry a good deal about the use of television . . . I know how anxious you are to develop the medium, and I'd like to be useful. I have no axe to grind except of course for the enormous enjoyment I get from sometimes succeeding and sometimes no doubt making a mess of this exciting medium.

Five months later he wrote a letter to Barnes headed 'For yourself alone', recommending a new discussion programme, based on a regular team, 'which won't talk about politics or at any rate won't talk about them on party-lines . . . Of course we could talk about economics or peace and war, but purely as a matter of personal opinion and in what I might call a Third Programme spirit.' He suggested that MPs be excluded altogether: 'If you put on Mugger-idge, John Betjeman and me, you'd only need one other to make an effective team.' The following May, after he had been 'rested' from 'In the News', he returned to this idea, suggesting Isaiah Berlin, Stephen Spender – 'always ready to ramble on any subject' – or Robert Blake as possible fourth members of the team. '"In the News" was the most enjoyable experience I ever had in my life and I want some more.'[12]

In July the BBC broadcast 'Private Opinion', an 'informal' and 'intimate' 'conversation piece' recorded in the MP Peter Smithers' home. Apart from Alan the guests were Marghanita Laski, John Newsom and Mary Grieve. This was his only appearance on the programme.

Alan's relations with Eve deteriorated. They quarrelled frequently. His children were a source of tension; Alan missed them, and wanted them to spend at least some of the holidays at Holywell Ford; it was after all their home, where each of them except Giles had been born. Sebastian in particular was frequently there, being a weekly boarder at Magdalen College School. Eve was fifteen years younger than Alan; she had no children of her own and found it hard to accommodate someone else's. It did not make it easier for her when Margaret telephoned, seemingly every day, with advice or instructions. When Margaret and Alan discussed the children's needs, it was as if Margaret was still there, wife as well as mother. Alan felt that Eve's attitude was unreasonable. He continued to see Margaret, dropping in to take tea with her at Park Village. 'I'm trying to win him back,' Margaret told friends. She still referred to him as 'my husband'.* Since things were going so badly with Eve Alan saw no reason why he and Margaret should not resume 'family life' together, if only for the sake of the children. Dylan's death had removed the primary source of friction between them. In September 1952 Alan explored the Isle of Wight for a few days on his own, and decided that Yarmouth, though not as good as the Lake District, was a good enough place to spend family holidays. The sea was warm and clean, and inland there was an opportunity for long walks on the Downs. He would give up Holywell Ford, and spend the school holidays with Margaret and the children, in the snug little Yarmouth house she had found for them. In term-time he would spend one night a week, usually Saturday, with Margaret in London.

In the summer of 1953 Alan left Holywell Ford and moved into a set of rooms in the college, keeping only the little garden hut where Dylan and Caitlin had lived.† He stayed a week with Margaret in London, and then they took the children to the Isle of Wight for the summer. Eve moved to a basement flat north of Regent's Park; Alan assumed that their marriage was over. She started looking for work again; she wrote to Wadsworth and Hamilton, and applied for a job with the BBC,‡ but nothing materialised. Eve persuaded Alan to introduce her to various literary editors, in the hope that she might get reviewing work. On these occasions Alan grinned maliciously and said nothing. Friends said she spent all day in the flat reading novels. They were concerned that she seemed painfully thin. Alan felt he could not completely abandon her. He began to spend one night a week with Eve, and took her to concerts and the opera. She often accompanied him on his trips away from home.

---

*'I am not now legally married to my husband,' she wrote to Dylan's solicitor in December 1953.
†He had been renting this out to a succession of tenants. The rent was £3 with sin, £2 without.
‡She told Hamilton that she had a first-class degree. In fact her degree was an upper second.

This was the beginning of Alan's 'life in compartments'. In the week he lived the life of an old-fashioned bachelor don, inhabiting a set of three large rooms in Magdalen's eighteenth-century New Buildings, where Edward Gibbon had spent fourteen months which he later described as 'the most idle and unprofitable of my whole life'. Alan's rooms provided views both north over the Deer Park and south over the open quadrangle. He could shift between the rooms to avoid the draughts, depending which way the wind was blowing. The rooms were heated by electric radiators and two coal fires, much enjoyed by his pupils, though sometimes it was hard to stay awake. On the walls were a stuffed owl and an L.S. Lowry. The rooms smelled of stale pipe tobacco and Gauloises; Alan rationed himself to one cigarette a day. There was no bathroom: the nearest was up two flights of stairs and along a corridor. He rose very early and took a cold bath every morning, a legacy of his prep school days. Then he went out for some fresh air – in winter he would take a stroll down Addison's Walk; in summer, he took a dip in the Cherwell from the diving-board by the Fellows' Garden. Afterwards he tramped over to the summerhouse at Holywell Ford, where he cooked himself breakfast before returning to his rooms to write. One pupil whose rooms faced the New Buildings often stayed up all night working on his essays; as he gazed blearily out of his window at about six o'clock in the morning, he would often see Alan come running into the college and disappear up his staircase; a few moments later the light came on in his rooms as Alan sat down at his typewriter to work.

On Thursdays Alan left Oxford and came down to London, usually staying with Eve. Often he would spend the evening with Kingsley Martin at the Players' Club, an old-time music-hall. Friday was his day for journalism and 'In the News'. On Friday nights he would go to Margaret's house, only a few hundred yards from Eve's flat. There he would stay until Sunday afternoon or Monday morning, when he returned to Oxford.

Alan shuttled between these three homes in a succession of large convertible Zephyrs. He still drove very fast, veering recklessly into oncoming traffic, stamping down on the accelerator to engage the overdrive, sometimes forcing the cars he was overtaking to brake. Not surprisingly, he did not escape unscathed; in 1953, for example, he smashed up the car, leaving Eve with a head wound which required stitches.

On another occasion two young hitchhikers in a hurry to reach London were disappointed to be picked up by an elderly driver whom they were sure would dawdle. Their dismay only increased when Alan insisted that they wear seat belts, rarely used in those days. They were therefore unprepared for the speed at which they were transported to the capital, arriving sooner than they thought possible.

Two more jobs came up in 1953. Namier retired from the Chair of modern history at Manchester to concentrate on the *History of Parliament*, a vast undertaking which promised biographies of every known MP. It seems that Alan was offered the post as his successor; he turned it down because Manchester was too far from London. Then came a Chair in international history at the London School of Economics; it had been founded by a member of the UDC, Sir Daniel Stevenson, as part of the campaign against 'war-guilt'. Alan went for an interview, and was asked why he wanted a job in London: 'Only an hour on the train from Brighton,' he joked. The LSE Director, Sir Alexander Carr-Saunders, had a horror of personal publicity. In the 1930s LSE dons, Harold Laski in particular, had often expressed their views in public; some of their colleagues had felt this could be misinterpreted and a compromise had been reached that any letters written to the press should not give the LSE as the address. Rightly or wrongly, Alan believed that Laski had been forbidden by the then Director, Sir William Beveridge, from contributing to the *Daily Herald*, the paper for which Alan was even then writing.* He decided to take the bull by the horns, and sought reassurance that he would not be 'muzzled', as apparently Laski had been. He did not get the job. It was permissible for a don to operate on two, or even three levels, Carr-Saunders told Keith Kyle. 'But I couldn't take a man who operated on seven levels.'

---

*Kingsley Martin published a biography of Laski in the same year; this may well have been what caused him to raise the matter at the interview.[13]

A chair meant recognition and a higher salary; it would also bring a relief from teaching. Professors supervised only graduate students. The teaching load on ordinary Oxford dons in those days was heavy by comparison with those at other universities, and courses in modern history were popular. Alan might have as many as twenty pupils to pack in – until he left Holywell Ford in 1951 he often asked undergraduates to come for tutorials at nine o'clock on Saturday mornings.

In 1953, however, the History Faculty Board appointed Alan to a special lectureship, which limited his teaching to a maximum of ten hours each week. There were five of these lectureships at the disposal of the Board, and their purpose was to allow the holder more time for advanced research, lecturing and the supervision of graduate students. To guard against the tendency for such posts to be awarded on the grounds of seniority rather than merit, the Board decided in 1953 that, from that date, the lectureships should be tenable for five years in the first instance, and not more than ten years in total. One such lecturer, who had already held a special lectureship since 1949, was reappointed in 1953 on the new terms, and thus gained a windfall of the four years he had already served. This was Alan's colleague Bruce McFarlane.

K.B. 'Bruce' McFarlane was the other senior historian at Magdalen.[14] He was a very different personality. McFarlane was a medievalist, accustomed to the driest and most intricate study of rolls and other documents. He enjoyed this kind of drudgery and it became dear to him to an almost dangerous degree. He weighed his words carefully, dispensing them only in small quantities. It was said that Alan had once met McFarlane in the snow, early in the New Year. Alan asked him if he had had a happy Christmas. There was a long pause. McFarlane at last said that he had spent what he supposed might be called a family Christmas. He thought that in future he would spend Christmas in college.

Immensely learned, McFarlane published only one book in his lifetime. He could be a stylish writer, with a lively interest in 'medieval gossip'; but he could never quite bring himself to believe that his manuscripts were ready for publication. His coruscating reviews of other men's work were enough to silence them for good.

Touchy, proud, aloof, McFarlane was not an easy conversational-ist. His pupils regarded him with awe. He often referred them to obscure learned journals without any indication of where these might be found. When he died, one joked that it was like going off the gold standard; a delegation of them was supposed to have gathered outside the dead man's study before anyone could get up the nerve to enter. Not for nothing was he known to undergrad-uates as 'the Master'.

McFarlane and Alan were polar opposites. Between them arose a rivalry that from time to time erupted in animosity. This was most keenly felt by the undergraduates, for whose attention the tutors competed. McFarlane was the patron of a history essay society in the mid-1950s. One winter day the undergraduate who had founded the society asked him if he thought Mr Taylor might come and give them a paper. 'Oh yes, certainly,' replied McFarlane: 'if you pay him a fee.'

In fact Alan had established an earlier version of the same, known as the Historians' Essay Group, which met on Tuesday evenings in his rooms. The students would assemble after dinner. Alan provided Yugoslav wine – then very exotic – and an under-graduate would read his essay, followed by about an hour's general discussion of the topic. When the clock struck ten Alan would enter the conversation; it seemed to his listeners like a Rolls-Royce sweeping past.

It was not just that McFarlane and Alan occupied opposite ends of the curriculum. They had radically different ideas about what constituted history. McFarlane counted himself a Marxist, but this meant simply that he gave an economic interpretation to historical events; he eschewed any active interest in contemporary politics. McFarlane was a pure scholar; by contrast, Alan seemed like a journalist. McFarlane believed that scholars should not be tainted by any activities other than the pursuit of learning; in his study, books and papers, some of them untouched for years or even decades, covered every surface. Only when he was absolutely certain he knew all that could be said on a subject would he pronounce; and he refused to go an inch beyond what he knew.

Alan, on the other hand, kept his rooms meticulously tidy. There were no books or papers on his desk, except a Stock Exchange

Edwardian outing. Small boy Alan leans nervously against his mother's knee. Joshua Blackwell stands at the back, his wife in the black hat by his side. Their daughter Eunice is the other child seated at front.

Alan, dressed in a sailor suit, at the wedding of his uncle John to Sara Fraser. Alan's grandmother Martha Thompson sits on the left of the picture; his father Percy is the man standing on the left, and next to him stands Alan's uncle Harry, hair parted in the middle. The other child is Alan's cousin Karin.

Percy, Alan's father.

Connie, Alan's mother.

Henry Sara.

'Little Dolly'.

'Henry Sara spoke on Clapham Common . . . resolutions were passed emphasizing that a Fascist dictatorship in Germany would seriously affect the position of the working class of the whole world, and declaring the solidarity of British workers.' *Daily Worker*, 25 July 1932.

Percy Taylor and comrades at a meeting of the Preston Independent Labour Party (ILP), *circa* 1924. The table is draped with a flag emblazoned with the hammer and sickle. Note the bust of Lenin on the table and the portrait of Stalin on the wall. *Harris Museum & Art Gallery, Preston.*

Alan aged ten, Christmas 1916, a month or so before he was sent away to boarding-school.

Nature study at The Downs. Alan sits cross-legged on the right, another boy's arm around his shoulder. The Headmaster, H.W. Jones, stands above him.

'An *enfant terrible* . . . almost always the smallest, and scruffier than most of the other boys.' (p. 36). Alan in 1921, aged fifteen.

'George Clazy and I had been at school together for a long time without noticing each other. Suddenly I fell in love with him.' – *A Personal History*, p. 60. Alan grins behind the Headmaster; Clazy, on his right, looks more solemn.

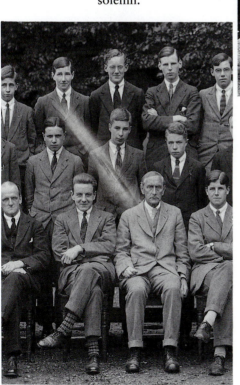

'Alan was now a figure of some substance within the school.' (p. 48). Here he sits with arms crossed next to the Headmaster, Arthur Rowntree. Note the tartan socks.

Oriel Second Torpid, 1926 – perhaps not the most impressive eight on the river. Alan sits in the middle, 'Innes' (J.I.M.) Stewart at his feet. *Provost and Fellows of Oriel College.*

Alan in his early twenties,
around the time he went to
Vienna.

Margaret Taylor in the
mid-1930s.

Alan in his early thirties,
photographed around the time
he arrived at Magdalen.
*President and Fellows of
Magdalen College.*

Margaret Taylor outside
Holywell Ford.

Robert Kee.

Holywell Ford. *Vera Collingwood.*

'A sort of middle-class Ottoline Morrell'. Margaret Taylor (fourth from left) plays hostess at Holywell Ford to Stephen Spender, Peter Watson of *Horizon*, the Hon. Gay Margesson (later Lady Charteris), and Cecil Day-Lewis.

Alan and Margaret bicycling with their sons Giles and Sebastian.

The scholar. . .

. . . and the poet. *Lee Miller Archives*.

Eve Crosland, the second Mrs Taylor. *Solo.*
K.B. 'Bruce' McFarlane, photographed around the time he arrived at
Magdalen in the late 1920s. *President and Fellows of Magdalen College.*

Yarmouth Mill, where Alan holidayed with his ex-wife Margaret and her
children. *PM Colour Library.*

Malcolm Muggeridge.

A.P. Wadsworth. *Guardian/John Rylands University Library of Manchester.*

Lewis Namier, photographed in 1942. *Elliot & Fry.*

Hugh Trevor-Roper, photographed for *Tatler* in August 1957, just after he had been appointed Regius Professor. *Mark Gerson.*

Encaenia, 22 June 1960, New Buildings in the background. The area in front was used for the Magdalen quincentenary party which Alan had organised two years earlier. *President and Fellows of Magdalen College.*

Alan in 1961, when the row over *The Origins of the Second World War* was at its noisiest. *Michael Peto/Observer.*

The 'In the News' team: W.J. Brown, Robert Boothby MP, Michael Foot MP, and Alan Taylor. The chairman on this occasion was Dingle Foot. *BBC Photograph Library.*

Alan leads the Aldermaston March, 1960. *Express Newspapers.*

The Honorary Director of the Beaverbrook Library stands in front of
Sickert's portrait of the Lord. *Observer*.

Alan in the garden at
Twisden Road, 1985.
Toby Glanville.

Eva Taylor. *Sue Adler/
Observer.*

Yearbook, which he kept by the telephone – itself unusual enough to be an object of comment. Pens were lined up ready for action. Alan launched into print without hesitation, just as he launched his car into oncoming traffic. 'Think of an essay like a leading article,' he told one undergraduate who had some experience of journalism; 'or like a concerto – statement, development, conclusion.'

'Whenever you hear or read a sentence beginning with the word "surely",' Alan remarked one evening at High Table, 'prepare yourself for ignorance or prejudice or both.' Alan enjoyed giving as good, or better, than he got. Like C.S. Lewis, he was capable of crushing another in an argument, or indeed in a review, without realising how much offence this might give. Alan often made waspish comments about his colleagues, and these tended to reach the ears of those stung. But though he adored gossip, he had none of the poisonous malice that so often afflicts dons, particularly in the 'snakepits' of the two ancient universities. His talk was entirely free of the tittle-tattle about promotion or seniority which makes up so much academic conversation. 'His pugnacity made him many enemies among those who failed to see the warmth and kindness behind the brusqueness,' wrote one obituarist.[15] For Alan, vigorous debate and free comment was fun: not so for some of his colleagues.

Alan was by now the most famous don in Britain, greatly in demand as a speaker. He had printed a postcard which read: 'Mr A.J.P. Taylor much appreciates your invitation to address the [space left to handwrite the name] and regrets that he is unable to accept it.' When Anthony Howard became President of the Oxford Union, he asked Alan to speak. Back came one of the standard postcards with a P.S.: 'Never have spoken at Union, never will'.

The score against Alan in Oxford gradually mounted. McFarlane was not the only don to disapprove of his journalism and television appearances, not to mention his wives. Nor was Alan the only one to be criticised. Not long after the War Noel Annan, for example, was told that he could never be taken seriously in Cambridge if he wrote for the *New Statesman*. No doubt there was an element of jealousy. One don who had criticised Alan for his journalism was asked to appear on television for the first time. The invitation specified the fee. 'Thank you very much for your kind invitation, which I am delighted to accept,' replied the don: 'I enclose a cheque for £35.'

Alan was the first* to publicise the term 'the Establishment', by which he meant the governing classes, or what Cobbett called the THING. 'The THING gets hold of you, even if you kick against it,' Alan lamented in the *New Statesman* in 1953. 'The Establishment draws in recruits from outside as soon as they are ready to conform to its standards and become respectable. There is nothing more agreeable in life than to make peace with the Establishment – and nothing more corrupting.'[16]

Alan was disappointed in the young people arriving in Oxford from the social classes which had not previously sent representatives to university. They were not having the effect he had hoped for. Instead of undermining the place, they simply, with dismaying rapidity, adopted the habits and points of view that had always been characteristic of Oxford. They learned to speak differently from their parents, to eat different food at different times. Alan and his more radical middle-aged colleagues found themselves in the queer position of being further to the Left than their students.[17] One of his pupils at this time was Kenneth Baker, a meritocrat then active in the University Conservative Association and a future Tory Home Secretary.

On the other hand Alan enjoyed some of the forms of Oxford, even when he disagreed with the substance. Like almost all the other atheist dons, he mumbled grace at High Table.† When Sebastian had a trial to become a chorister in the Magdalen chapel, Alan went to see the recently elected Dean of Divinity, Arthur Adams. 'My name's Taylor,' he said to the Dean, who took him to be Philip Taylor, the organist. 'I hope you give my son a good run for his money when you see him this morning.' In the event Sebastian was successful. Alan confessed to being 'enormously pleased',[18] and thereafter occasionally attended evensong in col-

---

*Henry Fairlie's piece in *The Spectator*, often credited with publicising the term, was not until 23 September 1955.
†One exception was G.D.H. Cole who refused even to pretend to say grace.

lege chapel; but once Sebastian had left, he advocated turning the chapel into a swimming-pool. There is an echo here of 'blow it up after I have come down'.

Alan would meet one undergraduate who had neighbouring rooms each morning, as the young man hurried off to Dean's Prayers at 8.30 a.m.; when his turn came to study with Alan, his tutorial hour was set for 8.30. Alan started early so as to pack all his pupils into the part of the week he spent in Oxford.

Invited to participate in a radio discussion comparing Oxbridge with the redbricks, Alan claimed to be impartial. 'In my opinion the reformers ought to have closed down Oxford and Cambridge a hundred years ago. The only reason for not doing so now is The Fleshpots – food, drink, and obsequious servants.'[19]

In 1952 the college decided to hold a dinner at which each Fellow could ask one distinguished guest. Alan invited Wadsworth. 'The list of distinguished guests', he wrote, 'starts (as invited by the President) with the Duke of Wellington – just back from the Peninsula, I suppose.'[20]

'I am sorry to say that I find I get more idealistic as I get older,' Alan told Wadsworth in 1952. 'I am always getting into disputes with Labour MPs because they no longer believe in Socialism, and I do.'[21] The following year, he poked fun at Spender's new periodical, *Encounter*; 'the culture, whose freedom we are defending . . . is getting a little thin on top'. He spotted that the principal reason for the journal was anti-Communism, long before its CIA funding was revealed. 'Communism may still be an intellectual movement in the US, though even this seems doubtful. It is dying in Europe, and has never seriously been alive in this country.'[22]

In 1953 Alan was invited to give a talk at the John Rylands Library in Manchester on 'John Bright and the Crimean War'. This was a nostalgic exercise. Alan told his listeners how he had been educated at Bright's old school, where he had heard Bright's great speeches against the Crimean War recited a score of times in the library which bore his name. In the 1930s Alan, like Bright, had opposed the notion of British participation in war overseas. Alan reminded his audience that Bright had represented Manchester in Parliament. He praised Bright as the greatest of all Parliamentary orators. Then he turned the knife.

> Once it was agreed that the Crimean War had been a mistake, it was easy to draw the conclusion that all wars were a mistake. The moral law which Bright invoked turned out to be the doctrine of the man who passed by on the other side. It was no accident that Bright, at the end of his life, had Joseph Chamberlain as his colleague in the representation of Birmingham. There was a continuity of ideas from Bright to Joseph Chamberlain and from Joseph Chamberlain to Neville. The Munich settlement of 1938 was implicit in Bright's rejection of the Crimean War.[23]

Subsequently Alan was asked to repeat this talk on the Third Programme, to be followed by a reading of some of Bright's speeches in fairly broad Lancashire. Alan promised to practise a Lancashire intonation. He asked Wadsworth to listen and tell him if he sounded authentic. Wadsworth demurred. He had consulted an old man who had heard Bright speak in the 1880s, and who remembered his speaking 'the best English in the best English way', i.e. with no Lancashire accent. This was perhaps not what Alan wanted to hear.[24]

'No truth in it whatsoever' was a typical 'AJP' phrase. Though his Lancashire accent had all but disappeared, the cadences of his speech lent themselves to opinions firmly expressed. He became dogmatic when challenged, or bored. During tutorials he would often pace up and down, and if he was bored he would take out Percy's gold watch, which he kept on a chain in the waistcoat of his corduroy suits, and look at it. If very bored, he would resort to invention, making up the names of title-holders of high office which credulous undergraduates scribbled down. One of his most outrageous claims was to suggest that Kitchener had not drowned on the way to Russia during the First World War, but simply assumed a new identity: Josef Stalin. This was why, he explained, Churchill greeted Stalin when they met in August 1942 as 'my old war comrade'. Or he would make cracks about other historians. He once said it would be fun to write a really bad book under a pseudonym. 'What name would you use?' asked an undergraduate. He snapped back: 'Hugh Trevor-Roper'.

In 1953 Alan's *Manchester Guardian* review of a history of France, translated and edited by A.L. Rowse, caused a falling-out with an old friend. Wadsworth wrote to tell Alan: 'I have had a very abusive letter from Rowse. I extract the less libellous sentences.' Alan replied proposing the following appendix to Rowse's letter: 'Every friend of Mr Rowse will appreciate this latest effusion of his pen.'[25]

A *Times Literary Supplement* piece Alan wrote in 1954 compared the condition of historical study in England unfavourably with history in France: 'If we ask what is wrong with English history at the present time we perceive a simple answer: there is not enough bitterness and dispute.' He decried 'this soft lotus-land of English history, compounded of complacency, timidity and incompetence in equal parts'. In France, he said, there are historians 'still confident they have a vital duty to perform and therefore eager to dispute over every historical question, great or small. To be an historian in France is to be a combatant, to be also a politician, and even (in the old-fashioned sense of the term) a prophet, a moral teacher.'[26] 'In France', he had written in 1948, 'a professor, and especially a professor of history, enjoys the standing and the influence of an elder statesman, and every historian assumes that his work contributes to the public life of France.'[27]

In March 1954 Alan went alone to Vienna, where he stayed with Nicholas Henderson, now a diplomat. There he encountered Donald Maclean, later notorious as a Soviet spy. Alan commented how strange it was to walk down the street without being recognised. One evening Alan telephoned his old girlfriend Else, to discover that she was now married and once again living in Vienna after spending the war in Czechoslovakia. Alan persuaded her to abandon her husband for an evening and together they went to a restaurant they had known in the late 1920s. 'It was unchanged and in our affection so were we . . . It was a magical experience . . . our

old intimacy was restored as though it had never been interrupted
. . . Then the past once more disappeared into the mist.'[28]

In 1954 *The Struggle for Mastery in Europe* was published.
Originally Alan had intended to give the book to Hamilton, but
when he was approached to contribute to the Oxford History of
Modern Europe series for Oxford University Press, then being
planned, he found the opportunity too good to resist. He wrote
apologetically to Hamilton. 'This will not be a profitable venture
for me; but I feel that, if a number of leading Oxford historians take
part, I should not stay out . . . a scholar is in a rather different
position from an ordinary writer: he has obligations to the University which cut across his literary activities.'[29]

In fact the invitation to write for the series had been issued only
with reluctance. The Oxford University Press is a department of the
university; its governing body, known as 'The Delegates', is a
committee of dons, chaired by the Vice-Chancellor. Naturally
enough, its decisions often reflect attitudes prevalent within
Oxford. When the series was first discussed in 1947 Alan's name
was on the initial list of possible authors; others mentioned
included Maurice Bowra and Isaiah Berlin. Eleven volumes were
planned, covering the period 1789–1945; some of them would be
general histories of the individual nation-states, and there would be
three volumes of diplomatic history. But before Alan or any of the
others had been approached, Dan Davin, recently appointed as the
Press's senior editor*, and A.L. Poole, the President of St John's and
the history Delegate, had agreed that 'AJPT would not do'.

Davin inhabited two worlds. A New Zealander, he had read
'Greats' at Balliol, emerging with a First in 1939 before serving in
the Army during the War, when he was three times mentioned in
dispatches. In 1945 he published his first novel. A tough, hard-
drinking literary man, Davin was attracted towards 'Fitzrovia', a
term used to describe the literary and artistic clique which gathered

---

*Davin's official title was Assistant Secretary and, later, Academic Publisher. In
effect he was chief editor for the Clarendon Press – the scholarly side of OUP's
publishing.

in northern Soho, close to Alan's wartime flat in Percy Street. But from 1945 Davin was based in Oxford, an employee of the Oxford University Press. When Dylan Thomas, himself on the fringes of Fitzrovia, arrived at Holywell Ford, Davin found him a congenial companion, one who shared his tastes for local pubs and free talk. Almost certainly Davin would have encountered Margaret; perhaps Dylan had boasted about her infatuation for him. Alan was sensitive on this score.[30]

Davin retained the fragrance of Bohemia until his retirement. In later years, when the Press aspired to change from an agreeably collegiate, somewhat ramshackle organisation into a modern, businesslike, international publisher, young executives deplored his appearance, socks worn inside sandals in the office. Yet Davin's style was as much that of don as poet. He was very much an OUP man. Far from siding with his authors, he took the view that it was a privilege to be published by the Press. A patrician attitude predominated in its Walton Street headquarters; complacency lurked in its long corridors. Davin's authors were charmed by his intelligent understanding of their work, his unbureaucratic informality, and, sometimes, his unscrupulousness; but irritated by his lack of punctuality and, seemingly, of commercial nous. 'To be published by the Oxford University Press is like being married to a Duchess,' remarked one wit: 'the honour is greater than the pleasure.'

Of course, the Press took its colour from the university. Like a party manager, Davin kept in close contact with the dons who mattered. He was known throughout all the colleges and the faculties – less so, perhaps, in the science subjects. He absorbed their opinions and their prejudices. If the Press sometimes seemed insular, even arrogant, it was a true reflection of Senior Common Room sentiment.

The Press's procedures for quality control were elaborate; the Delegates met infrequently, and decisions were often postponed. Nothing much happened about the Oxford History of Modern Europe volume until the following year, when Davin had relented enough simply to note that Taylor 'would need firm handling'. Woodward was suggested instead: 'from our point of view this has the advantage of removing AJPT from the immediate foreground'. Six months later Alan was back in the frame; Davin had agreed with the newly appointed editors of the series, Alan Bullock and F.W. 'Bill' Deakin, that Alan was 'the right man. He would not be as dangerous on this subject as he would be on Germany.' Bullock approached Alan, and received an encouraging response. In due course Davin sent Alan an offer of terms. Alan responded with a 'no nonsense' letter, dealing point-by-point in numbered paragraphs; and concluding 'I know the Press prides itself on driving a harder bargain than any other publisher; and I have agreed to your general terms. All the more reason to meet me over the details.'[31]

Davin was flabbergasted. He delayed a response for a month until he 'felt sure of not replying in a manner that would be less than ill-tempered'; meanwhile he had written to Bill Deakin, co-editor of the series:

> Words fail me for this gratuitous offensiveness . . . What exasperates me . . . is the general tone . . . We are not engaged in gypsy horse-trading, after all, and if negotiations are going to be carried on in the atmosphere of suspicion which the whole of Taylor's letter breathes, I for my part would sooner he returned to the kind of publishers with whom he appears to have been accustomed to deal.[32]

Alan and OUP were on different wavelengths. Perhaps it was fortunate that at this stage Alan introduced his new literary agent, Spencer Curtis Brown, to carry on negotiations, though the Press disliked agents on principle. Davin was disconcerted to find Curtis Brown acting for another four authors in the series, including Deakin himself. Curtis Brown had a bet with Davin that Alan would be the first to deliver. Arthur Norrington, Secretary to the Delegates and Davin's senior, commented: 'AJPT is such an infernal nuisance and timewaster that I should be glad to see him dropped from the team'; Davin described him as 'of course the most troublesome of all the authors'. After a meeting of all the proposed contributors to the series, Davin reported that Alan was the chief trouble; but 'I found that if one jumped on him fast and hard he becomes much less formidable'.[33]

Nevertheless, of the original dozen or so authors initially approached to write for the series Alan was the first to hand in his manuscript, in 1953; and the resulting book, *The Struggle for*

Mastery in Europe, 1848–1918, was published a full twelve years before the next volume in the series. (He had of course made an earlier start.) Davin admitted that Alan had shown himself an admirably efficient author. While the book was still in press the editors were seriously considering whether Alan might write another book in the series, the volume on the diplomacy of 1789–1848. 'The only embarrassment,' wrote Davin, 'might be that he would finish this also before any of the others have come up to the start line. But the prospect of this ironic result might be one of its attractions for him.' And so it proved. After Bullock had sounded out Alan, he reported back: 'A.J.P. says he is prepared to write all the volumes in the series provided that it be called Taylor's History of Modern Europe . . .'[34] This was too much for OUP to contemplate.* In 1965, by which time Alan had written another big Oxford history, his name came up again as a potential author of yet a third volume in the series, this time the volume on the diplomacy of 1918–39. 'Over to A.J.P.T' reads the note on the file, but it seems he was never asked.

Before *The Struggle for Mastery in Europe* had appeared Alan wrote complaining about OUP to Hamilton. 'I expect it will be late. They are dilatory and treat their authors with great discourtesy. For instance, they refuse to give presentation copies to certain continental scholars whom I suggested.'[36] A few weeks later he wrote provocatively to OUP's publicity department: 'I suppose the Oxford Press is too grand to think of giving a launch party for the publication of my book even though it launches a new series.'[37]

The Struggle for Mastery in Europe is the most substantial of Alan's books, the one most admired by professional historians. In intricate detail it traces the diplomacy of the Great Powers of Europe, by a comparison of the diplomatic documents. The story of the seventy years before the end of the First World War is presented entirely from the point of view of the diplomats and the foreign ministers controlling them. Everything else is in the background, or altogether invisible. Social and economic forces are ignored, except

---

*In 1957 Henry Kissinger was being considered for the same 1789–1848 volume. 'Too much on his plate' was the eventual verdict. Kissinger, of course, became the Metternich *de nos jours*.[35]

in the introduction. Wars and revolutions are dealt with only as expressions of the changing Balance of Power, not as events significant in themselves. Public opinion is generally a nuisance; the people barely get a look-in. Indeed, Alan conceded that throughout he had used terms such as 'France' or 'the Germans' to mean no more than those particular Frenchmen or Germans who happened to shape policy at that particular moment – sometimes literally two or three men.[38]

Underlying the book are two assumptions. One is that Great Powers are machines for making war, or deterring it; by definition they are in a state of constant struggle.[39] Europe has known considerable periods of peace thanks only to the 'perpetual quadrille' of the Balance of Power.* Ideas count for little in the process. In this sense *The Struggle for Mastery in Europe* – as well as Alan's two pre-War monographs – can be described as a 'conservative' history. The second premise is that after Bismarck's fall from power in 1890 there was nothing left except the alliance of the lesser Powers to restrain the German bid for hegemony on the European mainland. The 'struggle for mastery' is really the German struggle for dominance, and the struggle of the other Powers to restrain Germany, culminating in the disaster of the First World War. Until 1914 most men assumed that the Balance of Power was self-regulating, 'the political equivalent of the laws of economics. The First World War discredited the laws both of economics and of politics. The self-operating laws failed to operate.' In 1918 Europe ceased to be the centre of the world, and the new Great Powers were no longer exclusively European.[40]

Alan did not suggest that the War was inevitable. 'No war is inevitable until it breaks out.' War had threatened several times in the years before 1914, and been averted.[41]

The methodology of the book led Alan to stress the permanent factors in European history. 'Where most of Europe felt over-shadowed by Germany, she saw the more distant Russian shadow; and many Germans thought of anticipating the Russian danger almost as genuinely as others thought of combining against the weight of Germany.' It also led him to attribute national character-

---

*'That foul thing', as John Bright called it.

istics: sharp practice to the Russians, aggression to the Germans, dishonesty to the Italians, lying to the French, hypocrisy to the British.[42]

Among the details of the diplomatic ebb and flow are some crackling epigrams and typical Taylor paradoxes: 'what men think is more important in history than the objective facts'; the 'attribution of unworthy motives . . . is characteristic of the intellectual in politics'; 'the Cabinet was resolute for inaction'; 'mutual fear, not mutual aggression, caused the Crimean War'; 'colonial expansion was . . . the result of weakness, not evidence of strength'; 'Germany and France were involved in an auction for Russia's friendship; an auction in which each wished to avoid bidding'. And so on.[43]

No prospectus for the series had been issued, and some reviewers regretted the strict concentration on diplomatic history. Nevertheless most of them praised the way Alan had not only mastered an enormous quantity of detail but also kept his eye on the ball, in the sense of presenting the major developments of the period clearly to his readers. This favourable opinion was not unanimous. W.E. Mosse, writing in the *English Historical Review*, deplored the mixing of opinion and fact; 'its general tone is iconoclastic rather than authoritative'. This was a common reaction to Alan's work. 'All too often,' Mosse went on, 'real flashes of insight are marred by Mr Taylor's straining after effect; time and again commonsense and accuracy are sacrificed on the altar of the neat epigram, the clever paradox or simply the memorable phrase.' (This reviewer then fell back on a list of typesetting errors, always the last resort of a pedant.)[44]

Several of the reviewers compared the book to the American historian William L. Langer's work on the same period, which, they agreed with Alan, was too sympathetic to Germany. Langer, it will be remembered, was a fellow-pupil of Pribram's in 1920s Vienna. Alan had used the bibliography to attack the 'Germanic age of history-writing which is ending'.

The *Grosse Politik* was a great political stroke. It was not the least of the factors which made possible Hitler's destruction of the Versailles system. In the decisive years when interest in the origins of the First

World War was high, it held the field alone; most works of diplomatic history are still based on it . . . Perhaps the version of European history, created by seeing everything through German eyes, will never be wholly eradicated.[45]

The bibliography to *The Struggle for Mastery in Europe* begins with a lively essay. 'All sources are suspect,' Alan wrote; 'all politicians have selective memories; and this is most true of politicians who originally practised as historians.' He discussed the limitations of printed sources, and the inequity of governments making sources available to some but not others. But the historian must do the best he can. 'If he waited until he possessed all the evidence, he would never write at all – a doctrine favoured by some scholars.'[46]

Alan's own verdict on his *magnum opus* was to describe it as 'a fascinating recital of diplomatic episodes, each chapter suited to appear as an article in a learned journal and adding up to an unreadable book'.[47]

Shortly after publication of *The Struggle for Mastery in Europe* Woodward, who had been knighted in 1952 and was by this time based at the Institute for Advanced Study in Princeton, wrote to OUP expressing 'great surprise' at seeing a statement in the preface that he had 'scrutinised' the manuscript; he did not remember having seen it, and asked the Press to 'correct this wrong impression'.[48] Davin took this up with Alan. Woodward's complaint 'delights me more than I can say', Alan replied. He explained that Woodward had seen and commented on an earlier manuscript of about a hundred thousand words which he had written during the War and which had become incorporated into the Oxford History of Modern Europe volume.* He offered to write to the *Times Literary Supplement* withdrawing 'my acknowledgement, though not my thanks'.[49]

This was not enough for Woodward, who sensed a chance to humiliate Alan. In a ten-page, handwritten letter, he threatened to

---

*The Struggle for Mastery in Europe is about 250,000 words.

instruct a solicitor if a full and public retraction was not made and the acknowledgement deleted.

> For the last seven years I have had what I can call only a long series of malicious attacks – directed also against my colleague Rohan Butler – from Taylor in regard to the editorship of the *Documents on British Foreign Policy, 1919–39*. These attacks have gone far beyond reasonable criticism – to which of course I do not object; in the earliest and worst of them, I had to insist on a public withdrawal of personal allegations against Butler and myself, and, if I had not had this withdrawal, we should have taken legal steps to get it. The attacks continued, though they now keep outside (sometimes not very far outside) the range of slander.[50]

Alan bristled when Davin suggested that the Press would be forced to withdraw the acknowledgement.

> I will not tolerate demands. It is still not clear what he objects to. Is my name so discredited that a mere suggestion of acquaintance with me is libellous? Is Woodward afraid of being thrown out of the United States because of guilt by association with me? . . . You really must bear in mind [he wrote to Davin] that I am an author of yours just as much as Woodward; and you have no right at all to doctor my text or even to suggest doing so without my express permission.[51]

The affair rumbled on for two months. The Delegates, caught in the middle, refused to reprint the book until the dispute had been resolved. Woodward and Alan refused to communicate with each other directly. Eventually Alan agreed to withdraw the acknowledgement from subsequent printings.

Another person acknowledged by Alan as having scrutinised his manuscript – less controversially – was Nicholas Henderson. It was typical of Alan to seek the views of someone outside the academic world. He realised that Henderson, as a professional diplomat, could offer a special insight into diplomatic history, beyond the experience of ordinary scholars.

In a Third Programme talk on the outbreak of the First World War Alan stressed its moral impact, 'the thing that made it difficult for men to think rationally about it'. It came after a longer period of peace than any known in the recorded history of Europe. The resulting shock made it imperative to discover the causes of the War; and the controversies over the origins of the First World War helped to bring about the Second.

'We like to think that history runs only one way, that great events have great causes,' he wrote later. 'The First World War changed the destiny of civilisation; therefore we believe that its coming was long-announced. It would be humiliating to admit that the outbreak of war was an accident.'[52]

In his talk he traced the arguments about the origins of the War, questioning whether what happened was inevitable. On 28 June 1914, for example, all six assassins at Sarajevo missed their mark; the Archduke Franz Ferdinand was shot only because his driver had taken a wrong turning and stopped, enabling Princip to step on to the running-board and correct his earlier mistake. Great events did not necessarily have great causes. If there was any one single reason for the War, Alan argued, it was the Schlieffen Plan, which determined that Germany must knock out France quickly before turning with all its strength against Russia. 'It made certain that any war in Europe must be a general war – it could not be localised; and it also made certain that, once Germany began to mobilise, war was inevitable.'[53]

In May 1955 Eve discovered she was pregnant. This was a shock to Alan, who had believed her unable to have children. He felt committed to Margaret, even though he was no longer married to her. Now he felt committed to Eve too. He took the firm line that he must lead a double life, for the sake of the children of both marriages. With Eve's mother he bought a house in East Finchley for Eve and his second family; and Margaret bought a house in St Mark's Crescent, close to Primrose Hill, for his first. Alan and Margaret sold the house in Yarmouth and bought instead a large tidal mill outside the town overlooking the sea. In December Eve gave birth to a boy, whom they named Crispin. Alan agreed that if she was going to have a child she should have more than one, and another boy, Daniel, was born twenty months later.

'Marx would rank as the most unattractive character in nineteenth-century history,' Alan had written in 1948, 'were it not for Bismarck, who had the same repellent qualities even more intensely.'[54] Nevertheless he agreed to write a life of Bismarck when invited to do so in 1953 by Knopf, the American publisher.* Knopf was at that stage a husband-and-wife concern, and Blanche Knopf had been courting Alan for some time. Five years before she had rather clumsily declined an opportunity to publish an earlier work of his in America. 'Your writing is of such a high quality', she gushed, 'that I fear we would have difficulty in finding a market for *The Habsburg Monarchy* here.'[55]

He sat down to write the book while on holiday with Margaret and the children in the Isle of Wight. It was to be a brief summary, using nothing but printed sources: later he admitted that he had never seen an original document in Bismarck's own handwriting. As he progressed he was embarrassed to discover that he was presenting Bismarck as a moderate, pacific statesman and an attractive character. In fact he 'fell mildly in love' with Bismarck. He explained afterwards that he had been suddenly captivated by events and swept into unexpected waters. 'Historians often have this experience, and very exciting it is, though frightening if you are not used to it. The facts get up, hit the historian on the head, and make him go where he did not intend to go at all.'[56]

Alan's conversion was not so sudden as he later made out. One quality Alan disliked especially was humbug; Bismarck too had a profound contempt for political moralising. In a 1950 piece entitled 'Bismarck's Morality' Alan had celebrated this quality: 'Bismarck did not lack morality; what he lacked was uplift. He could not make his voice quaver with unselfish zeal, as Gladstone's voice quavered when he occupied Egypt . . . When men dislike Bismarck for his realism, what they really dislike is reality.'[57]

Alan conceded that Bismarck aspired to control events, and was prepared to go to war to achieve his ends. 'But Bismarck's planned wars killed thousands; the just wars of the twentieth century have killed millions.'[58] What distinguished Bismarck from other politicians, particularly other German politicians, was his moderation.

---

*Hamish Hamilton published the British edition.

'His only object was to maintain the peace of Europe. Those who admire this call it operating the Balance of Power; those who do not, condemn it as dishonest jugglery.' And Bismarck had been supremely good at what he did; as one professional to another, Alan could not but admire 'the undisputed master of the diplomatic art'. Bismarck had that essential quality of the significant figure, Alan had written in 1950: 'he can be made to sparkle whichever way you look at him.' Even in 1948, Alan had thought of Bismarck as the lesser evil. 'The history of modern Europe can be written in terms of three titans: Napoleon, Bismarck and Lenin. Of these three men of superlative political genius, Bismarck probably did least harm.'[59]

Alan poured scorn on those who saw Bismarck as the evil genius behind Germany's bid for mastery of Europe. Far from encouraging this process, Bismarck had restrained it. The fact that he had made her strong enough to contemplate a general war did not mean that he planned such a war. 'The future is a land of which there are no maps; and historians err when they describe even the most purposeful statesman as though he were marching down a broad highroad with his objective already in sight.' Bismarck had been credited with profound foresight where there had been only a quick instinctive response to events.[60]

Alan's enthusiasm for Bismarck went beyond mere approval of his politics, however. Bismarck for him was of all the great public figures of the past the one whom it would be most rewarding to recall from the dead for an hour's conversation. Alan admired him as a master of German prose; and as a father who gave his children the affection he had been denied by his own mother. Moreover there was something in Bismarck which reminded Alan of himself. Alan depicted Bismarck as the product of an easy-going, slow-witted father and a mother with a sharp, restless intellect, who, denied an intellectual life of her own, centred all her hopes on her sons. 'She gave her children encouragement without love. She drove them on; she never showed them affection.' Bismarck was not grateful that he had inherited her brains. 'He wanted love from her, not ideas; and he was resentful that she did not share his admiration for his father. It is a psychological commonplace for a son to feel affection for his mother and to wish his father out of the way. The results are more interesting and more profound when a son, who takes after his mother, dislikes her character and standards of value. He will seek to turn himself into the father with whom he has little in common, and he may well end up neurotic or a genius. Bismarck was both. He was the clever, sophisticated son of a clever, sophisticated mother, masquerading all his life as his heavy, earthy father.' Bismarck had a horror of feminine cleverness.[61]

Bismarck was an instant success, outselling all Alan's previous books on both sides of the Atlantic. It was equally popular with the reviewers. Harold Nicolson, for example, enjoyed his irreverence and his 'sharp snaps of paradox'. Michael Howard found his work 'as stimulating as champagne . . . how refreshing it is to read a historian who is not afraid of patterns, epigrams and judgements!'[62]

In his biography of Bismarck Alan had attempted to show that statesmen rarely work to a preconceived plan; the best or worst intentions were constantly thwarted by chance occurrences or misunderstandings. Arguably, this was a more realistic view of how politicians behave in practice than the grand master-plans sketched by politicians in their memoirs and confirmed by historians anxious to see a pattern in otherwise random events. In 1955 Alan wrote a substantial essay on Hitler's seizure of power.* He argued that there had been no seizure of power in 1933, when Hitler became Chancellor. The path to dictatorship had lain through intrigue; and was possible only because of the supine posture of democracy in Germany. At times the path was blocked, and Hitler could make no progress until a chance event, like the burning of the Reichstag, enabled him to move forward. Not until 1938 did he finally concentrate all the powers of the state into his own hands. Far from having any preconceived plan, Hitler took opportunities as they came.[64]

Alan's instinctive direction was against the grain. His guiding principle was *je suis contre*. Orthodoxies were there to be chal-

---

*The piece originated in a Unesco conference on Fascism held in Monte Carlo, the 'crackpot idea' being that 'next time we should recognise it in advance'.[63]

lenged; consensus was next to complacency. As a debater, he
anticipated the arguments of his opponents. In his writing, he
delighted in proving himself wrong. Thus he would tend to latch on
to evidence which weighed against his own political prejudices. He
had a love, some said an excessive love, of paradox; he delighted in
constructing historical sandcastles and then kicking them down
again. 'In private life I am an English radical and a socialist,' he
wrote in the introduction to the German edition of *Bismarck*: 'as an
historian my only aim is to discover the truth about the past.'

After the 'Sulky Don' episode, Alan was rested from 'In the News'
for nearly a year. Then he was brought back, but only for a handful
of appearances, the last in December 1954. After that he would not
be seen on BBC Television for another six years. The pressure on
the BBC from politicians continued, and Barnes continued to defer
to them in the nomination of speakers to appear on the programme.
Nobody lobbied for Alan except Lustgarten and Irwin; Alan was
useful not merely as a member of the team, argued Lustgarten, but
also as an irritant. But Alan's champions were themselves on the
way out. Barnes had decided that such a sensitive programme could
no longer be trusted to men not employed by the Corporation. In
December their contracts ran out, and were not renewed. They
began planning a rival programme to appear on commercial
television, provocatively called 'Free Speech', with the old team as a
permanent fixture. The idea found a warm reception from Norman
Collins, Vice-Chairman of the new Associated Broadcasting Company (later to become ATV), who had initiated the programme
when Controller of BBC Television. After his resignation Collins
had become a central figure in the campaign to end the BBC's
monopoly – it was said that he did more than any other single
individual to bring commercial television to Britain.[65]
   It is difficult now to imagine the distaste with which the prospect
of commercial television was viewed. The Great and the Good were
almost unanimous in their disapproval. A National Television
Council was formed to resist commercial television, with Lady
Violet Bonham-Carter in the chair; Vice-Presidents included E.M.

Forster, Lord Beveridge, Professor Julian Huxley, Sir Harold Nicolson and Bertrand Russell. They were supported by two Archbishops and fourteen Vice-Chancellors, including the Vice-Chancellors of Oxford and Cambridge. The Labour Party opposed the bill to legalise commercial television, and Attlee told a miners' rally that if the Conservatives handed over television to private enterprise, Labour would take it back.

Alan took an active part in the campaign *for* commercial television. He became Vice-President of the Popular Television Association – other Vice-Presidents included the England cricketer Alec Bedser and the actor Rex Harrison – and his presence undoubtedly lent intellectual credibility to what otherwise might have seemed a low-brow and self-interested pressure group. Alan depicted it as a struggle against respectability, for 'the freedom of the mind'. Under George Barnes, 'In the News' had become 'a balanced forum of orthodoxy'; the BBC, he said, was 'highly tolerant in whatever does not matter'.[66] His *Daily Herald* column frequently mocked 'that ridiculous farce, the British Broadcasting Corporation'; commercial television, he said, had put the monopoly in a fright.[67] After one such attack Barnes, now Sir George Barnes, complained to Alan that 'your typically rude comment is based on a total inaccuracy'.[68] Alan became a *bête noire* within the BBC. Internal BBC memoranda reveal how the resentment persisted; several years later there are references to 'blasting' Alan and 'giving him HELL'. Senior BBC executives began to consider whether it was right to continue to offer him broadcasting opportunities in sound.[69] Alan was broadcasting much less often anyway – between 1956 and 1961 he gave only six radio talks. The nature of radio broadcasting was changing, with a shift away from talks towards current affairs. The Third Programme split in two, and there was no longer the same demand for speakers.

Commercial television began on 22 September 1955. Three days later the first 'Free Speech' went out on ITV. Back in the summer Alan had written to tell Wadsworth that the 'old firm' was coming back: 'commercial TV justified'. 'It will be very nice to see you advertising detergents,' Wadsworth replied, 'giving demonstrations, I suppose.'[70]

In 1954 Alan had written excitedly to Wadsworth to tell him the 'amazing' news that he had been made Ford's Lecturer for the academic year 1955–56. It was a prestigious appointment. Recent Ford Lecturers had included Bruce McFarlane and Richard Pares and, somewhat earlier, Lewis (Sir Lewis since 1952) Namier. The main duty of the lecturer was to give six lectures in the Hilary term, on a subject of his choice within the field of English history. Alan told Wadsworth that he inclined towards 'Dissent in Foreign Policy', a subject which Bullock had suggested, and one Alan had studied briefly before going to Vienna in 1928. He asked Wadsworth for help or suggestions. 'It really is the most exciting thing that ever happened in my life. And yet, if I were asked to choose whether to be Ford's Lecturer or to return with the old team to IN THE NEWS, I'd hesitate. That no doubt is why some people wouldn't have me as a professor.' Wadsworth wrote back to congratulate him, and offered his thoughts on the subject.

> What I suppose you mean is the nature of the opposition to Government policy at particular times. And since it largely concerns the same people it would be English Radicalism and Pacifism against the fashionable notions. After Bright and Cobden in the Eastern Question there would be the anti-Imperialists, the pacifist Radicals of 1908–14 (including Persia) and so on. You could probably find some guiding thread although I should find it rather a matter of ingenuity.[71]

In the eyes of some it was a strange subject to choose. By its nature it was possible to work entirely from printed sources, pamphlets, speeches in Parliament, and so on – the kind of sources which Namier had dismissed as irrelevant. Alan proposed to tell the story of dissent in foreign policy from Charles James Fox to Arthur Greenwood, a span of 150 years. By the normal standards of such lectures the coverage would be thin and sometimes the thread would be tenuous. 'I don't think you'll like my Ford Lectures which will be a relief to all concerned,' Alan wrote to Trevor-Roper.[72]

At the beginning of 1956 Alan published another review article in the *Times Literary Supplement*.

Forty years ago . . . historians set out to write the history of international relations purely from the Foreign Office archives. More important, they claimed to be able to write about contemporary events with as much detachment as they had written about more distant periods. Their claim may have been justified. But it would be foolish to pretend that their sudden interest in contemporary history was detached and 'scientific'. It was a political interest, forced upon them by events and particularly by the event of the First World War. The twentieth century would have shown less concern with diplomatic history if the Bismarckian peace had endured. The diplomatic history of our time has always been a study of war origins, by no means to its advantage.

Historians seek to be detached, impartial. In fact no historian starts out with his mind a blank, gradually to be filled by the evidence . . . The historians of the early twentieth century had lived through the First World War; and nearly all of them lamented it. Their reactions took different forms. German, and to some extent French, historians were anxious to prove that their Governments had been right. British and American historians were anxious to prove that their Governments had been wrong. Soviet historians were a class apart. They were delighted to distribute the blame among 'imperialist' Governments, the old Russian Government most of all.

Alan then traced the history of the published documents. The years between the peace settlement and Hitler's victory were the great days for the 'pure' diplomatic historian. 'Men wanted to understand the contemporary world; and historians assured them they would do so if all diplomatic secrets were "revealed".' The most successful of the publishing ventures inspired by this desire was the German; and 'the "received idea" of the world before 1914 still rests on *Die Grosse Politik*, though this origin is forgotten'.

The results of all this disclosure were disappointing. For the most part it confirmed what men thought already. Perhaps historians were asking the wrong questions; attention turned away from diplomatic documents towards the more profound forces which shape the affairs of men. 'Pure' diplomatic history was in retreat. Moreover, in the modern age statesmen no longer played by the rules. Hitler and Mussolini had contributed to the depreciation of diplomacy. During the War itself, and the Cold War period that followed, diplomacy seemed of little moment. Yet it had been still possible for Namier to write a masterpiece on the outbreak of the Second World War. Diplomatic historians would have to learn new tricks, but there remained a place for them.[73]

Taylor's Law held that 'the Foreign Office knows no secrets'. This was a *double entendre*. On the one hand, Alan maintained that the Foreign Office knew little, and understood less, of what was going on abroad; on the other, that it disguised its ignorance by closing its archives to historians for absurdly long periods. When the archives were opened, the cupboard was bare – historians found they knew almost all of it already, and embarrassing secrets seemed not to have been filed. Alan liked to say that all official secrets are in print; after 1950 he did very little archival work.[74]

Alan's Ford Lectures were his most virtuoso performance. They were held in the largest hall of the Examination Schools, which then* could seat almost a thousand; even so, the hall was packed and listeners had to get there early to be sure of a place. As usual, he had decided to give them without notes. But it was one thing giving routine lectures to undergraduates without a script; quite another giving the Ford Lectures, with most of the History Faculty present. He prepared carefully, and had written a draft beforehand which he showed to the Third Programme producer who proposed to broadcast the lectures afterwards.[75] His son Sebastian, then a boarder at Magdalen College School, was with him in his rooms in the half-hour before he gave his first talk. Alan's confidence crumbled: 'I can't do it, I can't do it,' he moaned; 'the biggest mistake of my life.' Sebastian sustained him; together they walked down to the Examination Schools. He was a little late. The doors were already closed on an expectant full house. Alan hurried in, and climbed up on to an empty stage. There was no microphone, no lectern. He turned to face the audience, and there was a gasp of surprise as the watchers realised he was going to speak without notes. He began, in short, perfectly constructed sentences. 'Occasionally he pulled a postcard from his jacket pocket, and read out a quotation: a passage from Bright speaking to the House of

---

*Fire regulations have since reduced its capacity.

Commons, a piece of soaring rhetoric by Gladstone at Midlothian. They were more than quotations. For a moment, the lecturer almost became Bright or Gladstone. The voices, the gestures, the timing, the emotional power and the reciprocal relation created between audience and performer were those of a great actor. It was a histrionic masterpiece.'[76]

The content was more controversial. 'Many of us are very disappointed in the Ford Lectures, and indeed in the Ford Lecturer,' commented McFarlane. Alan himself wrote that the lectures were a 'gesture of repentance' for having recently written a substantial volume of respectable diplomatic history.* In that volume he had written of 'the British' as synonymous with the few members of the Foreign Office who happened to concern themselves with the topic in question. Now he would lecture on 'The Other Foreign Policy', the policy advocated by the Dissenters. Who were they? To Alan, dissent was too normal and too sensible to demand explanation. But for the sake of his listeners, he defined dissent by analogy with religion.

> A conforming member of the Church of England can disagree with Bishops and, I understand, often does. A Dissenter believes that Bishops should not exist . . . A man can disagree with a particular line of British foreign policy, while still accepting its general assumptions. The Dissenter repudiates its aims, its methods, its principles. What is more, he claims to know better and to promote higher causes; he asserts a superiority, moral or intellectual.

The Dissenters, distinguished by generous emotion, rejected the notion of the Balance of Power. They rejected 'foreign policy' itself. 'No foreign politics!' was their rallying-call.[77]

The Dissenters were the Englishmen whom 'I most revere'. Indeed they were Alan's spiritual ancestors. But they did not escape criticism in his lectures. The Dissenters had championed German claims against the Versailles settlement; and Hitler had advanced to a mounting chorus of dissenting applause. The opposition to Munich had come from the high-minded and the respectable – men

---

*i.e. *The Struggle for Mastery in Europe*.

like Namier – not from the Dissenters. The hero of Munich was Duff Cooper, not Attlee or Cripps or Pollitt. Indeed, Neville Chamberlain himself was a Dissenter gone sour.[78]

The Ford Lectures were both an affectionate tribute to Alan's intellectual forefathers, and an indictment of their inadequacy. They encapsulated both his intellectual origins and his revolt against them. It was a very personal exercise, perhaps all the better for it. Small wonder, then, that *The Troublemakers*, the published version of these lectures, became his favourite book.

The subject gave Alan plenty of opportunity for sideswipes at his colleagues. Men 'persist in having ideas and ideals, despite the exhortations of Mr Trevor-Roper and Professor Pares and Sir Lewis Namier'. He ridiculed the *History of Parliament*.*

> When I heard of the project, I couldn't help reflecting that a History of Parliament existed already, at least for more modern times. We call it *Hansard*, or – more grandly – *Parliamentary Debates*. No doubt the accumulated biographies will be of much interest to the social historian . . . But the history of parliament is to be found in what members heard and said, not in what they were.[79]

The Troublemakers is exhilarating to read; memorable phrases lie scattered on almost every page. Even when it does not convince, it stimulates. Perhaps it shocked his audiences in the Examination Schools. Alan was very disappointed about the volume of applause. Eve telephoned Raymond Carr and asked him if he would bring along people to clap.

Alan remained on very good terms with Hamish Hamilton. They began to address each other as 'Alan' and 'Jamie'. By 1956 their relations were good enough to survive the catastrophe of a lost typescript. Alan never kept copies of his typescripts, delivering them to his publishers in person. This he had done with his third volume of essays, *Englishmen and Others*; and when the printers

---

*Harold Macmillan too was sceptical about the *History of Parliament*, at least from the commercial point of view. On 10 January 1952 he scribbled a note to his son Maurice: 'Have *nothing* repeat *nothing* to do with this project.'

announced that the typescript had been lost, Hamilton was forced
to grovel. 'Don't worry,' Alan replied. 'These things happen; and I
never worry over past accidents . . . now that I reflect I am rather
glad. I was wondering how I was going to occupy the summer
vacation. Now I know all right!'[80] 'Very nice of him!' wrote Roger
Machell on the letter. Six weeks later the incompetent printers
found the typescript anyway.

In the preface to the book Alan had defined himself. 'I am not a
philosophic historian. I have no system, no moral interpretation. I
write to clear my mind, to discover how things happened and how
men behaved. If the result is shocking or provocative, this is not
from intent, but solely because I try to judge from the evidence
without being influenced by the judgements of others.'[81]

Alan had ceased to believe in Progress.[82] The historical figures he
depicted sympathetically were often Tories, such as Salisbury or
Disraeli, and he had a contempt for Gladstonian high-mindedness,
which to him was humbug. Reflecting in the *New Statesman
and Nation* on J.A. Hobson, he wrote that Hobson and Brailsford
were

> our sort. We think like them, judge like them, admire their style and
> their moral values . . . Yet . . . they were wrong . . . They expected
> reason to triumph . . . It is the high-minded and inspired, the
> missionaries not the capitalists, who cause most of the trouble.
> Worst of all are the men of power who are missionaries as well.[83]

In July 1956 Alan wrote to tell Wadsworth that he had been thrown
off the *Daily Herald* at twenty-four hours' notice. 'As a compensation of a sort I have been elected a Fellow of the British Academy!
A farce indeed.'[84] Fellowship of the British Academy, then limited
to 150, is the highest honour the academic world can bestow on the
historian. In the humanities and the social sciences the Academy is
the equivalent of the Royal Society.* Alan's election had been
initiated by G.N. (since 1953, Sir George) Clark, Alan's longstand-

---

*In 1965 he wrote to Kathleen Tillotson to congratulate her on being elected to
'this absurd institution'.

ing patron, and Sir Charles Webster, whom Alan had first met at a conference in Paris to mark the centenary of the 1848 revolutions. They wanted more modern historians to balance the medievalists in the Academy, and elected E.H. Carr, an historian much admired by Alan, in the same year. Galbraith, the Regius Professor, also supported Alan's election, partly because he admired the bibliography in *The Struggle for Mastery in Europe*, but partly too because he disliked Trevor-Roper and was anxious to prevent him becoming his successor when he retired the following year. Making Alan an FBA would advance Alan's claim to the Chair in preference to Trevor-Roper.[85]

'If British policy ever reached its goal of a federation of Arab states,' Alan had written in a letter to the *Manchester Guardian* during the War, 'the result would be disastrous; for the first aim of this federation . . . would be to deprive us of all control of the Suez Canal.'[86] On 26 July 1956 the 'disastrous result' occurred, when Colonel Nasser, the Egyptian President, nationalised the Suez Canal Company.

Nearly forty years later it is hard to appreciate the uproar Nasser's action caused. The Left thought of the Suez Canal as an international waterway; the Right thought it belonged to Britain. The British Government prepared for war, supported, it seemed, by the Labour opposition and even by the *New Statesman and Nation*. Indeed it was Hugh Gaitskell, the Labour leader, who compared Nasser to Hitler and Mussolini in the House of Commons on 2 August. There was much wild talk about 'appeasement' on all sides.

Alan's instincts were that this was all claptrap. He turned the argument on its head. At a meeting of the Movement for Colonial Freedom at Caxton Hall in London, Alan compared the British Government's planned aggression against Egypt over the Canal with Hitler's attack on Poland over Danzig. Left-wingers who had condemned the Germans for not resisting Hitler had a chance to stand up and be counted. Prepare for war resistance, he urged. Plan sabotage against British aggression. 'It was', he said later, 'one of my good speeches.'

Before he went in to speak, Alan had encountered Kingsley Martin, 'lurking outside like a clergyman hesitating whether to go into a brothel'. Alan told Martin he was going to take a stand against British aggression, and persuaded him to come in and hear what he had to say.[87] The next morning Martin charged up the stairs of the *New Statesman* two at a time. He bustled into his office and rang bells. 'Tear up that leader!' he ordered a group of his colleagues accustomed to these dramatic changes. 'This is the Boer War all over again' – another of Alan's analogies made the night before – 'and we are going to fight the British Government and its plans for aggression.'[88]

Alan was excited too. In the Isle of Wight he informed his assembled family that he might be ruined and sent to prison. He told his son Giles, then doing National Service in the Army, that it was his duty to sabotage the preparations for war, or at least to refuse to participate in them. 'I thought that the Boer War had come again and that we faced a long period of unpopularity, persecution and perhaps imprisonment,' he wrote later.[89]

Two days after the Commons·debate, Alan wrote to Wadsworth congratulating him for his line on Suez. 'The Labour Party, I think, must be raving mad,' he said. 'They would build up a great triumph, at the risk of some present unpopularity, if they opposed the whole lunatic business.'[90] Michael Foot was then editor of *Tribune*, and he commissioned Alan to write a thundering piece blowing away the smokescreen of 'international control' of the Canal. 'We allow ourselves to be hypnotised by the blessed word "Internationalism",' Alan wrote. 'No war for national interests! That's easy. But war, or at any rate sanctions, for the international control of the Canal. How idealistic and romantic that sounds! . . . If we want to practise internationalism we should do it with our own property not with that of others.' He suggested that Britain might begin by handing over Singapore and Gibraltar to international control.[91]

When Alan returned to London after the summer holidays he resumed his place on 'Free Speech'. As the summer turned into autumn and invasion loomed the debates polarised; on 4 November, the day before the first British troops finally landed on Egyptian soil, the atmosphere between the two sides, normally so convivial, was savage. Both before and after the broadcast Alan and Foot refused to speak to their opponents, and the debate itself was brutal.

A month later British troops withdrew from Egypt. Alan was in London with some time to spare and on a whim went to the Commons, the first time he had been there since 1913. There he saw the Conservative Prime Minister, Sir Anthony Eden, on his first day back from convalescence in the West Indies. 'It was eerie. There was a cold hostility on the Conservative benches against the man who had somehow let them down. Labour in comparison was almost sorry for Eden. It was clear that he was not long for this world as prime minister. I witnessed the end of a statesman and in a sense the end of an empire.'[92]

The Suez fiasco heightened Alan's dislike of 'superficial parallels' with the past, particularly parallels with the appeasement of Nazi Germany, which then cast a long shadow over British politicians, particularly Conservative politicians, as it arguably continues to do. Such historical analogies were 'profoundly misleading and did nothing but harm'. 'I have long thought that we learn too much from history rather than the reverse,' he wrote in 1951.[93] His Bismarck biography carried the same message. 'Great disasters are caused by trying to learn from history and correct past mistakes. Men being what they are, it is probably better to think about the present, not the past – or the future.'[94]

In his Ford Lectures he developed this theme. 'We learn nothing from history except the infinite variety of men's behaviour. We study it, as we listen to music or read poetry, for pleasure, not for instruction . . . The present enables us to understand the past, not the other way round.'[95] Any idea that history served a purpose, he argued, was just sales talk. This attitude, even if not intended to be taken wholly seriously, infuriated some historians, particularly in the United States. If history was of no value, of what value were historians?

In October 1956 Wadsworth retired. His wife had died the year before, and Wadsworth himself was very sick – he died in early November, five days after his official retirement date. Before that, however, tributes flowed in to the paper; among the many printed, Alan's praised him as 'a great editor . . . his Radical spirit has never faltered'. He described his feelings of 'love and gratitude' to Wadsworth. 'For my part, I have valued a casual word of praise from APW more highly than anything else in life, even though an instruction for some new task has always been hooked on to it.'[96]

Tradition as well as sentiment demanded that the Ford Lectures be offered to the University Press for publication in book form*, or so Alan imagined. The Delegates were consulted, and welcomed the idea; but after terms had been agreed, Alan queried the price. When Davin suggested twenty-one shillings, he replied, 'I am afraid I must decline your terms. In the ordinary way the Ford Lectures ought to come to you. But mine have a general interest and I owe it to the ordinary, unhistorical reader to publish them as cheaply as possible . . . no ill-feelings on either side, I hope.'[98]

There was some ill-feeling. 'This is very annoying,' Davin wrote to Poole in December 1956. 'It is some small consolation that one or two people have told me the lectures were not as good as they might have been.' 'I am not surprised,' Poole replied, 'he is always a difficult customer and a hard bargainer.'[99]

Three months later Davin told Poole the bad news that R.C.K. (now Sir Robert) Ensor had pulled out of the final volume in the Oxford History of England, covering the period 1914–1939, which ostensibly he had been writing since 1946. The series had been conceived in 1929 by G.N. Clark, who remained the editor, and like many such Oxford series had been remarkable for the dilatoriness of its contributors. For a while Clark, now Provost of Oriel, contemplated writing the volume himself, but in the end he decided it required somebody younger. During a walk with Alan in Wytham Woods, Clark burst out abruptly that he really must do something about the Oxford History of England. What about me? asked Alan. 'Would you?' said Clark, relieved. 'That would be

---

*Namier, for example, had felt obliged to offer his Ford Lectures to OUP, even though, as he wrote to Harold Macmillan, 'I specially dislike dealing with the Clarendon Press'. In the event he never wrote them up.[97]

marvellous.' Alan thought he could write the book in five years. Davin and his colleagues swallowed their annoyance. 'Taylor is not perfectly equipped on topics like philosophy and "thoughts",' Davin minuted C.H. Roberts, who had succeeded Norrington as Secretary to the Delegates, 'but he has as good a range as anyone we are likely to get, and we think we should get a successful book, at least from the publisher's point of view.' Alan's name duly came up for approval by the Delegates, who expressed 'some qualms about him in home politics' and deferred a decision. Clark, who had wanted to meet the Delegates before the suggestion was considered and had assumed the Delegates' approval to be a formality, was embarrassed. 'If it is rejected this will be a very serious blow to the Oxford History of England and, I think, to the position in historical publishing which the Press has built up, in the face of competition, during the last twenty-three years. Taylor is a close friend of Sir Lewis Namier, who is, or has been, Macmillans' chief historical adviser.' Clark would make sure that the book could not be open to criticism on political grounds. He hinted that he might resign as general editor of the series; and after much careful lobbying the Delegates were won over at their next meeting.[100]

The Troublemakers was published by Hamish Hamilton at eighteen shillings. In offering the book to Hamilton, Alan described it as 'much the most exciting and interesting book that I have written'.[101] Thanking Muggeridge for his comments on the book, Alan remarked 'I might almost say it was written for you – at least you were constantly in mind as I wrote. Apart from being funny, I meant it to shed new light on our immediate predecessors, to say: maybe they were often mistaken, but you can see why they made their mistakes.'[102]

The reviewers enjoyed the *bons mots*, but had doubts about the substance. Kingsley Martin himself reviewed the book for the *New Statesman and Nation*, and he likened Alan to 'this generation's Bernard Shaw, at once its unrelenting preacher and its irrepressible debater'. They had made successful lectures, Martin felt, but retained their epigrammatic, rather inconsequential quality in book form. Attlee, no longer Labour leader and now elevated to the

Lords, gave the book a typically downbeat review: 'Mr Taylor has a lively style and has written an interesting book, though I think he tends to over-stress the importance of the intellectuals as is natural in an academic writer.' The anonymous *Times Literary Supplement* reviewer reprimanded Alan. 'If he believes, as the dust-cover suggests, that an invitation to deliver the Ford Lectures is the highest honour which an English historian can receive, one can only wish that he had been more thoughtful about returning the compliment.'[103]

'In my innocence I didn't realise how much my academic colleagues would hate this book,' Alan told Machell. 'Namier got cold feet and pretended that he was too busy to write about it in *The Spectator*. He certainly does not act on the eighteenth-century principle of standing by his friends.'[104]

The horror of the Nazi years had knocked the gaiety out of Namier. He remained bitter towards the appeasers; some felt he could no longer view pre-War Europe coolly. Though he had been knighted in 1952, he still did not feel accepted by the academic establishment. In particular, his failure to obtain an Oxford Chair ate into his soul.[105] He became more anxious, more stuffy, less adventurous. Having been a strong supporter of an Anglo-Soviet alliance, he became alarmed lest he was viewed as pro-Soviet. When an anonymous review in *The Economist* of one of his books accused him of moralising about individuals at the expense of rational analysis, Namier complained to Alan that it must have been written by a hysterical woman. In fact the reviewer was Max Beloff; when Namier discovered his identity he struck Beloff off his list of friends. Tired of Namier's complaints, Alan defended Beloff: 'I not only think he had the right to review it, I think he was probably right.'

Alan himself had given offence by writing an 'insufficiently respectful' review of a collection of Namier's essays.[106] 'Poor Alan,' concluded Namier. 'He is losing his gifts.' But Alan, unlike Beloff, regretted Namier's wariness about Russia, as he had written to Wadsworth back in 1948, commenting on a Namier broadcast.

It is curious how he gets cold feet. He has never previously condemned Russian policy (wisely, I think: if the historian once begins to talk about war-guilt he has got to throw some on nearly everybody). But Beloff's review in *The Economist* frightened him, though he knows who wrote it; and he wanted to get rid of the charge of being pro-Russian. Hence the denunciation of Stalin at the end of his talk; really quite inappropriate, unless you also talk of the war-guilt of the feeble democracies. It's always the same with him: in just the same way he backed away from Zionism as soon as he saw it was going to become really unpopular with the governing classes. There is something Jewishly sycophantic about him with all his great qualities. No doubt, as a hereditary Lancashire radical, I exaggerate the virtues of independence and dislike of the established order; but they are virtues all the same.[107]

In 1953 Alan had written a piece for the *Times Literary Supplement* about Namier's view of history; whether Namier ever knew that Alan was the author is unknown. The article gave Namier qualified praise.

Sir Lewis has always disliked intellectuals in politics . . . it bewilders and irritates him that men should uphold some abstract ideal . . . Darwin was accused of taking mind out of universe; and Sir Lewis had been the Darwin of political history . . . Every modern historian of the younger generation must regard Sir Lewis as his master; and yet we must beware of the flaw. Sir Lewis has wielded every weapon except one. He has exploited Marx and Darwin and Freud; he has appreciated both tradition and revolution. He has ignored the liberal spirit.[108]

They remained friendly. Namier was incapable of guile, and he was genuinely fond of Alan. In 1954, for example, Namier wrote to say that he hoped to come to Oxford during the summer term, and 'I should very much like to see you'.[109] Alan was already engaged in preparing a *Festschrift*, a volume of essays in his honour. They were presented to Namier at a ceremony in Oxford in 1956. Alan was joint editor, with Richard Pares, and contributed an essay on 'The War Aims of the Allies in the First World War', which nicely complemented his work on Allied war aims during the Second

World War. Other contributors included E.H. Carr, Lucy Sutherland and Hugh Trevor-Roper.

Early in 1956 they had an amicable exchange about the Ford Lectures; Alan told Namier that he was holding his audience, though he doubted whether he had strengthened his reputation as 'a steady reliable figure'.[110] Perhaps Namier had some misgivings about Alan, for early in 1957 he declined the opportunity to write his obituary for *The Times*, pleading pressure of work.[111] Alan's lecturing style disturbed Namier, who was not an exciting speaker. Most of all, he could not understand how Alan could lower himself to write for the popular press. He regarded 'journalistic prostitution' as one of the three enemies of scholarship, the others being amateurism and obsession with doctrine. Journalism, by which he meant the desire to *épater*, to entertain, to be brilliant – was, in a man of learning, mere irresponsibility; and 'irresponsible' was one of the most opprobrious terms in his vocabulary.[112]

In April Alan asked Namier to contribute to a letter to *The Times* about saving from closure the Wiener Library, a collection specialising in totalitarianism and Jewish affairs. He referred to a talk he had given at the Athenaeum. 'I was *very* respectable, though of course a little frivolous here and there.' Namier was embarrassed by the appeal; he considered the continued separate existence of the Wiener Library a mistake.[113]

'It is awkward for us both to be in this mutual admiration society,' Alan wrote to Hugh Trevor-Roper in 1955, praising a review he had written: 'but damn it! apart from old Namier (who often writes atrociously nowadays) there are only you and me who are any good; and there's no way of hiding it.'[114] The following year he told Hamish Hamilton that Trevor-Roper was 'the ideal man' to write a life of Cromwell. 'It would have a fabulous sale . . . If I was you, I'd offer him the earth.' Four months later he told Hamilton that 'Hugh is nibbling at the idea of doing Oliver Cromwell and might do it if given a strenuous push'.[115]

Trevor-Roper was an immensely gifted historian and a witty, sophisticated writer. Like Alan, he was sometimes too sure of himself to be wholly popular; unlike Alan, he moved easily in high society. In 1954 he had married the daughter of Field-Marshal Earl Haig. Alan declined to attend the wedding; he told Trevor-Roper he would not fit in with 'the quality'. Moreover, Trevor-Roper was an astute politician. He later became a member of 'The Club', the group of a dozen dons which exerted a strong influence on Oxford appointments. Other members included Carr, Blake, Berlin, Masterman and the Warden of All Souls, John Sparrow.

Thus when speculation began about who would become Regius Professor after Galbraith retired, Trevor-Roper was one of the first names mentioned. *The Observer* put him alongside Alan as a frontrunner; Mr Taylor, it said, was often referred to among undergraduates as 'the Welfare State's Dr Johnson', whereas Trevor-Roper was known as 'the Rich Man's Lucky Jim'. The *Oxford Mail* added Rowse to the list, but quoted an anonymous don: 'You could make a very good book on this, with just as much certainty as on a horse race. Those who seem to have decided on the starters have forgotten the handicappers.'[116]

Regius appointments are in the hands of the Prime Minister, acting on behalf of the monarch. The Prime Minister consults the Chancellor, who in turn consults the Vice-Chancellor. At the same time an official known as the Appointments Secretary, commonly known as the patronage secretary, canvasses the opinion of those whom it is thought fit to consult. These include members of the History Faculty and representatives from the college where the Chair was based, Oriel.

At the end of 1956 Alan believed he had the appointment in the bag. He was said to be the college's preferred candidate. The Prime Minister, Sir Anthony Eden, had taken the advice of the Vice-Chancellor, Alic Smith, that Alan should be the next Regius Professor. Smith had himself been advised by Bullock that the History Faculty thought the Chair should go to Alan. But then both Eden and Smith resigned on the grounds of ill-health. The new Prime Minister was Harold Macmillan, and the new Vice-Chancellor 'that quintessential Establishment figure', J.C. Masterman.[117] Masterman lost no time in contacting Macmillan to the effect that his predecessor's judgement was not to be relied upon.

Macmillan was inclined to ask the advice of his old friend Namier. Indeed Namier might have had the Chair himself had he not been too old at sixty-eight. A few days after Macmillan became Prime Minister Trevor-Roper wrote to tell Namier that his application to give the Ford Lectures in 1958 had been spurned. Trevor-Roper referred to his failure to get the 'Third Chair' in 1951, and explained that Galbraith had prevented his election 'by a three-month campaign of absolute resistance'. Namier consoled him: 'snap your fingers at Oxford and write the great work I know you are capable of'.[118]

Alan was distracted. He wanted the Chair very badly. Becoming Regius Professor meant going back to Oriel, which would round off his Oxford career: although he remarked that he might find it awkward conversationally. He annoyed one of his brightest pupils, David Marquand, by interrupting while they were talking about Suez: 'Let's talk about something important. What about the Regius Professorship?' 'No question about it,' Marquand said provocatively, 'it should be Bruce McFarlane.' 'McFarlane!' Alan expostulated. 'What's McFarlane ever done, except point out there was a comma missing on page thirteen?' Alan was endearingly innocent about the academic rat-race. In May he suggested that Hamilton might send a copy of *The Troublemakers* 'to the Prime Minister, who is a member of your profession'.[119]

There are conflicting accounts of what happened next. Namier is said to have given Macmillan an alphabetical list of four names, and provided separate comments on each one, indicating no preference. Another version has it that the patronage secretary handed Namier a shortlist of four names, asking him for comments. According to the first account Alan's name was on the list; according to the second, it was not, and Namier was therefore not called upon to express an opinion about him. One name that *was* on the list was that of Lucy Sutherland, Principal of Lady Margaret Hall. She was one of Namier's brightest protégées, a specialist in eighteenth-century history. Macmillan proposed to appoint her, and she was inclined to accept, provided that no objection arose to her remaining Principal of LMH. But when the Appointments Secretary, David Stephens, took soundings in Oxford, he encountered strong opposition from the new Vice-Chancellor, who said that the office concerned was so important it ought not be held in plurality with the headship of a college. Another historian wrote to the Prime Minister expressing the same view. Miss Sutherland declined to step down from Lady Margaret Hall; and so another candidate had to be found.[120]

In his autobiography Alan relates a telephone call from Namier. Namier, he says, proposed at this stage to recommend him to Macmillan as Regius Professor. 'While I made embarrassed noises, Namier went on "Of course you must give up all this nonsense of appearing on television and writing for the *Sunday Express*".' It would have been in character; Namier had a fastidious distaste for 'the enemies of learning'. But what casts doubt on the accuracy of Alan's account is that at the time the appointment was made he had not yet begun writing for the *Sunday Express*; since he had been 'thrown off' the *Daily Herald* a year before he had been without a regular column on a popular newspaper. In the year past he had written only three articles for *Reynolds News*, a left-wing Sunday newspaper, the last of them in November. Perhaps, rather than issuing a threat, Namier was trying to convey to Alan that a Regius Professor who insisted on continuing to write for the gutter press would not be acceptable. In any case, Alan was very sensitive to any suggestion that he might be 'muzzled'. 'What I do in my spare time is no concern of yours or of anyone else,' Alan apparently replied: 'your standards and mine are no longer the same.' The conversation ended angrily.[121]

Two days before the appointment was announced, Alan wrote to Trevor-Roper.

> Sir Lewis asked me to tell you that he had not – as alleged in the press – supported the claims of any one candidate for the Regius Chair to the exclusion of others; and that in particular he had always mentioned you and me in the same breath as Lucy Sutherland. I am sorry to say that I do not give an unquestioned adherence to his statement – but I do not count it against him.[122]

The Chair was offered to Masterman's former pupil, Hugh Trevor-Roper, who accepted. Namier wrote to Trevor-Roper offering his congratulations. Trevor-Roper replied with his thanks. 'I must admit, I felt a bit of a fraud. I remain stubborn in my belief that Alan

Taylor ought to have had the Chair, and that politics ought not to have excluded him; but I suppose he was *vix papabilis,** so I must try to wear with dignity the mantle which has been stolen from him.'[123] Trevor-Roper also received a telegram of congratulation signed 'Alan', and wrote to Alan Taylor thanking him. In due course it emerged that this telegram had come from Trevor-Roper's former pupil, Alan Clark.

Alan was hugely disappointed. Namier, he felt, had 'betrayed' him. He seemed to believe that Namier had not only failed to promote his cause, but had spoken against it.† He wrote a 'hideous' letter to Namier, who returned it, not wanting Alan's angry outburst to stay on the record. But Alan broke off their friendship; they never spoke again. Namier was grieved by the split. In his convoluted way he tried to extend an olive branch. He asked Hamish Hamilton to send Alan a proof of his essay 'The Downfall of the Habsburg Monarchy', which was to be included in his forthcoming book, *Vanished Supremacies*. The implication was that he would value Alan's criticisms; but Alan was unmoved. 'I return the proofs of Sir Lewis Namier's essay,' he wrote back immediately, 'on which I have no comment to make.'[125] Two years later, when he was dying, Namier wrote directly to Alan saying he should like to see him again. Alan did not reply.

'The Regius Chair is a matter of unreserved pleasure to all concerned,' Alan wrote a few days later to Sir George Clark. 'It will give just as much pain in many quarters as my appointment would have done; and yet I'm spared all the trouble. Everyone, including Hugh, knows my qualifications are better than his; and being vain but not ambitious, this suits me down to the ground.'[126]

The Troublemakers was published in the same week that the new Regius Professor was announced. Readers could hardly fail to notice passages which seemed to refer to recent events in Oxford. 'Conformity may bring you a quiet life; it may even bring you to a university chair'; 'another sentence nearly lost him [Freeman] appointment to the Regius Chair'; 'It was no mean achievement for

---

*'Hardly the sort of person to be made Pope'.
†Commenting on an *Observer* profile in 1961, which reported that Namier 'had not recommended him for the post', Alan wrote to Roger Machell: 'his behaviour over the Regius Chair was much worse than that'.[124]

Hobson to anticipate Keynesian economics with one flick of the wrist and to lay the foundations for Soviet policy with another. No wonder that he never received academic acknowledgement nor held a university chair.'[127] Of course the book must have gone to press long before the choice of Regius Professor was announced; it is impossible to know whether these remarks formed part of the original lectures. In retrospect, Alan concluded that they had damaged his academic standing. '*The Troublemakers* is my best book,' he wrote to Hamish Hamilton three years later, 'though I think it cost me the Regius Chair.'[128]

Alan persuaded himself to behave graciously towards Trevor-Roper. A month after the announcement, a 'London Diary' written by Alan appeared in the *New Statesman* (no longer the *New Statesman and Nation*), praising Trevor-Roper for an essay in *Encounter* which had savaged Arnold Toynbee's *Study of History*. In October he reviewed a volume of Trevor-Roper's essays. 'Professor Trevor-Roper writes like an angel,' he commented. 'Each piece has a zest and perfection of a Mozart symphony.' There was a sting in the tail, of course. He observed that the book would enable Trevor-Roper 'to conceal for some time the fact that he has not yet produced a sustained book of mature historical scholarship.' Trevor-Roper thanked Alan; and Alan replied that 'the praise was not flattery but truth – though not grudgingly given'. He lamented that he would miss Trevor-Roper's Inaugural, owing to an engagement in Dublin.[129]

Alan's failure to become Regius Professor was the climax of his academic career. Was it an Establishment plot?

Many people saw it that way. Alan was a left-wing rebel, squeezed out of his rightful inheritance by lesser men jealous of his worldly success and frightened by his ideas. According to this version, Trevor-Roper was the well-connected candidate who would not rock the boat. When Trevor-Roper played a leading part in the successful campaign to make Macmillan Chancellor of the University in 1960, many saw it as a *quid pro quo*. A graffito at the time had it that 'A Vote for Macmillan is a Vote for Trevor-Roper'. Alan was the victim of a conspiracy.

Of course it was more complicated than that. Neither Alan nor Trevor-Roper was an orthodox follower of a party line. Nor was it unusual for left-wingers to obtain preferment in Oxford. Christopher Hill, for example, though an avowed Marxist, was Master of Balliol from 1965 to 1978; there are many other examples. Alan liked posing as an outsider, but he was an Oxford man through and through, and accepted as such. He was not universally liked, but nor was Trevor-Roper. Many of the more old-fashioned dons disapproved of Alan's journalism, but Trevor-Roper was also prominent in the public prints. Robert Blake, one of the dons consulted by the patronage secretary, who recommended Trevor-Roper, was at the time the newspaper magnate Lord Beaverbrook's 'court historian'.

A more informed conspiracy theory has it that Alan was outdone by the 'Christ Church mafia'. Before becoming a tutor at Christ Church Trevor-Roper had been an undergraduate at the college, where he had been taught by Masterman; so had David Stephens, the patronage secretary. Between Christ Church and Magdalen there was an historic rivalry, manifest particularly in the teaching of history. Macmillan and Namier were both Balliol men. But these are arcane college politics. One does not need to look so deep to find the reasons why Alan failed to become Regius Professor. Both the Vice-Chancellor and the Prime Minister had perfectly understandable, though not necessarily noble, reasons for preferring the successful candidate. Masterman was Trevor-Roper's old tutor; Macmillan his publisher. Both had reasons to dislike Alan. Possibly Namier's own disappointment at never returning to Oxford made him less keen than he might otherwise have been to promote the cause of his former protégé. But though Namier may not have campaigned for Alan, it seems he may have been ready to recommend him. If Namier gave Alan the impression that he had blocked his appointment, that may have been no more than his clumsiness in personal relations. It would have been ironic if Namier, having himself failed to come back to Oxford as Regius Professor despite Alan's support, had been the instrument which smashed Alan's hopes. Some of the other historians who were consulted felt that Alan would be a loose cannon within the History Faculty, incapable of the necessary administrative work and unlikely to supervise the postgraduate students properly. The fact that Alan later proved to be a capable administrator when Vice-President of Magdalen does not mean this concern was not genuine. On the other hand the administrative duties of the Regius Professor are not particularly onerous.

Alan muddied the waters by claiming never to have wanted the job in the first place. Indeed, he wrote in his autobiography that he would never have accepted such a post from 'hands still stained with blood', referring to Macmillan's role in the Suez affair. It is difficult to deny something that did not happen. But the evidence at the time strongly suggests that Alan hoped to be offered the post, and his behaviour during the contest and afterwards reinforces this interpretation. It is incredible that Alan would have acted so harshly towards Namier had he not been bitterly disappointed. He was fiercely competitive, in his career as in his driving. Like Lucy Sutherland, he might have chosen not to accept the Chair when it was offered to him, but he wanted to be recognised as the best in his class.

Yet it does seem hard that Alan failed to become Regius Professor, and extraordinary that he never became a full professor at all. Trevor-Roper was a fine scholar, but Alan was the senior man and his published work was more substantial. At any other institution Alan's achievement would have earned him the recognition of a chair of one sort or another. But Oxford was like that; C.S. Lewis, too, was disappointed not to be offered a chair and left Oxford as a result.* In the words of his former pupil and Magdalen colleague, the medieval historian Karl Leyser, Alan was 'too big a figure' for Oxford.

The irony is that wherever Alan went throughout his life people took it for granted that a man of his eminence would be a professor, and addressed him as such, to such an extent that he tired of correcting them. Perhaps, then, he was a 'people's professor', a professor by popular election. He would have relished the title.

---

*Lewis took up a Chair in Cambridge in 1955.

11: *In the Presence of the Lord*

In the preface to his volume in the Oxford History of England, published in 1965, Alan acknowledged the help of Sir George Clark, who 'honoured me by his invitation to write this book and sustained me when I was slighted in my profession'. The interpretation of this startling last phrase has been the subject of much speculation. What did Alan mean? The correspondence between the two men suggests that he was referring to his failure to win the Regius Chair. Only a week before Trevor-Roper's appointment was announced, Alan wrote to Clark, anxious that he had received no commitment in writing from the OUP. Perhaps he had some inkling of the qualms expressed by the Delegates, for he went on: 'I should like to be sure that the Delegates will not snatch this prize away from me – if prize it is.' Twelve days later he replied in the affirmative to Clark's offer of a contract: 'University bodies are notoriously fickle; and I wouldn't like to find that the Delegates had forgotten me.'[1]

Alan knew that the tide was running against him in Oxford. The Ford Lectures, though a popular success, had been much disliked by other historians. Clark had needed to fight to overcome the fears of the Delegates.* It seemed to Alan that Oxford was reluctant to grant him the recognition he had earned. Thus when he failed to become Regius Professor, he felt not just disappointed, but slighted. It was a turning-point in his career. He reacted by boasting

---

*'At the day of judgement his courage in inviting me to write *English History, 1914–1945* and thereafter in supporting me will atone for his earlier acts of timidity.'[2]

that he was more distinguished than 'more successful historians'. He managed to contain his bitterness, but he realised that he could never aspire to a professorial chair within Oxford. If he had any inhibitions before, he lost them now. He had nothing further to lose; he was free to do whatever he wanted. Since his colleagues thought of him as beyond the pale, he became reckless.

In the early 1950s Alan had begun what was to be a long association with the *Observer*. Edward Crankshaw had recommended him as a reviewer to Terence Kilmartin, the Literary Editor; Kilmartin was already familiar with Alan's contributions to the 'Books in General' page in the *New Statesman*. 'How many books would you like to do?' asked Kilmartin. 'As many as you like.' Alan continued to turn out book reviews at an impressive rate, keeping his name constantly before readers of the left-leaning press. In 1956, for example, he reviewed forty-six books; in 1957, fifty-five. the *Observer* had first call on his services, but he also reviewed regularly for the *Manchester Guardian* and the *New Statesman*.

His literary editors found Alan an ideal contributor. His reviews were always punctual, and he could write them at short notice, as was often required. They nearly always came in on the other side of a page of discarded typescript, almost always exactly the right length – if anything a little too short. His accompanying letters were brisk and businesslike. Occasionally he would put something outrageous in a review to test the Literary Editor's alertness; once he suggested that Ferdinand de Lesseps, architect of the Suez Canal, was the greatest man of the nineteenth century. If challenged, he yielded immediately: 'Oh no, I don't mind taking it out.'

Alan often came into the *New Statesman* offices in Great Turnstile to deliver his copy or to look at the books received from publishers. Sometimes he would lunch with Janet Adam Smith, the Literary Editor. Trevor-Roper too was a regular reviewer for the weekly. In 1958 Miss Adam Smith asked him to review a biography of Cromwell; he asked to be spared. 'As I recall, the radical hagiographer for your radical saints is that excellent "professional historian turned public entertainer" Alan Taylor. I remember he did a splendid turn on the tercentenary of Charles I's execution, saying tersely that whatever is radical is *ipso facto* (or *ipso dicto*) right. Why shouldn't he do it?'[3]

Whatever his colleagues thought of Alan, journalists rated him very highly as a reviewer. His opening sentence was always arresting. 'Good people, I am the Protestant whore!' began a review of Keith Feiling's *A History of England*. Alan was not a brutal reviewer, like Muggeridge; but he was not a kind reviewer either. He did not spare friends, colleagues or former pupils; disarmingly, he sometimes praised his enemies. He tended to write about the subject of a book and often gave only one sentence to the book itself. By bringing more to the piece than was in the book, he demonstrated his authority over the author under review.

Early in 1956 he was asked by the *Observer* to review a biography of Lord Beaverbrook, by Alan's Oxford friend Tom Driberg. It was a delicate project. Beaverbrook had once helped Driberg escape a homosexual scandal; Driberg had for many years been employed by Beaverbrook on the *Daily Express* as the gossip columnist 'William Hickey'; the newspaper was serialising the book, even though it was described by the publishers as a 'hostile' biography, and Beaverbrook's lawyers had applied pressure which had 'mutilated' the text.[4] To Kilmartin's surprise, Alan sent in a review which Kilmartin considered 'rather too obliging' about Beaverbrook. When Kilmartin told Alan this was unacceptable – Beaverbrook had a feud with the Astors, who owned the *Observer* – Alan was not perturbed. 'The editor is always right,' he said. 'Send it back.' He then wrote another review, the thrust of which was in the opposite direction. Headed 'Sound and Fury', it praised the biography as wonderfully entertaining, while belittling the subject. 'Though Lord Beaverbrook has often made news, it has not been news of any significance.'[5]

This was a very different tone from the one he had adopted in an exchange of letters with Beaverbrook the year before. Beaverbrook had written to Alan querying a couple of references in *The Struggle for Mastery in Europe*, which he described as 'this splendid book'. Alan replied supplying the references. 'I am very flattered by your kind words about my book. It is agreeable to please historians; but even nicer to satisfy those who have made history.'[6]

In November 1956 Alan reviewed a book by Beaverbrook himself. Entitled *Men and Power, 1917–1918*, it took up where two earlier volumes, *Politicians and the War*, had left off, providing a first-hand account of the politics of those years. Beaverbrook was revealed as playing a not inconsiderable role. Reviewing Driberg's book, Alan had mocked Beaverbrook's self-importance; he 'once played some part in politics when he brought Lloyd George and Bonar Law together against Asquith; but the only person who supposes this part was decisive is the author of *Politicians and the War*'. Now he praised Beaverbrook as 'the wise counsellor of everyone except himself'. *Men and Power* showed 'his supreme ability as a narrator of political conflict'; it was exciting and entertaining. The review was headed 'Lord Beaverbrook as Historian'. 'He may sometimes exaggerate the part he has played in events. No one could exaggerate his gifts in chronicling them.'[7]

Lord Beaverbrook was a man much abhorred. He occupied a position in British demonology not unlike that of Rupert Murdoch today. Like Murdoch, he was an outsider, a Canadian; unlike Murdoch, he had been a successful politician, a minister in both World Wars, transforming himself in the process from Max Aitken into Lord Beaverbrook. But he was regarded as a mischief-maker, a rogue elephant in British society. He controlled some of the most successful newspapers in Britain, over which he maintained absolute dominance; through them he exerted what many believed to be a malign influence. Their popularity, not to say vulgarity, was itself a source of distaste. But the causes he supported were almost all failures, and the individuals he championed (and indeed bankrolled) were generally second-rate, like Hoare or Bonar Law. Only in Winston Churchill did he finally pick a winner, and even then he had the gall to see himself as a possible replacement for Churchill during the War.

Most Englishmen regarded Beaverbrook as more ridiculous than sinister. Most progressive, left-wing Englishmen thought of him as a fossil, a crusader for lost causes. And most historians regarded his 'histories' with suspicion. He seemed to regard the past as a succession of shoddy political intrigues concerning almost-forgotten political figures. His style was bombastic and jejune. He was an absurd old man, a wilful megalomaniac egotist, puffed up with self-importance and sustained by malice, hopelessly out of touch with the modern world.[8]

It was surprising to find Alan praising such a man in the *Observer*. Readers searched in vain for the ironic twist. Beaverbrook himself was exhilarated; he had a real interest in history, and to be praised by a proper historian was delectable. 'I'm not a real writer, I'm a chronicler,' he told Michael Foot; but he was willing to be contradicted.

In May 1957 Alan had written to Beaverbrook with 'an impertinent request. *Politicians and the War* is an unrivalled authority for this period, as well as being a wonderful book. It is now hard to come by. If you happened to have a spare copy, I should indeed be grateful.' Beaverbrook sent him the two volumes – the first of many presents – 'which I shall treasure', Alan wrote gratefully. Beaverbrook invited Alan to lunch, and bombarded him with questions about himself and his work. He was a good listener, who liked a good talker. 'You spoil me, you do indeed,' Alan wrote to Beaverbrook afterwards. 'I never passed a more fascinating hour than in our lunch together last Friday.'[9]

Alan was intoxicated by the company of this wicked old man. 'A meeting with you is always a red-letter day in my life,' Alan told him in 1959. Beaverbrook had gaiety and zest; 'volcanoes of laughter' erupted around him. He had a gift for making you feel you were the most important person in the world, Alan said later; when he wanted to please he could be courteous, charming and hospitable – though when he chose he could be very unpleasant.

Alan had an appetite for luxury, which Beaverbrook had the means to indulge. Alan would often be invited to dine at Beaverbrook's country house, Cherkley, near Leatherhead, or at Beaverbrook's London flat behind the Ritz, in Arlington House; a car would be sent to pick him up, and to drive him home afterwards. At dinner there were glittering company, sparkling conversation, and champagne or fine wines; between invitations Beaverbrook draped Alan with presents, like a mistress he was trying to seduce. 'He stole my heart,' Alan wrote in his autobiography; some said he had bought it.

Beaverbrook became, in Alan's own words, the second of his two
'masters' – the first, repudiated only weeks before Alan met
Beaverbrook, had been Namier.[10] It was not an equal relationship,
nor could it be. Alan could not reciprocate Beaverbrook's *largesse*
by sending lavish presents in return – though a couple of years
before Beaverbrook's death he and Eve did start sending him
flowers on his birthday. Nor was Beaverbrook invited to dine with
the Taylors, either at Fordington Road or St Mark's Crescent. The
nearest Alan came to offering Beaverbrook hospitality was to
suggest a walk on Hampstead Heath.[11]

'How did so subtle, ironic an intelligence ever come to be
captivated by so preposterous a caesarkin?' wrote Muggeridge
many years later.[12] Perhaps Alan was feeling rejected. Beaverbrook
had a keen sense of grievance; chippy himself, he noticed and
perhaps encouraged resentment in others. 'Not enough recognition,' he wrote to Alan. 'More should be your portion.'[13] Not for
nothing did Alan call him a 'foul-weather friend'. Alan wrote later
that Beaverbrook's 'nature compelled him to hold out a hand to
one who had been in distress'.[14] W.J. Brown, cruelly dropped by
Beaverbrook after he lost his seat in Parliament, might not have
shared Alan's view.

But what Muggeridge and others missed was how much the two
men had in common. They shared a taste for brevity, clarity and
mischief; an interest in history, politics and journalism. Both were
romantic, inconsistent, energetic*; both were small men with large
personalities. Though generous, Beaverbrook was also frugal,
sometimes absurdly so, like Alan. Alan persuaded himself that
Beaverbrook was a Radical, an affectionate description he applied
also to Churchill. In a letter to Beaverbrook about Baldwin, Alan
wrote that 'he had that peculiar characteristic of the upper middle
class. You can never be sure when he is deceiving you and when he
is deceiving himself. I suppose there is something to be said for
softness in public life. At any rate everyone except old Radicals like
you and me seem to think so.'[16]

If it was special pleading to call Beaverbrook a Radical – a term
Michael Foot used about him too[17] – neither was he a conventional

---

*Both were demon drivers.[15]

Tory. He had long believed in better relations with the Soviet Union, for example, and during the War he had annoyed Churchill by campaigning alongside the Communists for an early Second Front. He was no Cold War warrior. Though of course a capitalist, he believed in high wages and Keynesian-style government intervention in the economy. Not being born into the British class system, he disliked snobbery and privilege. At Cherkley there were none of the class barriers which English people are liable to erect between each other. Alan was not the only left-winger who enjoyed his company; there were many others, including Michael Foot, Aneurin Bevan and Tom Driberg. When Alan dined with Beaverbrook it was often in the company of 'the Feet', Michael Foot and his wife; after dinner Beaverbrook liked to hear them sing the Red Flag.

'Of course Beaverbrook likes to corrupt the Left,' Alan told his pupil David Marquand in 1957; 'he's tried to corrupt Michael Foot, he's corrupted Bob Edwards*, and now he's trying to corrupt me.' Two years later Marquand, who had spent the intervening period in America, was shocked to find Alan referring to Beaverbrook incessantly, almost obsessively, as 'the old man'. 'My old man' was the term he used more and more, long after Beaverbrook's death. The analogy should not be pushed too far, but there was certainly a paternal element in Beaverbrook's relations with his young, left-wing friends. Michael Foot, for example, loved him, 'not merely as a friend but as a second father'.[18] Beaverbrook's own son could not share his passions for politics, newspapers and history.

Beaverbrook was a confidant of the powerful, and Alan relished the political gossip that radiated around his dinner-table. For Beaverbrook, politics were all about personality and anecdote; Alan was drifting towards the same approach. Robert Blake had been Beaverbrook's 'court historian', until he wrote an insufficiently respectful review of *Men and Power* for the *Evening Standard*. Now Alan inherited his place.

---

*Robert Edwards was Editor of *Tribune* from 1951 to 1954. From 1957 he was Deputy Editor of the *Sunday Express*, and he was Editor of the *Daily Express* in 1961 and from 1963 to 1965.

In 1957 John Junor had only recently become Editor of the *Sunday Express*, a Beaverbrook newspaper then more highly regarded than it is now. He commissioned Alan to write a three-part series on the late King George VI, and soon after offered him a contract to write twenty leader-page articles a year on an exclusive basis; Alan affected to hesitate before accepting. He wrote to Muggeridge explaining that he had become acquainted with Beaverbrook. 'Now I am being lured two ways. Shall I sell myself to the *Observer*? Or the *Sunday Express*? You might say – to neither. But I can't resist my merchant parents. I love buying and selling even myself.'[19]

In the event Alan was not forced to choose. Junor had no objection to his continuing to review for the *Observer*, or indeed anywhere else. He simply wanted to retain Alan's services for leader-page articles. Contracted contributors – others included George Gardiner, Harold Wilson, and Enoch Powell – were prevented from writing similar pieces elsewhere, and this rule was rigorously enforced. In return they were entitled to payment for the contracted number of articles, even though this was invariably well in excess of the number required in practice. There was therefore none of the normal rancour about articles being spiked, and indeed Alan was often used as a reserve when there was some doubt about a more important contribution. Alan was paid for articles as they appeared, and at the end of each year he would promptly telephone the paper with news of the balance owing. Staff were amused by the clockwork regularity of these accounts.

Alan's first *Sunday Express* piece, 'Why must we soft-soap the Germans?', received what *The Times* described as 'wide and angry publicity'. He had attacked the official Western line, endorsed by the Labour Party, that reunification of Germany was desirable. The division of Germany, though unintended, was 'a stroke of luck . . . splendid for the rest of us.' The basic cause of the two wars was the same, he went on: there are too many Germans, and Germany is too strong. 'Now we are handed a solution on a plate.' German reunification, on the other hand, would be only the start, leading to territorial demands on Czechoslovakia and Poland. 'Whoever commits himself to the reunification of Germany commits himself to the Munich settlement and to the demands which Hitler made on

Poland in August 1939.' Fifteen to twenty years after German reunification, he warned in a *New Statesman* piece, 'Namier's Law would begin to operate': there would be a resurgence of pathological nationalism.

Alan's views caused dismay. *The Times* reported that the 'indivisible Germany' organisation had invited him to visit Germany in the hope of persuading him to revise his views on reunification. But Alan was unrepentant. 'The kindest thing for the Germans is not to encourage their nationalist ambitions.'[20]

'I don't read you in the *Sunday Express*,' Kilmartin confessed to Alan. 'Well, I should hope not,' Alan replied. His *Sunday Express* pieces were just as crude as his work for the *Daily Herald* or the *Sunday Pictorial*; one of his recurrent themes was that people did not drive fast enough on the roads. He would cheerfully admit that what he wrote for the *Sunday Express* was 'rubbish', and affected to be annoyed when anyone took it seriously. 'A good journalist is he who pleases his editor,' he told his 'reserve' Alan Watkins. 'What do you think of Junor?' Watkins asked – 'A blockhead'. Junor was surprised to find Alan so 'biddable', ready to write on any subject he proposed. After briefing Alan over the telephone, he was nonplussed to find his own ideas regurgitated word-for-word. Alan would dash off his *Sunday Express* articles within ten or fifteen minutes of Junor's call.* When Alan was in Oxford, Junor would telephone at one o'clock wanting an article from him; it would arrive in London on the four-thirty train. Later, when he and Junor worked in the same building, Alan used to tell his secretary to keep back the typed article for an hour or so before getting the office boy to take it round to the Editor.

It shocked Alan's friends and colleagues that he felt able to write for a Tory newspaper like the *Sunday Express*. 'Why do you write for the *Sunday Express*?' Elizabeth Pakenham asked him after dining at Magdalen, as the port came round on the railway line built for the purpose. 'Surely you could write for a paper more suited to your political views?' Alan put on a mock melancholy

---

*Sometimes he came into the *Sunday Express* offices to compose his articles on a spare typewriter; during more than thirty years in journalism, Watkins has never seen anyone prepare a leader-page article so fast.

voice. 'It's the money I need.' Certainly he was paid well: in the early 1960s he told one of his friends that for a *Sunday Express* leader-page article he received £100; for a *New Statesman* review of similar length he received £12.

'You're pretty well a crypto-Communist,' Kilmartin observed one day. 'But, sometimes, one would take you for an extreme right-winger.' 'Sometimes extremes meet,' Alan replied. Though Alan continued to call himself a socialist, his views were too libertarian for the orthodox 1950s Left. His support for commercial television was one example; another was his attitude to the financing of the press. 'Newspapers have a right to exist only if they can meet their bills,' he wrote in 1959[21] – hardly a popular view in the late 1950s, when left-wing newspapers were struggling to survive.

Alan's detractors thought that he had sold himself to Beaver-brook. So, in a sense, he had. He was not free to bite the hand that fed him. In his autobiography he strongly denied that he owed his newspaper contract to Lord Beaverbrook's patronage. He claimed that he settled into the *Sunday Express* before he ever met Beaver-brook. In fact he lunched with Beaverbrook before his George VI series which inaugurated his relationship with the paper, and Beaverbrook certainly knew about these articles, because he sent Alan material for them.[22] But Alan was a professional journalist, who had done this sort of work before, and indeed he carried on working for the *Sunday Express* for many years after Beaver-brook's death. Correspondence between Alan and Beaverbrook over seven years rarely mentions Alan's work for the newspaper. Perhaps Junor was not averse to employing one of his proprietor's intimates. But it is just as likely that Junor was interested in Alan because he had again become prominent as a television star.

In August 1957 Alan had 'started a revolution on television'. On three successive Monday evenings at six o'clock ITV broadcast his lectures on the Russian Revolution. These were delivered straight to the camera, with no props or voice-overs. Conventional wisdom held that a television audience would not tolerate the necessary concentration. 'To see a man talking ought to be easier to take in than simply hearing him on the radio,' Alan maintained. 'It's not only me on trial,' he wrote, 'but the whole idea of lecturing on TV . . . It is conceivable that I will be so bad that some of them will switch over to the BBC, but that is setting my sights very, very low.'[23]

The idea had come from John Irwin, Alan's producer on 'In the News' and 'Free Speech'. He and Bill Brown had come up to Oxford to attend the last of Alan's Ford Lectures*; Boothby and Foot had been invited too, but were unable to attend. Irwin and Brown were surprised to find Alan holding the attention of such a large audience. Irwin decided to try something similar on television.

The first lectures were recorded on the vast stage of the Wood Green Empire, a cinema converted into a studio. The curtains were drawn back to reveal a dark and empty stage. Alan waited in the wings for a signal, then walked slowly into the spotlight, eyes downcast to avoid tripping over the microphone cables. When he reached a chalk mark on the floor, he looked up and began talking, hands clasped at the front. He had no notes or autocue, and the lecture was recorded 'live', in one take. From time to time the camera looked away to shots of an invited audience, but that was all.† After half an hour he concluded and walked off the stage, trailing the microphone cable behind him.

It was a bold experiment, and it proved a triumphant success. The lectures on the Russian Revolution were followed by many others: on the nineteenth century, on prime ministers, the 1920s, the 1860s; by the mid-1960s he had delivered more than forty, including two BBC series. His 'astonishing ease and naturalism before the camera is a *tour de force*', commented the *New Statesman* in 1963. 'Sitting and listening to Taylor's monologues in real life is one of the most satisfying of civilised pleasures'; thanks to television, the public 'can now share that satisfaction'.[24]

He would appear to be listening to his own argument; sometimes he would stop and deliberate, then contradict what he had just said. It's not often you can see people thinking on television, one critic

---

*Brown brought an inflatable cushion to sit on.
†This was felt to be a distraction and dropped after the first series. From then on viewers saw Alan alone on the screen throughout the half-hour lecture.

later commented[25]; and perhaps the technique was as compelling as the content. Not least of Alan's achievements was to wind up his argument to end bang on time. Initially Irwin had drawn a finger across his throat to indicate that Alan should stop talking; later Alan kept an eye on a large clock hanging behind the cameras.

How did he do it? He gave different answers at different times. He practised for hours in front of the mirror; he memorised six points and improvised around these; he prepared only the beginning and the end; he had three conclusions prepared, and decided which to use only as the lecture advanced. Maybe he liked to encourage the mystique. He certainly prepared the opening and closing lines in advance, because he had to recite these to cue the sound engineers. One habit may provide a clue: before the recording he would lie down for twenty minutes. Perhaps this was the equivalent of a stroll round Addison's Walk before lecturing in the Examination Schools; perhaps it was just relaxation. One observer who knew Alan well gave this explanation of his technique: most people think in phrases, or maybe in complete sentences; Alan thought in *paragraphs*.

Alan meant the lectures to be serious. They would be like his university lectures, only shorter and faster, he told a *TV Times* interviewer. He hoped the lectures might contribute to bridging the gap between the university-educated and 'the people, who have not yet found the means of confronting the governing class . . . I want to help them get the destiny of this country in their hands.' He believed that the public had an appetite for programmes which were intellectually interesting and stimulating, one underestimated by the broadcasters. 'I expect we shall have a tremendous university of the air in no time,' he said with a smile, 'and the variety programmes will have to be put on in the dead hours of the afternoon because of the queues of viewers waiting to look at lecturers.'[26] His first lectures drew a television audience of 750,000, a good figure in those days. By the early 1960s, close to four million people were said to watch him.[27] Alan enjoyed his popularity. One series of lectures was broadcast on Saturday evenings. 'I have had a number of complaints from teenagers,' he informed a television executive, 'that Saturday is their one night to go out dancing and that they miss the lectures much to their regret.'[28]

Alan's television lectures made him even more famous. 'No longer was I addressed at random as Bill Brown or Sir Robert Boothby.' He was the man who did those talks on TV, something nobody else did nor, for that matter, has done since. He was still participating in 'Free Speech', which continued until ITV decided to kill the programme in 1961.* Tom Driberg, an occasional contributor to 'Free Speech', sent the team a photograph from a tropical island which showed Driberg being garlanded with flowers by a pretty girl. 'Bottom, thou art translated,' remarked Alan.

There was one irony about his screen success; Alan himself did not possess a television set.

In September 1957 a profile of Alan appeared in the *New Statesman*. Entitled 'The Seventh Veil', it described Alan as the only intellectual in the country whose name was a household word, who was a *star*.

> But why be a troublemaker? A Fellowship at Magdalen is as near the heart of the Establishment as you can get. With the columns of the *English Historical Review* open to you, let alone the *New Statesman*, why bother about Free Speech? . . . Perhaps the answer is an old one: a sense of insecurity caused by the nagging suspicion that Oxford never really accepts the clever invader from below. But in the end the question seems unanswerable. However much one tears off the veils, however deep one penetrates beneath the surface mask, one returns at last to the starting point; the exuberance, the gaiety, the perverse charm, the human warmth. The man of many faces turns out to have the same face all the time. The star in his studio is no different from the don in his study. The seventh veil conceals only what the first did not conceal.

Alan wrote to thank Kingsley Martin for a charitable portrait.

---

*In January 1961 Alan offered 'Free Speech' back to the BBC! 'I daresay I sometimes cause trouble. But I also give value for money.'[29]

Your contributor did not seem to be able to decide whether there is a
mystery about me. There is none except that conjured up by his
intellectual snobbishness. He wonders why I appear on Free Speech
when I am already a Fellow of Magdalen and write for the NS. John
Junor asked me the same question the other way round: why do you
waste your time on obscure publications such as the *New Statesman*
when you can write for the *Sunday Express*? The answer is the same
in both cases: because I enjoy doing what I do well. As to wondering
whether the Establishment has really accepted me, such ambitions
had not crossed my mind. I like the good food and drink that the
Establishment provides; and it amuses me to outpace its members on
their own track – as for instance by being a Fellow of the British
Academy. But as for its esteem . . . ough, *conspuez-le*.[30]

Alan was upset when Martin rejected a piece he had written about a
new book* by Milovan Djilas, the imprisoned Yugoslav dissident.

You have every right as Editor to criticise me and to reject what I
write. I hold firmly to the view that the Editor is always right – he
knows how things read and what gets across to the reader. What you
are not entitled to do is to invent motives for me and to lecture me on
my carelessness or hastiness. I do not write to shock; and I never have
– particularly when writing about a book . . . If you go on repeating
that I write to shock, I shall return the compliment and accuse you of
cold feet in not publishing what I write.

Martin thought Alan was exaggerating when he saw the evils Djilas
described – bureaucracy, planning, conformity of thought – as
nascent in Britain. Alan defended this view forcefully:

Nothing prevents us from going the same way except constant
kicking. And not humbugging ourselves. For instance, you go on that
we have been able to make a hell of a row about phone-tapping. Yes,
and what good has it done? Phone-tapping goes on, and is given
official approval by the Labour front bench . . . You think (or appear
to think from your letter) that there is some innate virtue in the
British character, the British constitution, or the British climate,
which makes it impossible for us to develop the evils of Communism.

---

*Probably *The New Class* (1957).

I believe that (brutality apart, which is not an issue between us) Tom O'Brien,* Hugh Gaitskell, George Barnes, Lord Bridges†, would behave as Communist bosses do if they got the chance. At any rate, it seems to me that for the English lover of liberty the main enemy is here, just as for the Russian it is in Russia. One should dislike one's own Establishment most and first.[31]

In an exchange of correspondence early in 1958 Alan and Martin debated 'the German problem'. This was an issue which preoccupied the Left in the 1950s, particularly in the early 1950s when the American-led North Atlantic Treaty Organization (formed in 1949) started to press for German rearmament. It was a staple subject for discussion at Labour Party conferences. Could the Germans be trusted not to start another war? Was there something innately bellicose in the German body politic, or had this been expunged by the Nazi experience? It was common in progressive circles to argue that the essential difference between the Germans and the British derived from one people being situated in the middle of Europe surrounded by enemies, and the other being protected as a result of inhabiting an island. Alan refuted this argument in a letter to Kingsley Martin.

I don't think our anti-war groups are merely a luxury, granted to us by the Channel. They also spring from our having a long tradition of government by discussion, and especially from the tradition of dissent in religion. By and large the political Dissenters drew their inspiration from the religious Dissenters of an earlier date. I don't believe that anyone reared in the Church of England can be a true Radical . . .

He rejected the Marxist bias which dominated Martin's thinking about the causes of the First World War. 'Capitalism, particularly finance-capitalism, made for peace, not war.' Alan then returned

---

*Tom O'Brien, General Secretary of the National Association of Theatrical and Kine Employees (1932–70) and an MP (1945–50 and 1955–59), was prominent in the campaign against left-wing dissidents within the Labour Party.
†Edward Bridges, son of the poet Robert Bridges, former Secretary to the Cabinet (1938–46) and Permanent Secretary, HM Treasury (1945–56), had been an undergraduate at Magdalen and was now a Fellow of All Souls. He was created Baron Bridges in 1957, and became Chancellor of Reading University in 1959.

to the argument about the irrelevance of colonial questions which
had permeated his work since the mid-1930s: 'In fact capitalist
imperialism worked against war . . . I'd say the two strongest
forces in British Imperialism were the missionaries and Fabian
do-gooding . . . The causes of war were non-economic and were
in Europe.'[32]

Alan discovered that elaborate plans were being made to prevent
his becoming the next Vice-President of Magdalen. Since Boase was
at the time Vice-Chancellor of the University as well as President of
the college, the Vice-Presidency assumed extra importance. This
was especially so in 1958, for that year had been designated to
celebrate the 500th anniversary of the college. Plans had been made
for a party ten years earlier, and McFarlane had waited until
preparations were advanced before announcing that the true date
of the foundation was 1458, not 1448.

Normally the post of Vice-President rotates every two years
according to seniority, and Alan was next in line; but Boase, Driver
and some others were trying to block Alan's turn. Alan appealed to
Weldon, who threatened the President with a contested election if
Alan were not appointed. Alan duly became Vice-President. To
everybody's surprise, he enjoyed the necessary administration and
indeed excelled at it. His watchwords were relevance and dispatch.
Timewasters at college meetings were cut short by his curt interruption, 'We are not here to discuss *that*'; one lasted fewer than ten
minutes, a record. Joyce Payne, the college secretary, found him full
of fun and very efficient. He came into the college office as it opened
at 9.30 in the morning, having dealt with his own letters and
perhaps a review or two in his rooms beforehand; when she arrived
there was a pile he could point to proudly.

Alan's term of office began with a modest reform. On 12 March
1958 the college abandoned the custom of proceeding to hall in
order of seniority; Alan observed that no unseemly scramble
ensued. A few days later was Ladies' Guest Night, another reform
instigated by Alan; his guest was Ann Fleming, aristocratic wife of
the creator of the James Bond novels, who smoked continuously in
the Common Room during the drinking of port, a tolerance not

extended to the Prince of Wales when he had been a guest in 1934.* There followed a series of junkets organised by Alan, including a pious procession to the Founder William of Waynflete's tomb in Winchester Cathedral, with Alan and Driver leading the Fellows to the accompaniment of a special anthem from the choir. The Quincentenary revels climaxed in a party in the college grounds on 21 July, the eve of the Festival of St Mary Magdalen, for more than a thousand old members and their guests. It began with evensong in the chapel, followed by a buffet supper in the colonnade of New Buildings and in the marquees on the lawns in front of the Cloisters. Alan laid on lobster and two thousand bottles of champagne, all of which were consumed during the evening. Guests were entertained both by the Choir and the band of the Second Parachute Regiment, and after dark there was an extravagant fireworks display (costing £200), including screaming jet-planes and flying saucers, as well as the more traditional salvos of rockets. Unfortunately the operators were so drunk that the sequence was destroyed, and the traditional toast 'Floreat Magdalena', outlined in cascades of golden and silver fire and intended as a finale, went up in the middle of the display, not at the end. Alan had selected the fireworks in February; some of the best pieces, including elephants walking along the banks of the Cherwell, were hidden by the trees. Some Fellows commented that the pyrotechnics were typical of the man.

One old Magdalen man who did not attend the celebrations was the Duke of Windsor, the former Edward VIII. Alan sent him a formal invitation and followed this with a personal message: 'It would be a particular pleasure and a great honour to myself and my colleagues if you could both be present.' The reference to the Duchess must have pleased her husband; but he did not come.

One of Alan's tasks in 1958 was to look after the visiting American politician, Richard Nixon. Boase's smooth introduction – 'Ah, Vice-President Nixon, let me introduce you to Vice-President Taylor' – left the quick-witted American temporarily confused, wondering whether he had misunderstood the British

---

*'I had only met Professor [sic] Taylor once and was flattered and curious; he is a clever man who makes a great donkey of himself.'[33]

system of government. Alan liked Nixon, and was impressed enough to want him to defeat Kennedy in the 1960 Presidential election. Nixon, he felt, had the 'courage and the capacity' to overcome the defects of the Eisenhower administration. Nixon, it seemed to Alan, was 'not insincere in politics'.[34] As Alan saw him off into a taxi outside Magdalen, Nixon asked a question. 'I've got to go on television this evening. They tell me you're a TV performer. Any tips?' 'Yes, I have, Mr Vice-President,' Alan replied. 'Just one thing. Tell the truth – it'll be a sensation.'

That autumn Boase's duties as Vice-Chancellor kept him from attending the Restoration Dinner, the first such absence since Tizard had been stranded abroad in 1943. 'Then our President was engaged in fighting the Germans,' noted Alan; 'this time he was entertaining them.' In January Boase was able to return the compliment, inviting Alan to entertain a visiting party of German journalists lunching at the Mitre Hotel with senior members of the university. 'Mr Taylor is even better known in Germany than in England,' noted the *Oxford Mail*, perhaps a little unconvincingly, 'mainly for his highly unpopular opinion that reunification would be a bad thing for the West.'[35]

In October Alan had written to ask Beaverbrook to be his guest at the college feast on 21 March next. 'It would give me very great pleasure to entertain you, particularly as I shall still be Vice-President.' He commented on Boothby's elevation to the peerage: 'Lord Boothby is resplendent in his new glory.' Beaverbrook regretted that he could not come. 'If Bob Boothby keeps his health he will now expand and certainly he will live to do a great deal of mischief and much harm to the Conservative Party – which might not be a bad thing.'[36]

Alan was a demanding tutor. He was impatient with pupils who were unable or not sufficiently interested to put in the necessary effort. One socialite who yawned in an early morning tutorial found himself presented with an alarm-clock. 'It's no good going to that man with an essay cribbed from one of his books,' a pupil commented bitterly. 'He's against it even if he wrote it himself.' When another produced a Taylor-like essay, Alan commented that he'd heard of the dog returning to its vomit, but never of the vomit returning to the dog.

But tutorials with Alan were fun. He had a habit of dropping his voice and retailing some perception of a politician's motivation in a near murmur, as if it were a secret to be used discreetly. Nine-tenths of the explanation of an event or episode could be discovered from an examination of the characters and the motives of the individuals concerned; or to put it another way, history was full of racy gossip.[37] This interest in people was a feature of his history. 'The Congress of Vienna', he began one of his lectures, 'was the period when, as Metternich's carriage drew away from the doorstep of his mistress, Talleyrand's carriage could be seen arriving.'

On mornings when he was lecturing, Alan used to go into the Senior Common Room early to plan what he was going to say. Raymond Carr often joined him there around eight o'clock in an attempt to break his train of thought; but never succeeded.

> The hour has hardly struck the hour of nine [a profile in the *Observer* reported], and the last undergraduate is still struggling to find a place when Taylor appears on the dais, a stocky, rather rumpled figure, wearing a baggy suit and a shabby gown. He walks with mock diffidence to the rostrum, pushes it aside to show that, unlike lesser mortals, he has no need of notes, puts his hands on his hips, peers over the top of his spectacles, suppresses a grin as if he were about to tell a delightful, but rather rude, story, and starts.
>
> He talks quickly but clearly, making his points by the brilliance of his phrasing rather than by gesture or eloquence, using no tricks except an occasional spontaneous chuckle when he recalls some endearing folly by some long-forgotten British statesman. He stops promptly at five minutes to the hour and disappears rapidly, pausing only to buy the *Guardian* in the High before returning to his college.[38]

Alan's early-morning lectures became a legend within Oxford; no other lecturer could pack a hall at that hour. Undergraduates had been known to turn up at the Examination Schools to hear him speak still dressed in pyjamas and dressing-gowns.

It was obvious to his pupils that Alan was a busy man. Often when they arrived for tutorials he would be concluding a telephone conversation or putting the finishing touches to a review. But despite the many demands on his time, Alan was a conscientious tutor. He was always prompt, and gave his pupils exactly one hour. He concentrated too, listening beneath hooded eyes as his undergraduates read their essays, interrupting only occasionally. Sometimes the trace of a smile would flicker across his face. He was not fooled when a desperate student rewrote another's essay. At the end he would discourse fluently and dogmatically on the subject in question. He had a way of delivering criticism with a tight smile, as if to say, if only you knew.[39] Before the hour was up he would set the topic for the next essay.

Almost invariably he wore a bow-tie and a grey corduroy suit, neither too formal for the day, nor too informal for High Table – the sort of suit a man chooses who is too busy to worry about his daily appearance. The opening of the Trinity Term was marked by his appearance in corduroy shorts and open-necked shirt.

Alan was not much interested in those historical figures who had resisted change. One of his pupils never forgot the contempt with which Alan greeted his proposal that his next essay should be on the Oxford Movement. David Pryce-Jones was still a schoolboy at Eton when he went up to Magdalen to sit the scholarship, part of which was a viva interview. He had just sat down when Alan leaned across the table and said aggressively, 'Why are you wearing a tie?' Pryce-Jones was taken aback. 'Because I thought it appropriate.' 'That just shows what a conventional type of boy you are.' Pryce-Jones had the impression Alan was deliberately trying to unsettle him. Perhaps it was the school which irritated Alan; a reference he wrote for another pupil began 'You can see his typically Etonian faults at a glance . . .' Pryce-Jones when an undergraduate had to read an essay on the Jacobins to Alan. Suddenly Alan picked up a poker and said, 'I'll show you what the meaning of liberty is!' He struck at the chair where Pryce-Jones was sitting. Pryce-Jones ducked and ran out of the room, returning only the following week.

But though Pryce-Jones's tutorials with Alan often degenerated into shouting-matches, Alan was not vindictive towards him. One evening after hours Alan came into Pryce-Jones's rooms to find a girl there – this was then considered a serious offence, for which an undergraduate could theoretically be sent down. Alan affected to take no notice; he stayed and talked for a while, then left and never mentioned the matter later.

Martin Gilbert was another candidate who came up to Magdalen for interview. He had been sent across from Balliol, having puzzled the examiners by insisting that if he could not have a Brackenbury Scholarship he did not want any other; his schoolmaster had told him to say this. 'Why do you want to come to Magdalen?' one member of the interview panel asked. 'I don't,' the schoolboy replied, now thoroughly confused: 'I want to go to Balliol.' Alan chortled. He asked some penetrating questions, with the result that Gilbert was awarded a Magdalen Demyship – a unique form of scholarship dating back to the time of the Founder.

Like other dons, Alan supervised graduate students as well as undergraduates. One of these was William Roger Louis, an American who arrived at Magdalen with an M.A. from Harvard. He wanted to study the German Central African colony Ruanda-Urundi. 'You probably won't know the territory I'm interested in,' said Louis; 'Oh yes I do,' replied Alan, to Louis's surprise. When Louis later proposed to write a book arising out of his postgraduate studies, Alan gave him some sound advice. 'Just tell the story briefly,' he said; 'try to make it detached, precise and rather dull.'[40]

Postgraduates found him a first-class supervisor: efficient, kindly and inspiring.[41] He was modest as well. When Alan Sked came down from Glasgow to undertake research on Austria-Hungary he received a letter of welcome from his new supervisor. 'It is many years since I wrote anything on the Habsburgs and I have forgotten everything I ever knew. I look forward to learning it again from you.'

As an examiner he insisted that no thesis should be more than a hundred thousand words. He used to weigh those he received on the kitchen scales. If they proved too heavy, he would return them to the Examination Schools, *without stamps*. Alan often made the lesser award of a B.Litt. rather than a D.Phil., particularly to those whose work was not based on original sources. Americans suffered at his hands; it seemed to mean nothing to Alan that it was practically impossible to pursue an academic career in the United States without a doctorate. Many distinguished British historians – E.H. Carr, for instance – did not possess research degrees; in the smaller society of pre-War academia it had been possible for an outstanding student to establish a reputation while still an under-graduate. In 1960 Alan told one of his pupils not to 'waste his time' on a doctoral thesis: 'The thing is to do your research and write your books, and find a provincial university in which to teach.' When the same pupil was elected to a Fellowship at Merton, Alan lamented that here was 'another whom I've seduced and misled into staying in this moribund place'.

Alan kept aside one evening a week when students could come to his rooms in the New Buildings for a glass of wine and a chat while he played records on his horn gramophone. He seemed a little isolated; his more perceptive pupils realised it might be more of a kindness than an imposition to drop in on him. In fact few did so, perhaps because they were in awe of this famous and intellectually forbidding tutor. One who did noticed a pile of *Superman* comics by the bed.

Early in 1958 Alan got into another fight. A piece in the *New Statesman* announced the formation of a new organisation, the Campaign for Nuclear Disarmament (CND). Alan telephoned Kingsley Martin and offered his services; he was immediately co-opted on to the Executive Committee. There was to be a public meeting at Central Hall, Westminster, on 17 February; on the night far too many people turned up and several overflow halls had to be used. The speakers included Bertrand Russell, J.B. Priestley, Michael Foot and the Chairman of CND, Canon John Collins. Alan spoke last. He described the magnitude of a Hydrogen Bomb explosion – so many miles of total destruction, so many miles of uncontrollable fires, so many miles of lethal fall-out – pacing about the rostrum. Then he discussed the effects on human beings – the charred bodies, the hideous wounds, and the cancers caused by lingering poisons. Finally he enquired squeakily: 'Is there anyone here who would want to do this to another human being?' No one came forward. 'Then why are we making the damned thing?'

The crowd was excited. Alan, remembering his parents' stories of suffragettes breaking up political meetings with cries of 'Votes for Women', recommended heckling Cabinet ministers with cries of 'Murderer'. As the meeting ended more than a thousand people, though not Alan, made their way to Downing Street, where they stood outside No. 10 crying 'Ban the Bomb' and 'Murderer' until the police arrived with dogs.

For Alan, unilateral nuclear disarmament was 'the biggest issue in politics'. Like many of the CND Executive he had been concerned about nuclear weapons for some years. But in the late 1950s a number of different factors brought the issue to the fore. Atmospheric nuclear tests provided a vivid demonstration of the potential destruction that nuclear war could bring; and the fall-out which began to be detected throughout the world was a source of profound anxiety, particularly as its effects were so little understood. Britain had developed its own atomic weapons, and in 1957 appeared to have conducted successful H-bomb tests.* Large sums had already been spent developing the 'Blue Streak' ballistic missile delivery system; the 'independent deterrent' would soon be in place.

Alan knew how easy it was for war to start by accident, 'to sleepwalk into war'. In 1958 he published a pamphlet, *The Great Deterrent Myth*, followed a year later by another, *The Exploded Bomb*. It was a moral, not an emotional issue, he argued: nuclear weapons were wicked. But even in amoral terms, the deterrent was illogical. Who is safer from H-bombs, he asked – the Swiss or ourselves? 'The Swiss, because they have not got them.' The British weapons were out-of-date; since they were not protected by silos they would be destroyed in a first strike. Therefore they could be useful only as aggressive weapons. Britain could not compete in 'a contest of destruction'; there was no defence against nuclear weapons. He mocked the Government line – it was like saying 'this waterproof will keep you dry so long as it does not rain'. 'Would you feel safe with a fire extinguisher which was guaranteed to burn the house down if it were ever used?' It was no good getting rid of the British bombs and sheltering under the American nuclear 'umbrella' – this would make Britain less, not more, secure. 'The Americans can no longer rely on geographical isolation. Therefore they accumulate so-called allies, satellites, whose real function is to

---

*It now seems that these may not have been true H-bombs.[42]

serve as hostages and to be sacrificed on the outbreak of modern war.' The Americans should be told to quit their bases in Britain.

Unilateral nuclear disarmament should not be confused with pacifism, Alan declared. Indeed, he was described as 'shaking with anger' when Boothby accused him of being a pacifist on 'Free Speech'.[43] Getting rid of nuclear weapons would make Britain more prosperous, remove the danger of nuclear attack, and leave more resources for conventional weapons.* 'It is a disgrace that, apart from nuclear weapons, this country is now more dangerously disarmed than it was at the worst time in the 1930s.' Even though the Soviet Union had not advanced the frontiers of its power an inch since 1945, wrote Alan, we should take careful and accurate precautions against a Communist attack. 'The H-bomb is not a weapon of conquest, because there is nothing left to conquer . . . The H-bomb is a weapon of isolation . . . No one should be misled by the talk about negotiating bomb in hand. There is no way you can negotiate with a bomb, unless you are prepared to use it.' This was a crack at Aneurin Bevan, who had rejected unilateral disarmament at the 1957 Labour Party Conference with the argument that it would send a British Foreign Secretary 'naked into the conference chamber'.

Aside from the logical argument against nuclear weapons, 'there is just a tiny chance that our example may spread . . . There can be no harm in trying morality for a change.' He used the analogy of the slave trade; after Britain had renounced it unilaterally in 1806, other countries followed suit. If Britain disarmed, the moral pressure on the Russians would be far greater, Alan argued, than the deterrent effect of our few nuclear bombs.[44]

Alan became one of CND's most regular speakers. He addressed crowded meetings across the country, his audiences ranging from a few hundred to three or four thousand. In the early summer of 1958, for example, while the Magdalen Quincentenary celebrations reached a climax, he spoke at Sandown Pavilion, the Isle of

---

*In a debate with Alan in December 1958 C.M. Woodhouse, the prospective Conservative candidate for Oxford, neatly reversed this argument; according to Woodhouse, abolition of nuclear weapons would mean the restoration of conscription and at least a shilling on income tax.

Wight (23 April), the Congregational Hall, Guildford (5 May), the Town Hall, St Pancras (11 May), the Town Hall, Birmingham (12 May), the City Hall, Sheffield (16 May), the Town Hall, Cheltenham (19 May), the Free Trade Hall, Manchester (21 May), the Guildhall, Southampton (30 May), Central Hall, Bristol (2 June), the Wesley Central Hall, Portsmouth (6 June), the Co-operative Hall, Leicester (9 June), the Guildhall, Salisbury (26 June), and the Dome, Brighton (9 July).[45] A typical evening that summer found Alan travelling up the A1 on the bench seat of a Volkswagen Dormobile, with the novelist and journalist Mervyn Jones and CND General Secretary Peggy Duff. Alan was 'always on better form when going North'. 'Don't drive too fast, Mervyn,' he said. 'We don't want to arrive early.' The meeting, at the old Mechanics Institute in Bradford, was packed, and Alan gave a very good speech. Afterwards they dined in a local hotel before driving back to London as dawn was breaking.

It was a romantic exercise. The Troublemakers who had run the anti-slavery campaign and in particular the Anti-Corn-Law League were fresh in his mind. For Alan it was a 'wonderful experience' to speak in every great hall in the country, 'particularly as Bright had been there before me'. He spoke in Birmingham City Hall exactly a hundred years after Bright had made one of his most famous speeches there, ridiculing British foreign policy as 'a gigantic system of outdoor relief for the aristocracy'. Leslie Gilbert, Alan's history master from Bootham, was in the audience, and over dinner afterwards Alan cried when Gilbert told him 'God spoke through you tonight'. A year later Gilbert described what he had heard to a meeting of old scholars from Bootham and The Mount. Alan, he said, had made the finest speech of the evening, full of close argument and vigour. As a boy Alan had been critical of many of the things the school stood for, of 'John Bright and all that'. But in Birmingham City Hall 'he reminded the audience of the great speech Bright made in that Hall and how he was proud to have been at Bright's school, and he finished with a peroration which echoed the very accent* and words of Bright.'[46]

---

*Clearly Alan had taken little notice of Wadsworth's reservations on this subject – see page 216.

Alan was a thrilling orator. His moral passion and rhetorical art had made the most lasting impression of all those who had spoken at the inaugural Central Hall meeting. His CND speeches that followed struck Keith Kyle, by now an experienced political commentator, as the finest he had witnessed. This was a cause in which Alan believed one hundred per cent; later he described his involvement with CND as 'extremely enjoyable . . . the best political time I have ever had'. For a while Alan believed that CND might 'sweep the country'. He attacked the Labour Party leaders, who were 'racking their brains how they can get the Party to agree with the Government'. Alan's speech at the Central Hall meeting had offended at least one future member of the Executive Committee because of his 'sneering remarks' about all the political parties. Despite this, Alan agreed to speak to fringe meetings at both the Labour Party Conference and the TUC Conference in 1958.

One of the tactical issues which most exercised the CND leaders was whether or not to work through the Labour Party. Alan was frequently disappointed by Labour under Gaitskell's leadership, which seemed to be dominated by middle-of-the-road public schoolboys. Of course there is a difference between the Conservative and Labour Parties, he had remarked sardonically early in 1957: 'it is the difference between Eton and Winchester'.[47] He proposed that CND should run independent candidates for Parliament. Others on the Executive Committee – Michael Foot, for instance – believed that the Campaign could succeed only if it captured the Labour Party.

In 1960 Alan joined the annual fifty-mile march from the Weapons Research Establishment in Aldermaston to Trafalgar Square in London. (The first march, in 1958, had been in the opposite direction.) At the rally on Easter Monday he spoke to a huge crowd, estimated at up to a hundred thousand people. In his speech he alleged that a prominent member of the Labour Party had been threatened by Hugh Gaitskell with expulsion from the Shadow Cabinet if he joined the march.

Later that year the Labour Party Conference passed a motion in favour of unilateral disarmament, despite the bitter opposition of the leader, who vowed to 'fight and fight and fight again to save the

Party we love'. A Campaign for Democratic Socialism was formed to reverse this decision; its secretary was Alan's former pupil, the future MP, Cabinet minister and peer, William Rodgers. At Conference the following year the resolution was overturned.

Alan detested Gaitskell. In January 1961 he had written a sarcastic letter to the *Guardian*:

> The Labour Party should weigh seriously Mr Gaitskell's warning that, should it support unilateral nuclear disarmament, the results would be disastrous at the polls. A leader who puts electoral calculations first always adds to his reputation. It was for this reason that Baldwin was so highly respected at the end of his life . . . Mr Gaitskell speaks with unique authority on the art of winning elections. He stood high in Labour counsels in 1951 and 1955; he led the party in 1959. Labour's success was staggering on all three occasions.[48]

Alan was now established in two London homes, which he kept entirely separate. Eve sometimes referred to 'The Others'; Margaret to 'The Enemy'. Eve was forbidden from contacting him when he was with Margaret. Even when she gave birth to her first child Eve had to wait until Alan telephoned her before giving him the news; he had not told Margaret that she was pregnant. His daughter Amelia was unaware that the children from the second marriage existed. Margaret described herself as 'Mrs Taylor', and behaved as if she were still his wife; Alan went along with this deception. Hosts found it disconcerting to find Alan arriving at social functions sometimes with one wife, sometimes with another. In 1959 he warned Beaverbrook that he was bringing Margaret rather than Eve to dinner that evening. 'So don't be surprised that you have not met her before; and don't be cross with me. What's more, going off to the Isle of Wight tomorrow, I have no black tie.'[49]

The Isle of Wight 'is my real home now', Alan wrote in 1957.[50] The Mill – originally a tidal mill – was a large seventeenth-century brick building situated on an estuary, very close to the river mouth. Bathing was easy. Giles and Sebastian raced sailing dinghies during the summer. Alan spent the school holidays there with Margaret and the children; the girls were there so much of the year that they began to acquire the local accent. Yarmouth was deserted in the evenings when the day-trippers had gone home. The house was big enough to accommodate whole families of visitors – nobody was ever quite sure how many bedrooms it contained, but they were estimated at twenty-five. There was even congenial company; the Priestleys lived nearby, as did Margaret's cousin, the barrister Patrick O'Connor. Inland the Downs offered good country for walking.

To outsiders visiting Yarmouth Mill or Margaret's London house in St Mark's Crescent Alan appeared like the paterfamilias; he ruled the roost. While Alan was there his word was law; everyone else had to fit in with his routine. Saturday evenings were sacrosanct; the children were made to stay in and Margaret would cook a special meal. After he left on Sunday evening everything reverted to 'normal'. When Carlton Lake, an American art collector, advertised in the *New Statesman* for a house to rent in London, it was Alan who answered the advertisement, and Alan who showed him round St Mark's Crescent. Alan had his own bedroom there, and his own study behind the sitting-room, overlooking the Regent's Canal; he let himself in and out with his own key. To Lake, the house seemed very untidy, with dumpy furnishings and decorated in execrable taste (mauve was a favourite colour). Nevertheless he took it for several summers in succession.

Alan was devoted to his children. By this time Sebastian was at Cambridge; Giles had dropped out of Westminster and was working for a Lyons Corner-House. Giles was active in Youth CND, and after the Aldermaston marches there would be young people sleeping all over the house. To his daughters, now in their early teens, Alan was a more remote figure. They were not old enough to remember much about the time before their parents had split; and he had been absent most of the time since. He took them for walks in Regent's Park and talked to them about the Kings and Queens of England, more like a teacher than a father.

Alan's complicated domestic arrangements did nothing for his career. In 1958, for example, his name came up in conversation between Dame Lilian Penson, the nineteenth-century historian who had been the first woman Vice-Chancellor, and Alan's old friend Kathleen Tillotson, who had recently been elected Hildred Carlile Professor of English in Bedford College. Professor Tillotson suggested Alan as a suitable person to deliver the Stevenson Lecture. 'I think not,' Dame Lilian said. 'He is not really sound. You know, his private life is quite a mess. Although he is divorced from his first wife he apparently still goes back to her.'

Perhaps because of his own experiences, Alan disliked sexual intolerance. In March 1958 he was one of the signators to a letter published in *The Times*, supporting the recommendations of the Wolfenden Report that homosexual acts between consenting adults should no longer be a criminal offence. The previous year he had ridiculed a police campaign against 'saucy' postcards. 'Why can't we leave people to regulate their own private affairs?'[51]

'I fear the waiting-list for professorial chairs at Brighton University [sic] must already be full,' Alan's 'London Diary' lamented in November 1958. If this was a hint, it was not taken up. Sussex University was the first and most fashionable of the new 'plate-glass' universities to open in the 1960s, followed by Essex, Kent, Lancaster, East Anglia and York. Competition for teaching posts was keen; it was said that the entire English Department at Aberdeen applied for places at Sussex. Alan liked Brighton, and thought he might be given a free hand if he went there. He approached John Fulton, Principal of the new University College and soon to be Vice-Chancellor of the new University. Might he find a place for Alan? But Fulton had already appointed two professors of history; he could not accommodate any more. A little later a swingeing attack on the new universities appeared under Alan's name in the *Sunday Express*.[52] The scientists were particularly upset, for they found that according to Alan's piece science would not be taught at Sussex.

Alan was invited to give the 1959 Raleigh Lecture at the British Academy. He chose as his topic 'Politics in the First World War', marking a move away from European to English history,* and

---

*In *Europe: Grandeur and Decline* (1967), a selection of his essays on European history, the latest is dated 1955.

from diplomatic to political. He wrote telling Beaverbrook that he intended to 'trespass into your field . . . It will be hard going to compete with those wonderful books of yours.'[53] Like his Leslie Stephen Lecture delivered a couple of years later, 'Lloyd George: Rise and Fall', his Raleigh Lecture was derived from his work on the Oxford History of England volume. Yet both lectures were pioneering studies. 'Politics in the First World War' identified the underlying conflict between freedom and organisation as the profound force which broke Asquith's Government and brought in Lloyd George as the head of a coalition. 'Could the War be conducted by 'Liberal' methods – that is, by voluntary recruiting and *laissez-faire* economics? Or must there be compulsory military service, control of profits and direction of labour and industry?' The American historian Alfred Gollin, writing nearly twenty years later, described this piece as a contribution of vital consequence. 'It opens up the subject in a way that has not been done by anyone else.'[54]

'Lloyd George: Rise and Fall' resurrected the reputation of the Welsh Wizard, a process of rehabilitation which has continued ever since, until today Lloyd George is recognised as a great Prime Minister.* There has been a corresponding decline in the reputation of Lloyd George's political rival Asquith, described by Alan in 1966 as 'one of the most disastrous prime ministers in British history'.[55] Alan was the first historian to reveal that during the First World War Asquith – 'Squiffy' – was often helpless with drink on the front bench.[56]

In 'Politics in the First World War' Alan went out of his way to praise Lord Beaverbrook's historical works, which he described as 'splendid volumes. Their brilliant presentation, wealth of material and deep understanding of men's motives, stir the admiration of the professional historian, not his jealousy.' His lecture was a 'supplement' to Beaverbrook's work, or, 'in a phrase which he has used in a different connection, "another version of the same".' It was one thing to praise Beaverbrook in the *Observer*, quite another to do so within the walls of the British Academy.

---

*The process has been enhanced by access to Lloyd George's papers in Beaverbrook's collection, and particularly by John Grigg's monumental biography.

Viscount Stansgate, father of Tony Benn, was in the audience for the Raleigh Lecture. He had been a Liberal MP during the First World War. After the lecture was over he said to Alan: 'I had no idea it had been like that.'

At a CND meeting in Brighton during the summer of 1958 Alan had become very angry with a speaker who asked what was obviously a pro-Soviet question. It was only a few weeks after the Hungarian leader Imre Nagy had been executed, having been in hiding and then imprisoned after the 1956 Hungarian Uprising. 'Don't imagine for one moment that this Campaign is a front for the murderers of Imre Nagy,' he said furiously. Over dinner afterwards Alan was unrepentant about his outburst.

The Hungarian Uprising had been crushed by the Soviet Army, resulting in perhaps 20,000 deaths, at the very moment when the Anglo-French force was landing at Suez. For some years afterwards Hungary was a pariah state, shunned by Westerners, just as many refused to visit Spain while Franco was still in power. But in 1960 Alan decided to accept an invitation to go there with two other Academicians. Perhaps he saw it as an act of defiance against the Cold War. He took a sleeper to Vienna, where he and Else had lunch together one last time. Then he travelled on to Budapest, to lecture in the University on the origins of the Second World War. He visited the Karolyi Palace, now a museum; his old friend Michael Karolyi had died in exile five years earlier. Tears stood in his eyes as he peered into the hall and saw the grand staircase beyond. His guide on these sightseeing trips was a young Hungarian historian who specialised in nineteenth- and twentieth-century British history, Eva Haraszti.

They spent a great deal of time together, and Alan found himself drawn to this thoughtful young woman. Eva was seventeen years younger than this famous English historian whom she had always admired. She was married, with two small children. But she felt attracted to Alan; and she was moved when, as they sat together on the banks of the Danube, he told her of his two unhappy marriages. On Alan's last evening in Budapest they dined alone, and held hands in the car back to the hotel.

On his return Alan wrote a piece for the *New Statesman* entitled 'Too Good to be True?' which gave a generally sympathetic picture of life in Hungary after the Uprising. He admitted that it was hard to be sure, but he judged the stories of mass arrests and hangings to be exaggerated. 'Conditions in Hungary were certainly much better than I expected them to be.'[57]

Before his visits to Hungary Alan had described the Soviet action in 1956 as 'shameful' and 'foolish', though 'they are not likely to repeat it'. Reviewing a book on the Communist subversion of Czechoslovakia only two months before his trip, he had written that 'it is impossible ever to co-operate with Communists or to trust them'.[58] But afterwards he came to believe that the anti-Communist forces in Hungary had brought repression on themselves. Better a Communist government than a reactionary one, he argued. 'The Hungarian rising of 1956 was a rising by all the most reactionary forces,' he said in 1983. 'I think in every way what happened in Hungary in 1956 was fortunate.'[59]

Raymond Carr was with Alan in 1960 on the night Namier died. The telephone rang; it was the *Observer*, wanting an obituary. 'Give me five minutes to think,' said Alan. Five minutes later the telephone rang again and Alan dictated his piece straight down the line. Namier, he said, had a unique place among English historians.

> Whatever subject he handled came out not merely illuminated but transformed. The political history of England in the eighteenth century, especially, will never look the same again . . . His new interpretation was not only valuable in itself. It was even more important because of the method by which it was arrived at. This method was the 'Namierisation' which has since been used by others, and extended into other fields from the fifteenth to the twentieth centuries. Essentially, Namierisation meant a rigorous substitution of accurate detail for the generalisations which had contented older historians . . .
>
> Namier knew in his blood the complexities of European nationalism and class conflict; and he interpreted these complexities to English audiences with dazzling clarity.

I was his colleague at Manchester for eight years; and for twenty-six* his close friend. I loved and admired him as a man as well as an historian. We had our differences. I thought he had an excessive contempt for ideas and principles in history . . .

He was . . . a master of English prose-style. He loved England, particularly the traditional England of the governing classes. Most of all, he loved the University of Oxford. The University repaid this great historian by according him recognition only after he had passed retiring age.[60]

There was another break with the past three months later, when Kingsley Martin retired as editor of the *New Statesman*. 'The end of an era! It is most distressing,' Alan lamented to him, 'to think that the *NS* may now follow a consistent line two weeks running.'[61]

In 1960 Alan wrote an article for the magazine *History Today*. 'Who burnt the Reichstag?' was based on research by a retired German civil servant, Fritz Tobias. The Reichstag fire on 27 February 1933 had been extremely convenient for the Nazis, so convenient that most historians assumed the Nazis must have started the fire themselves. Hitler had been appointed Chancellor at the end of January, but the Nazis and their allies did not have a parliamentary majority. The burning of the Reichstag provided a perfect pretext for the suspension of constitutional freedoms; and by blaming the Communists the Nazis were able to whip up a Red scare. Few neutral observers believed the Communists were responsible. Alan, like most historians, assumed the Nazis must have done it.

Tobias's research challenged this consensus. He argued, in Alan's opinion conclusively, that the fire had been the work of a lone Dutchman, Marinus van der Lubbe. For Alan the conclusion was clear:

The affair should change our estimate of Hitler's methods. He was far from being the far-sighted planner that he is usually made out to appear. He had a genius for improvisation; and his behaviour over

*i.e. until 1957

the Reichstag fire was a wonderful example of it. When he became Chancellor, he had no idea how he would transform his position into a constitutional dictatorship. The solution came to him in a flash as he stood among the smouldering ruins of the Reichstag that February evening . . . That is the way of history. Events happen by chance; and men mould them into a pattern.[62]

After publishing four books in as many years – *The Struggle for Mastery in Europe* (1954), *Bismarck* (1955), *The Troublemakers* (1957) and a book of essays, *Englishmen and Others* (1956) – Alan had paused. There was his volume in the Oxford History of England: but that would take years, and he had told Clark he could not start writing until the beginning of 1960, when he was free from his duties as Vice-President of Magdalen. Meanwhile he had started reading and collecting material as soon as he felt sure of OUP's commitment. In June 1957 he wrote to Captain Basil Liddell Hart, the military expert: 'I am very anxious to consult you some time. I have undertaken to write a volume in the Oxford History of England on the period 1914–45; and am very much in search of guidance on the military side.' Liddell Hart agreed to help; and Alan sent him a preliminary letter full of questions about the First World War: about movement, tanks, horses and conscription, among other issues. On 4 July they met for the first time; a month later Alan wrote from the Isle of Wight: 'I am most grateful for the papers you sent me which started my mind off in all sorts of ways.'[63]

Hamish Hamilton tried to get Alan to write another book in the meantime. He put various ideas to him, among them biographies of Metternich ('worked out') and Adam von Trott, but Alan was not tempted to write a book just for the money. 'You little know what it would cost you to compensate me for articles and television, I daren't tell you how many thousands a year!' He told Hamilton that his intellectual capital needed replenishing. Perhaps he had been hurt by criticism of *The Troublemakers*, for in October 1958 he wrote to Hamilton: 'I doubt whether I shall write any more. The more one writes, the more one is ignored or slighted in the academic world, until one becomes embittered as I have.'

However, it seems that this mood was only temporary, for six weeks later he mentioned a book on the origins of the Second World War which he planned to write in 1959, when his duties as Vice-President would be less time-consuming.[64] The subject had preoccupied him for at least the past ten years; he had explored it repeatedly in book reviews and other short pieces. Reading dozens of volumes of diplomatic documents and memoirs for review had caused Alan to think about the problems of the 1930s as they appeared to statesmen at the time. They moved 'in a moral and intellectual fog — sometimes deceived by the dictators, sometimes deceiving themselves, often deceiving their own public'. Alan had become so sceptical of explanations offered by statesmen after the event that he was inclined to dismiss them altogether. The historian, he argued, must try to 'push through the cloud of phrases to the realities beneath'.[65] He was irritated by facile parallels with the 1930s; now he wondered if the 1930s had been like that anyway. He knew the temptation to look back into the past and see a pattern where none had existed, or at least where none had been apparent to the protagonists. His biography of Bismarck made him believe that statesmen rarely follow a preconceived plan; even when they do, their best or worst intentions are constantly thwarted by chance occurrences or misunderstandings. His work on the origins of the First World War had led him to the conclusion that great events do not always have great causes. His study of the Nazi 'seizure of power' made him disinclined to believe Hitler's own boasting. What if Hitler were an opportunist, taking advantage of events which occurred at random? What if the war of 1939, far from being premeditated, were a mistake, the result of diplomatic blunders?

This was the conclusion Alan had reached in principle. His short pieces anticipated many of the arguments which were to cause such shock when published in book form. In November 1959, for example, he reviewed a volume of the German diplomatic documents:

> The war of 1939 seems in longer retrospect to have been the result of miscalculation, not of deliberate policy . . . [Hitler's] success seems mysterious; his secret was not to have one . . . Hitler did not plan his victory. It was presented to him by the statesmen of Great Britain,

France and Soviet Russia. Such are the advantages of being at the centre of Europe and having strong nerves. The lesson has not been lost on Dr Adenauer.[66]

At the beginning of October 1959 Alan wrote to Liddell Hart explaining that he had put his Oxford history aside for a year or so in order to write a book on the origins of the Second World War; 'mainly to make the point that it was not planned by Hitler but that he scrambled into it by mistake – some his own mistakes but also the mistakes of others. I'm sure this is right; but it will disturb received notions.' Liddell Hart replied that he was

> most interested . . . Your conclusion that it was accidental rather than deliberate coincides with my own . . . In a discussion at the first annual Conference of the Institute for Strategic Studies this last weekend, I had come to see that most wars were detonated accidentally rather than deliberately. I emphasised this to correct some arguments that the best way to check any frontier incursions by the Russians or their satellites was to start dropping some atomic bombs.[67]

Liddell Hart had put his finger on one of Alan's reasons for writing the book. Thermonuclear war loomed large in Alan's mind as night after night he trod the boards of city halls speaking on behalf of CND. One of the strongest arguments for nuclear disarmament was the danger of unintended war in the age of nuclear weapons. This fear influenced Alan as he wrote; indeed it was a reason for writing such a book now, rather than waiting another ten or fifteen years. 'The few survivors may have given up reading books by then, let alone writing them.'[68] If the Second World War had started by accident, then so could a Third. To put it another way, if Alan could show that the War had begun in error, it would be a powerful propaganda stroke for CND. Alan had long ago decided that one of the causes of the Second World War had been the mistaken conclusions drawn by historians about the causes of the First. Perhaps a Third World War would arise because of mistaken conclusions about the causes of the Second. In particular, Alan was anxious to refute what he saw as a specious argument: that it was necessary to take a tough stand against the Soviet Union because failure to take a tough stand against Germany in the 1930s had led to war. On the contrary, Alan believed that Anglo-Soviet friendship was a necessary condition for peace in Europe.

The origins of the Second World War had excited comparatively little interest from other historians. Ever since the early days of the War itself there had been a consensus about the events which had led up to it. Left and Right united in the view that the policy of appeasement was doomed because Hitler had planned a war from the beginning; only the blindness of a few Western politicians – and the treachery of the Soviet Union – had allowed him to get so far. When war broke out, and a weak French government collapsed, as much from internal corruption as external assault, Britain stood alone. This was the national myth.

Alan had a keen eye for hypocrisy. Appeasement had been a popular policy, certainly until after Munich. It had originated in a high-minded attempt at the impartial redress of grievances; only later did it become synonymous with craven surrender. Those who had pointed a finger at the 'Guilty Men' in 1940 had for the most part opposed the National Government's attempts to rearm. Many anti-Bolsheviks had welcomed Hitler as a strong man who would stand up to the Soviet Union. Alan resented the way the national myth had been employed, often by those whose records were less than clean. Fresh in his mind was the example of Suez, when British politicians had seen in Nasser a reincarnation of the Fascist dictators of the 1930s. CND, said its critics, was another form of appeasement. The Campaign had been running for less than a month when Priestley complained in the *New Statesman* of attempts to 'smear us by making use of false analogies and of vague references to what happened in the 1930s'.[69]

The myth about Hitler required him to have had a plan for war. It was part of the prosecution case against the leading Nazis at the Nuremberg Trials that they had conspired to commit 'crimes against peace'. If it could be proved that Hitler and his immediate circle conspired to make war, it would help to rehabilitate the German masses, who presumably had been tricked into fighting. Various documents, including the Hossbach Memorandum, were produced to support the idea that such a conspiracy existed. Alan pointed out these were collected hastily, and almost at random, as a basis for lawyers' briefs. 'This is not how historians would proceed. The lawyer aims to make a case; the historian to understand a situation.'[70]

'I wrote this book to satisfy my historical curiosity,' Alan wrote afterwards. He tried to present the events leading up to the War in a detached manner, setting aside all partisan feelings: 'The present-day historian should seek to anticipate the judgements of the future rather than repeat those of the past.' He admitted that the record, considered in detachment, often pushed him towards conclusions different from those which other men, including himself, gave at the time. 'This has not weighed with me one way or the other. I am concerned to understand what happened, not to vindicate or condemn . . . In retrospect, though many were guilty, none were innocent . . . This is a story without heroes; and perhaps even without villains.'[71]

Alan was not interested in the profound causes, which explained everything and nothing. Wars, he said, are much like road accidents.*

> They have a general cause and particular causes at the same time. Every road accident is caused, in the last resort, by the invention of the internal combustion engine and by men's desire to get from one place to another. In this sense, the 'cure' for road accidents is to forbid motor cars. But a motorist, charged with dangerous driving, would be ill-advised if he pleaded the existence of motor cars as his sole defence. The police and the courts do not weigh profound causes. They seek a specific cause for each accident – error on the part of the driver; excessive speed; drunkenness; faulty brakes; bad road surface. So it is with wars. 'International anarchy' makes war possible; it does not make it certain. After 1918 more than one writer made his name by demonstrating the profound causes of the First World War; and though the demonstrations were often correct, they thus diverted attention from the question why that particular war

---

*He could speak as an authority on the subject. In the 1950s he had at least two serious smashes; and early in 1961, a couple of months before *The Origins of the Second World War* was published, he was convicted of dangerous driving and fined £25 after a collision. The other driver was Peter Plantagenet Somerset Fry, who not long before had won £1000 answering historical questions on a television quiz show.[72]

happened at that time. They are complementary; they do not exclude each other. The Second World War, too, had profound causes; but it also grew out of specific events, and these events are worth detailed examination.[73]

Alan's method was similar – though much less detailed – to the one he had used in *The Struggle for Mastery in Europe*. *The Origins of the Second World War* picked up where *The Struggle for Mastery in Europe* left off, in 1918. Each step on the road to war, each crisis, was examined, using all the published documentary evidence available. It was like analysing a game of chess; when one side made a move, you turned the board around to consider how the situation appeared to the opponent. Even the time taken to respond could be significant. Examining the Anglo-Soviet negotiations before the Nazi-Soviet Non-Aggression Pact, for example, Alan showed that, far from stalling the British, as might be expected as evidence of insincerity, the Soviets had always responded very swiftly to British proposals; it was the British who had dragged their feet.[74]

Viewed close up, the events leading up to the War seemed very different from the way they had hitherto been presented. Munich emerged as 'a triumph for British policy'; everyone agreed that the Sudeten Germans should be allowed self-determination, and Hitler had been forced to accept much less than he had hoped. Far from operating by a master-plan, Hitler improvised, and like other politicians often blundered. The *reductio ad absurdum* of this approach was Alan's conclusion: 'Hitler may have projected a great war all along; yet it seems from the record that he became involved in war through launching on 29 August a diplomatic manoeuvre which he ought to have launched on 28 August.'[75]

Hitler, too, seemed different. Alan started with the idea that Hitler's foreign policy was capable of rational explanation. He deliberately used the word 'statesman' to describe Hitler, something which riled his critics. According to Alan, the mainspring of Hitler's foreign policy was no different from that of his predecessors: the destruction of Versailles. 'He wanted to free Germany from the restrictions of the peace treaty; to restore a great German army, and then to make Germany the greatest power in Europe from her natural weight.'[76]

Alan did not doubt 'the unspeakable wickedness of the gas chambers'; but he was much more doubtful that it was wicked to use force, or the threat of it, to achieve one's aims in international affairs. This is what he meant when he made one of the statements which most antagonised his critics. 'In principle and in doctrine, Hitler was no more wicked and unscrupulous than many other contemporary statesmen.' This sentence has often been quoted without the one which immediately follows: 'In wicked acts he outdid them all.'[77]

Alan discounted all Hitler's talk about remaking the world. In his view Hitler was a dreamer. 'If only people had known how to handle Hitler properly,' Alan told Keith Kyle, 'he'd probably have ended his days at a German Chatham House.'* Neither *Mein Kampf* nor the Hossbach Memorandum should be taken seriously. 'When Hitler talked to his generals, he talked for effect, not to reveal the workings of his mind'; 'Hitler did not make plans – for world conquest or for anything else. He assumed that others would provide opportunities, and that he would seize them'; 'he was always the man of daring improvisations; he made lightning decisions, and then presented them as the result of long-term policy'.[79] But if Hitler did not plan the War of 1939, how did it happen? Alan's explanation was that human blunders do more to shape history than human wickedness; war was caused as much by the blunders of others as by the wickedness of the dictators themselves.

Facing the dictators were the appeasers. Alan, who had excoriated the appeasers in the late 1930s, now produced the case for the defence – or at least a plea for mitigation. Whatever he thought of politicians, Alan was remarkably sensitive to the problems they faced, perhaps because he had spent so much time looking at their documents. Neville Chamberlain was a Nonconformist Radical gone sour; so, in a different way, was Alan. When Alan wrote that Munich was 'a triumph for all that was best and most enlightened in British life', it was of course meant ironically; but it was not altogether a joke. It was 'a triumph for those who preached equal

---

*'In England, Mussolini, the vain and discontented schoolteacher, would have been, no doubt, an eager member of the Left Book Club.'[78]

justice between peoples', he went on, 'a triumph for those who had courageously denounced the harshness and short-sightedness of Versailles. Brailsford, the leading Socialist authority on foreign affairs, wrote in 1920 of the peace settlement: "The worst offence was the subjection of over three million Germans to Czech rule."'[80] This is what Alan's father had believed, what Alan himself had believed, what almost all Progressive people had believed in the 1920s and early 1930s. Chamberlain's mistake was not to have changed his mind.

Another important element in the book, one often overlooked by his critics, is Alan's attention to Soviet affairs. It was part of the British myth to denounce Soviet treachery, as it was to lament French weakness. Alan attempted to show that the faults were not all on one side. Given that Soviet statesmen regarded all foreign Powers with intense suspicion, and given that the prime motive of Soviet policy was to be left alone, it was perhaps not so surprising that they acted as they did. When the Soviet attempts to form an anti-Fascist alliance were continually rebuffed, they chose what seemed to them the only available option, a non-aggression pact with Germany.

> It was no doubt disgraceful that Soviet Russia should make any agreement with the leading Fascist state; but this reproach comes ill from the statesmen who went to Munich and who were then sustained in their own countries by huge majorities. The Russians, in fact, did only what the Western statesmen had hoped to do; and Western bitterness was the bitterness of disappointment, mixed with anger that professions of Communism were no more sincere than their own professions of democracy.[81]

Alan worked hard on his new book. The result is perhaps the most perfect of all his writings, so simple and clear that its conclusions come as a shock. The style alone – sparse, laconic, controlled – makes it worth reading. He had completed the manuscript by the summer of 1960. 'It will annoy the old boys who thought they had settled everything about the Second World War years ago,' he told Hamilton.[82] He sent a draft to James Joll to check for howlers;

though Joll did not wholly agree with the argument, he found it stimulating. Alan knew that a storm was brewing. 'We shall have some silly reviews,' he warned his editor, Roger Machell, on the eve of publication: 'paradoxical, wrong-headed and so on, they'll say.'[83]

The Origins of the Second World War was published in April 1961. Critics descended on the book like hungry birds. Several reviewers praised it as a masterpiece; others as perverse, dangerous, disgraceful and intellectually deplorable. Some seemed to believe it was an exercise in deliberate perversity. 'Strange how people think it was deliberately wrong-headed,' Alan commented to Sir George Clark: 'such a book would be impossible to write.'[84] A correspondence began in the *Times Literary Supplement*, where the book (and its favourable review) was attacked by critics as varied as Isaac Deutscher, Elizabeth Wiskemann and A.L. Rowse; an exchange of views was printed in *Encounter*; there was a televised debate. Of course it became a bestseller. When the book was published in the United States, the reaction was even more extreme. Alan was accused of whitewashing the Nazis; the magazine *Horizon* printed a 'Memorandum from Adolf Hitler' congratulating Alan!

The most powerful of Alan's critics was Hugh Trevor-Roper, who launched a devastating polemic against the book in *Encounter*. He accused Alan of sharing the views of the appeasers; more seriously, perhaps, he accused Alan of selecting, suppressing and arranging evidence to support his thesis, and of ignoring the programme which Hitler had laid down for himself in *Mein Kampf* and elsewhere. In a subsequent issue of *Encounter*, Alan issued a retort; he compared Trevor-Roper's use of his material with what he had actually said. Trevor-Roper had concluded that the book 'will do harm, perhaps serious harm, to Mr Taylor's reputation as a serious historian'; Alan repudiated this allegation and alongside it wrote: 'The Regius Professor's methods of quotation might also do harm to his reputation as a serious historian, if he had one.' Trevor-Roper protested that his summaries had been distilled from many quotations.[85]

The newspapers relished the 'feud' between the 'fighting dons of Oxford', particularly when Alan agreed to take part in a televised debate with Trevor-Roper. Before Trevor-Roper's *Encounter* review appeared, Alan was interviewed by *Reynolds News*. 'His review of my book should be very amusing,' he said: 'I look forward to reading it. He knows as much about twentieth-century history as I do about seventeenth-century history – which is not to say nothing at all.'[86] (This last sentence has often been misquoted, omitting the double negative.)

The television debate was chaired by Robert Kee. Given the sharpness of the printed exchanges, it was curiously subdued – 'often lively but never bad-tempered', in the view of the *Oxford Mail*.[87] 'Arguing with Hugh was like hitting a featherbed,' Alan complained to Hamilton. Most viewers thought that Alan won the contest, though some thought Trevor-Roper won the argument. Alan was the more polished television performer, and by using Trevor-Roper's first name when the latter addressed him as 'Taylor' he succeeded in making Trevor-Roper appear stuffy. Beaverbrook watched the 'TV encounter of the week' with Michael Foot and his wife Jill Craigie. 'If you will excuse a cliché, you wiped the floor with the young man, who is a Regius Professor,' wrote Beaverbrook. 'It was a pity the chairman interrupted so frequently. You should have clobbered him.' Alan thanked Beaverbrook for his kind words. 'I ought to have done better, but perhaps scholarly reserve was a good thing for once.'[88]

The main criticism of the book was to allege that it excused Hitler's crimes. A few critics went further and said that, by implication, Alan had exonerated the German people. Indeed, Isaac Deutscher thought it was intended to justify German rearmament. Others took the moral of the book to be that Britain should have stood aside and allowed Germany to dominate Europe unopposed. These critics showed a complete misunderstanding of Alan's viewpoint. Alan perhaps exaggerated when he wrote that he had been an anti-appeaser from the day Hitler came to power; but he could certainly claim to have been an active opponent of Germany 'when many of my critics were confining their activity to the seclusion of Oxford common-rooms.'[89] Far from denigrating the British decision to go to war, Alan took a far more populist line than most historians, frequently describing it as 'a good war' or 'a war of the people'. In 1958, for example, he had written in the *New Statesman* that 'Englishmen who remember the Second World War know that one war was right'. Alan believed that blaming Hitler alone for the War let the German people off the hook. The Germans sheltered behind the Nazis. 'All this about economic causes of war fine, but irrelevant,' Alan wrote to Kingsley Martin early in 1958. 'Cause of World War I: Germany. Cause of World War II: Germany. Now no Germany, so no war!'[90]

The error was not confined to academics. When Alan flew to Munich for another televised debate, this time with a Swiss professor, the taxi-driver who drove him in from the airport queried whether he knew a certain Englishman called A.J.P. Taylor. Alan was taken aback; he explained that he knew him well, being himself A.J.P. Taylor. The taxi-driver stopped in mid-traffic, explained that he had been part of Hitler's SS bodyguard, and extended a hand to congratulate Alan for proving that Hitler had not caused the War after all.

Yet one can see why the mistake was made. Alan had spent much of his career arguing that Germany should be held responsible for the First World War; now, it seemed, he was arguing that Germany might not be responsible for the Second. Alan's approach was so cool that hot-blooded critics missed the irony. His cynicism contrasted oddly with his romantic idealism, for example about nuclear disarmament. Alan admitted that 'my book *can* be read two ways'. Perhaps Trevor-Roper was right when he commented that Alan ran the risk of being considered 'too clever by half'.[91]

Alan's response to his critics was not to respond. After the fusillade in the *Times Literary Supplement*, Alan replied with a brief note: 'I have no sympathy with authors who resent criticism or who try to answer it. I must however thank your correspondents for the free publicity which they have given to my book.' Following a meeting of the Theodor Herzl Society at Zion House, Hampstead, at which the guest speaker, C.C. Aronsfeld, acting director of the Wiener Library, accused Alan of 'juggling with the facts of history' and condemned *The Origins of the Second World War* as 'possibly the start of a Nazi revival', the local paper asked Alan to comment. 'I have nothing to say,' he was reported as replying: 'people can read my book and judge for themselves.'[92]

Some years after the book was published, Martin Gilbert bought a copy of *The Origins of the Second World War* in a second-hand bookshop. He was disconcerted to find it was full of pencilled marginalia of a kind hostile to the argument. The letters 'FBA', standing for Fellow of the British Academy, appeared after Alan's name on the title-page; against them the owner of the pencil had placed an exclamation mark. When Gilbert turned to the fly-leaf, he found the previous owner's name: A.L. Rowse. Gilbert presented the book to Alan, who was very much amused.

When Gilbert apologised for one of the paragraphs in his *Time and Tide** review, which he felt, having sent it off, had been too harsh, Alan replied reassuringly:

> I should be ashamed to have pupils who were not disrespectful of me as of everything else . . . Never, never do I resent criticism; nor do I reply to it . . . of course I aim to write like a journalist if by that you mean that I aim to interest the reader without falsifying the issue. And it would do you no harm to have the same aim.
>
> Serious advice. As a reviewer, weigh your words carefully. But once you've settled them, stick to them. Never apologise or retreat. Above all, remember that as a reviewer, you have one duty and one duty only: to the potential reader. You must tell him the truth about the book without thought whether you are pleasing the author or offending him.
>
> At any rate, don't ever imagine again that you need to apologise to me. For one thing, I can defend myself.[93]

When the American edition came out in 1962, Alan took the opportunity to add a Preface for American Readers. The book drew particularly hostile, in his view abusive, reviews from Americans. 'Is there something in my writing peculiarly provoking to Americans?' he asked in 1964. 'If I were to return the abuse I could say . . . that my country declared war on its own choice. Citizens of a country which only got into the War when Hitler condescended to declare war on it are not entitled to reproach anyone except

---

*The Literary Editor was David Pryce-Jones.

themselves.'[94] His flippancy infuriated the more serious American historians. American professors resented his book, he often said, because they disliked the prospect of having to revise their lecture notes. Enthusiasts for the Cold War could not be expected to agree with Alan's vindication of the Soviet pre-War position, nor the book's implicit moral of rapprochement with Russia. To exonerate Hitler was to encourage Khrushchev. Perhaps Americans had invested more heavily in the cliché of appeasement, somewhat discredited in Britain after Suez. Yet there was another aspect of Alan's book which made it particularly provocative to Americans. 'In the American view war is justifiable only in self-defense against attack,' wrote Louis Morton, Professor of History at Dartmouth College. Alan's cynical emphasis on power politics was an affront to such idealistic sentiments.

In 1963 a second edition was published, which included a new foreword, 'Second Thoughts'. Alan took the opportunity to rebut some of the criticisms, and to support his argument with new data. He discussed in detail the provenance of the Hossbach Memorandum. 'All that survives', he concluded, 'is a copy, perhaps shortened, perhaps edited, of a copy of an unauthenticated draft.' As for *Mein Kampf*, 'Hitler merely repeated the ordinary chatter of right-wing circles'.[95]

Turning from Hitler to the appeasers, Alan wanted to understand them, not to vindicate or condemn them. They were not stupid or cowards. What were their alternatives? Alliance with Soviet Russia was the only option: an option few Englishmen were prepared to embrace in 1939. Alan had a distaste for cant.

> The British stand in September 1939 was no doubt heroic; but it was heroism mainly at the expense of others . . . In 1938 Czechoslovakia was betrayed. In 1939 Poland was saved. Less than one hundred thousand Czechs died during the War. Six and a half million Poles were killed.* Which was better? To be a betrayed Czech or a saved

---

*The Polish figure includes the three million Polish Jews murdered during the War; the Czech figure omits the 277,000 Czechoslovak Jews who died. I am indebted to Martin Gilbert for pointing out this alarming discrepancy.

Pole? I am glad Germany was defeated and Hitler destroyed. I also appreciate that others paid the price for this, and I recognise the honesty of those who thought the price too high.

It was no part of an historian's duty to say what ought to have been done.

His sole duty is to find out what was done and why. Little can be discovered so long as we go on attributing everything that happened to Hitler. He supplied a powerful dynamic element, but it was fuel to an existing engine. He was in part the creation of Versailles, in part the creation of ideas that were common in contemporary Europe. Most of all, he was the creation of German history and of the German present. He would have counted for nothing without the support and co-operation of the German people. It seems to be believed nowadays that Hitler did everything himself, even driving the trains and filling the gas chambers unaided. This was not so. Hitler was a sounding-board for the German nation. Thousands, many hundred thousand Germans, carried out his orders without qualm or question. As supreme ruler of Germany, Hitler bears the greatest responsibility for acts of immeasurable evil; for the destruction of German democracy; for the concentration camps; and, worst of all, for the extermination of peoples during the Second World War. He gave orders, which Germans executed, of a wickedness without parallel in civilised history. His foreign policy was a different matter. He aimed to make Germany the dominant Power in Europe and maybe, more remotely, the world. Other Powers have pursued similar aims, and still do. Other Powers treat smaller countries as their satellites. Other Powers seek to defend their vital interests by force of arms. In international affairs there was nothing wrong with Hitler except that he was a German.[96]

'Is it, as some have suggested,' wrote Trevor-Roper, 'a gesture of posthumous defiance to his former master, Sir Lewis Namier, for some imagined slight? If so, it is just as well that it is posthumous: otherwise what devastating justice it would have received!'[97]

Certainly *The Origins of the Second World War* revises the picture painted by Namier in *Diplomatic Prelude*. Yet a recent study of Namier has pointed to the similarities of approach and analysis between the two men's work on the subject.[98] John

Brooke, the keeper of the Namier flame, had 'no doubt' that if Namier were still alive he would have come out firmly on Alan's side in the debate with Trevor-Roper and others.[99] Like Alan, Namier paid very little attention to Fascism as an ideology; like Alan, Namier was profoundly cynical about the actions of Western statesmen and diplomats; like Alan, Namier believed an Anglo-Soviet alliance was necessary to contain Germany; like Alan, Namier saw Hitler's bid to dominate Europe as part of a continuous process in German history. He was sceptical of explanations which relied on Hitler's character and mental instability. For Namier, the Third Reich was not 'a gruesome accident or an aberration, but the correct consummation of the German era in history'; Hitler was 'probably one of the most representative Germans that ever lived'. Fascism was merely a doctrine; but Germany was the psychotic of Europe. 'States, like Planets, move in predestined courses.'[100]

In the same year that *The Origins of the Second World War* was published, the German historian Fritz Fischer published his *Griff nach der Weltmacht*. Fischer's book, which caused considerable distress in Germany, revealed the extent of German culpability for the First World War; and incidentally supported Alan's view of Hitler. Fischer confirmed that Hitler was pursuing, albeit by more violent means, the traditional aims of German foreign policy.[101] Fischer's work strengthened the idea that an unrestrained Germany, Fascist or not, was a menace to the rest of Europe. In his review of Alan's book, Geoffrey Barraclough noted that Adenauer was even at that moment speaking of the 'peaceful revision' of the frontier with Poland – 'a favourite phrase' – he quoted Alan's words with approval – 'of statesmen who are not ready to go to war'.[102]

The Origins of the Second World War was an international bestseller, and a *cause célèbre*. It was translated into French, Italian, German, Finnish, Dutch, Portuguese, Spanish, Norwegian, Danish, Swedish and Sinhalese. It became a 'set book' for students everywhere, from the Open University to the University of Texas, and inspired at least three published collections of criticism, the most recent, *The Origins of the Second World War Reconsidered*, published in 1986.[103] In 1985 the American Historical Association held a special session to discuss 'the A.J.P. Taylor Debate' twenty-five years on. Millions of words have been written in response to the book; no doubt more are to come. Though errors have been found in it, its effect on historical study has been described as 'iconoclastic and liberating'[104] – liberating because it freed historians from the prison of rhetoric and prejudice which surrounded the events leading up to the War. Alan's book was the first major 'revisionist' work on the subject. In a seminar on the origins of the Second World War, Alan used the analogy of the pebble, which if detached will release an avalanche. The job of an historian, he told Raymond Carr, is to identify and then release that pebble. According to Namier, the mark of a great historian was that after he had done his work, others should not be able to practise within its sphere in terms of the preceding era.[105] Such is the measure of Alan's achievement.

Despite the furore over *The Origins of the Second World War* the myth remains intact. Though historians have now accepted many of Alan's conclusions, the general public clings to an historical cliché. 'Men see the past when they peer into the future,' Alan wrote of pre-War statesmen;[106] today British, and for that matter American, politicians are still able to summon the ghosts of the Fascist dictators and to evoke the shame of appeasement to support military adventures. Any challenge to the received version of events elicits that note of deep indignation and outrage which is the reaction of the honest man to the destruction of long-held and long-cherished beliefs.[107]

Namier had once suggested that history should be for society what psychoanalysis was for the individual. Societies, like individuals, could become neurotically 'fixated' on experiences in the past, revisiting them endlessly because something in that event prevented the society, or the individual, from developing. The historian's proper function was to enable his readers to overcome the past, by understanding it.[108]

Britons have become dangerously and self-destructively fixated on a few years in their history. On the one hand, the 'finest hour'; on the other, Munich. 'Munich became an emotive word, a symbol of shame,' Alan wrote in *The Origins of the Second World War*, 'about which men can still not speak dispassionately.' In his book

Our Age, published in 1990, Noel Annan devoted a whole chapter to 'The Obsession with Munich'; 'the events that led to Munich left scars that never healed upon the minds of Our Age'.[109] In *The Origins of the Second World War* Alan picked at these scars; the howl of outrage that greeted his book was also a howl of pain.

12: 'What an opportunity!'

'You may like to know that I have started my volume for you,' Alan reported to Clark in October 1960: 'I can't promise that I'll ever finish.' The college had given him a year's sabbatical, but he groaned at the prospect of resuming teaching after that, particularly when his special lectureship ran out.

> The History Board proposes to terminate my university lectureship in three years' time; and I growl sometimes that I have been kept out of a chair three times. Not that I would have made a conscientious Professor; but I have stronger claims than anyone else in Oxford. If you can think of any way by which I can get more leisure, let me know; but I suppose that, with my character and background, it is useless.

As his sabbatical year drew to an end, Alan grew still more concerned. 'Somehow I propose to get out of being a College tutor in a year or two, either with the support of the College, which I think likely, or by becoming a slightly more committed journalist. I can make nearly as much money that way, though I'd prefer to keep a foothold in Magdalen.'[1]

Perhaps Clark was alarmed by such talk, coming at the same time as the obloquy heaped on Alan over *The Origins of the Second World War*. He asked Davin to confirm his authority over Alan as editor of the series, which Davin was happy to do.[2] It did not help Alan's reputation as a man of good judgement and discretion when he let it be known, wrongly it seems, that he had been offered the job of Provost of Worcester. The *Evening Standard* – a Beaverbrook paper – quoted Eve as saying that he had turned it down, principally because he enjoys teaching. He didn't want to exchange history for administration pure and simple. He can't bear to spend a lot of time on committees. And neither of us liked to think of bringing up a young family in the antiquated environment of an Oxford college – and in that big barn of a Provost's house.[3]

Even if this was fantasy, it was scarcely polite to Sir Oliver Franks, who had just been appointed Provost,* to suggest that he was the second choice. No wonder that when Beaverbrook wanted to use another of Alan's stories as a diary item, Alan refused; 'my record of indiscretions is already long . . .'[4]

In preparation for writing his Oxford history Alan had looked at all fourteen preceding volumes in the series, with troubling results. Where was the story line, he wondered? Most of them seemed to be collections of essays, the story interrupted by excursions into 'mental and social aspects', for example. Alan determined that his book should be a narrative, with the 'occasional pause for refreshment'. He also decided that 'English history' should mean just that, not Scots – or, as he insisted on calling it, Scotch – Welsh or Irish. When the series had been conceived in the early 1920s 'England' was still an all-embracing term; later historians had got round the problem by including separate chapters on the Scots and the Irish where their history deviated from that of the English and the Welsh. To follow their example would mean deviating from the narrative principle; Alan decided to tell the history of the English, including the history of the other peoples of Great Britain and indeed the British Empire when they were concurrent, but only then.

By the early spring of 1961 Alan had finished three chapters of the book, covering the period of the First World War in 40,000 words. 'I love it all,' he told Clark. 'My fault is compression, as in my volume in the other Oxford history: I get everything in, but so tight that it does not make sense to anyone except me.'[5] He had undertaken a series of ATV lectures on the War – 'possibly the most brilliant and captivating solo performances to be seen on tele-

---

*The previous year Franks had failed to become Chancellor of the University after Trevor-Roper's successful campaign on behalf of Macmillan, despite the fact that the heads of almost all the Oxford colleges had signed a round-robin in favour of Franks.

vision', remarked the *Sunday Times*.[6] After the first of these, Liddell Hart wrote to congratulate him on a 'brilliant crystallization of the course and key factors of the 1914 campaign. I marvel at the way you manage to maintain such a consecutive run of points without apparent reference to notes.' 'I haven't a note, hardly an idea when I start talking,' Alan replied. He sent Liddell Hart transcripts of the first two lectures. 'The scripts are gradually put together by a stenographer – raggedly and often incorrectly.' In fact ATV stopped sending him scripts when it was announced that his next television series would be for the BBC – a revelation that, given Alan's well-known views on the Corporation, caused more than one pair of raised eyebrows. 'Well, who would have thought it of AJP?' was the headline announcing the story in the *Daily Mail*; 'it is as though the head of the Salvation Army should announce his conversion to Rome.'[7] Actually the reason was more prosaic; John Irwin had left ATV and Alan went with him. At the end of the series Liddell Hart wrote again to tell Alan he had watched his 'masterly' lectures 'with intense interest'.

Liddell Hart had sent Alan scripts of his own lectures on 'The Military Balance-Sheet of World War II'. As a result of this exchange the two began a debate on the Allied policy of unconditional surrender: one which Liddell Hart deplored as 'contrary to the basic principles of strategy', making it hard for any resistance to develop in Hitler's Germany. Alan believed that the 'so-called resistance would have been satisfied only if they could have kept the post-Munich frontiers and probably Danzig as well'. The opposition to Hitler, Alan argued, opposed his methods, not his aims. Both Alan and Liddell Hart sought to support their arguments by analogy with the First World War. Liddell Hart expressed the traditional view, the view Alan had learned as a schoolboy, that the Treaty of Versailles had left Germany with justified grievances. Alan denied that Versailles was a hard or severe peace.

It was strictly in accordance territorially with the Fourteen Points which the Germans had accepted. Reparations were not fixed in the Treaty, and the Germans could have got a low figure quite early on. Basically they objected to any peace which expressed their defeat. So maybe it would have saved trouble to march to Berlin in 1919 and so prevent the Second World War.

Summing up, Alan remarked that 'the great feeling of the Second World War was that we must not repeat the mistakes of the First; and it was widely believed that the great mistake was to make an armistice with the Germans instead of imposing unconditional surrender. As usual men learned from past mistakes how to make new ones.'[8]

As a result of his television lectures, Alan was approached to write a short illustrated history of the First World War for the book 'packagers' George Rainbird. Packagers specialise in putting together illustrated books, which they then sell on to publishers. Alan asked a literary agent, David Higham, to handle the negotiations. 'I'm already making £6000–£9000 a year,' he told Higham; for a 10,000-word serial in the *Sunday Express* he could earn 1200 guineas, more than an ordinary university lecturer earned in a year.* When Higham made a lucrative contract with Rainbird, Alan's publishers became anxious about this interloper. 'I am ready to follow your advice without question or demur,' Alan reassured Machell: 'a publisher always knows better than an author whether a book will go or not.' Hamilton annotated this letter '*what* a good author!' and evidently expressed his appreciation to Alan, because just over a week later Alan replied: 'What delightfully appreciative letters you write to me. If only everyone appreciated me as much, how different life would be.' But a month later he commented to Higham, 'Publishers are all so casual – so much less prompt and efficient than I am.'[9]

Higham made the contract; and Alan surged ahead. Early in 1962 he was able to send Liddell Hart his first four chapters; Liddell Hart returned them with six pages of notes: 'In sum, it is a brilliant outline of, and commentary on, World War I.' By May Alan was able to express his appreciation of Liddell Hart's 'wise comments' on the whole manuscript: 'I shall not thank you in the book so that you may be free to attack it or even praise it.'[10]

The First World War: An Illustrated History is an extraordinary

---

*The average wage for a manual worker in 1961 was £798 p.a.

feat of compression. 'No one but Mr Taylor,' wrote Robert Kee in the *Observer*, 'could have written such a short history of the First World War as this without it being almost meaningless historically and a mere filler for photographs. In fact, Mr Taylor manages in some two hundred illustrated pages to say almost everything that is important for an understanding and, indeed, intellectual digestion of that vast event.'[11] Even more remarkable, the book is wonderfully entertaining; Alan's sardonic humour is never far away. Thus, when Hindenburg was called out of retirement, he buttoned himself 'into an old uniform that was now too tight'. 'After the sinking of the *Lusitania*, the only menacing sound heard from Washington was the rattle of the President's typewriter.' There is even a poignant side. Alan describes how, in June 1914, Archduke Franz Ferdinand went to inspect the army in Bosnia because this was the only occasion at which his socially inferior wife could be publicly acknowledged. 'Thus, for love, did the Archduke go to his death.'[12]

One of the most enjoyable aspects of *The First World War* is Alan's captions. Most authors of illustrated books evince little interest in these. Rainbird's chief editor, George Speaight, had prepared some draft captions to accompany their selection of suitable photographs, but when Alan saw them, he said, 'I think we can do something more lively.' The result is a rarity: an illustrated book in which the text and the pictures complement each other. Some of Alan's captions are very funny* – perhaps the best-known being 'Lloyd George casts an expert eye over munition girls'.

Alan was concerned to make two serious points. One was to explain how Soviet Russia became an outcast, not 'recognised' by the non-Communist world; 'hence all our problems at the present day'.[13] The other was to show the danger of relying on a deterrent.

> Nowhere was there conscious determination to provoke a war. Statesmen miscalculated. They used the instruments of bluff and threat which had proved effective on previous occasions. This time things went wrong. The deterrent on which they relied failed to

---

*Beaverbrook, too, was noted for his pithy captions. To accompany a picture of the indolent Baldwin, he had written: 'Mrs Baldwin called him "tiger".'

deter; the statesmen became prisoners of their own weapons. The great armies, accumulated to provide security and preserve the peace, carried the nations to war by their own weight.

No one reading these words in the early 1960s, when Superpower tension reached near breaking-point, could fail to draw the moral.[14]

In *The First World War* Alan outlined a theory which he later developed in a separate short book, *War by Time-Table: How The First World War Began* (1969). 'Though there were, no doubt, deep-seated reasons for disputes between the greatest powers, the actual outbreak of the First World War was provoked almost entirely by rival plans for mobilisation.'[15] The inexorable logic of railway timetables meant that mobilisation in the face of a presumed threat had to be all or nothing; so that once one Great Power mobilised, the rest had to follow suit or risk being caught napping. The Germans had evolved a plan of a swift knock-out blow against France, to avoid the dreaded 'war on two fronts' against both France and Russia. It was because of railway timetables that the assassination of an Austrian Archduke by a Serb terrorist led logically to general war in Europe.[16]

Alan was still working on his Oxford history, and by Christmas 1961 he had reached the halfway mark. Then he stopped, unable to see a way forward.

In November CND had staged a rally in the Albert Hall, organised by the pioneer of street theatre, Joan Littlewood. The rally mixed politics with jazz, folk songs (including *The Misguided Missile and the Misguided Miss*) and comedy, not unlike more recent events for the benefit of Amnesty International. The Alberts, a slapstick duo with whippet and trumpet, were a hard act to follow, but Alan carried it off. Britain, he said, should emulate Austria: a Great Power which had successfully settled down to become a happy little country. Though the hour was late, Alan's oratory mesmerised his audience.

Alan's involvement in CND further undermined his reputation

within Oxford. He was 'Senior Member'* of the Campaign in Oxford for Nuclear Disarmament, which quickly developed into the largest of all the undergraduate societies. It did not enhance his standing within the college when undergraduates painted the walls of Magdalen with CND symbols. The Campaign was thought by many to be subversive; Alan was now, in the words of more conservative dons, 'off the rails'. Wits compared him to Dr Henry Sacheverell, the Tory Fellow of Magdalen in the early 1700s who had made a reputation as 'The Modern Fanatick' for his incendiary pamphlets and sermons attacking in violent terms dissenters, low churchmen, latitudinarians and Whigs.

In fact Alan was becoming disillusioned with CND. He had seen it as a single-issue campaign which, like the Anti-Corn-Law League, would 'argue its way to victory'.[17] The wild talk of anarchy and utopia was anathema to him. Like Canon Collins he was suspicious of the methods of Direct Action, the movement of extra-parliamentary protest which existed uneasily alongside CND. When the Committee of 100 was formed without reference to the Executive Committee to pursue a policy of civil disobedience Alan was outraged; 'never heard anything so dirty, so underhand'. From the start CND had been run by a small clique of like-minded friends, including Kingsley Martin, Canon Collins, J.B. Priestley and his wife Jacquetta Hawkes, Michael Foot, the playwright Benn Levy and the journalists Mervyn Jones and James Cameron. It was informal enough that Margaret Taylor, though not officially a member of the Executive Committee, often attended their meetings, even when Alan was absent. This self-appointed committee of 'big names' was manifestly unrepresentative; pressure came from the regional offices to create a more democratic institutional structure. Alan did not welcome this tendency. He was unwilling to hand over control to the teachers and social workers who made up the foot-soldiers of the Campaign; while for their part, many of the younger radicals thought Alan (and some of the other members of the Executive Committee) slightly fogeyish, his talk of the Anti-Corn-Law League antiquarianism. Canon Collins tried to draw the two sides together at a meeting in his study, where the 'old guard',

---

*All undergraduate societies must have a Senior Member.

including Priestley and Levy as well as Alan, confronted the radical activist Pat Arrowsmith. But any reconciliation was brief; in the autumn of 1960 there was an embarrassing public row between Collins and Russell, who resigned as CND President. Alan was unhappy with the way things were going and withdrew from the Executive Committee.

Alan was not enthusiastic about civil disobedience. But when Adam Roberts, one of his pupils who was active in the Committee of 100 and the son of his friend Janet Adam Smith, was sent to prison after being arrested for sitting down outside the Soviet Embassy and refusing to be bound over to keep the peace – i.e. promise not to repeat the offence – Alan proved sympathetic. He wrote to Roberts saying that he well understood what he was trying to do, but that he should remember a year at Oxford was sacred. To interrupt it was not a good idea. Alan advised him to sign on the dotted line and return to his studies.*

Events marginalised CND in any case. The Cuban Missile Crisis in 1962 took much of the steam out of the Campaign. An early CND pamphlet had urged *Let Britain Lead!*; in 1958 Alan had written that the movement offered Labour 'moral leadership of the world'. Now Alan, and many others too, realised that whatever Britain did could have little influence. The cancellation of Blue Streak emphasised this point. Britain henceforth would rely on American weapons; it had no 'independent' deterrent. If Britain was irrelevant, so was CND. Or, as Alan himself had asked, 'If we threw away our bombs, who'd notice?'[18] The Treaty banning atmospheric testing in 1963 removed one source of anxiety, and suggested a relaxation in the tension between the Superpowers.

In the mid 1970s Mervyn Jones, who was having dinner with Alan and Margaret, asked him: 'Looking back, do you think we were wrong? Do you think the deterrent has kept the peace?' 'Of course not!' Alan snapped, 'Of course we weren't wrong!' When Michael Howard made a disparaging comment about CND in a 1975 review, he received an angry broadside from Alan. 'I am ashamed that one whom I esteem so highly should write in such

---

*Adam Roberts is now back at Oxford as Montague Burton Professor of International Relations.

ignorance. You see, we happened to be right and you marvellous pundits were entirely wrong.'[19]

'History is the great propagator of doubt,' Alan had written in 1960. 'It is sceptical of the authorities; of historians; of our own views, and of those of others.'[20] In October 1961 he reviewed a book about history itself, based on the George Macaulay Trevelyan Lectures given in the University of Cambridge by E.H. Carr. His respect for Carr knew no bounds; he had hailed Carr's *History of Soviet Russia* as 'an achievement without rival in our age', which 'challenges comparison with the greatest works of the classical historians'. But he was less enthusiastic about *What is History?* which to him was just 'sales talk'. He could not understand how knowledge of the past enabled us to behave more sensibly in the present and to foresee the future.

> It does not work when tested against the facts: historians are not wiser politicians or more sensible in their private lives than other men – often indeed the reverse . . . My view of history is more modest than Carr's. The task of the historian is to explain the past; neither to justify nor to condemn it. Study of history enables us to understand the past; no more and no less.[21]

T.F. Tout, the grand old man of the Manchester History School, had preached that 'we investigate the past not to deduce practical political lessons, but to find out what really happened'. Reviewing *The Death of the Past* by J.H. Plumb, another work on the philosophy of history, some years later, Alan expressed himself in very much the same terms that he had used when reviewing Carr: 'History enables us to understand the past better – no more and no less. Any historian who is dissatisfied with this conclusion should take up some useful profession such as knitting.'[22]

In 1961 Alan crossed the Atlantic for the first and only time. Beaverbrook was Chancellor of the University of New Brunswick, at Fredericton, Canada, and he tempted Alan with the offer of an honorary degree. Alan's response was to pretend it was an order: 'It had not entered my mind that I should ever cross the Atlantic, but it is now clear to me that in September next I shall be on my way to New Brunswick.'[23] Beaverbrook paid for Alan to fly across first-class. At the annual convocation Beaverbrook bestowed the honorary degree on his friend; by this ironic route Alan became Dr Taylor.

While in Canada Alan visited St Andrews, and was able to look across the bay to Maine. This was the closest he ever came to the USA. When asked later whether he had visited the United States, he would reply 'I have seen them'. Why did he never cross the bay? He certainly was not prejudiced against individual Americans. One of his favourite postgraduate pupils, Roger Louis, was an American; so was Arthur Marder, one of the historians whom he admired the most. He became friendly with other Americans later on, Stephen Koss and Alfred Gollin, for example. He wrote enthusiastic reviews of books by George Kennan and Arthur Schlesinger Jr. But he affected not to see any reason to go to America; the Americans he liked he could meet in England. Neither the architecture nor the food attracted him, he insisted, though how he made this judgement is hard to say. Even when he was offered large sums to lecture there, he was not tempted. Perhaps he felt that, as a former Communist and someone who had visited the Soviet Union, he would not be welcome. In the McCarthyite period this would certainly have been true. He may not have wanted to give his ideological enemies the satisfaction of refusing him a visa. Perhaps he did apply for a visa at some stage, and was rejected. No evidence has emerged either way, except for this fragment. When one of Alan's colleagues, Leslie Sutton, applied for his own visa in 1957, the clerk at the American consulate in Berkeley Square remarked: 'I see you're from Magdalen College. You have a chap there called Alan Taylor, don't you? He's a Communist, isn't he?' 'I don't think so,' Sutton replied. 'He's an old-fashioned Manchester liberal who plays to the gallery.'

'You're the last of the Whigs,' Bullock is said to have told Alan. But if Whiggism means anything, it means patrician rule; this was far from being Alan's philosophy. For him the last of the Whigs was

Bertrand Russell.[24] Bullock liked to say that Alan had two moods, one for each of his role models, Bismarck and Beaverbrook. In his Bismarck mood, he believed everybody can be bullied; in his Beaverbrook mood, that everybody can be bought.

That same year Macmillan announced Britain's intention to join the European Economic Community, and on his return from Canada Beaverbrook threw himself into the campaign against 'that blasted Common Market, which is an American device to put us alongside Germany. As our power was broken and lost by two German wars, it is very hard on us now to be asked to align ourselves with those villians.'[25] Alan was an eager recruit. He had already spoken against the Common Market in the summer, when he addressed a meeting in Oxford on the subject. The Common Market, he said, 'seems to many people to be another name for Germany running the economy – and running it for her own interest'. In December Beaverbrook wrote to thank him for a 'helpful' article in the *Sunday Express*, which praised the Commonwealth in preference to the countries of the EEC. 'The fact remains,' Alan had written, 'that the nations of the Commonwealth are our brothers and sisters and that foreign countries are not.'[26] A year later de Gaulle vetoed Britain's application. 'Now we are not in the Common Market,' reported Alan early in 1964, 'we are more prosperous than ever.'[27] The Common Market became one of Alan's staple targets for attack in the *Sunday Express*; others were German reunification, the United Nations, the BBC, opinion polls, breathalysers, speed limits.

Alan had been puzzled by a description in *Men and Power* of Lloyd George descending on the Admiralty in 1917 and seating himself in the First Lord's chair. This seemed to Alan unlikely and he wrote to Beaverbrook requesting his evidence for the statement. Beaverbrook promised to ask Churchill, but never did, and Alan came to realise that it was an invention, inserted in the proofs to enliven the narrative – what Beaverbrook called 'balancing'. Far from being shocked at this discovery, Alan thought what Beaverbrook had written was 'symbolically true'. He repeated the story in *The First World War*.[28]

When the one-volume edition of Beaverbrook's *Politicians and the War* came out in 1960, Alan had praised it warmly as 'a historical work of the first importance', a brilliant piece of sustained narrative, studded with 'dazzling' portraits of individuals, 'as though Tacitus and Aubrey were rolled into one'. Alan made a public retraction of his earlier criticisms. In the great struggle between Lloyd George and Asquith, 'nearly everyone agreed that Lord Beaverbrook had exaggerated his part in the affair. The two volumes fell out of print. But they could not be disregarded. Every subsequent revelation confirmed the essential truth of Lord Beaverbrook's account; and every historian of the period draws heavily on Lord Beaverbrook, though not always with acknowledgement.' The two volumes 'occupy a place of unique importance in our historical literature . . . It is too soon to assess Lord Beaverbrook's place in history. But his place as a historian is secure.'[29] Beaverbrook glowed when he read these words. His investment in Alan had paid off. Interviewed in 1964, Beaverbrook said that this review had given him more pleasure than any other event he could recall.[30]

In 1962 Beaverbrook asked Alan if he would read the manuscript of his new book and give an opinion 'for or against publication'. He offered a fee of £500. Alan refused to accept any money, but suggested that instead Beaverbrook might like to pay for an operation Eve was due to have on a vein in her leg.* He read the galleys of Beaverbrook's book 'with great excitement. I have no doubt at all that it should be published. It is full of revelations; it is an important piece of your political autobiography; and it is also extremely entertaining.' When the book came out he reviewed it enthusiastically in the *New Statesman*; cynical readers may have reflected that their reviewer enjoyed a lucrative contract with a Beaverbrook paper. But perhaps that was not it at all; perhaps treating Beaverbrook as a serious historian was merely the latest act of Taylor perversity. Beaverbrook thanked him for a 'thrilling

---

*In contrast, Aneurin Bevan had in 1932 refused an offer from Beaverbrook to pay his medical costs.[31]

piece' which 'gave me great happiness'; 'without your encouragement I would never have brought it out'.[32]

It was a reciprocal process. Alan often dined alone with Beaverbrook; one summer evening in 1962 Beaverbrook was in poor
shape – his gout so painful that he could hardly walk, and his head
dropping on to his chest during the meal. After they had eaten he
asked Alan what he was doing. Alan explained that he was stuck,
unable to make progress with his Oxford history because he could
not work up any interest in the financial crisis of 1931 and the
subsequent Depression, which had seemed to dominate the 1930s.
Beaverbrook woke up, kicked off his gout shoes, jumped to his feet
and marched up and down, scarcely able to contain his excitement
as he rattled off his memories of the period. Alan was inspired,
more by Beaverbrook's enthusiasm than by what he said. 'What a
chance you've got!' exclaimed Beaverbrook. 'What an opportunity! I'd give anything for the opportunity to write about the
1930s. Have the revenge I never had!'

For Alan, Beaverbrook was living history; for Beaverbrook, Alan
was his passport to posterity. Through Alan, and Alan's writing, he
could once again fight old battles, settle old scores, reshape the past.
In his review of Driberg's book, for example, Alan had dismissed
Beaverbrook's crusade for Empire Free Trade as 'knockabout
comedy', not worth a footnote in the textbooks; but by 1961 he
was assuring Beaverbrook that it deserved a book in itself.[33]

Alan became even more important to Beaverbrook later in the
year, when he began to suggest that he might write Beaverbrook's
biography after his death. Beaverbrook's great-nephew, Jonathan
Aitken, an undergraduate reading history at Christ Church, often
dined at Cherkley; Robert Blake persuaded him to tell his great-
uncle that Alan was not a suitable person to write his biography
because he would be too favourable. Beaverbrook was not
impressed by this advice.[34]

The dust stirred up by the controversy over *The Origins of the
Second World War* had not settled when, early in 1962, Martin
Gilbert began to canvass potential contributors to a *Festschrift* in
Alan's honour. It is typical of the many legends about Alan in

circulation that some Oxford dons believe to this day that he asked for the *Festschrift* himself. In fact, it originated in the anger and resentment felt by some of Alan's recent pupils at the way he had been depicted. Alan was neither consulted nor informed. The whole idea of the volume was to surprise him – pleasantly, it was hoped.

The project soon ran into trouble. There was some feeling in Oxford that it was presumptuous of a young whippersnapper like Gilbert to undertake a project that should belong to his seniors. Moreover, some believed, perhaps reasonably, that there was no occasion for the volume. It was not to be expected that Trevor-Roper should agree to contribute; but it was disappointing when Bullock declined to do so. Berlin was too busy*; Beloff felt embarrassed to be the only relatively senior Oxford contributor. The economic historian Paul Einzig thought it would be a 'huge joke' if he were to contribute an essay, having castigated Alan's television lecture on the Depression in two letters to *The Listener* – 'never in the history of human relations has anyone with so little knowledge on the subject displayed such a degree of cocksureness'.[35]

Gilbert began to feel that he had done the wrong thing. He feared Alan would be further upset when he discovered the reluctance of his colleagues to pay tribute to him. He went to see Alan at his Magdalen rooms to tell him what had happened. As usual, Alan was brisk and businesslike. After saying how flattered he was at the *idea*, he deprecated it, and said that he was happy to take the will for the deed.

Gilbert determined to continue. When Alan heard that he had decided to ignore his advice and was pressing on with 'this flattering, though foolish project of yours', he asked Gilbert to his Magdalen rooms and suggested some other possible contributors and two possible publication dates: September 1963, when his special lectureship elapsed; or March 1966, his sixtieth birthday, the date Gilbert settled upon. He suggested a meeting early in the summer: 'I shall be fascinated to learn whose zeal for print is such that they are prepared to commemorate even me.' Six months later,

---

*See p. 341.

after Gilbert had told him something of the continuing saga, he asked to see the burgeoning and sometimes acrimonious correspondence. 'It will make a delightful pamphlet,' he wrote: 'perhaps published by the Country Bumpkins Press?'[36]

It was around this time that Alan invited Gilbert to accompany him to Salisbury, where he was due to address the local Historical Association about the origins of the Second World War. Driving through Tidworth on Salisbury Plain, Alan was stopped by the police for speeding. 'I'm Alan Taylor and I'm on my way to give an Historical Association lecture,' Alan said importantly. The confused policeman saluted and waved him on. They arrived at the meeting, and Alan mounted the platform. 'We are very honoured to have Professor Taylor here tonight,' began the Chairman, 'who is going to talk to us about Ramsay MacDonald, the man who betrayed the Labour Party.' Gilbert was alarmed. Would Alan try to change the topic? Alan got to his feet. 'First of all,' he said, 'I want to say that I am not a professor. Secondly . . .' He paused. 'Ramsay MacDonald was *not* a traitor . . .' Alan continued just as fluently.

In March 1962 Alan travelled once more to Hungary. When Michael Karolyi had died in France in 1955, the Hungarian press had marked his death with just one sentence. Now Karolyi was being rehabilitated, and his remains were returned to Budapest for a State Funeral, shown on Hungarian television. Alan marched in the cortège behind the coffin. Tears flowed down his cheeks as he made the funeral oration.

Alan was excited at the thought of seeing Eva Haraszti again. In his imagination she embodied the blend of socialism and sexuality which Muggeridge had described so evocatively in *The Thirties*. As soon as he arrived in Budapest he telephoned her, and they arranged to meet. Though flattered by his attention, she was astonished when he presented her with a photograph of himself. She discouraged his advances. He gave her one of his books, in which he wrote a loving dedication; she tore it out on the way home.

'I was stuck for a long time in a fit of depression,' Alan told Clark later that summer. 'Now I have broken through . . . there will be a respectable book, maybe too many ideas and too few facts.'[37] All he needed was time. He was determined not to return to full-time teaching – fifteen hours a week rather than the eight or ten which were required of a special lecturer – when he could be doing something more valuable.* Contrary to what Eve had told the *Evening Standard*, Alan was bored by teaching. He was more and more intolerant of his less able pupils. One unfortunate had not reached the end of his first sentence when Alan interrupted: 'What a *horrible* way to begin an essay!' He enjoyed lecturing, and he was extremely good at it, perhaps the best lecturer within the university. But there were plenty of other people who could teach as well as he could.[38]

On 12 October Alan sent a private note to Alastair Hetherington, who had succeeded Wadsworth as editor of the *Guardian*. 'I enclose a news item which may be of interest to you. No enquiries or comment until Wednesday please.' The item was an announcement of what he intended to say before his lecture at nine o'clock the following Wednesday: 'The History Board have informed me that they do not intend to renew my lectureship when it runs out next summer. These are therefore the last lectures which I shall give at this university.'[39]

On the morning of Wednesday, 17 October, the Examination Schools were unusually crowded. Among the 400 or 500 undergraduates who regularly attended Alan's lectures were photographers and representatives of the press, some of them in borrowed gowns. Hetherington had obviously not been the only one to receive advance warning of Alan's bombshell. Several newspapers had scooped the story and published an item the same morning. But it was on the following day, after the reporters in the Examination Schools had trooped back to Magdalen to interview Alan, that the story really broke. 'I'm not sacked but I'm hurt' was the headline in the *Daily Mail*; 'TV Don loses his big job' reported George Gale in

---

*University lecturers usually reckon on a multiplier of about three times as much work as time spent teaching – though the Oxbridge tutorial system, which obviates the need to mark essays, makes the load somewhat lighter.

the *Daily Express*, which also printed an interview with Sir Charles 'C.P.' Snow. The author of *The Masters*, a novel of High Table intrigue, speculated that Alan had been 'victimised' for the 'terrible crime' of 'talking to ordinary men and women – in writing and in broadcasting'.

The quality papers too made it a big story. Alan was on the front page of both the *Guardian* – 'A Flurry at Oxford' – and the *Daily Telegraph*; both carried editorials – 'The Stormy Petrel' and 'Mr Taylor's Place'. There was even a waspish piece in the 'Peterborough' column: 'The news that Mr Taylor is now to give more time to writing will be greeted with mixed feelings. There are those who believe him to be a better lecturer than historian.' The same morning another Magdalen don, Gilbert Ryle, found Alan in the Senior Common Room studying the newspapers. Alan looked up and grinned. 'Isn't it marvellous?' he said, pointing to the pile of papers around him.

Both the *Sunday Times* and the *Observer* carried the story at the weekend. Unless Magdalen creates a new research fellowship, reported the *Observer*'s 'Pendennis' column, A.J.P. Taylor will leave Oxford next summer. Was he, perhaps, asking for special terms? 'Of course I'm asking for special terms,' retorted Alan: 'I'm a rather special historian.'

The *Sunday Times* 'Atticus' piece was cooler. The uproar

> seems a little excessive when we remember that Mr Taylor's special lectureship which is all that he is losing, was always due to expire in 1963, [and] that Mr Taylor has known this since he accepted it in 1953 . . . From the rumpus one would think that Mr Taylor was being silenced or starved; in fact (like others in his position) he will only have to teach undergraduates – Sir Charles Snow's 'ordinary people' – for a few more hours a week, unless he can persuade the University or his college to create a new post for him.

In the interviews he gave to the press after the story broke Alan gave a true picture of the situation, but in the announcement sent to Hetherington and others before the event, he had been disingenuous. 'Professors are appointed for life, i.e. to the retiring age of 67,' it read. 'Readers and lecturers are appointed for five years and are normally renewed until they reach 67, unless there is a specific University regulation to the contrary. There is no such regulation in regard to Mr Taylor's lectureship. Mr Taylor is 56.' The implication was that he had been singled out for exceptional treatment, or, in plain language, sacked. This was the impression given to the casual reader; it was a public relations disaster for the University, and for the History Faculty Board in particular. Sir Isaiah Berlin, then a visiting Professor at Harvard, was upset when he heard the news and expressed his concern to another Magdalen Fellow on sabbatical in America. 'What a way to run a university!' wrote Paddy Monkhouse, by this time Hetherington's deputy.[40]

Alan's behaviour offended his colleagues. They disliked the way he had orchestrated the press outcry. They were irritated by the way he had allowed the case to be misrepresented. They were repelled by his boasting, and indignant at the suggestion that they too would be journalist-historians if only they were up to it. Alan had transgressed the unspoken professional code. He had let the side down.

Elsewhere the matter looked different. Noel Annan, for example, then Provost of King's College, Cambridge, in a letter written a couple of years later, said he thought Alan had been 'scandalously treated'; 'it is iniquitous that you have never been made a Professor'.[41] 'Things might have worked out differently', Alan wrote in his autobiography,

> if Oxford University had created a Professorship *ad hominem* for me, as Cambridge did for Geoffrey Elton and Jack Plumb in similar circumstances.* Then I should have been more than content and should have gone on lecturing at Oxford until I reached the age of retirement. Instead Oxford, meaning the Board of the History Faculty, did nothing for me, nothing at all, and indeed went out of its way to hound me out of all university work.[42]

In fact the History Faculty Board felt it had little choice. It had no *ad hominem* Chairs or Readerships at its disposal, and its readerships were not senior posts but purely functional in specialised

---

*Both had failed to get the Regius Chair at Cambridge.

fields – palaeography or Indian history, for example. It could not raise sufficient funds to make the special lectureships permanent, and its application for an additional seven such lectureships plus two readerships in foreign history had been rejected. There had been talk of making an exception for Alan, but this was felt to be invidious. It was perhaps unfortunate that the one individual to hold a special lectureship for more than ten years should have been Bruce McFarlane.

'I've shaken off my teaching commitments here after next summer, as you may have seen in the public prints,' Alan told Clark. 'I'm glad, though I think it is a bad thing that a great institution such as Magdalen (or the history faculty) cannot strike a halfway house between teaching and research . . . However no one wanted me except as a fulltime tutor, so I gave up with relief. I'll have to make more money in the marketplace, and I can.' He sent Clark the chapters covering the period up to 1931. 'Thought and Art will get more, though within the existing frame. They will be put in for their importance in history, not because I have anything valuable to say about them in themselves. I don't think I shall include science – I don't understand it.' As always, Clark read these chapters quickly and provided copious helpful comments. Alan thanked him warmly. 'Your letter was really kind. It is an inspiration to have an editor so encouraging and so critical in a constructive way.'[43]

College rules prevented anyone from holding a research fellowship at the same time as a special lectureship. Alan wrote to President Boase explaining that he had decided not to continue as a college tutor but that he wanted to carry on with his research. Boase had been anxious to see the back of Alan for some time. He was a vigorous advocate of the college system, and resented university appointments which, he felt, undermined college loyalties. When Alan's letter arrived, Boase saw his chance to be free of him, and wrote on the agenda for the next college meeting: 'Resignation of A.J.P. Taylor'. Alan's friends managed to get this changed before the meeting. Early in December 1962 the *Daily Telegraph* was able to tell its readers that Alan had been made a Fellow by Special Election. 'It isn't what I should most have liked,' he was quoted as saying: 'I should have preferred to go on teaching for eight or ten hours a week.' Bruce McFarlane, who had hoped to be rid of Alan, was disappointed. 'I shall never take any interest in the college again,' he told A.L. Rowse.[44]

Six months later the *Daily Telegraph*, along with the rest of Fleet Street, reported Alan's valedictory lecture, delivered at the unusual (for him) hour of five o'clock in the afternoon. He chose as his subject *Oh What a Lovely War!*, the title of the satirical musical then showing at the Theatre Royal, Stratford, in London's East End. Alan had seen the show several times; he was so impressed that he dedicated his book *The First World War* to its director, his old Manchester friend Joan Littlewood. She travelled up to Oxford to hear him speak; afterwards he entertained her in his rooms. Despite the fact that so many books had been written on the 1914–18 war, Alan said, no historian had ever given a satisfactory explanation of its origins and causes. *Oh What a Lovely War!* did what the historians had failed to do.

The cause of the 1914–18 War, he went on, was the deterrent: the belief that if you are strongly enough armed you can prevent a war. When you say the deterrent can prevent war, you have the example of the 1914–18 war to prove you wrong. His only criticism of *Oh What a Lovely War!* was its failure to show that there was mass enthusiasm for the War at its outset; the belief everybody had that their country was in danger. The men who marched in 1914 were the same men who came out on strike in 1926, he concluded. These were the two most honourable days in the history of the British people.

'It was a flawless performance,' reported the *Oxford Mail* the next day, 'delivered in his usual style, with the passing side-long dig and the self-deprecating witticism as paradox was piled on paradox and the rockets went up shedding a sudden light.' At the end he walked off 'to a rousing and sustained burst of applause'. Their correspondent felt it was 'extraordinary to think that an Oxford institution has come to an end and that undergraduates will in future only be able to enjoy the star lecturer in the History Faculty on television. The University is bad at meeting special cases.'[45]

The same day a valedictory piece by Alan himself appeared in the *New Statesman*. He looked back on thirty-three years of university lecturing with both regret and relief. As a profession, the life of a university teacher was beyond compare. But he deplored the fact that English universities, particularly Oxford and Cambridge, set out to be schools of manners and morals also.

> I cringe with embarrassment every time an undergraduate is sent down for having a girl in his rooms . . . The great delusion of our universities is to suppose that it is their duty to turn out 'good citizens'. This would only be true in a perfect society. In our society, who is the good citizen – the man who kicks against it, the scientist who makes H-bombs or the marcher for CND? Turning out 'good citizens' inevitably implies that society is already perfect; and this is what in fact most university teachers believe. Otherwise, like me, they are at war with their consciences. In Heaven, no doubt, the universities conduct courses in playing the harp and walking on streets paved with gold. They turn out angels, not men who think for themselves. But even in Heaven, Satan was sent down. Reports say he was the only Archangel in the running for a First. I am on Satan's side; and this has made me uncomfortable in my earthly paradise.[46]

In a *Daily Express* piece headed 'My Farewell to Oxford', Alan paraphrased the First World War song:

> When this bleeding term is over,
> No more lecturing for me.[47]

In July 1963 Alan reviewed a book by an old friend. Innes Stewart was now both J.I.M. Stewart, a distinguished don at Christ Church, and Michael Innes, the crime writer. Under his first hat he had written the final volume in the Oxford History of English Literature, *Eight Modern Writers*, covering the twentieth century. Alan made fun of the fact that a history of English literature should end with studies of eight separate writers, only two of whom were genuinely English, three of whom were Irish. Joyce and Yeats were all very well, but where, he asked, was H.G. Wells, 'to my mind the most characteristic writer of the twentieth century?' He criticised Stewart for treating writers as if they appeared in a vacuum, without dealing with the society in which they appeared; as a result, the book was 'the most flagrant manifesto of unbridled individualism ever penned'.

> Reviewers are sometimes accused of flattering books which their friends have written. My practice is the opposite. I hesitate to wound strangers. Old friends, I know, will not mind. J.I.M. Stewart and I have been close friends for nearly forty years. He thinks me brash. I find him precious. This book confirms my judgement, as the review will, no doubt, confirm his.[48]

Soon after this review appeared in print Alan dined at Christ Church as a guest of his former pupil, William Thomas. Thomas was uneasy about Stewart's reaction to the review, and took the precaution of warning him beforehand that Alan would be there. The two did not confront each other during the meal, but only as they filed out of the hall through the small panel-door leading to the spiral staircase. At that point, Stewart held out his hand and greeted Alan: 'Dr Leavis, I presume.' 'Innes, how nice to see you again,' replied Alan, and took his arm. For the rest of the evening they chatted affectionately, two old friends delighting in each other's company.

In 1964 Penguin Books decided to bring out a paperback edition of John Reed's *Ten Days that Shook the World*, and asked Alan to write an introduction. He stressed the confused and accidental nature of the Russian Revolution. Reed's book had become unacceptable to the Soviet Union, Alan said, because it ignored Stalin, and, worse still, made clear Trotsky's central role in events. Reed's widow had given the copyright in the book to the Communist Party of Great Britain. Alan's introduction was submitted to their publishers, Lawrence & Wishart, and came back covered with objections. Alan attempted to modify his statements or, where he felt this would be impossible without error, deleted them. The revised introduction was again submitted, and again found to be full of errors, which the publishers now refused to specify. They proposed that the job should be given to someone else. Penguin preferred to publish the book without an introduction, and so it remained until 1977 when, the copyright having expired, Alan's introduction could at last be used.[49]

'Thank you for the Burgundy. I cannot think what I have done to deserve it,' Alan wrote to Beaverbrook in June 1962. In fact he had written an article for the *Sunday Express* entitled 'Why Do I Write For This "Awful Newspaper"?' The piece was little more than an affectionate sketch of the newspaper's proprietor, ending 'Lord Beaverbrook has always been on the side of life'. 'My last article in the *Sunday Express*, unlike most I write, was my suggestion, not the Editor's,' he told Beaverbrook. 'I have never written an article with more satisfaction or sincerity.'[50] As Christmas approached, the flow of presents turned into an avalanche. On 7 November Alan thanked Beaverbrook for a box of cigars; on the 21st a cheese; on 18 December some more wine; and three days later more cigars. 'Don't hesitate to summon me if I can ever be of use, either as a historian or merely for company,' Alan told Beaverbrook, thanking him for this latest present. Beaverbrook issued his invitations in lordly fashion; 'I shall be so glad if you will dine with me'.

'It was kind of you to remember my birthday,' wrote Alan in March 1963, as yet another present arrived: not a very difficult feat of memory for Beaverbrook, as Alan had mentioned his birthday in a letter to Beaverbrook only four days earlier. The following month Beaverbrook invited Alan and Eve to join him for Easter at la Capponcina, his villa at Cap d'Ail, on the French Riviera; unfortunately Alan was due to lecture in Rome, but he suggested calling for a couple of days on the way back. This seemed to suit Beaverbrook, and Alan made the travel arrangements with George Millar, always known as 'Mr Millar', who ran Beaverbrook's private office. 'We don't mind', Alan notified Millar, 'moving up from tourist to first class as Lord Beaverbrook's guests!'[51]

After the stay in France Alan expressed his gratitude to Beaverbrook. 'I am content to have won your friendship, which is the most precious experience of my life.' 'Do not hesitate to say when you would like our company,' he wrote a month later.[52] In October Beaverbrook published an article in the *Sunday Express* about

Alan, 'The Man Who Likes to Stir Things Up'.* 'His learning and his brilliance are not in doubt, but he is far from being Oxford's favourite son,' Beaverbrook informed his readers.

> The reason is obvious. Taylor writes an enormous amount, and much of it is written for ordinary, intelligent people who make no claim to be scholars. This is highly distasteful to the kind of don who writes a little monograph once every ten years to be read only by other dons and maybe a few young men who are trying hard to become dons themselves.

'You make me blush,' Alan wrote to him afterwards, 'and I should be the more embarrassed if I did not reflect that your article will give almost as much pain to others as it gives pleasure to me. There are few people whose good opinion I value. You are one of the few . . . I'll ring soon to propose a visit.'[53]

At Christmas Beaverbrook again invited the Taylors to visit him in April at Cap d'Ail, and sent Alan a case of claret and a box of cigars. 'In return I can send only good wishes,' Alan replied. 'One, that (with the help of de Gaulle) you may resist the Common Market in 1964 as effectively as you did in 1963 . . .' After his birthday in March Alan had cause to write yet another thank-you letter. 'I have much to thank you for and hardly know where to begin. Thank you for the claret. Thank you for the cigars. Thank you above all for the privilege and the delight of your friendship.'[54]

Eve had approached Beaverbrook with great suspicion; when she first visited him she acted as though she was entering the house of the devil. But soon her suspicions were replaced by a glutinous ingratiation. 'Dear Max,' she addressed him in 1961, 'Little did I think that I should live to the day when I could address "the lord" in so familiar a fashion!' 'Dear, dear Max,' she wrote after her operation, 'I feel overwhelmed to have won your friendship. Believe me, it is reciprocated a hundred times over.' 'We miss you very much,' she lamented to him while he was in France: 'this country seems quite empty when you are away.' Beaverbrook disapproved of women smoking, and became quite cross when Eve

---

*This article had been commissioned by Martin Gilbert for the delayed *Festschrift*.

wanted a cigarette one evening. 'Dear, dear Max,' she wrote to apologise: 'my friendship with you is something unique, and I treasure it too much to do anything to spoil it'. In May she wrote once more, feeling 'very very proud and honoured that for the past few years you have counted me as a friend'. Knowing and talking to Beaverbrook was one of the most enriching experiences of her life, she told him. 'Thank you, dear Max, for the many lovely times you have given me. Thank you for letting me be your friend.'[55]

Beaverbrook often preferred to meet Alan alone. In June 1963 he married 'Christofor', the widow of his friend Sir James Dunn. Beaverbrook was now a very old man, grumbling and wayward; one of the few pleasures left to him was exercising his power over others. On 25 May 1964 Alan attended a gala dinner to celebrate Beaverbrook's eighty-fifth birthday: Alan had written a tribute to mark the occasion for the *Sunday Express*, 'The Man Who Deals in Sunshine'.[56] The next day Beaverbrook thanked Alan with one last case of Château Latour – perhaps an unnecessary extravagance, since he had already paid for the article. He died two weeks later.

A couple of days after Beaverbrook's death, while his body was still lying in state at Cherkley, Alan wrote to David Higham about his biography, as well as 'a complication'.

> Just before his death, old Max asked me to chair a small committee which should decide all requests for access to his collection of papers. I hope this offer will stand and indeed I shall try to expand it, giving me real control. In that case, there will be a salary as well as terms for the book to settle . . . Among other things, Max's death has been a great grief to me, as you can imagine, and I can't think straight at present.[57]

Later that month Alan lunched with Lady Beaverbrook, and they discussed the archive as well as the biography. In a subsequent letter he set out the basis of their agreement about the biography, and included a proposal for 'The Beaverbrook Institute for Twentieth-Century History'. 'Alan is fired with enthusiasm for his new idea. It will wane,' commented Beaverbrook's eldest son, Max Aitken. 'I think first things first and that the biography is number one.'

There was some confusion to begin with about the degree of control the Beaverbrook family should have. 'The book will be my copyright, the independent production of a historical scholar, which, as we know, is what Max wanted,' Alan had written after his lunch with Lady Beaverbrook. She replied that she was delighted he was going to write the biography: 'as you will recall, you stated that on completion before publication you would delete anything Max or I did not approve of'. 'We must be careful to avoid confusion,' Alan wrote back. 'The Beaverbrook papers are your property and of course cannot be printed without your permission. If there is anything I come across which you don't want published, you can say so and have it taken out. Apart from this, the book will be my affair . . .' A month later he reminded her about the Institute. 'Max, as you know, was strangely modest about his achievement as a historian, and it would be a great vindication to have him acknowledged by the profession . . . I gave my heart to Max, and I'd gladly devote the rest of my working life to keeping his memory green.'[58]

Beaverbrook's funeral was a curious affair, with few of his close friends in attendance. Alan was not invited. Three months later a ceremony took place in Beaverbrook Town Square, Newcastle, New Brunswick. Beaverbrook's widow laid an urn, apparently containing his ashes, into a chamber inside a plinth, which itself supported an enormous bust of her late husband. Alan wrote to Lady Beaverbrook regretting that he could not be present.

> Not a day goes by when I do not miss Max, but it is with pride, not with sadness. It is a wonderful task to give him his true place in history, and I feel unworthy of it. Love for him is my only qualification . . . I wish I could have been there to say: Goodbye, old friend. I'll do my best for you.[59]

13: *Little England*

'The Beaverbrook family rushed out the announcement of an official biography before I had agreed on terms,' Alan informed Sir George Clark on 18 July 1964. 'However this probably strengthens my hand. I have insisted on no payment from the family and complete freedom of access, together with full copyright for me. Of course if I find anything really discreditable, I should just not write the book – I loved the old man too much. But he told me he had nothing to hide.'[1]*

Alan had finished his Oxford history, though he was still revising it in response to Clark's comments, 'even sacrificing reluctantly Lloyd George's habit of breaking wind'. Earlier in the year he had again been stuck, though only briefly. 'I see my way through to 1941,' Alan had written to Clark in February 1964. 'Then somehow British history comes to an end – eclipsed by the Great Powers. And one feels what's the point of going on? But then what was the point of World War II? I remember feeling very strongly at the time that it had a point and now I can't see what it was. Or nearly so.' That same day he told Liddell Hart that he was struggling to reduce the War to manageable compass. 'At present I am rather stuck, partly because I was myself emotionally involved in World War II and cannot look at it objectively. I think it will baffle posterity much more than World War I.'[3]

By June Alan had reached the last page. The paragraph which concludes the book is one of the best-known and most quoted pieces of historical writing. 'I want to say that I like the English

---

*On Beaverbrook's instructions, a box of secret papers was burned immediately after his death. Whether this contained anything significant is disputed.[2]

people very much and have a poor opinion of those who claim to guide them,' he told Clark. 'I'll get it right in the end.'[4]

> In the Second World War the British people came of age. This was a people's war. Not only were their needs considered. They themselves wanted to win. Future historians may see the War as a last struggle for the European balance of power or the maintenance of empire. This was not how it appeared to those who lived through it. The British people had set out to destroy Hitler and National Socialism – 'Victory at all costs'. They succeeded. No English soldier who rode with the tanks into liberated Belgium or saw the German murder camps at Dachau or Buchenwald could doubt that the War had been a noble crusade. The British people were the only people who went through both world wars from beginning to end. Yet they remained a peaceful and civilised people, tolerant, patient, and generous. Traditional values lost much of their force. Other values took their place. Imperial greatness was on the way out; the welfare state was on the way in. The British empire declined; the condition of the people improved. Few now sang 'Land of Hope and Glory'. Few even sang 'England Arise'. England had arisen all the same.[5]

English History, 1914–1945 has been described as disguised auto-biography. It is certainly a very personal book. Alan's opinions, sometimes controversial, sometimes outrageous, are scattered everywhere. Charlie Chaplin is described as 'England's gift to the world . . . as timeless as Shakespeare and as great'. The League of Nations 'provided a useful meeting-place where statesmen could express benevolent sentiments about nothing in particular'. Sir John Simon 'lacked the air of puzzled rectitude which enabled a Grey or a Halifax to lapse from the highest moral standards without anyone complaining or even noticing.'[6]

The book is, of course, the history of Alan's own lifetime, or at least the first half of his life. He could hardly avoid being more engaged with his subject than, say, Jacob on the fifteenth century. Yet, even allowing for this, Alan let himself go in a way that few academic historians would have dared to copy. Like Beaverbrook, who had 'balanced' passages which he considered needed livening up, Alan added 'embellishments' at proof stage. At the end of a footnote giving factual details of George V's career, for example,

Alan added the words: 'his trousers were creased at the sides, not front and back'. Alan had an eye for telling detail. To illustrate the conservatism of the Labour Chancellor of the Exchequer, Philip Snowden, he noted that Snowden had restored to its traditional position the furniture in the Chancellor's room, which his predecessor had rearranged.[7]

Another footnote described Churchill's career in conventional terms, until the end, where he added the words: 'the saviour of his country'.* Churchill is one of the heroes of the book. During the Second World War 'no other man could have done what he did' – perhaps a fair judgement, but again one that few historians would venture. The passage dealing with the 'finest hour' is intensely personal, and moving.[9]

Yet Alan's book was much more than opinion and sentiment. Orthodoxy after orthodoxy is challenged, none more vigorously than those of the Left. Appeasement, according to Alan, 'never sat comfortably on Tory shoulders. It was in spirit and in origin a Left-wing cause, and its leaders had a Nonconformist background.' The 'Guilty Men' were not guilty, at worst incompetent. 'English people showed little enthusiasm for a dynamic leadership even if it were offered to them. Essentially rulers and ruled had the same outlook . . . Both were trying to operate old concepts in a changing world. Both hoped that the storm would not blow or at least that it would blow elsewhere.' MacDonald was accused 'unjustly' of betrayal; later attacks on him were 'scurrilous'. Baldwin 'truly represented the decade'. Chamberlain, 'more than any other leader, laid the foundations for British fighting power during the Second World War'.[10]

It was typical of Alan's approach that he should make a case against the strategic air offensive. In his view, British bombing did more damage to Great Britain than to Germany, in terms of casualties and of resources better used elsewhere. Worse, it was unacceptable on ethical grounds. 'The British outdid German frightfulness first in theory, then in practice, and a nation which

---

*Apparently inserted in the proofs on the day of Churchill's funeral. 'I still regard that as the best sentence [sic] in my book however much the new generation of historians think we ought to have fought on the other side.'[8]

claimed to be fighting for a moral cause gloried in the extent of its immoral acts.'[11]

In private he took a less moral line. In 1963, when David Irving's *The Destruction of Dresden* had first excited public interest in the subject, a guest at Magdalen High Table leaned across and asked Alan: 'Professor Taylor, isn't it terrible to learn of the intensity of these bombing raids?' 'Intensity?' Alan exclaimed. 'They should have bombed Germany sooner and harder.'

Alan had been stuck at the onset of the great Depression, until Beaverbrook helped him to move on. The conventional view of the 1930s was: misery. Alan asserted, on the contrary, that for those in work, there had been no better time to be alive.

> The nineteen-thirties have been called the black years, the devil's decade. Its popular image can be expressed in two phrases: mass unemployment and 'appeasement'. No set of political leaders have been judged so contemptuously since the days of Lord North. Yet, at the same time, most English people were enjoying a richer life than any previously known in the history of the world: longer holidays, shorter hours, higher real wages. They had motor cars, cinemas, radio sets, electrical appliances. The two sides of life did not join up.[12]

Alan's previous books had been confined to high politics. Now he explored the lives of ordinary people. Observing that only five per cent of private households had a resident domestic, he linked this statistic with 'lamentations from the comfortable classes about the decline of civilisation. The lamentations only mean that professional men were having to help with the washing-up.'* The English were the only European people who sorted themselves out by class at mealtimes, he wrote; the masses took their principal meal at midday, their betters in the evening.[14]

Alan's inquiry extended into the bedroom. Concluding a startling passage about contraception, in which he listed Dr Marie Stopes 'among the great benefactors of our age', Alan wrote:

---

*Alan always believed in making a joke work hard for a living. The present talk about the decline of civilisation, he had written in 1959, 'means only that university professors used to have domestic servants and now do their own washing-up'.[13]

The historian should bear in mind that between about 1880, when
limitations started, and 1940 or so, when the use of the sheath at any
rate became more general in all classes, he has on his hands a
frustrated people. The restraint exercised in their private lives may
well have contributed to their lack of enterprise elsewhere.

Another footnote dealt with the word 'fuck'. 'Its use', he decided,
'seems to be approaching literary, though not conversational,
respectability.'[15]

Alan had fun with some favourite Aunt Sallies. The university
constituencies of Oxford and Cambridge, he said, could be relied
on to return reactionary members.* Broadcasting was a dictatorship; 'in no time at all, the monopolistic corporation came to be
regarded as an essential element in "the British way of life" '. The
British Legion was 'a conservative paramilitary organisation'.
Clark, who was connected with the Oxford British Legion,
objected to this last passage and Alan agreed to delete it.[16]

The reader searching in Alan's book for information about the
University of Oxford would discover that it had been the preserve
of the privileged classes, and a bastion of the Established Church,
that it had discriminated against women, had succeeded in out-
doing the worst achievements of the Victorians with the new
Bodleian building, and had 'frivolously' given an honorary degree
to P.G. Wodehouse. Only one cause for pride is recorded: the
production by an Oxford scientist in 1932 of an effective contraceptive jelly.[17]

Reviewers dubbed the book 'Taylor's England'. 'In his
impatience of humbug, especially of lofty humbug, in his radical
warmth and unashamed humanity,' wrote Max Beloff, he 'comes
closest to those things which are in the end most admirable about
the English'.[18] *English History, 1914–1945* was Alan's tribute to
the English people. It was a work of reclamation. Conservatives, he
said, had appropriated patriotism.[19] He aimed to take it back.

---

*Only partially true. A.P. Herbert, for example – very much an independent – was
Burgess (i.e. MP) for the University of Oxford from 1935 until the practice of
having University Members of Parliament was abolished (except 1939–45).

'There are no words to express my gratitude for all your aid and encouragement,' Alan wrote to Clark when he had finished. Six months before publication he wrote again: 'I can't thank you enough for giving me this great opportunity. It has been a wonderful experience, and I shall die content if I do not write another book.'[20]

Other books in the Oxford History of England were presented with pale blue dust-jackets; but OUP planned to issue Alan's book with illustrations on the cover. The background colour was a deeper blue, on which were superimposed five black-and-white photographs. Alan wrote to protest.

> I hope I am not too late to raise my voice most strongly against it. I have acquired, I think undeservedly, the reputation of being a journalistic, unscholarly writer. This jacket will confirm the reputation. People will think that the book is another piece of provocative, paradoxical display by an elderly enfant terrible . . . I have put years of labour into this book, partly with the intention of showing that I was a serious scholar. This jacket will ruin all my efforts.

It was too late to recall the review copies, but OUP agreed to re-jacket the remaining stock, reverting to the typographical style of the other volumes in the series.[21]

English History, 1914–1945 was published in October 1965; the Oxford University Press held a cocktail party at Claridge's to celebrate. It was an instant bestseller, and despite an initial print-order of 40,000, copies were soon unobtainable in many book-shops. After the criticism directed at *The Origins of the Second World War*, this book was greeted with almost unqualified praise; all noted his literary craftsmanship. For Alan Bullock, it was 'compulsive as well as compulsory reading', a *'tour de force'*; a term also used by Noel Annan, who believed that it deserved, 'like Macaulay's history, to supersede for a few days the latest fashionable novel on the tables of young ladies'. For David Owen this was 'vintage Taylor'; for Max Beloff, a 'masterpiece'. The reviewer in the *Times Literary Supplement* thought it must be the most readable book of its size for many a day: 'his talents are at last happily yoked, not only with his accustomed brilliance as a stylist, but also with the balance and sensibility of a mature historical mind.' 'The style is a perfect model, hard and vivid,' wrote Maurice Shock,

> the sentences short but with few failing to carry a point and punch of their own. There is not a dull page in the book. But the style is only a reflection of the method which essentially consists of bringing before the reader a rapid succession of events, each of which is caught momentarily, but sharply, under the microscope. It is this skill which makes Mr Taylor such a master of the condensed narrative.[22]

In a letter to Annan about his review, Alan denied any intention to 'demythologize' the era. 'I wrote to find out what happened and why it happened. I have no more interest in debunking than in bunking.' And in a letter to the anonymous *Times Literary Supplement* reviewer, Alan denied that he was 'deliberately revisionist'. 'I am neither revisionist nor orthodox – I don't think about the question one way or the other.'[23]

In his preface to the book Alan had concluded by thanking three people. One was Clark. Another was Kenneth Tite, Fellow of Politics at Magdalen, who had himself been commissioned to write a volume for the Pelican History of England, which he had been forced to abandon due to ill-health. Tite read Alan's manuscript twice, saved him from many mistakes, questioned some of his judgements and tempered the dogmatism of Alan's style. 'One other historian gave me inspiration and guidance. I had hoped to place this book in his hands. Now I set down in bereavement the name of Max Aitken, Lord Beaverbrook, my beloved friend.'

By the late summer of 1965 Alan was spending a couple of days a week at Cherkley working on the Beaverbrook papers. Beaverbrook had acquired a considerable archive, including the private papers of Lloyd George and Bonar Law. There was steady pressure from scholars for access to these papers; in his lifetime Beaverbrook himself had decided who could see them. Now Alan was the only person qualified to do this. But Cherkley, deep in Surrey, was a private home, not a suitable place for researchers; Alan groaned

that he had to spend three hours on the road every day he worked
there. Agreement in principle was reached that the Beaverbrook
archives should be moved to a new building in London, where Alan
would be installed as Honorary Director. A smart new library was
being prepared at the back of the Express Building in Fleet Street,
due to open in 1967.

In October 1965 Alan wrote to thank Evelyn Waugh for the gift
of a copy of his *Sword of Honour* trilogy, which had just been
released in one volume. Alan referred to his own work on the life of
Beaverbrook, and mentioned that Beaverbrook professed never to
have read any of Waugh's books, though he showed a surprising
awareness of their contents – especially the adroit answer, 'Up to a
point, Lord Copper'.* Waugh replied:

> I am not surprised that the late Lord Beaverbrook had read nothing
> of mine. I used to meet him quite often in the late 1930s and I noticed
> that though he went out of his way to be civil, he always got names
> and titles wrong. He liked to get information at second-hand from
> hangers-on . . . But I don't think he had the patience to plough
> through a new novel.[24]

Alan enquired about the fate of Trimmer, one of the characters in
Waugh's trilogy. In subsequent printings of *English History, 1914–
1945* the bibliography ends with the following note:

> If future generations want to know what the Second World War was
> like for English people, they can safely turn to *Sword of Honour* by
> Evelyn Waugh, the greatest work of a great English novelist.† Its
> admirers will be interested to know that Trimmer married a Johan-
> nesburg Jewess and is greatly scared about his safety and fortune.

Late in 1965 readers of the *New Statesman* competition were asked
to provide an extract from Alan's history of the years 1946–1965.

---

*Lord Copper, the dictatorial and preposterous press lord in *Scoop*, bears some
resemblance to Beaverbrook.
†He had made the same point in a 1961 *Observer* Christmas round-up, when he
had praised *Unconditional Surrender* – the final book in the *Sword of Honour*
trilogy – as 'the best book of the year, alas'. It may have been this which prompted
Waugh to send the one-volume edition to Alan.

The winning pastiche came from the hand of another historian, Henry Pelling:

In January 1965 Sir Winston Churchill died. He was given a state funeral – a distinction reserved for royalty since the Duke of Wellington. He had saved his country twice – once by vigour, in 1940; once by sloth, in 1951–4, when England could have joined the Common Market. It was to no avail. With his death, the last vestige of national greatness disappeared. Prime ministers still flew to Washington; opposition leaders lectured at Harvard. No one in the White House or the Pentagon took any notice. Ambassador Lodge attended a 'teach-in' in Oxford, probably to keep the Rhodes scholars in line rather than to instruct the natives. Even the Embassy library in Grosvenor Square was dismantled. British public opinion no longer mattered. British diplomacy faltered. A month's war took place between India and Pakistan. Whitehall ran a firework display in St James's Park. Rhodesia declared independence. The Queen gave the governor a decoration. The Conservatives, if anything, were keener 'Little Englanders' than the government. But there was not much in it. Still, there were the Beatles; if it had not been for them, no foreign schoolchild would ever have heard of England.[25]

In 1966 Alan tried his hand at parody. The book under review was Cornelius Ryan's blockbuster *The Last Battle*.

A bell rang insistently in the quiet room. Hack historian Taylor looked at his watch. It was precisely 11.43 hours. He reached listlessly for the telephone. Then his face changed. A book to review? A bestseller? Send it out at once. Down by the Thames secretaries and messengers sprang into action . . .[26]

In April 1966 the *Times Literary Supplement* devoted most of an issue to an attack on traditional history.[27] In a keynote article Keith Thomas proclaimed 'the coming revolution', when social history would take the place of political history as the central subject around which other branches of history were likely to be organised. Alan's approach in *English History, 1914–1945* had been to put politics centre-stage: 'the rest – culture, economics, religion and so on – are refreshing interruptions, like drinks at the bar during the interval'. Thomas described Alan's volume in the Oxford History of England as 'a brilliant swansong for the dying concept of history as past politics, and social history as undemanding subsidiary'.[28]

Thomas was indeed a prophet. In the late 1960s and the 1970s Alan's style of history came to seem old-fashioned, as the new disciplines of the social sciences, sociology, social psychology, anthropology and demography, carried all before them. Just to be interested in kings, statesmen, generals or diplomats seemed 'ideologically unsound'.

This dethronement of politics, Thomas had predicted, would encounter much resistance. Alan was certainly irritated by Thomas's attack. He had long thought that 'sociology is history with the history left out'.[29] Reviewing a book by a member of the French *Annales* school, which Thomas had held out as a model for British historians to copy, Alan wrote: 'I wish I could understand all this or be as confident about anything as M. Morazé is about almost everything. A great deal of this book, I am ashamed to say, washes over my head, and I come up spluttering.'[30]

Towards the end of 1967 Clark – perhaps inspired by the *New Statesman* competition, perhaps not – suggested that a revised *English History, 1914–1945* might be extended forwards in time. 'My book was deliberately shaped to end in 1945, and I doubt whether an epilogue would improve it,' Alan replied.

> At present I am fully engaged in writing Beaverbrook's life and I cannot foresee how long this will take me. When it comes to an end, I should like to plunge into the rich resources of the Lloyd George and Bonar Law papers which we have. My ultimate intention is to provide a completely revised edition of *English History, 1914–1945* when others have explored the papers now opened under the coming thirty-year rule. Whether I shall ever have time to do all this is another matter.[31]

Five years later he mentioned this plan to Davin.[32] In 1978 Davin retired; his successor was Robin Denniston, a very different character. In 1979 Alan wrote to Denniston after reading the announcement of a New Oxford History of England:

> Looking through *The Periodical*, now defunct, I was surprised to read that the Oxford History of England, edited by Sir George Clark, was completed in 1961. I have in my possession a copy, indeed more than one copy, of Volume XV, published in 1965. I had indeed thought of preparing a revised edition. However, now there is to be a New Oxford History of England, incorporating I hope such modern trends as sociology and psycho-history, I have laid any such thought aside.[33]

In July 1966 Alan had been able to review the second book in the Oxford History of Modern Europe series, Raymond Carr's volume on Spain. 'A single volume appeared twelve years ago. Now the authors seem astir at last.'[34]

Alan had reached the height of his fame. If his books did not sell in such huge numbers as those of G.M. Trevelyan and Arthur Bryant, he was much better known, because of his regular appearances on television. Like many famous people, Alan enjoyed the sensation of having a familiar face. He was quite put out when someone stopped him in the street and said: 'I know who you are – you're A.P. Herbert, aren't you?'

One result of his fame was an abundance of commercial offers. In the 1960s and early 1970s he was constantly in demand to lend his name to works aimed at the general reader, so much so that despite his need to support two families in some style he was able to reject offers which did not interest him. His letters to his agent David Higham in this period frequently refer to efforts to reduce his surtax. In 1967 he turned down the opportunity to do a 'Jackdaw' – a wallet containing facsimile historical miscellanea, then very fashionable for schoolchildren. 'I've made more money this year than I need and I don't feel like making more merely for the pleasure of paying surtax at the top rate,' he told Higham. 'There may come a time when I am short of money. By then I hope I'll be dead. So no more projects at the moment.' When Higham raised the possibility of a lecture tour in America, Alan wrote that it was very unlikely he should ever contemplate such a thing, 'unless my finances fall into ruin'.[35]

'I have long experience of publishers who parade their poverty while drinking champagne,' Alan told Higham in 1968. He became very irritable about a demand from Atheneum, his American publishers, for a separate manuscript of one of his books. 'If Atheneum complain any further you may tell them that their complaint will be met and you should add that in no circumstances will any future book of mine be offered to them.' He had the typescript photocopied, at a cost of £20.4s. When he heard that Atheneum had decided to offset from the British edition – meaning that they had no need for a separate manuscript – he was livid. 'There have been too many mistakes of this kind,' he wrote to Higham: 'This is to give notice that I do not propose to call on your services as agent in my future dealings.'[36] He soon calmed down, however, and asked Higham to negotiate a fee for an introduction to a new edition to Keynes's *Economic Consequences of the Peace*. This was one of many projects which Alan was too busy to complete; other books he was prepared in principle to write included one on Britain in 1940 and another on the Decline and Fall of the British Empire.

In 1966 Alan published *From Sarajevo to Potsdam*, a volume in Thames and Hudson's 'History of European Civilisation' series, edited by his Bootham contemporary Geoffrey Barraclough. Though a mere 40,000 words, it was far from bland; the *Times Literary Supplement* reviewer described it as

a fine romp . . . There is the familiar combination of non-fact and debatable statement which irritates the professional historians – but there is also the striking probe, the brilliant summation and the arresting choice of word and phrase which will always excite their envy and admiration . . . This is the kind of book Mr Taylor can now write with his left hand.[37]

In the same year he agreed to act as Editor-in-Chief for Purnell's ninety-six-part 'History of the Twentieth Century', which was published in magazine form – known in the trade as a 'partwork' –

between 1968 and 1970. In the early 1970s he acted as advisory editor to Nelson's *Dictionary of World History*, and edited a series for Weidenfeld and Nicolson on 'British Prime Ministers'. Though none of these was a work of original scholarship, Alan set high standards. His popular writings were always provocative, crediting the general reader with a critical intelligence and a serious interest in historical issues. So many historians took the opposite line, fearful of exposing historical controversies outside the profession in case of being 'misunderstood'. Alan and Liddell Hart regularly exchanged 'unacademic' greetings.

Since 1965 Alan had been teaching one afternoon a week as a special lecturer at University College, London (UCL). But he was out of the academic mainstream, and he lamented that his influence was diminishing. When a former pupil asked him to support his application for a Chair, Alan replied that 'you should always quote my name if you think it will bring you advantage, but of course on some occasions it may be the kiss of death'.[38] 'I am extremely busy writing letters of commendation,' he advised another young historian: 'I hope, indeed I am confident, that one of these days one of them will come off.'[39]

In 1966, the year of Alan's sixtieth birthday, Gilbert's *Festschrift* was published, under the title *A Century of Conflict, 1850–1950: Essays for A.J.P. Taylor*. Among those who agreed to contribute but who failed to reach the finishing-post were Raymond Carr, Richard Crossman, Michael Foot, Henry Kissinger and Arthur Schlesinger Jr. Nevertheless there was an unusually wide range of contributors, including Max Beloff, Hugh Thomas, Edward Crankshaw, and Liddell Hart, now Sir Basil Liddell Hart. Sir Isaiah Berlin, who when first canvassed had been too busy, had also written an essay. Alan himself reviewed the book in *The Observer*; 'I am the one man who can be impartial', he told Machell. He praised in particular an essay by the economic historian Paul Einzig which criticised Alan strongly: 'the most slashing attack I have ever read on an historian's accuracy, and the maddening thing about it is that most, though not all of it, is justified'. Einzig wrote to Gilbert that he was 'very favourably impressed' by Alan's reaction to his essay.[40]

Berlin's piece, a 'Personal Impression' of Namier, could be taken as a back-handed tribute, though Alan did not see it this way. Berlin referred explicitly to the breakdown in relations between Namier and his former disciple. In his review, Alan did the same. 'All who loved Namier must have experienced the same fascination, tempered by occasional impatience. No man was more perceptive, and none so blind.' In his later days, Alan wrote, Namier 'grew more respectable, using that word in a pejorative sense, and indeed this caused estrangement between us. He was certainly very far from respectable when he first came to Manchester and graced parties at Malcolm Muggeridge's flat.' Berlin must have been concerned that Alan had taken his piece badly, for Alan wrote him a reassuring letter:

> You are quite wrong to think that I resented what you wrote about Namier and me, or that I thought you had done it to embarrass me. On the contrary I greatly esteemed it and thought you had done it perfectly. There again, you almost made me feel I had been unjust to Lewis – but not quite. In my opinion he slightly misinformed you, but maybe he did not realise himself how badly he had behaved, and perhaps I behaved badly in taking any notice. If he put snobbery ahead of academic values, why should I set myself up to judge him? At any rate I appreciated every word, without exception, of your piece in the Festschrift.[41]

In 1967 Sir Isaiah Berlin raised the possibility of Alan's autobiography. This, Berlin felt, would be 'an intellectual odyssey . . . one of the most exciting unwritten books of our time'.[42] It was not the first time he had suggested it. At Berlin's prompting, Hamilton had written to Alan in 1956 to suggest such a book. 'What extraordinary ideas you do have!' Alan had replied. 'I had thought of writing "memories" for some time for my own amusement, and you shall have them if I do. But it won't be until I have accumulated the experiences of a few more years.'[43] When Berlin again mentioned the idea eleven years later, Alan told his agent that few men are gifted enough to write their memoirs – 'witness Macmillan, who was thought to be quite clever till he tried. Nothing interesting has ever happened to me; I have known no one of any interest; and the few episodes I might record would give universal pain. How would the great like a picture of Dylan* treating human beings as a boy pulls the wings off a fly?'[44] Alan wrote to Berlin saying that he had turned down the proposal. 'To adapt Namier, you must be a very clever man to find anything interesting in me . . .† My memoirs would be duller than Maurice's‡, and one can't say worse than that.

'I don't think I have travelled much intellectually, indeed far too little. I was at sixteen much where I am at sixty-one.' Of course this was not true. At sixteen, and at twenty-six, Alan was still a starry-eyed Marxist, waiting for the Revolution, a rigid adherent to the Materialist Conception of History. 'I have a blind spot for religion and philosophy,' he continued.

> They are as meaningless to me as, I suppose, witchcraft is to you. When I am asked to contribute to volumes entitled What I Believe, I can only reply: I don't *believe* anything. I make certain practical assumptions in life, as that most drivers keep to the lefthand side of the road in this country or that seeds sown in fertile soil will germinate. I have moral habits just as I have appetites and pay my bills with the same routine as I eat my dinner. I like keeping to the rules, but I do not condemn others who break them. Indeed I do not claim any right to judge others and equally deny their right to judge me. Professionally, I am an old-fashioned narrative historian with no gift for analysis or social techniques.
>
> I don't like hierarchies and am for the poor against the rich. I can't find much interest in politics except when the call comes unmistakably, as it did for me in the General Strike, Suez, and CND. Then, I think, I'm as good a speaker as Bright was, but this is a technical accomplishment I am not particularly proud of. I like making money, not because I want to spend all that much, but simply for the operation of making it. All my life I have driven fast, rather showy cars and am now beginning to fear the days when I shall no longer be able to do so.

---

*David Higham was also Dylan Thomas's agent.
†The reference is to a comment made by Namier to Berlin: 'You must indeed be a very clever man to understand what you write.'
‡Sir Maurice Bowra's *Memories* (1966).

These are outside characteristics. I doubt whether anyone can write honestly about the inside since Freud. He turned us into psychological hypochondriacs. I can never have intimate relations with women without noting the symptoms, and it really makes a mess of things. Some strange things have happened in my private affairs, but I don't think it would be a kindness to write about them. My marriage with Margaret was torn apart by two affairs – the first a war-hero, the second a poet, now, I am glad to say, dead. I ought to have accepted these fantasies, as Lutyens did under similar circumstances. Instead I resented them as irrational and pursued a course which was as destructive for me as for others. Such stories are better left alone.

Evidently Berlin did not give up, because six weeks later Alan wrote to thank him for an 'endearing' letter. He promised to think again when he had finished with Beaverbrook.[45]

In December 1966 Penguin asked Alan to write another introduction, this time to *The Communist Manifesto*. It was to be published on the sixtieth anniversary of the Russian Revolution, the beginning of a new wave of vulgar Marxism, and the edition was soon to be found on every student bookshelf. Alan received a small royalty; ironically this became his 'best money-spinner'.[46] Alan's introduction was longer than the manifesto itself, written in a satirical style: 'me at my iconoclastic worst', he told his former pupil William Thomas.[47] He referred to the manifesto as a 'religious book', and described himself as a 'non-believer'. He gave a brief account of the careers of its two authors, Marx and Engels. In retrospect, Alan concluded, Marx 'appears as a respectable Victorian gentleman of scholarly disposition'. He teasingly exposed the contradictions in Marxist thought. The great capitalist crisis of the Depression, for example, 'passed over without a single Marxist revolution'. The Marxist explanation of imperialism – super-profit – had not proved convincing; 'everyone knows,' he wrote, 'that the British working class would be better off if the British Government did not insist on clinging to the tattered remnants of a dead empire.' But some of the manifesto had proved triumphantly vindicated. 'Nearly everyone now accepts the principle that ideas and beliefs grow out of and reflect existing society rather than lead an independent life.' It was characteristic of Alan to put forward a controversial assertion as if it were accepted fact.

Alan had long since renounced his faith in Marxism. But he remained sympathetic to the Soviet Union, and frequently stated his opinion that the Cold War was 'an American invention'. 'Anti-Communism causes more trouble in the world than ever Communism does or did.' 'Anti-Communism as a militant aggressive creed is still virulent, as Vietnam witnesses,' he wrote in 1967. He still believed that the Soviet Union might be proved economically right, though politically wrong. Even in the mid-1970s he thought that most countries in the world would adopt some form of Communist economic system, though without the political dictatorship. The revolutionary zeal he had first experienced in short trousers never completely departed; in 1970, for example, he described Lenin as 'a very great man and even, despite his faults, a very good man'.[48] In his enthusiasm for the Revolution there is an echo of Charles James Fox on the French Revolution: 'How much the greatest event it is that ever happened in the world! And how much the best!' – a line which Alan quotes again and again in his writing.

Around this time Alan was invited to give a lecture on the Russian Revolution at Birmingham University. The large lecture-hall was packed. When Alan arrived, he was given a microphone to hang round his neck. A few moments later he was called to speak. He advanced to the edge of the platform. 'Don't pay any attention to all this stuff about my being the greatest living historian, or the most famous,' he said, referring to the complimentary introduction. 'What I've written hasn't been particularly original or even particularly important. But it has always been said in a loud, clear voice, and I certainly don't need this' – so saying, he took off the microphone.

A few years later he contradicted a statement made in a review by the young historian Cameron Hazlehurst, whose postgraduate work Alan had supervised. 'You are wrong to call me Britain's best-known historian,' he wrote. 'Rowse, Veronica Wedgwood, Arthur Bryant and perhaps Trevor-Roper are better known.' Hazlehurst did not accept the correction: 'I imagine your *total* sales would be greater than Wedgwood's, vastly greater than Trevor-Roper's, and not far behind Rowse's.[49]

In 1967 Liddell Hart wrote to remonstrate with Alan about a piece he had written for the *Sunday Express* attacking the newly imposed seventy-mile-an-hour speed limit. Indeed Alan had advocated raising the speed limits in built-up areas. 'I have been driving a car for 45 years,' Alan wrote: 'I have consistently ignored all speed limits. Never once have I encountered the slightest risk as a result.' Alan was an 'ancient-rights driver', one who had begun driving before tests were introduced in 1934 and therefore had never submitted himself to one. Alan told Liddell Hart that he was 'not shaken by your advocacy of the speed limit . . . our over-burdened police have better things to do'.[50] In fact he was irritated when others, especially other historians, took his *Sunday Express* articles seriously.

Alan was equally dismissive of the breath tests introduced to control 'drink-driving'. He continued to drive after he had been drinking; one evening he was so drunk that Eve had to help him crawl from the car to the door on his hands and knees.

On 25 May 1967 – Beaverbrook's birthday – the Beaverbrook Library opened its doors. 'I have come into an empire,' Alan wrote to his old friend Noel Fieldhouse. The Library was on the first floor of an impressive modern extension to the main *Express* building, with a separate entrance in St Bride's Street. As one walked up the stairs one could hear the noise of printing machinery and glimpse huge rolls of paper. Then, once through the Library doors, one left the bustle behind and entered the air-conditioned tranquillity of the Library itself. Dominating the entrance was the large Sickert portrait of Beaverbrook; framed Low cartoons hung on the walls; books by and about the great press lord sat on oak shelves; and glass-fronted cabinets displayed documents and photographs. Polished wood tables provided seating space for half-a-dozen or so

researchers; sliding shelves housed the archive. An elderly Scots-
man put out to grass by the Beaverbrook Newspapers retrieved the
documents. Off the main room were several offices: two smaller
ones occupied by an archivist and a secretary, a larger one by the
Honorary Director.

Alan came running up the stairs of the Library at around nine-
thirty every morning. His first act would be to go through the post,
dictating clear and concise replies. He found it strange having a
secretary, he told his cousin Karin, with whom he had resumed
contact after many years. 'I can't bring myself to let her write my
books or even my private letters. But she does everything else, and it
is tremendous to have someone who looks up the times of trains for
me or makes hotel reservations. She even makes excuses if I don't
want to lecture somewhere. I suppose all tycoons have such
luxuries but it is a new and very funny experience for me.'[51] The
secretary was Veronica Horne, a glamorous import from the *Daily
Express*, a distraction for all but the most conscientious scholars.

Apart from fielding requests for access to the archive, Alan's
prime duty, the one he found most onerous, was to deal with
requests to publish material held in the Library; he was endlessly
having to remind applicants that copyright belongs to the writer
and not the owner of the document. He became irritated with those
he thought over-scrupulous: 'copyright permission is a lot of
nonsense in a scholarly book'. Alan treated his post like a job,
keeping regular hours and even asking leave before going on
holiday. But he maintained his distance from the Beaverbrook
Foundation, receiving no more than a retainer for his permissions
work. 'I run the library though I take care not to get paid for it,' he
told his cousin.[52]

The doors opened to researchers at ten o'clock. Alan took a lively
interest in their work, and visitors were often invited into his office
for a chat. During the university terms there were never more than
two or three people working there, but during the vacations,
particularly in the long summer break, the Library was often full.*
Many of these were foreign scholars, especially Americans. For

---

*The visitors' book shows 972 entries between 1967 and 1975.

Alan the contact with younger historians was stimulating; for the young apprentices Alan was an inspiration, suggesting new lines of inquiry and encouraging fresh thinking. His friend Richard Ingrams described Alan as 'the Beaverbrook Professor of History'.

Alan worked all morning on his Beaverbrook biography, typing it himself. He also wrote his reviews and *Sunday Express* articles in the Library. He refused almost all invitations to lunch; 'I am not a lunching man' – making an exception only for old friends like Dan Davin, with whom any awkwardness had long since evaporated. His normal lunch was just bread or a couple of high-bake water biscuits and cheese, washed down with Malvern Water, which he kept in a fridge in his office. Then he attended a lunchtime concert, or took a walk in the City, sometimes looking at churches with his old friend John Betjeman. Afterwards he might go on to the London Library, or stroll to Hampstead Ponds – a good hour's walk – for a swim. If he returned to the Library he would take china tea at four o'clock when the readers left.

The Library even had its own notepaper, though in frugal Beaverbrook fashion it was not at all 'fancy'. Betjeman described it as 'very funny, it looks as if it was done by a nice local printer in Haltwhistle, if there is one there, and he has made the best use he can of what display type he has. Did you design it yourself, you dear old thing? Never get rid of it, it has naive charm and individuality.'[53]

In *English History, 1914–1945* Alan had described Lloyd George as the most inspired and creative British statesman of the twentieth century. 'Mr Taylor is clearly intrigued by Lloyd George,' wrote Geoffrey Barraclough, reviewing *Politics in Wartime*, another collection of Alan's essays: 'perhaps it is natural that the great "rogue" of English political life should appeal to the great "rogue" of English history.'[54] Alan drew the same parallel in his personal life: like Lloyd George, he would have a wife and a mistress. The only difficulty was to decide which was which.

Alan was still oscillating between his two wives. Now that his teaching commitments in Oxford had ended, he was able to spend more time in London. In 1966 he and Eve moved to Croftdown

Road, just by Hampstead Heath in Parliament Hill Fields. They were now quarrelling frequently. Eve likened him to Casaubon, the dried-up scholar with a much younger wife in George Eliot's *Middlemarch*; he accused her of profligacy. She did not care for walking; he did not care for tennis, which for Eve became a consuming interest. Visitors to the house noticed a 'sticky' atmosphere. When Alan's secretary came to tea, she was surprised when Eve suddenly left, announcing that she had to take a bath. Those who stayed to dinner found that conversation was stilted and the food unappetising. Later he joked that he had left Eve because of her cooking.

'We historians are dull creatures, and women sometimes notice this,' Alan told Paul Addison, whose thesis he was supervising. 'I've had more than my share of troubles and, on balance, an unhappy life outside my work.'[55]

Eve felt she was losing Alan to Margaret. He refused to make a break with his ex-wife, something Eve could not accept. Though the children of his first marriage were all now grown-up, Margaret was frequently seen with him in public, and often described as his wife. When his daughters were married in a joint ceremony at St Pancras Town Hall in 1966, for example, the press covered the wedding of 'the AJP girls' without mentioning that their parents were no longer married. Perhaps to compensate, Eve introduced herself to people as 'Mrs A.J.P. Taylor'. Sometimes she would appear to become hysterical and shout at Alan; he did not retaliate.

One afternoon in September 1968 John Grigg was working in the Beaverbrook Library when Alan left early. As he passed where Grigg was sitting, Alan tossed a screwed-up note over Grigg's shoulder. Then he left. Grigg smoothed open the note, which read: 'I am leaving Eve tonight. I hope you and Patsy [Grigg's wife] will be able to see her some time.' Two days later an article appeared in the *Daily Mail*. 'He left this morning,' Eve was quoted as saying. 'He has gone back to his first wife . . . I have known this was going to happen for a long time.'[56] Two days later he advised Machell that he had moved to St Mark's Crescent. There was some press speculation that he planned to re-marry Margaret; Alan made 'no comment'. To those friends who asked he said he had gone back to Margaret because he needed a home for his books. In fact he soon drifted into the habit of spending Sundays with Eve and her children, and they took holidays together. It was the 'double life' in reverse.

At Christmas-time, Alan wrote to his cousin Karin:

> My second marriage broke up in the autumn mainly because my second wife became increasingly jealous of my first brood of children. Well it was sad. I was fond of her and very fond indeed of my two young sons. But there came a time when I was weary of being . . . nagged at. I'd like to think things would go right again one day, but I doubt it and in a way I don't much care. I'm so busy that I am never at home until late evening, and then it does not much matter where I am . . . It was Henry Sara over again, and in each case I thought – I'm not standing for what my father did.'[57]

In 1968 Alan was consulted by Douglas Johnson, Professor of History at Birmingham, who had been asked to write a general history of France. They went together to a Lyons' Corner-House café in Tottenham Court Road. During the course of the conversation, Johnson quoted to Alan something his own father had said to him: 'There comes a time in the life of every man when he looks in the mirror and sees his father's face looking back at him.' Alan was intensely interested, seemingly moved to the brink of tears.

That same year Alan began the first of a series of long-distance walks. He and his second son Sebastian tackled the Pennine Way, a two-hundred-and-fifty-mile tramp along the backbone of England. They completed the walk the following year, when the thriller-writer Len Deighton joined them. Deighton had bought the film rights in *Oh What a Lovely War!*; Joan Littlewood recommended Alan to him as an adviser. They quickly became friends; Alan appreciated Deighton's single-mindedness and technical expertise. On the walk, Deighton's feet succumbed to his new mountaineering boots, and he spent the day resting with Margaret, who joined the walking party at hotels in the evenings. He assumed Margaret to be Alan's wife, and no one disabused him.

The walk on the Pennine Way was followed by others: along the Offa's Dyke Path which separates England and Wales, with Crispin, Giles and Daniel; along the Pilgrim's Way, the traditional route to Canterbury, with Giles and Crispin; and along the South

Downs Way, with Giles. Once he had exhausted these routes, he took to following the routes described by Wainwright in the Lake District. The children of the two families, who accompanied him on these walks in various permutations, were reconciled, though their mothers were not.

In August 1968 Russian troops invaded Czechoslovakia and crushed the reforming government of Alexander Dubček. When Cameron Hazlehurst mentioned to Alan that he found 'this Czech business' very distressing, Alan replied that 'the best comment on the Czech affair was a banner at Sunday's demo – "Schweik Lives"'.[58] A few years later Alan wrote a joint letter to *The Times* with Hugh Trevor-Roper, protesting about the treatment of Czech scholars under the new regime; their protest inspired a leader.[59]

In 1969 Alan heard from the British Council that Eva Haraszti was coming to England for a month, in connection with the book she was writing on appeasement. She had 'particularly asked whether we could arrange for her to meet you'.[60] He had not seen her since 1962, though in 1965 both had attended the Vienna conference of the International Association of Historians in the hope of meeting, but had failed to find each other. Their relations had reverted to a more formal footing; he signed his letters 'Yours sincerely'.

Now, however, Alan decided to press his suit. He sent flowers to her hotel, and pursued her to the Public Record Office, where he 'fell in love with her again in one of the waiting rooms'. Alan embarked on a whirlwind courtship. He took her in the evenings to smart restaurants. He escorted her to Oxford where he showed her his rooms, and they walked down the Cherwell to Holywell Ford. They drove out to see the Chartist settlements at Minster Lovell, lunched in Burford, and walked round Blenheim Palace together. Eva hugged Alan by Churchill's tomb at Bladon, overcome with emotion. That evening he entertained her at Magdalen High Table. Back in London, Alan took Eva to see his favourite City churches. He was excited and frisky. 'My divorce will go through next year,' he advised Eva after her return to Hungary. 'Thereafter, if you are ever free and want to marry me, I shall be waiting. Or even if you are free for a shorter time, I am available.'[61]

Eva's husband, who had been seriously ill with stomach cancer, died that same winter. Alan wrote to console her, and they began a passionate correspondence. He addressed her as 'Darling', 'Dear Heart', 'My Dearest One', 'Beloved', 'Lovely Mine', and 'Lovey Dovey', often finishing his letters 'love, love, love'. As a fellow-historian, Eva was able to share Alan's interests, and his love letters were interspersed with reflections on his work and historical gossip. There were frequent misunderstandings; Alan confessed that he was 'frivolous at heart', whereas Eva was a serious Marxist historian, who had referred to Alan in one of her books as an excellent representative of bourgeois historiography. 'I have no objection to making money by speculation as long as capitalism lasts,' he confessed.[62] And though she had lived in London before, in the late 1940s, cultural differences divided them. But Alan was convinced that he had found a soul-mate. They arranged to meet the following September at an historical conference in Königs-winter, organised by the German *Ranke Gesellschaft*.

The Beaverbrook Library became what one historian has called 'a kind of alternative Public Record Office'.[63] The opening of the Library coincided with the relaxation of the fifty-year rule, which gave an impetus to the study of early twentieth-century political history. Twenty years of public records, covering the period from the First World War almost up to the Second, became available at a stroke. These records neatly complemented the holdings in the Beaverbrook Library. From 1968 the Library was host to a weekly Thursday evening seminar in the university vacations, attended at one time or another by most of the leading scholars in the subject. Someone would give a paper, generally lasting about fifty minutes; Alan became annoyed if these trespassed over the hour. While the paper was being read he would sit with his head on his shoulder, eyes closed as if asleep. When the speaker had finished, Alan came to life. He thanked the speaker and then provided a scintillating appraisal of the subject, full of provocative ideas and lively, sometimes shocking judgements. This led into a general discussion of the subject, which often continued over a drink in the pub or a meal in a local restaurant afterwards.

Martin Gilbert spoke to the seminar on 'The Politics of Gallipoli'. In a wicked mood, Gilbert decided to try a spoof: he presented all the previously recorded facts as new, and all his real findings as old hat. Alan thanked him for his talk which, he said, had contained several important discoveries. No one seemed to notice anything amiss.

The Beaverbrook Library came to function as a small research institute, with Alan as its elder statesman. Its activities centred on the Lloyd George papers, the largest and most significant holding in the archive. Alan edited three books arising out of this collection: *Lloyd George: Twelve Essays* (1971), a volume of papers presented at the Library seminars; *Lloyd George: A Diary* (1971), by Frances Stevenson, and *My Darling Pussy: The Letters of Lloyd George and Frances Stevenson, 1913–41* (1975). Frances Stevenson had been Lloyd George's secretary, mistress and confidante; after Dame Margaret Lloyd George died in 1941, she became his second wife. Alan was fascinated by her; even in old age she remained, in Beaverbrook's words, 'an appetizing woman'. Twenty-five years younger than her husband, she did not die until 1972. 'I never knew any woman more pleasantly aware of a male's presence and more attentive to his needs,' he wrote to the editor of the Lloyd George letters, Kenneth O. Morgan, some years after her death. 'I understood for the first time what was meant by "a mistress by nature". The result for the male was both flattering and sympathetic.'[64]

In fact the archive was full of sex; as well as those of Lloyd George, Beaverbrook's numerous affairs were amply documented. Alan was pleased to find that Asquith, too, had a craving for a much younger woman not his wife: Venetia Stanley, to whom he wrote almost every day and who, to escape him, became engaged to another member of his Cabinet. She had shown Beaverbrook copies of Asquith's letters, and later lent him some of them to help with his histories.

A coterie of young scholars formed around Alan at the Library. Alan enjoyed their confidences, and even relished competition amongst them. When Stephen Koss reviewed a book by Cameron

Hazlehurst which attacked Koss's work, Alan wrote to congratulate him on his piece, 'a very fine example of turning the other cheek
in the most devastating manner'.[65] He was able to do this without
taking sides or losing the confidence of either man.

In 1971 Koss urged Alan to come and lecture in New York; there
was a possibility of a fee of upwards of $10,000 for five lectures. It
was a very attractive offer. Alan thanked Koss for the suggestion,
'but I fear it is out of the question'.[66]

In 1969 Alan became involved in another row, this time over his
contribution to a book on Churchill.[67] Dial Press, the American
publishers, controlled the rights; and the agent acting for them,
Anthony Sheil, proposed to sell a serialisation to the *Observer*. The
Sunday Express refused to release Alan from his exclusive contract
and attempted to block the serialisation. Sheil sent a solicitor's
letter to Alan demanding an indemnity on behalf of the *Observer*
against action by the *Sunday Express*. The matter seemed absurd,
particularly as Alan's reviews appeared in the *Observer* every other
week. In the end, the *Sunday Express* withdrew because they found
they had no legal power against the *Observer*. But Alan was very
annoyed; he sent a furious letter to Dial: 'I deeply resent this
discourteous negligence and immediate resort to legal threats.'[68]

Alan had been intrigued by the psychiatrist Anthony Storr's
contribution to the Churchill book. He told another contributor,
the historian Robert Rhodes James, that he had found Storr's
contribution 'very interesting, though I am in general a believer that
people are born with their dispositions, not shaped by lack or
excess of parental love during childhood'.[69] He invited Storr to
dine with him, in the hope that he might provide some insight into
the workings of Beaverbrook's mind. Later, without naming Storr,
Alan described their conversation that evening. Alan had outlined
Beaverbrook's character, his zest for power, his enjoyment for
making money, his inner uncertainty and his craving for affection
which he often mistakenly thought money would win him. 'He
must have been a neglected only child,' Storr is supposed to have
said. In fact he was nothing of the kind, Alan wrote triumphantly:
'henceforward I left psychology alone'.

Storr's recollection is rather different. 'I let him down completely', he wrote, 'because I hadn't read anything about Beaverbrook and wasn't prepared to give an instant diagnosis on the basis of ignorance.'[70]

Alan was very sensitive to criticism of his relationship to Beaverbrook. He insisted that his book was not an authorised or commissioned biography, but the work of an independent scholar. He was not beholden to the Beaverbrook Foundation; his position at the Beaverbrook Library was an honorary one. But not everybody appreciated these distinctions. Early in 1970 he delivered six Waynflete Lectures on various aspects of Beaverbrook's life.* On the day before his last lecture – 'Lord Beaverbrook as Historian' – a diary item appeared in the *Guardian* under the heading 'Daily Excess'. In the junior common room of one Oxford college, it reported, an alternative title for the series had been offered – 'How I Learned to Stop Worrying and Love the Ruling Classes'. The senior common room of the same college had appended a seventh lecture to the list: 'Lord Beaverbrook, Patron'. Alan was furious. He wrote to Alastair Hetherington demanding a withdrawal of the 'smear'. It implied that he had derived 'material benefit' from his friendship with the late Lord Beaverbrook, a suggestion which was 'totally false'. 'The paragraph reflects gravely on my standing as an independent scholar, and I am advised that I could claim heavy damages for it.' The following day, at the close of his final lecture, he referred to the report. 'As to the unnamed senior common room,' he said in conclusion, 'I will respect its witticisms more when any of its members produce work comparable in distinction to Lord Beaverbrook's or even my own.'[72]

In December 1970 Alan complained to Roger Machell that Macmillan had brought out a book called *The Origins of the Second World War*. The book was an anthology of criticism of Alan's own work, and the sub-title 'Historical Interpretations' appeared on the title-page, but Alan felt this was not enough to distinguish it from

---

*These were a stopgap; the man who was due to deliver them – 'some frightful American sociologist' – had failed to come at the last moment.[71]

his original. Its editor was Esmonde M. Robertson; Alan claimed to have been asked why he had employed Robertson 'to edit my book. Is this a case for complaining to Macmillan? I should like to get some money out of them, and if we could compel them to withdraw the book, this would be even more delightful. Here is a real treat for Christmas.'[73]

Machell pointed out in reply that there was no copyright in titles, but offered to protest all the same. Alan did not expect to get any money out of this, he told Machell, but he did think Macmillan had 'behaved very badly'. Hamish Hamilton duly protested; Macmillan replied 'regretting any unintentional discourtesy'. Alan described this as an 'impudent' apology, but he did not press the point further.[74] A couple of years later Alan's former pupil Roger Louis brought out a similar book, having consulted Alan beforehand. As a result of this publication the original *Times Literary Supplement* reviewer of Alan's book identified himself to Louis – not E.H. Carr, as Louis had speculated, but C.M. Woodhouse. 'Apart from the fact that I was practically the only non-professional historian who presumed to write on the subject at the time, you may like to know that I was, at any rate on this side of the Atlantic, the only reviewer with any personal experience of the process of political decision-making, and the only one who actually fought in the war against Hitler.'[75]

By April 1972 Machell was able to send Alan an advance copy of *Beaverbrook*. 'The book is beyond praise!' Alan replied: 'I mean in appearance. I still think it is dull, though good as history.'[76] James MacGibbon, Sophia's father-in-law, had read the typescript and sent Alan pages of detailed comments. 'What a good friend you are,' Alan replied. 'Of course, I'm a historian, not a biographer' – and took no notice. 'I am no Boswell,' Alan wrote in the introduction. He quoted a comment from Kenneth Young, another of those who had read the book in typescript, that he had written a history of Beaverbrook, not a biography. But Machell, in a private report on the typescript to Hamilton, had described it as 'marvellously lively', 'a superb monument to its hero', 'one of the great biographies of our day'.

Alan made no attempt to disguise his affection for his subject. Beaverbrook was 'the dearest friend I ever had'. 'For me Max could do no wrong,' Alan admitted, and then continued with a sentence deleted from the final typescript: 'I hope this is not a disqualification for his biographer.' Alan quoted his own remark to a friend after Beaverbrook's death: 'I loved him more than any other human being I have ever met.' Curiously, these words were ones Beaverbrook himself had used (and Alan had quoted) about Bonar Law: 'I loved him more than any other human being.' For Beaverbrook, Bonar Law had been a 'hero', a 'father figure'. Perhaps for Alan, Beaverbrook was the same – though Bonar Law, a dull and solid character, was very different from Beaverbrook. In his autobiography, Alan was to cite the very sentences which Beaverbrook had used to describe his friendships with Bonar Law and Churchill: 'I have served two masters. One was faithful unto death; the other betrayed me.'[77] For Alan the master who was faithful unto death was Beaverbrook; the master who betrayed him, Namier.

'He would not be a subordinate unless he could turn his leader into a hero,' Alan wrote of Beaverbrook. 'You're like him on Bonar Law,' Crossman told Alan during a television discussion about political biography. 'You make him your hero. Therefore he can't be at fault.'[78]

Alan's declared aim was to print an accurate story, confident that readers would warm to Beaverbrook if they saw him warts and all. He did not therefore suppress stories which might show Beaverbrook in a less favourable light. Of course the same story might be viewed differently by different people. Alan delighted in Beaverbrook's mischief-making, for example. 'The drawing-pin on the chair gave him pleasure as a boy, and its political equivalent gave him pleasure as a man. If he saw two naked wires he could not resist putting them together, whatever the resulting explosion.'[79] Others saw Beaverbrook as capricious, even wicked.

Alan cheerfully recorded Beaverbrook's unscrupulous manipulation of his newspapers, and his dictatorial attitude to subordinates. To Alan, it was these qualities others disliked so much which had made Beaverbrook 'one of the architects of victory' in 1940. As Minister of Aircraft Production, his unorthodox methods and persistent demands had worked miracles when miracles were needed. He provided the planes; Dowding provided the pilots. Together they had won a victory 'comparable only to Trafalgar'.[80]

Alan made allowances for Beaverbrook's philandering. Beaverbrook, he wrote, 'could not help switching people on and off according to his mood ... When he needed someone, no trouble was too great for him. When he turned to something else, his closest friends and even his wife ceased to exist for him.' He was 'a loner', something Alan himself could appreciate. When Alan described Beaverbrook's uncertainty before his marriage, perhaps he recalled his own hesitation about marrying Margaret: 'such doubts often assail men on the eve of matrimony'.[81]

Five years before the book was published Alan had written to tell his postgraduate pupil Paul Addison about a letter Beaverbrook had written on 8 May 1940, encouraging Neville Chamberlain, then still Prime Minister, to challenge a division in the House of Commons. Alan had little doubt that Beaverbrook was encouraging Chamberlain to his doom. 'I regret this letter though I shall publish it. My old friend was a very bad man.' But in the final version Alan did not present the letter as reprehensible. Beaverbrook had been trying 'simply to force a decision one way or the other'.[82]

'I'm afraid that he too often heightened the drama,' Alan confessed to Driberg, 'and occasionally invented anecdotes.'[83] Alan affectionately related numerous examples of Beaverbrook's 'romantic imagination'; in one such, Beaverbrook described to his intimate friend Arnold Bennett how he had made a triumphant speech in the House of Lords. Bennett used this episode in his novel *Lord Raingo*. In fact, as Bennett found, the speech was never delivered.

> Beaverbrook, like the true romantic he was, had imagined the whole episode. No doubt his feelings of anxiety were real, and no doubt he experienced the triumphs of oratory in his dreams. As often happened with him, the imaginary became more real to him than the reality. At any rate, despite Bennett's discovery, Beaverbrook repeated the original story to me in the last years of his life with admirable embellishments, and, like Bennett, I believed it.[84]

It was hard to reconcile such a flexible attitude to the truth with Alan's claims for Beaverbrook as 'a great historian'. By making such extravagant claims, as Machell in his report pointed out, Alan had erected a fence too high for even him to jump. 'I see now why you love Beaverbrook being a romancer,' Crossman told him. 'Because you yourself are a romancer.'[85] Alan admitted in his introduction that 'occasionally I have followed his [Beaverbrook's] example and have put in a remark or story because it seemed to me funny without implying that it was significant or true'.[86]

Reviewers praised the literary qualities of the book, while some of them questioned its impartiality. 'A loving biography' was one verdict; 'a work of scholarship – and friendship' another. The *Times Literary Supplement* reviewer described the book as 'a work of art', its author as 'often idiosyncratic, frequently iconoclastic, sometimes wrong-headed, occasionally very wrong indeed, but always interesting, always provocative and always exciting'. 'Only a biography of extraordinary quality could recapture the zest and fascination of this contradictory man,' wrote Kenneth O. Morgan, 'but that is the achievement of this compelling book by our greatest living historian.' Robert Blake made the point that Alan's friendship with his subject had enriched the book. 'This combination of energy, charm, fun, wit, gaiety and impish malevolence would never survive in the archives.' Richard Crossman, however, was less favourable; for him, the book 'provides the last and most crowning example of the most potent and most potentially corrupting quality which its subject possessed – his gift for spotting talent, and for making it his willing slave'. For Muggeridge, 'perhaps it was just one more case of love being a great deceiver'.[87]

Alan 'loved' Beaverbrook while he was still alive. 'Now that I have learnt to know him better from his records,' he wrote in the introduction to his biography, 'I love him even more.' His work on the book had produced 'an embarrassing result', he informed the novelist C.P. Snow just as he was finishing. 'I started by thinking that he was not much more than a political hobgoblin, as he called himself. Now I think he was right on almost everything.' 'Politically I came to admire him more and more as I went on,' he told Driberg a few days later. 'I think he was right about everything except Empire Free Trade.'[88]

'Everything' extended even to Beaverbrook's pre-War policy of isolation, backed by great armaments. Though Alan had previously condemned the hypocrisy of British and French guarantees to countries they could not defend, he had always before argued for an alliance with Russia against Germany instead. Now he was convinced that isolation was 'not only the wisest course to follow in a world full of dangers but also more honourable than to distribute guarantees which we could not fulfil'. These guarantees 'lured the guaranteed countries to disaster'.[89] In a letter to the naval historian Stephen Roskill, Alan argued that greater rearmament 'might have enabled us to keep out of the War altogether, and this in my opinion would have been the wisest course'.[90]

'Beaverbrook would have been on stronger ground in 1939 if he had argued that Hitler's tyranny had destroyed the British sense of judgement,' Alan wrote in his biography.

> People no longer asked: What can we do? They asked: What ought we to do? If they had been told that the price of overthrowing Hitler would be twenty-five million dead, they might have hesitated. They might even have hesitated, as some did, if they had been told that the price of destroying Germany would be Soviet domination of Eastern Europe. The question of peace and war was never put on this practical basis. It was considered solely in terms of moral obligation and emotion.[91]

'I wrote the book with my heart as well as with my head,' Alan confessed later.[92] Perhaps Alan was just a romantic biographer, inclined to fall in love with his subject, as he had fallen in love with Bismarck. While he was finishing the book, he had already begun to distance himself from Beaverbrook. 'I seem to have been enslaved to that old man for ever,' he complained to Eva. By the time the book was ready for publication, he was wondering whether it had been worth all the effort. 'Of course I did it because I loved him, but that memory fades too. Now I often remember the times when I found him exasperating and wondered why I ever wasted my time in his company.' Two years later, he had begun to resent having spent so much time on the book. 'I had to get him out of my system, but now I don't think he was worth it.' By 1976 the biography seemed to have been 'a waste of time'.[93]

But he remained very touchy about Beaverbrook. In 1979, for example, he left a dinner party early when he felt that a fellow-guest, the journalist Peter Jenkins, had insulted him. Jenkins expressed the view that Michael Foot, then Leader of the House in the last days of Callaghan's Labour Government, was not a serious politician. Anybody who had taken Beaverbrook's shilling was pretty disreputable, he said. Alan was so upset that he insisted on being taken home.

Alan had begun to write his memoirs as he finished the biography. In fact they were back-to-back; literally so, because he typed the draft of his autobiography on the flip side of his *Beaverbrook* typescript. 'I must try to write my autobiography for you,' he wrote to Eva. Partly, he meant, for her amusement; partly as a legacy, to be published after his death. 'I am writing my memoirs in my spare time,' he told Machell. 'I shall call them *An Uninteresting Story*. Unfortunately I can't leave out my private life and that means the memoirs can't be published while my two wives are alive. After that I shall be dead and everyone will have forgotten me. So there is something for you to mourn over.'[94]

In 1970 Alan began wielding a new weapon: an electric typewriter. He used this for the first time to write his Beaverbrook biography; later he claimed that it influenced his style. 'With a pen you write words. With a typewriter you write sentences. With an electric typewriter, which I use now, you write paragraphs. In military terms: bow and arrow, musket, machine gun. I try to keep up a continuous fire.'[95] Once he had started a book, he aimed to write a thousand words a day. At night he was often sleepless, and then he would go over what he had written during the day and think how it might be improved.[96]

In a sense, the typewriter had a life of its own. Alan often said that when he wanted to find out about something, he wrote a book about it. Even on a subject he knew well, he did not know what he was going to write until he started — and then his argument led him in unexpected directions. 'Writing books is a way of teaching myself and discovering ideas that I had never thought of before.'

The same was true of his lecturing. One benefit of preparing only casually, if at all, was that he could think on his feet; often his best ideas came to him in front of an audience.[97]

'I'd rather start with my mind a blank and let the story tell itself,' he claimed. He described himself as an old-fashioned narrative historian. But narrative history as a series of steps was pedestrian; Alan's history was never dull. His narratives were lit up by dazzling flashes of intuitive brilliance, ignited by his paradoxical wit. He believed that the politicians he wrote about worked the same way.

> Being sceptical by nature, I hesitate to credit statesmen, however able, with such foresight and deliberate purpose. In my view states-men are no more purposeful in their struggle for power than in any of their activities. They wait upon events and then act by intuitive genius – what Gladstone called 'the right sense of timing'.[98]

'I work very thoroughly and patiently,' he told Eva in 1971. 'Then I make up my mind. I take a risk. Ninety-nine times out of a hundred it comes off. The hundredth time I make a mistake. I get a reputation for being slightly careless, but this is deliberate. If you wait until every detail is right, you will produce nothing. I have a neat mind that likes to see results. Sometimes I make patterns too precise, but that is better than drifting in a fog. I drive a car the same way, usually a bit too fast rather than too slow. So far the risk has not caught up on me.'[99]

In December 1972 Alan responded to an Austrian reader who accused him of finding no one in history to admire.

> You are quite wrong . . . In *The Habsburg Monarchy* for instance I make clear my admiration for Masaryk and Michael Karolyi. I regard Garibaldi as the most wholly admirable political figure of the nineteenth century. I admire the German independent socialists and say so. My twentieth century hero is the German sergeant in Poland during the Second World War who persistently helped Jews to escape until he himself was detected and killed. But as to great men, which of them should I admire? Napoleon was a great man; Hitler was a great man. Bismarck, I admire, because he moderated his greatness. As to the merely rich and powerful, the Emperors in their fancy dress or the generals with their taste for slaughter, they do not

win my admiration . . . If you want a final expression of my
admiration I admire Willi Brandt. He is the living proof that there is
such a thing as a good German.[100]

Brandt, who had become Chancellor of West Germany in 1969,
was awarded the Nobel Peace Prize in 1971. His *Ostpolitik*, a
policy of seeking reconciliation between Eastern and Western
Europe, culminated in a treaty between East and West Germany
signed in 1972. It seemed the beginning of the end to the Cold War.
Though Alan remained implacably hostile to the idea of German
reunification, his longstanding hostility to Germany moderated. 'I
used to say we could never trust the Germans. Now I am becoming
soft towards them.'[101]

In 1973 he delivered the Creighton Lecture in the University of
London, where because of the size of the audience he was forced to
use a microphone, something he much disliked. The topic was the
Second World War; as usual he spoke without notes. 'The anti-
German coalition came to stand for the simple cause of humanity,'
Alan said. The gas chambers 'represented German* civilisation as
truly as Gothic cathedrals represented the civilisation of the Middle
Ages'. The full record of German crimes was not known while the
War was on. 'Even so, enough was known to rule out any ending
except unconditional surrender and make the Second World War
that rare thing – a just war.'[102]

The lecture was to form the basis of the first chapter of an
illustrated narrative history, a companion to the volume on the
First World War, which he published in 1975. In the preface he
remarked that he had been composing the book for more than
thirty years; during the War itself he had given monthly commentaries on its progress for the Ministry of Information, and immediately afterwards he had broadcast a potted history of the War, in
twelve programmes of five to seven-and-a-half minutes each, on the
European Service of the BBC. In fact *The Second World War: An
Illustrated History* was completely original; many writers would
have produced no more than a potboiler for such a commission, but
Alan used the opportunity to survey the whole War afresh.

*Changed to 'National Socialist' in the book.

It was misleading to see it as one war from start to finish, Alan suggested: rather, 'a number of small wars gradually coalesced into a great one'. The basic pattern of the War was a struggle between those peoples 'who were more or less content with the world as it was and those who wished to change it'. Hitler's aim was 'to transform Germany into a World Power'.[103]

Alan reiterated his belief that Hitler's actions could be interpreted as being based on rational principles. Because Hitler lost, Alan argued, he had been 'written off as a psychopath'. Hitler was an opportunist who took gains as they came. Only in deciding to attack Russia did he take the initiative. 'After talking fearsomely of Russia's strength, Hitler finally justified the invasion by announcing her weakness.'[104]

Alan emphasised the muddled and paradoxical nature of the War. Italy's defeat 'alleviated Hitler's problems', just as France's defeat made things easier for Great Britain. The Allies invaded first North Africa and then Italy because they had to do something and this was all they were capable of – 'they were there because they were there', an echo from the trenches of the First World War. 'Bomber' Harris was the Second World War's equivalent to Sir Douglas Haig, launching attacks that cost the RAF more than the Germans.[105]

The tone of the book is grudging towards the American allies, generous towards the Russians. Stalin 'thought only of defeating Germany'. Allied co-operation did not break down because of the Yalta agreements, Alan argued: 'it broke down because the British and the Americans repudiated them'. The Allies could not agree even on a day to celebrate their joint victory.[106]

This was a people's war, he wrote; civilians were in the front line.

> In Great Britain, for instance, until 1942 a serving soldier was more likely to receive a telegram that his wife had been killed by a bomb than his wife was likely to receive one that her husband had been killed in battle. Conscientious objectors serving in ARP (air raid precautions) were in greater danger than if they had been in the armed forces.[107]

'Three things distinguish his work from any other account,' wrote C.M. Woodhouse, reviewing the book for the *Observer*: 'his unfailing grasp of the details on every front, the marvellous succinctness of his narrative, and his acute use of anecdotes to concentrate attention on the crucial turning-points.' In Alan's account, wrote Hugh Thomas in *The Listener*, everything happens by accident: 'Practically no one has any idea of what they are doing . . . This is, of course, the reverse of Marxist history. The result is that the book is unfair to all in authority.'[108]

Alan had no vengeful feelings towards Germany. He disliked the Nuremberg Trials; 'there are few episodes of modern history more nauseating',[109] and actively campaigned for the release of Rudolf Hess, who had been sentenced to life imprisonment at Nuremberg for 'preparing to wage aggressive war, whatever that may mean, actually for trying to bring the war to an end'. He wrote five *Sunday Express* articles on the subject, the first – 'Must This Man Stay in Prison for Ever?' – in 1962. In a sarcastic letter to *The Times* in 1968, Alan wrote that Hess had been sentenced to life imprisonment 'for the sole crime of being a premature advocate of Nato'. Six years later another letter from Alan appeared, this time in the *Observer*, arguing that Hess had been 'harshly used', and countering the assertion that he had known anything about plans for the invasion of Russia.[110] When Hess's son came to England to campaign for his father's release, Alan received him.

Showing humanitarian mercy towards an old man who had been imprisoned half his life was one thing; consorting with an unrepentant Fascist was another. In that part of *English History, 1914–1945* which dealt with politicians' response, or lack of response, to the financial crisis of 1929, Alan had depicted Mosley, then a junior minister in the Labour Government, as the only man who rose to the height of the challenge: a point he frequently reiterated in his reviews. 'The rejection by Labour of Mosley's programme was a decisive, though negative, event in British history.'[111] In his Beaverbrook biography Alan praised Beaverbrook's intervention which had secured Mosley's release from internment in 1943.[112] Alan first met Mosley when the latter was writing his memoirs; Alan had urged him to be frank about his period as leader of the British Union of Fascists. When Mosley's autobiography came out, in 1968, Alan described him as 'a superb political thinker, the best of our age'.[113]

Mosley, who lived in France, often invited Alan to dine with him at the Ritz when he visited England. 'He is lonely, isolated, an insignificant figure,' he wrote to Eva. 'I accept his invitations because I am sorry for him, even though I am bored when we meet.' There was another reason: he liked going to the Ritz.[114] In 1975 he ran into his former pupil David Pryce-Jones in the London Library. When Pryce-Jones told him that he was writing a book about Unity Mitford*, Mosley's sister-in-law, Alan asked: 'How are you getting on with Oswald?' Pryce-Jones had interviewed Diana Mosley twice, but the Mosleys were now trying to prevent the book's publication. 'I'll put that straight,' Alan reassured him. 'I'm having dinner with him in three weeks' time. Come along too.' With some hesitation, Pryce-Jones agreed. 'You'll see. He's a wonderful man.' The evening was not a success. Pryce-Jones felt that Alan was pandering to Mosley's vanity, allowing his boasting to go unchallenged, even applauded – 'well done Tom'. Afterwards Mosley took out two injunctions against the book; when these failed, Pryce-Jones's lawyer received a threatening letter: if he did not withdraw it, 'we are not responsible for the consequences to him'.

Later that year Alan wrote a full-page review of Robert Skidelsky's biography of Mosley. Skidelsky had made Mosley the 'hero' of his earlier book *Politicians and the Slump*, which Alan had reviewed approvingly. Now he skilfully balanced condemnation of Mosley's Fascist period with praise for his early career and sympathy with his desire for reform. But this was too much for many critics, particularly Jewish academics, for whom Mosley's anti-Semitism put him beyond the pale. Alan's *Observer* review, which most people felt was too favourable to the former Fascist, was described by Mosley himself as libellous.[115]

In 1979 Alan received an unpleasant letter from one of Mosley's aides complaining at remarks he had made about the BUF in a review of a book about anti-Semitism in Britain. There was a P.S. in capital letters: 'NO MORE FREE DINNERS FOR YOU AT THE RITZ!'[116] In any case Mosley died the following year.

Unity Mitford: A Quest (Weidenfeld & Nicolson, London, 1976).

Alan and Eva had resumed their romance in Königswinter, and the following autumn they had spent three days together in Salzburg. For the next few years they met abroad at least once a year. By 1971 they were lovers. It was a clandestine courtship. Alan told neither of his wives about Eva; he asked her to write to him at the Library, and they could speak on the telephone only when he was there or in Oxford. After his early talk of marriage, Alan now appeared to retreat. He was a creature of habit, and his 'double life' was built around those habits. In particular, his social life revolved around his children – 'I have no friends in London'.[117] Crispin and Daniel were teenagers, still living at home with Eve. Margaret's children expected their father to care for their mother, particularly now her health was failing and she had become increasingly dependent. In each case Alan's access to his children seemed to depend on maintaining the *status quo*. Any disruption within the family threatened these arrangements. He knew that he could expect hysterics from Margaret, and bitter hostility from Eve. He hated 'fuss', and was apprehensive about 'scenes'. 'I have two women on my hands, both grasping at me all the time, blaming me for everything that has gone wrong.'[118] Moreover, he was still supporting both Eve and Margaret, and Eve was harassing him for increased maintenance. He worried that if he married Eva he might be unable to provide for her properly. Just as inflation began to erode his savings, his earning power appeared to be diminishing; 'as I get older people want me less'.[119] The *Sunday Express* cancelled his contract – though Junor relented and agreed a new contract based on fewer articles.

After Frances Stevenson died in 1972, Alan had decided to publish the love-letters between her and Lloyd George; when Alan was unable to read the handwriting, his own secretary, Veronica Horne, helped out. In his letters to Eva, Alan often discussed these love-letters, and even drew parallels between the two; 'you are My Lass as much as Frances was Lloyd George's Girl'.[120] In doing so, whether consciously or not, he was sending out ambiguous signals. 'Certainly Lloyd George loved her,' Alan told Eva. 'But he had no intention of ever leaving his family, and made out to her that he found them very tiresome when really he enjoyed life with them in the country.'[121] 'Lloyd George's letters are very passionate,' he commented in another letter: 'of course this was to console Frances because they were together so little.'[122] Lloyd George's wife was called Margaret.

Eva wished to resolve matters and several times appeared ready to break off relations, but Alan clung to her tenaciously, while stressing the difficulties which lay before them. After two failed marriages, he was determined to seize this chance of happiness for himself; but he was equally concerned not to make a third mistake.

Alan was a selfish man. It was not that he did not care about the feelings of others – on the contrary, he cared very much – but often it did not occur to him how they might react to what he said or did. Perhaps this was a result of being an only child; perhaps of being generally much more clever than those around him. This insensitivity was a strength as well as a handicap. He was not interested in the views of others. Those whom he admired in history – Bismarck and Churchill, for example – tended to be dictatorial. He often quoted approvingly Churchill's remark: 'all I wanted was compliance with my wishes after reasonable discussion'. He tended to think those who disagreed with him had failed to understand what he was saying. He was magnificently oblivious to orthodoxy, and deeply distrusted 'confederated learning'. Nothing was more likely to set him on the opposite course than an expression such as 'it is generally held that . . .' Other historians moved in schools, like fish swimming together; when they clashed, it was *en masse*, like army battalions. Alan, by contrast, swam solo. He fought his battles single-handed. He was an individualist, an iconoclast, an independent.

In the early 1970s Alan became very pessimistic about his financial future. A seemingly endless succession of strikes threatened to paralyse the economy, presenting a challenge to the Government. At first Alan was wholeheartedly on the side of the workers. 'I rejoice at the miners' victory,' he wrote to *The Times* early in 1972. 'Now the miners have avenged the defeats of 1921 and 1926 . . . February 19 will be long remembered as a glorious day in the history of the British working-class.'[123] He was convinced that socialism was the answer. But many of the strikes – in the mining, electricity, and transport industries, for example – affected Alan directly. He suffered power cuts, petrol shortages, delays. 'I am all for the working-classes asserting themselves but it is a great nuisance as well.'[124] The oil crisis, the miners' strike, and the 'Three Day Week' at the end of 1973 made matters still worse. Alan was 'terrified' by the economic situation; 'I feel the approaching hurricane'. His shares plunged. He foresaw total economic collapse – no oil, no coal, no heat, no light, millions of unemployed. 'I have been expecting the collapse of capitalism all my life,' he told Eva late in 1973. 'Now that it comes I am rather annoyed.'[125]

'There is no future for this country,' he wrote in April 1974, 'and not much for anywhere else.'[126] Though the Tories had been replaced by a minority Labour Government, Alan remained pessimistic. 'Pray for the recovery of capitalism,' he implored Eva, only partly tongue-in-cheek. Alan predicted a slump, unemployment, and some sort of National Government with a reactionary programme. 'You can't realise how near we are to catastrophe,' he wrote to Eva in July 1974: 'all our banks may close their doors in a few months' time.' He feared riots, possible revolution, civil war and Fascism: 'you are lucky to be living in a Communist country and safe from such things'.[127] 'We live in an economic tornado which somehow never seems to blow,' he wrote to his old friend Noel Fieldhouse in Montreal. 'As ruin advances everyone still appears in a state of undiminished prosperity. I have no idea what is going to happen.'[128]

Alan was not alone in his fears. The spurt of inflation in the mid-1970s and the defeat of the Heath Government by the miners suggested that the country was out of control. Retired generals began to talk about recruiting private armies to meet the national emergency. This was one of the subjects discussed in a new series of 'Free Speech', revived after fifteen years with a team consisting of Alan, Malcolm Muggeridge, the former Labour minister Lord George-Brown, and the journalist Peregrine Worsthorne. The first programme discussed whether democracy in Britain was doomed. Alan argued that democracy in Britain had never been stronger, 'particularly when the unions were doing so well'. Afterwards the producer told them that the debate had been 'splendid'. There was one little disappointment: the show did not go out, due to industrial action by the Post Office engineering workers.[129]

'I shall soon be ruined,' he told Eva in August 1974.[130] His highest earnings had coincided with a period of punitively high tax rates – which at one stage were close to 100 per cent – leaving him with fewer savings than might be expected. His two families had drained what the taxman had left. And because of his personal circumstances, he had not benefited from the enormous inflation in house prices of the 1950s and 1960s. His shares, which had been worth nearly £100,000 two years earlier, were now worth less than £20,000.[131] He had been relying on his investments to support him in his old age. Inflation, which was 'running wild', cut away at the value of his pension. 'It is all right for workers and such-like who can push up their wages, but it is ruin for those with fixed incomes.'[132] 'Prices go up every day.' He told Eva that he was no longer a rich man.[133] 'I dread the thought that I may be driven to go to America just to keep alive. Truly I'd rather be dead.'[134] He began divorce proceedings against Eve after they had spent a summer holiday together with the boys in 1973, and the divorce was made absolute the following April. But marriage to Eva was 'impossible unless circumstances change'; there were 'insuperable economic difficulties'.[135] 'You sometimes say I cheated you,' he wrote to her. 'Not so. Life has cheated us. If British capitalism had gone on being prosperous we should have arranged things by now.'[136]

Change made Alan anxious. 'However much one wants revolution in theory, it is no fun when you are old.' He became nervous, fearful of the future. Grievances erupted in his letters to Eva. He took refuge in self-pity, often absurdly melodramatic. When Crispin failed his driving test as a result of a faulty clutch, Alan blamed himself; 'I feel I have let him down'. 'I feel that I have failed all my children in not providing them with a stable family life,' he continued. 'I have been a bad father, not fit to have children. It seems a wasted life, devoted to my children and yet not good enough for them. Now even the two boys are growing up. They won't need me any more and won't bother about me.'[137]

Alan gave an interview late in 1975 in which he outlined his thoughts about the economic crisis. It had been touched off, he believed, 'when America stopped the Vietnam War, which it had been running on credit – and the money ran out, just as it had in 1929'. Alan urged 'a return to a standard of urgent need and no luxuries'. His solution was a four-point programme: a rigorously planned economy; putting the entire nation on rations; devoting the nation's resources to the country at large; and ensuring the disappearance of profit. 'The best time we ever had, in my lifetime, when the country was best run, the most egalitarian society and the most efficient, was during the Second World War.' Perhaps 'we might consider having a war with somebody – but it would have to be someone just big enough to give us a fright, and yet not big enough to defeat us'.[138]

Alan was also depressed by the worsening 'troubles' in Northern Ireland. To him they proved 'what I have always known, that two communities cannot live together once they become conscious of their separate existence. Different religions, like different nationalities, have to be sorted out.' He was amused when Yugoslav radio denounced the IRA as clerical Fascists, just like the Croat Ustachi. 'Nationalist sentiment does not fit into the Marxist analysis,' he told Eva, 'but it is the force which has kept European history going. I think there will be real bad trouble in Yugoslavia when Tito dies, if not before. They have nothing to hold them together except memories of the partisan war, and that was a long time ago.'[139]

In June 1974 Alan was the guest of honour at a dinner party given by his pupils in the House of Commons. Several MPs – Giles Radice, William Rodgers, David Marquand – were present, together with Keith Kyle, Robert Kee and Paul Johnson. Kenneth Baker was not invited. 'What are you most proud of?' Marquand asked Alan – 'The box'. Afterwards he wrote to thank Rodgers for 'a delightful evening'. 'I don't often get the chance to bask in a warm glow of flattery. How young you all look to me.'[140] That same year Alan was able to write to congratulate his old friend Michael Foot on becoming Secretary of State for Employment in the newly elected Labour Government. He referred to Beaverbrook's prediction that Foot would become leader of the Party. 'So Max was right after all. You have climbed to the top of the greasy pole or very near it.' Alan's brother-in-law, Tony Crosland, was Foreign Secretary. And in 1975 a former pupil, Malcolm Fraser, would become Prime Minister of Australia. Alan was not unknown to the President of the United States, Richard Nixon, and to his Secretary of State, Henry Kissinger. Alan was in danger of becoming part of the THING.

In October 1974, however, Alan suffered 'a catastrophic blow'.[141] Sir Max Aitken asked to see him; when Alan returned from their meeting, he seemed shrunken. The Beaverbrook Foundation had decided not to maintain the Library any longer; it was to be closed, and the papers dispersed. Alan was to be kept on with a secretary, handling the Beaverbrook permissions, but that was that. 'It leaves a sad gap in my life,' he wrote to Christopher Seton-Watson. 'I thought I had found for good a way of being useful to historians. Now I am at a loss, pushed aside when I still have so much to give.'[142] He felt bitter, and near despair. 'The killing of the Beaverbrook Library on top of my money worries and general political apprehensions has been almost too much for me.' 'I might as well be buried,' he wrote to Eva; 'my life is really finishing.'[143] Now nearly seventy, he worried about his health, and he suffered a succession of skin problems, not helped by his penchant for sunbathing naked.

He found a home for the papers in the House of Lords Record Office; the archivist, Katharine Bligh, went with them. The Low and Vicky cartoons went to the University of Kent. He sold most of the books he had kept at the Library, an act he later very much regretted. Alan and his secretary Della Hilton, who had replaced Veronica Horne in 1973, remained in their offices while the old Library was 'literally torn to pieces'.[144] The furniture was gone, the stacks had been torn down, the carpet had been taken up; only the portrait of Lord Beaverbrook remained, looking down on the ruins of the Library that was to have been his monument.[145] The advertising department took over the space the Library had occupied. A few weeks later Alan and Della moved to offices at the front of the *Express* building on Fleet Street; towards the end of the year they moved again, to an office in the *Evening Standard*, looking out on to Holborn Viaduct.

He faced the future gloomily. He had started writing a short history of Great Britain from 1901 to 1975, but found it hard to make progress. In 1976 he would be seventy, which meant that he would have to retire as Research Fellow of Magdalen and give up his rooms; 'another epoch in my life closing'.[146] 'I have lost faith in the future,' he lamented to Eva. 'I have spent a lifetime believing in Socialism and now I see that nobody wants it.'[147] He had planned to spend the next few years rewriting his Oxford history. But now he thought a revised edition might 'destroy the spirit'. 'When I wrote *English History, 1914–1945* I still had great hopes for the future. Now I have none.'[148]

All his children were now grown up; soon they would not need him. Crispin, the elder of Eve's sons, was in his final year at Cambridge and talked of becoming a chartered accountant; Daniel, the younger, was due to go to university the following year and had started reading the extreme left-wing journal *Militant*. 'Now my life is totally empty,' he moaned to Eva.

> I can't settle to anything. I come here every day. There are virtually no letters. I have nothing to do. I try to read, but again to no purpose. It is really the worst time I have had in years. When I was younger I could pull up the spirit to overcome my difficulties. Now I am overwhelmed by them . . . I hate life actively. I am bad-tempered with everyone, and particularly with everything that has happened to me. I truly see no way out. When you get to seventy and you feel your life is a failure, you can't help feeling that it is too late to begin again. This is not a plea for sympathy or consideration. It is just a statement of fact. I dread the day beginning. I dislike it while it is on. And I am glad when each day is over.[149]

14: *His Last Bow*

'Revolution is knocking at the door,' Alan wrote to Eva from Oxford in May 1975. 'Until now I had breakfast almost alone in the elegance of the Senior Common Room. Now I have to have it in Hall among the undergraduates.'[1] The following month he was feeling optimistic enough about the future to speculate in North Sea oil shares. He told Eva that his son Crispin was very disapproving, 'and quite right too'.[2]

In the summer he had been elected President of the City of London Music Society, in succession to Sir Arthur Bliss. He had been attending their lunchtime concerts for years, but the invitation to become President was unexpected. Alan accepted the position with humble gratitude, he told the Society, 'as long as you do not expect me to write a symphony'.[3]

'I shall never write a gloomy letter again,' Alan promised Eva in November.

> I am now much more clear-headed and cheerful . . . The strange thing is that I am desperately miserable in my present life even though I have difficulty in escaping from it. For years the company of my children saved me from complete unhappiness. Now they don't count any more, being too busy with their own. The older ones are friendly when we meet, but I can see I shall never have holidays with them, and now my holidays with Crispin are fading away. Next year Daniel will go to Manchester University and I shall lose him also. So there will be nobody to keep me from you or to be your rival.[4]

In 1974 and then again twice in 1975 he had visited Eva in Hungary. There he had been accepted by her sons as a member of the family. Alan realised that he could procrastinate not much longer about marrying Eva. 'The moment for decision, never a thing I liked, was coming closer.'[5]

William H. McNeill, editor of the *Journal of Modern History*, decided to devote a special issue to Alan, including assessments of his work by historians from Britain, Germany and America. This was an honour awarded previously only to Fernand Braudel. Alan was asked to explain what had shaped him as an historian; he referred to the resulting piece, 'Accident Prone, or What Happened Next', as his 'intellectual autobiography'. It 'shows, I fear, that I am incurably frivolous. I am sure American historians will be shocked by it'.[6]

'I have never supposed, as many earlier historians did,' wrote Alan, 'that men can learn any useful lessons from history, political or otherwise.' This kind of remark annoyed those academics, particularly American academics, who spent much time and energy arguing that study of history could help to anticipate the future. 'Of course you can learn certain obvious commonplaces, such as that all men die or that one day the deterrent, whatever that may be, will fail to deter. Apart from this, history is an art just like painting or architecture and is designed like them to give intellectual and artistic pleasure.'[7]

'Accident Prone' was accompanied by three other essays about Alan in the same issue. One was by Oswald Hauser, Professor in the University of Aachen, the historian who had invited Alan to the *Ranke Gesellshaft* in Königswinter. Hauser had there witnessed Alan and Eva embracing violently on a bench in a dark corner near the river. Such things often happen at academic conferences; and this aside, he had no special insight into Alan's life or work. 'I hope that, as Germans,' the professor wrote, 'we are no longer oversensitive but ready to listen to criticism from outside, most of all from persons who have tried to understand the particular and difficult situation of this country in the middle of Europe, which is surrounded by dynamic powers much stronger and perhaps more dangerous than those faced by the great insular or peninsular nations of the world.' Although Alan had avoided Germany for a long time, Hauser went on, 'I had the impression that he held no bias against my people and that he enjoyed being amongst us'.

Another piece was written by D.C. Watt, Stevenson Professor at the London School of Economics, the Chair which Alan had failed to make his own in the early 1950s. Alan was annoyed at his participation. Watt, a specialist on pre-War diplomacy, took it on himself to defend Alan's diplomatic histories against American critics. 'I am plausibly informed,' he wrote, 'that for a time the writing of destructive critiques of these works was a standard exercise in some American university Ph.D. seminars . . . Much of this criticism, of course, comes from adherents of the nineteenth-century Germanic dogma that the task of historians is to produce the definitive monograph.'

The third contributor was John W. Boyer, of the University of Chicago. Boyer decided to analyse Alan's methodology. It was a densely written piece, explicable, if explicable at all, as a sociological critique. 'Because of the relative absence of social and psychological contextual materials as part of the reactive process . . .' began one sentence. It was hard for the non-specialist to follow the argument, but the general drift was hostile. 'If one approaches *Mein Kampf*, for example, from the perspective of social learning theories of aggression one might argue the . . . statements in the book . . . had a dual functionality.' In a footnote Boyer thanked three of his colleagues for their 'helpful discussions'; sometimes all four authors seemed loose in the same sentence.

'Critical essays followed by other historians,' Alan wrote later, 'from whom I learned characteristics of my work that I had never been aware of or even suspected before.'[8] McNeill, who did not much like Alan, thought the whole A.J.P. Taylor issue was 'a dud'.[9]

In the spring of 1976 Eva came to England for three months. She had been sponsored by the Hungarian Academy to continue her work on appeasement in the British archives. Alan arranged to meet Eva at the air terminal, and took her to a hotel. He was still not ready to tell Margaret about their romance. When he took Eva to see his home, he introduced her to Margaret as a colleague. He left work early to visit Eva at her hotel, returning to Margaret as if he had come straight from the office. He and Eva took a series of covert excursions together; Eva accompanied him to Historical Association lectures, and they made trips to Oxford, Manchester and the Lake District. They spent several days in Manchester while Alan made a television programme. During their stay Alan took Eva out to Higher Disley, where he had lived with Margaret in the 1930s.

Eva came to a seventieth birthday celebratory lunch for Alan at the LSE, though not everyone there realised the special reason for her presence. Among the others attending were Michael Foot, Kathleen Tillotson, Robert, now Lord, Blake, and Tom Driberg, now Lord Bradwell. The *Sunday Express* reported that Driberg had been present at Alan's twenty-first party; readers were not told whether he kept slipping out as he had done forty-nine years before.

Malcolm Muggeridge was unable to attend the LSE lunch, but sent a friendly letter. 'I suppose no outside observer would appreciate the deep ties of affection that unite you and me,' Alan replied. 'If you were someone else you would be deplorable to me; as it is you can do no wrong in my eyes.'[10] Alan had resumed contact with Muggeridge through the revival of 'Free Speech'. Over the next few years he renewed many of his oldest friendships, some of them – for example, with his Oriel contemporary Charles Gott – going back half a century or more.

As well as the lunch, there was another *Festschrift* for Alan, edited by two of his former graduate students, Alan Sked and Chris Cook. The contributors were mostly younger historians, many of whom had attended Alan's seminars at the Beaverbrook Library. Plenty of people had refused to contribute. 'One *Festschrift* is enough for any mortal,' commented Sir Isaiah Berlin. When the Beaverbrook Library was closing, Alan had written to the editors telling them to forget the idea. There was nothing to celebrate, he told them; 'I've been a failure these last few years.' Sked persuaded him to change his mind. 'If you're a failure,' he said, 'how can the rest of us justify our lives?'

In April 1976 Alan caused a stir by giving an interview to Irish State radio in which he argued for British withdrawal from Northern Ireland. Later that week Lord Bradwell would propose a

similar motion in the House of Lords. The British presence in
Ireland had helped to create the conflict in the past and was now
serving only to perpetuate it, Alan said. He claimed that the best
solution would be an armed push by the 'Irish nationalist majority'
which would be strong enough to drive the Ulster Protestants out of
Ireland altogether. He cited the expulsion of the Sudeten Germans
from Czechoslovakia at the end of the War as an example of how
such a harsh and seemingly unacceptable solution had eventually
proved successful. 'Every day the British stay in Northern Ireland is
likely to increase the number who will be killed in the end. Because
there is no doubt, whatever British governments say now, there will
come a time when the British people will not be prepared to go on
having young Englishmen killed for a cause which does not concern
them in the slightest.' The *Guardian* printed a leader attacking
Alan's broadcast: 'to equate the leadership of the Provisionals
[IRA] with the colonial liberators is a profound misreading of
history'. Alan retorted in a letter.

> What exactly are we waiting for in Northern Ireland? For the
> Protestants to renounce their supremacy? For the Catholics to
> acquiesce in it? Neither is likely to happen.
>   If British troops withdraw the two contending parties will arrive at
> a solution even if it be a solution imposed by one party on the other.
> As long as British troops remain there will be no solution and the
> bloodshed will go on.
>   Do you wish this situation to go on indefinitely? If not, make an
> end of it.[11]

By the time Eva returned to Hungary at the end of June, she and
Alan had decided to marry. Eva would come to live with Alan in
England, but not until she had secured the future of her sons and
finished her doctorate.* Until then he would continue living with
Margaret. They agreed that even after Eva came to live in England,
Alan should be free to visit Margaret, and that he would continue
to holiday with her on the Isle of Wight.
  It was there, after Eva had returned to Hungary, that Alan broke

---

*The Doctorate in Historic Science, the Hungarian equivalent of the D.Litt.

the news to Margaret. She was 'hysterical', he wrote to Eva, 'driving herself into a nervous breakdown'. Later she tried to be co-operative, but then resumed 'almost constant hysterics'. 'She has also turned all the children against me,' Alan informed Eva; 'I shall have to move out if this goes on'.[12]

Alan had reached retirement age. He had been a Fellow of Magdalen for thirty-eight years, more than half his life. Now he was saddened at having to quit his rooms in New Buildings. But in November the college elected him an Honorary Fellow, a distinction rarely conferred. 'It means I can attend all the feasts,' Alan told the *Evening Standard*. A suite of comfortable guest rooms was available when he wanted to stay. The college had not acted without some prodding. Earlier in the year a story had appeared in the *Daily Mail* speculating that Alan would not be offered an Honorary Fellowship. An unnamed Magdalen member had been quoted as saying his success in the media had ruled out further academic honour.[13]

For many years Alan had been campaigning for the right of women to be admitted to the college. There was similar pressure throughout the Oxford colleges; several had already become co-resident. Alan's argument was based on natural justice, though perhaps too he enjoyed the thought of the pain that the admission of women would cause to his more traditional colleagues. Now, at his very last college meeting, Alan was successful.

Later in 1976 Hugh Trevor-Roper invited Alan to an Oriel dinner-party in honour of the Ford Lecturer. Any lingering bad feeling arising from their disagreement over *The Origins of the Second World War* had long since disappeared. In 1968 Alan had reviewed another book on Hitler's last days by suggesting that the effort was futile. Trevor-Roper was 'an incomparable scholar', his book on the last days of Hitler 'a triumph of intuition and scientific imagination', a 'brilliant book' which demonstrated 'how a great historian can arrive at the truth even when much of the evidence is lacking or, as in this case, deliberately kept from him'.[14] But Alan was still capable of inflicting glancing blows. In 1973 he ended a review of a book on the origins of the First World War with a dig he had long waited to use: 'Professor Trevor-Roper, an authority on English history in the seventeenth century, contributes a fore-word.'[15] Alan declined Trevor-Roper's invitation. 'They tell me Oriel is to be found somewhere off the High, but I have forgotten where.'[16]

As one door closed, another opened. In the spring Alan had received an indirect approach from the University of Bristol through the editor of the *Times Literary Supplement*, John Gross. Would he like to be Benjamin Meaker Visiting Professor for the academic year 1976–1977? 'I am attracted by the idea of acquiring a chair after all these years without one,' Alan replied.[17] He took up the post in the autumn, travelling down to Bristol by high-speed train to stay a couple of nights a week. John Vincent, head of the history department, gave him only a handful of students to teach; his main duty was lecturing. His lectures drew record numbers of undergraduates from all departments, filling the Reception Room, the largest hall in the University. Alan's stint was considered a success, and renewed for another year.

Alan's special lectureship at UCL also came to an end, but it was replaced by a similar lectureship at the Polytechnic of North London (now the University of North London), where Robert Skidelsky had assembled a powerful history department. Based in Kentish Town, it was easy for Alan to reach on foot. In 1977 the seminars on modern British history which Alan had run at the Beaverbrook Library started up again in a new London home, the Institute of Historical Research in Senate House, with Alan once again in the chair.

There was another new beginning for Alan in 1976, when he resumed lecturing on television. He had been approached by Eddie Mirzoeff, a BBC producer who had attended Alan's lectures as an Oxford undergraduate reading history. Why aren't you lecturing on television? Mirzoeff asked. Alan replied that the money had been a problem. They negotiated a fee of £250 per broadcast, later rising to £300 – since this was almost the only cost, it made cheap television. 'The War Lords', a series of six programmes on the individuals who had shaped grand strategy during the Second World War, was followed in 1977 by 'How Wars Begin', and the following year by 'Revolution'. Alan impressed Mirzoeff with his professionalism; he knew how to talk intimately to the camera. Most of the programmes were recorded in one take. Only once in the eighteen programmes did he lose his thread, a few minutes before the end; Alan was crestfallen.

'It is fascinating to watch a television personality of one's own name,' Alan wrote in a diary piece for *The Listener*.

> I have nothing in common with the screen figure whom I think of vaguely as Him. He has mannerisms which had never occurred to me. He says things that astonish me – sometimes penetrating remarks that I should never have hit on, sometimes rash general-isations that seem to me a trifle unscholarly – but he always seems to pull through somehow. Occasionally I think of something he ought to say and is going to miss. Just when I have despaired of Him, he says it after all. I rather like Him, though I am glad I am not Him or anything like it in real life.[18]

Alan adopted the device of turning the transcripts of his television lectures into books: 'rather sharp practice', as he confessed to his cousin Karin.[19] 'Anything Mr Taylor writes is worth reading,' wrote Geoffrey Wheatcroft, reviewing *The War Lords* in *The Spectator*; but the anonymous *Economist* reviewer of *How Wars Begin* was more severe. 'These reprinted television lectures are not likely to do Mr Taylor's bank balance any harm. They will do his academic reputation, which was high, no good at all.' The *New Statesman* review of the same book referred to 'unctuous asides'; and the *Sunday Telegraph* complained that the Americans 'are sneered at throughout'.[20]

Alan was not in demand everywhere. He had been invited to act as historical adviser to the Imperial War Museum for an exhibition on the Home Front during the Second World War. After Alan had agreed to do so, the Director, Dr Noble Frankland, vetoed the choice. Christopher Dowling, who had issued the invitation, was obviously uncomfortable at having to communicate the decision. 'I very much regret', he told Alan's agent, 'that Dr Frankland has instructed me to say that Alan Taylor's great fame would over-personalise the exhibition and that he wants us to use someone with a lower profile.'[21] In the event it proved too late to find anyone else.

Alan was one of the judges for the 1976 Whitbread Literary

Awards. The other judges were the novelist Susan Hill and David Holloway, Literary Editor of the *Daily Telegraph*, who had been one of Alan's pupils just after the War. There were three categories for the awards: biography, fiction and children's books. Alan told his fellow-judges that he was not going to read anything but biography, so Hill and Holloway decided the other two winners between them. Their choice for the fiction prize was Kingsley Amis's *The Alteration*.* When he heard this, Alan kicked up a tremendous fuss. He described the book as a monstrous perversion, and it was clear to the other two that he had read it after all. Eventually they adopted their alternative choice, a novel by William Trevor. All were agreed that the biography prize should go to Winifred Gérin for her book on Mrs Gaskell; but when it came to the awards ceremony Alan announced that he alone had been chosen to decide the biography prize and that he alone thought Gérin's the best book. Holloway stood up afterwards and contradicted him.

In September 1976 – seven years after he had first raised the possibility – Alan and Eva married in Budapest; Alan informed Margaret by letter. Then he returned alone to England, and took up residence once more at St Mark's Crescent. At first he seemed to believe that they might all three live there when Eva arrived, albeit in separate units, but soon it became clear that this was not feasible. Margaret 'is hysterically hostile towards you', he wrote to Eva: 'she flies into a tantrum at any mention of you'.[22] Alan himself was in a state of high anxiety, inclined to dither and then to act suddenly. He began to look for somewhere else to live, and having decided that what they really wanted was a flat, impulsively purchased a house in Twisden Road, a few streets away from his old home in Croftdown Road.

Almost immediately, Alan began to feel he had done the wrong thing. He was nervous about squatters moving into the house, which remained empty. He put it on the market for re-sale. 'If only Margaret would co-operate,' he moaned, 'things would be much easier. You could come to her house at first and we could look

---

*The novel is a satire, set in an alternative present, in which the Reformation has been defeated. Two officials of the Inquisition are named Foot and Benn.

together, finding perhaps a house for her as well.'[23] He was apprehensive about the scenes Margaret would make when the time came for him to leave; 'she is obviously still hoping it won't happen'. When it became clear that she would need an operation, Alan told Eva 'of course, if she becomes really ill she will have to live with us'.[24] He decided not to sell the house in Twisden Road after all, but when a buyer begged him to change his mind, he hesitated. Eventually the house in Twisden Road was sold, whereupon he promptly bought another in the same street. It needed some improvements, which Alan was happy for Margaret to supervise.

When Eva came to England for a few weeks in the summer of 1977, Alan allowed Margaret to dictate when he might see her. 'Please forgive me for being so weak,' he wrote to Eva.[25] She found it hard to avoid resentment, not just of Margaret, but also of Alan's secretary who opened his post and whom she suspected of reading her letters. After she returned to Hungary work on the house dragged on slowly, threatening to delay the date when Eva might take up permanent residence in England. In December 1977 Alan agreed that she should come to England before her visa expired. If the house was not ready in time, he would find somewhere else in London for her to stay – alone – until it was.[26] Only in April 1978, nineteen months after their wedding, were Alan and Eva at last able to start living together.

Reading the *Evening Standard* in his office one lunchtime Alan noticed a piece disclosing the identity of the controller of MI6; it was Maurice Oldfield, his Manchester pupil in the 1930s. Alan was enormously pleased. 'I taught 'M'!' he told his secretary, referring to the character in the James Bond novels. In fact Oldfield was generally supposed to have been the model for another fictional spymaster, John le Carré's George Smiley. They had often met at the Athenaeum over the years, but Alan had always understood Oldfield to work for the Foreign Office. Now he lost no time in reestablishing contact with his former pupil. He invited Oldfield to dinner more than once, and tried, unsuccessfully, to arrange a meeting between him and Len Deighton. One night, after they had dined out together and drunk several bottles of wine, they rang David Wiseman, another of Alan's Manchester pupils, from a telephone box. Wiseman had been a Communist. 'This is National Security here,' said Oldfield, trying to disguise his voice. 'We have reason to be very concerned about your continuing agitation.' Wiseman could hear Alan chortling in the background.

'Hitler was a medium for German national emotion, not a lone operator,' wrote Alan in 1977, reviewing yet another biography of the Führer.[27] He thought the public fascination with Hitler was in itself psychopathic; he was 'essentially a nullity, an empty man and the least interesting of the dictators'. David Irving's claim, in his book *Hitler's War*, that Hitler was unaware of the murder of the Jews, was 'too silly to be worth arguing about'. In June 1977, when Irving's book came out, Alan confronted Irving on television. 'Now, Mr Irving, let me see if I have this right. You say that the lack of any written order from Hitler concerning the Final Solution proves that he knew nothing about it. Is that right?' Irving assented. 'And yet you say that the lack of any written order from Churchill concerning the death of General Sikorski does not clear him from being implicated in his murder?' Alan praised Irving's next book, a 'prequel' to *Hitler's War*; its great merit was 'not in its novelty but in its careful repetition of the version, already accepted by sensible historians, that Hitler was an opportunist who took advantages when they offered themselves'.[28]

In 1977 Alan contributed to a *Times Literary Supplement* survey of the most overrated and the most underrated books. The most overrated, according to Alan, was Toynbee's *A Study of History*: 'neither history nor a study, but a vast miscellany of information, much like Burton's *Anatomy of Melancholoy*, though not so funny'. The most underrated book was the Authorised Version of the Bible, 'once the foundation of English prose, now never read in schools and rarely, I believe, in churches. If all knowledge of the AV is lost much of classic English literature will be incomprehensible and English prose style is doomed.'[29]

Alan remained very much an 'English' historian. He had defended the use of the term 'England' in his preface to *English History, 1914–1945*; and he rejected the use of the term 'Britain' in a piece for the *Journal of Modern History* in 1975.[30] Some of this was prejudice. When Kenneth Morgan was preparing the Lloyd George letters, Alan teased him relentlessly about 'Welsh procrastination'; Morgan had the good sense not to respond. In 1978, Alan delivered a lecture on 'Nations in History' to the University of St Andrews, in the course of which he referred, not once but several times, to Burns as an 'English' poet, on the grounds that he spoke a dialect of English. This was not well received. Mutters during the lecture were followed by indignant questions after. Worse was to follow. At a dinner that evening for the speakers and other dignitaries and guests, much wine was drunk, and speeches often interrupted. The Principal lost control of the proceedings. After the meal the diners mingled in small groups, and a few Scots, still smarting from Alan's lecture, came up to confront him. Eventually he could stand it no longer, and begged his friend Norman Gash to help him escape. They left hastily.

'I find the Lords a very cosy and friendly place,' Tom Driberg told Alan soon after he had been made a peer. 'That is, of course, part of its danger. It would be more fun if you were here also, so please get yourself a peerage as soon as you can.'[31]

In March 1976 Harold Wilson unexpectedly resigned as Prime Minister. There was some speculation in the press that Alan might be named in Wilson's resignation honours list, but this was not to be. It seems that Tony Crosland, for one, had put forward his name while Wilson was still Prime Minister.[32] 'I don't want an honour, but I should have liked the pleasure of refusing one,' Alan was quoted as saying afterwards. It seemed anomalous that while others of his generation and seniority were being awarded knighthoods and peerages, Alan remained without any kind of handle to his name. During the 1970s Blake, Bullock and Trevor-Roper were elevated to the peerage. Alan was always reading in the press that he had been offered something or other, he told his UCL colleague Douglas Johnson, but in fact he had never been offered a public honour of any kind. Referring to their Provost, Lord Annan, he went on: 'Wouldn't you like to belong to a club' – he meant the House of Lords – 'where you're paid to be a member?'

Alan had previously been scathing about the honours system. He quoted approvingly R.H. Tawney's remark on being offered a peerage by Ramsay MacDonald: 'What harm have I ever done the Labour Party?' Just after the War he and his Magdalen colleague David Worswick entered into a pact not to accept a life peerage were one offered to either of them. (Worswick later accepted a CBE.) The authorities who handle such matters might have been justified in assuming that Alan would refuse an honour if one were offered. His attitude towards those who could have recommended him for an award – Macmillan, Gaitskell, Wilson and Callaghan, for example – was not likely to endear him to them. An article in the *Daily Express* posed the question 'Why no honour for AJP?'; and came up with a possible answer, 'perhaps because he has never licked the boots of any politician'.[33]

A year after his resignation Wilson published a book about his predecessors, *A Prime Minister on Prime Ministers*, which Alan was given to review. 'The prevailing tone is *1066 and All That*,' he wrote. 'Sir Harold says that anyone who aspires to be Prime Minister should have the gift of falling asleep at a moment's notice. He has clearly followed this advice and often fallen asleep while writing this book . . . If a university student submitted these essays, I should mark them NS – *non satis*.'[34]

A couple of weeks after this review was published, Alan wrote to Eva in 'distress'. He had seen a photograph of members of the Order of Merit, 'our highest award', being entertained by the Queen. 'I thought "Why not me? I am more distinguished than most of them and a better writer. So why not me?" And I felt I had wasted my life.' The two historians who held the OM were Dame Veronica (C.V.) Wedgwood and Sir Ronald Syme, Alan's contemporary at Oriel in the 1920s. 'I am not anxious to join such a mediocre collection,' he told Eva in his next letter; though obviously his exclusion rankled.[35] In 1981, when Michael Foot was leader of the Labour Party, he tried to get Alan made an OM, but membership of the Order is limited in number to twenty-four and the list was full. Alan believed that the Establishment had contrived to fill up the list so that he might be kept out, knowing that he was approaching the age-limit of seventy-five.[36] In fact there is no such age-limit.

1978 was the quincentenary of the Oxford University Press. Among the many celebrations that year was a special Foyle's Literary Lunch. Alan was one of the speakers. 'The only distinction I have', he told his audience, 'is that I am one of the very few contributors to the Oxford History of England who is neither knighted nor dead.'

After 'Revolution' Alan proposed 'How Wars End' as a subject for a new BBC lecture series. Mirzoeff was not taken with the idea. Alan was convinced that he had been 'got at' from on high; nothing Mirzoeff could say would convince him otherwise. 'I shall look for employment elsewhere,' he told Machell. Eventually Alan took the series to the newly formed Channel 4. When the producer contacted Alan to discuss the logistics of production, Alan replied that there was 'no such thing'. 'I make them up as I go along.'[37]

He was still lecturing regularly to the Historical Association. After one such talk a schoolboy asked, perhaps facetiously, what could be learned from history. Alan stared hard at him and answered in one word: 'scepticism'.

'I fear Margaret may want to interfere in our lives, telling you how you should do things,' Alan wrote to Eva before they began living together. 'If so we can soon tell her to leave us alone. I should be glad to quarrel with her, which would relieve my conscience, but otherwise I must discharge my obligations to her.'[38] They had agreed before Eva arrived that Alan could spend one evening during the week with Margaret, and stay with her on Saturday nights. He usually left Twisden Road on Saturday mornings, not returning until midday on Sunday. He also spent one evening a week at the Beefsteak Club. For Margaret, things were much as they had been in the 1950s and 1960s; this was a similar routine to the one he had adopted after the early years of his second marriage. It meant that Eva was alone for three evenings each week. During the day Alan went to his office in the *Evening Standard* building, and Eva discovered that he often called on Margaret on the way home. He spent the summer holidays with Margaret on the Isle of Wight, where Eva was discouraged from telephoning. But Margaret telephoned Alan at Twisden Road almost every night.

Eva found this situation difficult to accept. Not surprisingly, she often suspected that he was hankering after the best days of his marriage to Margaret. A foreigner with few friends in England with whom she could discuss these problems, she was often lonely and homesick. Even when Alan was working at home, she was reluctant to disturb his concentration. She had sacrificed much to come to England; in particular, she missed her sons keenly. In Hungary she had a respected position as an historian; in England, she had no status. It was not an equal relationship, she felt; his love for her was a reflection of her admiration. She was seventeen years younger, and sometimes he treated her like a young girl. Her English was not fluent, and she found it difficult to keep up with family 'in-jokes'. It was easy for her to feel laughed at, and sometimes she reacted badly to flippant comments from Alan. At times she became terribly unhappy, something Alan did not fully appreciate. She struggled to overcome her very natural feelings of jealousy. It did not make it any easier that Margaret treated Alan as though he was still her husband, referring to him as 'my darling'. Eva noticed that when he was going to see his ex-wife he picked out a tie which Margaret had given him.

In Budapest Eva had lived in a modern flat; it took time for her to adjust to a Victorian house in North London. Margaret had furnished it cheaply, with a second-hand cooker, a second-hand fridge and cheap broken plates mended with glue. Eva disliked the scruffy old armchairs. Most of all she disliked the bed, its stained mattress a reminder of Alan's past.

Eva felt like a kept woman, not a wife. She had only half a life in England, perhaps only half a husband. He was still leading a double life. She noticed that after he had been away from home Alan was always anxious to rush off and tell Margaret what had happened on the trip. Margaret had lived with Alan for almost half a century, and they had children and grandchildren in common. Eva felt inferior, her confidence undermined. She began to fear that she might lose him to Margaret, as Eve had done. His evasiveness made her wonder whether she could trust Alan; she accused him of being a chameleon, of changing according to which woman he was with. Alan ridiculed her fears. She knew that he hated 'scenes'. Eva began to contemplate returning to Hungary for the rest of Margaret's lifetime.

In 1980 a huge bibliography of Alan's work appeared, compiled by Chris Wrigley, a young historian who had worked on the Lloyd George papers in the Beaverbrook Library.[39] It listed twenty-three books written by Alan, and another twenty-six he had edited or introduced; thirteen pamphlets; forty-five historical essays in books, and another one hundred and fifteen in newspapers and periodicals; four hundred and fifty-nine newspaper articles; and more than fifteen hundred book reviews. Also listed were more than four hundred and fifty broadcasts on radio and television. It was a staggering total, all the more remarkable since it was incomplete; some items had been forgotten or proved impossible to trace. And there was more to come. Wrigley's work resulted in a further selection of essays, *Politicians, Socialism and Historians* (1980), the fifth to be published.

Towards the end of 1979 a book was published which was to involve Alan in another big row. In *The Climate of Treason* Andrew Boyle alleged that the notorious traitors Philby, Burgess and Maclean had not been alone; there had been a 'fourth man'. Speculation about his identity caused questions to be asked in Parliament; and in November the new Prime Minister, Margaret Thatcher, told an astonished House of Commons that Sir Anthony Blunt, eminent art historian and former adviser to the Queen, had spied for the Soviet Union. The story was confusing; it emerged that he had confessed in 1963 and had been granted immunity, in the hope that he might be 'turned'. It was not clear that he had supplied information to the Soviet Union since the War — when Russia had been an ally — though Blunt had confessed to having tipped off Burgess and Maclean in 1951, enabling them to flee before they were captured, and to having subsequently protected Philby. Keen observers felt the story seemed 'fishy'; perhaps the full truth had not been revealed.

Blunt was immediately stripped of his knighthood, and he resigned from his Fellowships of both the Society of Antiquaries and Trinity College, Cambridge, when it became clear that if he did not do so he would be expelled. There remained another Fellowship. 'I wonder whether he will resign from the British Academy,' Alan wrote to Eva, who was visiting Hungary for the wedding of one of her sons. 'It would give me an excuse for resigning from it also.'[40]

The Council of the British Academy considered the matter the following spring.[41] Blunt was invited to attend a Council meeting and argue the case for his retention, but he did not come. A majority of the Council decided to recommend his expulsion to the 460 Fellows of the Academy. A counter-motion proposed by Lord Robbins and Dame Helen Gardner 'deplored' Blunt's conduct but proposed that the Academy should 'not proceed further in the matter'. Both these motions were on the agenda for the Annual Meeting of the Academy on 3 July. Meanwhile Alan told *The Times* that he intended to resign from the Academy if Blunt was deprived of his Fellowship. He believed it amounted to 'a witch hunt'. His announcement prompted a letter to the paper: 'The expulsion of Professor Anthony Blunt from the British Academy was hitherto a very remote possibility, but Mr A.J.P. Taylor's promise, so portentously reported in your columns today, to resign from the Academy if that event occurred has now rendered expulsion a virtual certainty.'[42] The letter was signed 'Max Beloff'; Beloff hastened to assure Alan that it was a hoax. Alan told the *Sunday Express* he found the letter 'very funny'; 'I thought the idea of expelling Blunt as a way of getting rid of me was quite brilliant.'[43]

The Meeting on 3 July was well-attended, and outside Burlington House a number of journalists gathered. Fellows were anxious that their discussions should be private; two sets of locked doors separated the Academicians from the rest of the world. The debate on the Council's motion to expel Blunt has been described as 'sulphurous'. After forty minutes' tense discussion, Lawrence Gower, the outgoing Vice-Chancellor of Southampton University, proposed that the Meeting should 'pass on to the next item on the agenda'. This proposal was carried by a large majority, and no further discussion of the proposal or the counter-proposal took place. Fellows emerging from the Meeting were disconcerted to find Alan talking to reporters on the steps outside. He hailed it 'a splendid outcome . . . a victory for good sense . . . It was just like McCarthy all over again. I believe in toleration and I am a freedom man. It is a wonderful thing to realise that we can show patience and tolerance and that we can tolerate the intolerable.' Professor Ralf Dahrendorf, Director of the LSE, echoed his sentiments. 'The British Academy is about scholarship, and that was the decision we took – by a handsome majority.'[44]

Over the next few days three Fellows resigned from the Academy in protest at its decision, one of them being Colin Roberts, former Secretary to the OUP Delegates. Another resigned in the first week of August. Alan wrote to Chris Wrigley that he had 'defeated an attempt to expel Blunt'[45]; a claim not endorsed by others present, who felt that Alan had little or no influence in the debate. A campaign hostile to the Academy had begun in the letters pages of the *Daily Telegraph*, and the paper printed several condemnatory leaders. *The Times*, perhaps chastened by the 'Beloff' letter, perhaps because, as it was rumoured, the paper had made an agreement with Blunt in exchange for access to his story, declined to publish letters on the subject. Blunt wrote to the President, the classicist Professor Sir Kenneth Dover, expressing his distress at the way the *Daily Telegraph* was using him as a stick to beat the Academy.

Dover was facing a crisis. Some Fellows unhappy with the decision at the Meeting were trying to organise a ballot, though nothing in the Academy's constitution provided for such a thing. Several other Fellows had threatened to resign if Blunt did not leave by the end of the year. Three of these were historians – J.H. Plumb, Norman Gash, and Alan's former pupil I.R. Christie. Dover believed that up to fifteen Fellows might go; in his reply to Blunt's letter, Dover asked him to 'give serious consideration' to resigning himself as a means of 'healing the wound' in the Academy. Blunt spoke to Dover on the telephone twice, and on the second occasion announced that he had decided to go.

The news of Blunt's resignation broke on 19 August. The same day Alan also resigned. In a letter to Dover he said that the decision taken at the Annual Meeting should have been the end of the matter. 'Instead, by requesting Professor Blunt to resign, you have revived the controversy and enabled a small group of Fellows to thwart the wishes of a substantial majority. I deeply regret this as I have regretted the controversy from the start. But I have no choice. I will not be party to a witch hunt and therefore tender my resignation as a Fellow.'[46] The press gave the matter attention not normally paid to Academy affairs. 'A.J.P. Taylor quits over Blunt "witch-hunt"' was the headline in the *Guardian*, and there were similar stories, and editorials, in all the papers. Some of the speculation was rather wild; a *Daily Express* reporter, knowing that Blunt was homosexual, asked whether there was a 'special relationship' between him and Alan.

Alan was the only further Fellow to resign, though Richard Cobb – another Oxford historian – resigned and then withdrew his resignation. The affair was debated for a long time afterwards, however; in *Encounter*, which published articles by Dover and Christie; in a *Policy Review* essay by Norman Gash; and in a long piece by George Steiner in the *New Yorker*.[47] The *Guardian* commented that the Academy had not come well out of the affair.[48] Strong feelings had been expressed on both sides. The nub of the argument for those trying to expel Blunt was that he had betrayed those values which the Academy stood for; those against his expulsion believed that it was not the Academy's business to police the political, sexual or moral behaviour of its Fellows. The former argued that the Academy was accountable to the British public; the latter that it was accountable to no one. Righteous indignation against Blunt collided with a refusal to be censorious. Dover observed that there was no correlation between Right and Left on this issue. Although the majority, if not all of those prominent in the campaign to expel Blunt were Tories, other Conservatives such as Hugh Trevor-Roper, now Lord Dacre, were opposed to Blunt's expulsion. Patriots referred to the Academy's Royal Charter – though the role of the monarch was one of the many cloudy aspects of the Blunt case. Some of those opposed to Blunt's expulsion reflected that the independence of the Academy was one of the aspects which differentiated it from similar bodies in authoritarian countries; expulsion was a tactic more often used by the enemies than by the defenders of scholarship.

Alan's position may have been based on a misunderstanding. It seems that he resigned believing that Dover had put pressure on Blunt to resign, and it seems that this may not be quite what happened. Perhaps he had wanted to resign all along, as he told Eva – but it would have been characteristic for Alan to say such a thing tongue-in-cheek. He remained in touch with Peter Brown, the Academy Secretary, and a few years later he enquired whether he might return. Brown had to explain that under the by-laws a Fellow could return only by re-election, and Fellows could be elected only under the age of seventy. 'Ah well,' Alan replied, 'I do these things, it is part of my life.'

Margaret died a few weeks after the Meeting of the Academy. She had been ill for some years, although doctors had never been able to diagnose what was wrong with her. Exploratory operations failed to reveal any specific ailment. Possibly she used her 'illness' as a lure for Alan's sympathy. Alan attended the funeral but not the wake afterwards; 'there had been enough hypocrisy already'.[49]

Margaret's death eased the strain on Alan's third marriage. Alan was committed now only to Eva; and he became increasingly dependent on her. When Eva made her usual summer trip to Hungary, he found it hard to cope on his own. He did not know how to light the oven. He was easily flustered about small things, like where to put his books or what to buy for supper. In 1981 she left behind the typescript of her autobiography *An English Husband* for him to read. Alan had not appreciated before how hurt she had been when he had continued seeing Margaret. 'The whole situation makes me very unhappy. I appear so utterly inconsiderate and selfish. It really is a wonder that you put up with me for so long.'[50] 'Only now are we properly married,' Eva noted in her diary six months later: 'Margaret's shadow has disappeared for ever.'[51]

Eva worked hard to make a new life for them both. Alan's old friends began to come to dinner, even though Alan was not always an easy host. Visitors complained that they were given only one glass of wine to drink, and that when Alan refilled his own he omitted to top up those of his guests. He was concerned, he told guests, that he might exhaust his stock of the wine Beaverbrook had given him before his death. After dinner the men were handed aprons and expected to wash up; Sir Isaiah Berlin and the Lords Longford and Boothby all wielded a dishcloth in Twisden Road.

Alan always went to bed at 10.15 p.m., whether or not there were guests present. After the lights were out he sang revolutionary songs to his radical wife. He began reading to Eva in bed, Macaulay's *History of England* – 'Alan enjoys it tremendously,' she noted in her diary[52] – the Beatrix Potter stories, and the *Diary of a Nobody*. Eva reflected that Mr Pooter's house sounded very much like those in their neighbourhood.

When Alan and Eva returned to Hungary together Alan was welcomed warmly by his stepsons, and fêted as a distinguished foreign visitor. In 1981 he became President of the British-Hungarian Friendship Society, which had started at the height of the Cold War after the visit of several hundred young Britons to the 1949 World Youth Festival in Budapest.

In 1981 Alan was seventy-five. It was also the seventy-fifth anniversary of the Historical Association, and Alan was asked to lecture – on the year 1906, their common birthday – at the climax of the celebrations on 25 November. Earlier that day there had been a reception at Stationers' Hall. Alan was presented to the Queen, the Patron of the Association. Eva, who was with him, made a point of not curtseying.

In September 1981 there was a gathering of fifty-seven Taylors at Ross-on-Wye. Alan gave a short speech, in which he talked about the grandfather they all shared, 'J.T.'. Alan insisted on presiding; as the eldest son of the eldest son, he claimed the title of Head of the Family. It was important to him to be recognised as such; on family occasions such as Christmas dinner he liked to make the first symbolic slice of the turkey, and he was irritated if anyone else inadvertently usurped this role.

A television series provided another nostalgic excursion. 'The Edge of Britain' was Alan's personal view of four towns on the North-West coast – Southport, Blackpool, Morecambe and Preston. The programmes mixed history and autobiography. While

Alan and Eva were in the area making the films they revisited many of the places of his childhood. He was able to show her the house in Birkdale where he had lived as a boy, and the infant school run by the Misses Filmer he had attended around the corner.

At a party for Hamish Hamilton Alan ran into Anthony Howard, former Editor of the *New Statesman* and *The Listener*, who had often used Alan as a diarist. 'What are you doing now?' Alan asked. Howard replied that he was planning to write a life of R.A. Butler. 'Fill your pockets with lead, get on a Channel steamer and get off halfway,' Alan advised, 'rather than write a life of RAB.'

In 1981 Alan gave the annual lecture to the German Historical Institute in London. He chose as his subject '1939 Revisited', a return to the themes he had discussed in *The Origins of the Second World War*. It was a strange, querulous piece, with none of the scintillating paradox or flashes of good-humoured wit which had marked Alan in his prime. Listeners were disappointed to find that he did not seem to have kept up with recently published scholarship in the area, particularly the German work.

He was becoming increasingly curmudgeonly. In 1978 he had received an honorary degree from the University of Bristol. 'I attach no importance to these things,' he told Eva, 'but it is nice to think that Bristol appreciates me and I also like to think of the pain that my honorary degree will cause to all those who have slighted me.' His reaction to being listed by *The Times* as one of the 'Brains of England' was to denigrate the others named.[*][53] Attending a party to celebrate the twenty-fifth anniversary of CND, he felt 'forgotten'. In fact he was the only 'founder' of the Campaign mentioned in an address by the General Secretary, Bruce Kent, who had also made a point of welcoming him personally.[54]

CND was experiencing a second wave of popular support, fuelled by the determination of the Conservative Government and its NATO allies to install a new generation of nuclear weapons. Arms limitation talks seemed permanently stalled. Large public demonstrations in favour of disarmament were held in London and several other European capitals. There was much discussion of 'limited' nuclear war in Europe; and of the ridiculous official plans

---

*They included Isaiah Berlin, E.P. Thompson and A.J. Ayer.

for civil defence. Alan wrote about these issues in bleak terms. A
Third World War seemed to him more likely than not. Early in
1981 he wrote that he had been rebuked for using the phrase 'the
next war' in a book review.

Alan's last big public occasion came when he was invited to give
the 1981* Romanes Lecture, delivered in the Sheldonian Theatre in
Oxford. To be appointed Romanes Lecturer is an exceptional
honour; the first, who delivered his lectures exactly one hundred
years earlier, had been Mr Gladstone. Alan chose as his topic 'War
in Our Time'. He was very tense beforehand; he felt ill and his
hands were trembling. When he looked back over his teaching
career, he began, he realised with some embarrassment that he had
been dealing with the subject of war most of the time. He confessed
that he could not claim any expert knowledge of war; the nearest he
had been to combat was to patrol round the Oxford gas works in
1940 as a member of a Home Guard platoon. But war had
dominated his life. When he had started studying history, the great
issue of the day, on which historians made their reputations, was
the origins of the First World War. Alan had reached the conclusion
that all the profound causes put forward as explanations were
inadequate. The colonial disputes between the Great Powers, for
example, were by 1914 on the point of being settled.

> The prime cause of the war lay in the precautions that had been taken
> to ensure there would be no war. The deterrent dominated strategi-
> cal planning before 1914. When one Great Power had threatened
> war, the other countries had climbed down, as in the Bosnian crisis of
> 1908–9. But if all the Powers used the deterrent simultaneously war
> followed automatically. That is what happened in August 1914. The
> deterrent did not prevent war: it made war inevitable.

Alan continued by discussing the Second World War and the Cold
War which followed. His conclusion was a sombre one.

> The deterrent starts off only as a threat, but the record shows that
> there comes a time when its reality has to be demonstrated – which
> can only be done by using it. So it was in August 1914 and so it will be

---

*Delivered in March 1982.

again. So far we have done very well. We have lived under nuclear terror for forty years and are still here. The danger increases every day. Without the abolition of nuclear weapons the fate of mankind is certain.

Some historians listening to Alan lecture were indignant. They had come expecting a lecture based on scholarly research; instead they were given propaganda. Most of the undergraduates, on the other hand, seemed to like what they heard.

In May 1982 Alan was awarded another honorary degree, this time by the University of Manchester. At the ceremony, the head of the history department referred to the oral legend of Alan Taylor, which persisted within the university more than forty years after his departure. Alan spoke after the Chancellor, the Duke of Devonshire. He seemed to be having difficulty walking, and had been forced to ascend the platform in tiny, shuffling steps, well before he was due. But his bite was as sharp as ever. He referred to his own time at Manchester: 'Then, as I suppose now, all professors were regarded as reactionary.' The Vice-Chancellor squirmed.

A month afterwards Alan delivered to Machell the typescript of his long-awaited autobiography, first discussed with Hamilton more than twenty-five years earlier. Margaret's death had removed one obstacle to publication. 'Eve Crosland,* my second wife, is my great problem,' he told Machell. 'I don't think she is libelled, but you never know. Shall I show her the relevant passages? Perhaps better still will you show them to her? I would not mind cutting her out altogether though it would spoil the story. I have taken out all the best bits already.'[55] After some discussion Machell wrote to Eve asking whether she wanted to see the parts of the text which concerned her, and if not whether she might confirm in writing that she did not intend to take legal action against the book. Eve's reply was searing. She knew, she said, of Alan's capacity to twist facts, tell half-truths, and make damning implications by omission. She refused to consent to the publication of anything in the book concerning her, nor would she give a guarantee not to take legal action if she thought it appropriate.[56]

---

*Eve had changed her name back to Crosland by deed poll.

'My second wife does not wish to be named or referred to in this book,' Alan wrote in the preface. 'I have therefore struck out all the passages relating to her even though it leads to some odd gaps. I had hoped to atone for some of my graver acts of selfishness and lack of consideration. But the opportunity has been denied me.' He also talked more generally about the problem of libel.

> At a first run through my publisher's legal adviser found seventy-six cases . . . There is one way out. If the person allegedly libelled is dead all is well. How eagerly I have gone through the obituaries killing off not only my enemies, not that I have any, but my best friends . . . If there is ever a second edition of this book I will gladly oblige anyone who would like to be struck out of my memories. I am afraid I cannot however consider requests to be included from those aggrieved persons whom I have left out.[57]

Though Eve was not mentioned at all in the autobiography, Alan felt able to be frank about his first marriage. In particular, he wrote a great deal about Margaret's passion for Robert Kee and Dylan Thomas. He linked Margaret's behaviour with his mother's infatuation for Henry Sara; and his own reaction with that of his father. His portrait of Connie is relentlessly hostile; in the whole book he has not a good word to say for her. His father, on the other hand, is described sympathetically.

> His position was in my opinion intolerable. He ought to have revolted. This never crossed his mind. I do not think he ever realised how things had worked out for him. I was entirely on his side . . . When later I resented the way the women in my life treated me, it was as much on my father's behalf as my own. I kicked because he failed to do so.[58]

Alan told Eva that he had written the autobiography for her. He had taken chapters with him to their assignations on the continent of Europe. She was anxious about his residual affection for Margaret; he was keen to allay these anxieties. If the picture of Margaret that emerges from his autobiography is unsympathetic, this may be one reason. He could never forgive Margaret, he told Eva. Her infatuation for Robert Kee had 'destroyed my self-confidence'.[59]

'I no longer feel the enthusiasm I once did for "the lads",' Alan wrote in the chapter which covered the ruinous inflation of the 1970s; commenting that trades unionists had become 'the principal exploiters of the poor and humble'.[60] Like many elderly men, he had ceased to believe in Progress. 'Men used to have hope for the future. Has any sane man now any hope that the future will be better than the past?'[61]

One striking aspect of his autobiography was his unwillingness to acknowledge any debt to his teachers. Leslie Gilbert 'had forgotten most of his advanced history'; he 'was not really interested'. G.N. Clark 'was bored by tutoring' – 'of the recent history to which I have devoted my life I learnt at Oxford precisely nothing'. Pribram 'never gave me any guidance'. Alan 'never learnt anything' from Namier 'except anecdotes beginning "When I was in the Foreign Office . . ." '[62] Almost without exception, other historians were ridiculed or belittled. He was 'much more distinguished', Alan told his readers, than Kenneth Bell, the don who had chosen not to award him a Brackenbury Scholarship at Balliol; 'the most distinguished and by far the best known' of the undergraduates awarded Firsts in history in 1927; 'among the most distinguished' scholars at Manchester University in the 1930s; 'more distinguished' than Cambridge historians awarded *ad hominem* chairs; 'the most distinguished historian of contemporary times' at Oxford.[63] Probably this was all true, but it irritated reviewers: John Gross, for example.

> Some of the boasting is merely harmless, perhaps endearing, vanity; some of it takes the form of an unseemly crowing over vanquished rivals and forgotten competitors. And, in retracing his career, Mr Taylor never seems happier than when recalling slights, setbacks and university feuds. The tone is suitably snide: reputations are nibbled away, and compliments wing their way through the air tipped with poison. In many of the disputes he describes Mr Taylor may well have been in the right, but that does not necessarily mean he is right to dredge them up now.[64]

Alan's autobiography – retitled *A Personal History* rather than *An Uninteresting Story* at the insistence of his publishers – was published in May 1983. It contained some very funny stories, very well told. David Holloway, reviewing the book in the *Daily Telegraph*, thought it 'wonderfully lively'; according to *The Times* reviewer, there was 'not a single dull sentence in it'.[65] But sometimes the rueful tone became self-pity, the candour rancour, the cantankerousness turned sour. The mask of self-mockery slipped, revealing the bitterness beneath. Oxford, for example, was 'a small provincial town', 'an inbred society', where he 'felt an outsider and was treated as such'. 'So far as Oxford was concerned, I did not exist.' He spent thirty-eight years there – not counting three earlier years as an undergraduate – 'without making a single intimate friend'.[66]

'I am glad you both think the autobiography funny,' Alan wrote to Machell. 'I thought it was tragic but I suppose cheerfulness kept breaking in.'[67] 'The book is full of good stories,' reported David Holloway. 'I hope they are all true.'

To mark the book's publication a group of a dozen or so, mostly old friends, assembled for dinner at a house in Camberwell, in south-east London. The hosts were Robert Kee, one of Alan's earliest Oxford pupils, and his friend and Oxford contemporary Sir Nicholas Henderson, who though not one of Alan's pupils had known him just as long. After dinner Alan's old sparring partner, Michael Foot, turned to Henderson and congratulated him on a wonderful party. Talking of Alan, he asked: 'Don't you agree that what he's really renowned for is the pursuit of truth?'

This was too much for Henderson. Alan was a terrific influence and a very stimulating one, he concurred, but 'I don't think that truth is what he's been particularly concerned with'. Perhaps it was unfortunate that Alan overheard, but it was not a challenge, and could easily have been laughed off or ignored; indeed it was the kind of irreverent criticism which Alan normally encouraged. This time, however, he was deeply offended. 'There are many things in your life and career I particularly dislike,' he snapped at Henderson. Nothing Henderson or the others could say would mollify him, and he insisted on being taken home early. He never thanked Henderson for the party, and never spoke to him again.

One of Alan's favourite phrases was that history is a version of events. 'The fact that there are other versions does not make any one of them wrong. It is just like taking different views about a human being.'[68] He wrote this in a letter to Eva, who realised that he presented different versions of the truth to the different women in his life; 'he gives each woman what she needs'.[69] 'In history, I'm committed to truth,' Alan told Robert Skidelsky, during a discussion of CND: 'in politics, I would lie to whatever extent is necessary.'

On the cover of *A Personal History* was a portrait by the artist June Mendoza. She had approached Alan in 1974, and he had agreed to sit for her. The portrait had been exhibited at the annual Portrait Painters' Exhibition, and had thereafter been hanging on the artist's dining-room wall. Magdalen had declined to purchase the painting, being engaged in raising money to restore its old buildings. A piece in the *Guardian* referred to the college's 'shabby stand'.

In 1981 Chris Cook organised a circular letter, soliciting £2500 to buy the portrait on behalf of the college. Some, including two former prime ministers, Sir Harold Wilson and Lord Callaghan, were willing to contribute. Others were not. 'He is stinking rich,' complained one former colleague. 'I would rather send a donation to some worthy cause such as Oxfam.' 'It sticks in my throat to subsidise one of the richest colleges in Oxford which is – apparently – too mean to buy this picture,' exclaimed another. 'We have just moved house and are frightfully broke,' wrote the best-selling novelist Jilly Cooper.

The contributions, which ranged from one thousand pounds to one, were sufficient to meet the asking price. At the last moment it was realised that VAT of £375 would also be payable; the college agreed to 'stump up' the necessary amount.[70] On 17 March 1984 an unveiling ceremony took place at Magdalen.

'My intellectual powers are undiminished,' Alan had concluded his autobiography, 'and I intend they should remain that way.' This was a brave statement; before the final proofs were passed for press he had been diagnosed as having Parkinson's disease. He had noticed for some time that his hand was trembling, making it difficult to use his cut-throat razor; now he was finding it difficult to walk, too.

Parkinson's disease attacks the parts of the brain which control movement. Its fundamental cause remains unknown and there is no cure, though the symptoms can be relieved. All sufferers react individually to the disease but they steadily deteriorate, faster in old age. Its onset is gradual, and sometimes the sufferer is unaware of symptoms which appear obvious to the stranger. Often the first indication of the disease is when a routine chore such as shaving becomes difficult.

The most conspicuous sign of Parkinson's disease is trembling, leading to impaired dexterity. Patients adept in a rhythmical technique such as playing the piano can often continue when apparently simpler activities such as holding a teacup become impossible. In Alan's case he remained able to use the typewriter long after the trembling became marked and his handwriting had deteriorated. Another classic sign of Parkinson's disease is shuffling rather than walking, something Alan had been doing for some time. For many years Alan had tended to drag one leg slightly; perhaps this too was an early indication. The other characteristic of Parkinson's disease is that the muscles and joints become stiff, producing a 'mask-like' face. The inanimate impression this conveys is accentuated by a tendency for the voice to become monotonous.

These physical symptoms can be alleviated by drug treatment, though the drugs made Alan feel nauseated. Occasionally they would produce an obfuscatory or even hallucinatory effect. Worse still, Alan was among about one-third of all those with Parkinson's disease who suffer mental as well as physical deterioration. Loss of memory is accompanied by diminishing drive, enthusiasm and curiosity. Drugs have no effect on these symptoms, and the struggle to overcome this loss of faculties causes intellectual as well as physical fatigue. Gifted people such as Alan can disguise the effects for a long time.

Alan faced this dreadful disease without complaint. He described the early stages in a 1983 *London Review of Books* diary.

> The principal symptom is shakiness, at first slight and then more and more troublesome. Often it affects one side more than another. Being congenitally left-handed, I can hold a teacup or a beer mug with my left hand and it does not shake at all, whereas I have had to give up

the use of my right hand almost entirely. One cheerful bit of news is that the disease does not affect my use of a typewriter. Even stranger, it does not affect my driving of a car. On the contrary, when I get out of my car after having driven for some time, I am much steadier than when I got in. But most of the time I am shaking more or less. The most difficult problem is to go downstairs – upstairs not so bad. It is worst when there is no banister or handrail to help me down. Then I have to creep down with my back to the wall, a humiliating process. In a more general way the disease slows me down physically, though not, of course, mentally. I start out for a walk in quite a sprightly fashion and suddenly notice I can proceed no further . . .

The workings of the disease are quite unpredictable. I cannot be sure whether I can lecture for a whole hour, indeed whether I can lecture at all. In the course of an evening party I suddenly feel that I can go on no longer and must shakily make my departure. Sometimes I stagger up to bed in the middle of the morning. At other times I go into London and spend most of the day happily reading in the London Library. Gradually I get more reluctant to go out for more than a few hundred yards. I can see that soon I shall be quite content to sit in the open air of my backyard or patio. I lose interest in what is happening further afield.[71]

In January 1984 Alan was knocked down by a car outside the Algerian Coffee Store in Old Compton Street. He spent two weeks in hospital, and when he was back at home told Eva that the end was not far away. Then he developed septicaemia and was admitted to hospital once more. The fever and the powerful drugs he was given to counteract it induced delirium; for a time he failed to recognise Eva and then spoke to her as if she were Margaret. He rattled off dates to confirm his grip on reality – 'Battle of Hastings, 1066'. When Alan rallied, he joked that since Betjeman's recent death he was now the nation's leading Parkinsonian.

He was no longer able to work. His typing became erratic, and his letters were not always coherent. His once magnificent memory had started to fail him, and he began to confuse names. His reviews had become shorter and shorter, and after Lord Carver had written to the *Observer* protesting at the inaccuracy of one of them Kilmartin stopped sending books to him. After his accident there had been only a trickle of work for the *London Review of Books*. 'I am crying out to wright,' he informed the editor, Karl Miller, late in 1985; but his spelling betrayed him.[72] 'I live in a state of total bewilderment,' he told Eva one morning; 'my mind is disorderly.'[73]

In March 1986 a dinner was organised at the Gay Hussar to celebrate Alan's 80th birthday. Alan was determined to make a short speech afterwards, and took special precautions to conserve his strength beforehand. It required a supreme effort, but he produced a typical waspish, donnish address and then left immediately.* Alan also received the accolade of a third *Festschrift*, this one edited by Chris Wrigley.[74]

The following November he had deteriorated to the point where Eva could cope with him no more, and he was admitted to Moss Lodge, a residential nursing-home in Finchley. He was confused, and hostile; on the first night he tried to run away. Later he seemed to settle. Eva brought many of his possessions – his armchair, his books, his typewriter and his pictures – to help him feel at home in his room. She also brought in his gramophone to enable him to play music, one of his few remaining pleasures. He pored over an album of old family photographs, which he cut up with a pair of scissors. Sometimes he pulled one of his books off the bookshelf and looked at it, though he could now barely read. 'All my books are running away from me,' he told a visitor.

Early in 1988 he sat for a portrait by the artist Maggi Hambling, now exhibited in the National Portrait Gallery. Friends and pupils visited him. Alan's conversational style remained the same, though the sense was jumbled and often he had to grimace to force out the words. Sometimes there would be a flash of meaning among the confusion. Sometimes too there was a grim humour. One day when Sebastian came to visit, Alan, emulating Lear, remarked: 'They tell me you are my son.' 'Yes, I am afraid I am,' Sebastian replied. 'Who was your mother?' 'Margaret.' 'Ah. Someone else came the other day and told me he was Margaret's son. She's got a lot to answer for.'

Alan's vitality made him physically resilient. Though his body

---

*The following day Alan could recall little about the dinner or what it was for. At Eva's prompting (she had not attended, being ill herself), a friend who had been present the previous evening came round and described it to him.

wasted under the attack of the disease, years of Spartan living and vigorous exercise kept him going much longer than might have been expected. He was courageous throughout his ordeal; his consultant found him a delightful patient.

Alan died on 7 September 1990. He was cremated at Golders Green Crematorium ten days later. Two of his most favoured pupils, Robert Kee and Pat Thompson, gave addresses. A memorial meeting was held in Magdalen College Chapel; originally planned for February, it was postponed after thick snow until April. The speakers were Michael Foot, Alan Sked, Robert Skidelsky, and the former Dean of Divinity, Arthur Adams. Kee's second wife Cynthia gave a reading from Beatrix Potter, and Rosa Howard, one of Alan's grandchildren, read Tennyson's poem 'Break, Break, Break'. There was music by Schubert and Lord Berners, and Richard Ingrams played an organ solo.

Alan's will valued his estate at £307,083. This was not a fortune, but it was a considerable sum, particularly after three years of fees for Moss Lodge. From 1972 his royalty income through David Higham Associates (which did not collect royalties from his two OUP volumes) was never less than £5,000 a year, reaching a peak of more than £25,000 in 1983. This was augmented – perhaps even doubled – by fees from other sources, including television and journalism. His fears of penury in the 1970s had proved unfounded.

Malcolm Muggeridge died in November 1990. In 1981 Muggeridge had asked Alan to speak at his funeral; 'a preposterous suggestion', Alan had replied.[75] After Muggeridge's death readers of the *Guardian* were slightly surprised to read Alan's warm obituary of his old friend. Alan quoted Muggeridge as having said that though they had never agreed about anything, they had never quarrelled: 'a rare tribute for Malcolm to pay'.[76] Alan must have written this obituary as much as ten years earlier, perhaps determined to have the last word.

Alan's final ambition had been to attend the 1988 Magdalen Restoration Dinner, the 300th anniversary of the restoration of the Fellows whom James II had expelled. It would also have been the fiftieth anniversary of Alan's first Restoration Dinner, when he had denounced the Munich settlement to the embarrassment of many of his listeners. Sadly he had been unable to attend. But perhaps his spirit still lingered around the college.

Some time after Alan's death the Governors of Magdalen College School sat down to lunch in the oak-panelled New Rooms. The Master of the School was at the head of the table, in front of Alan's full-length portrait by June Mendoza. When everyone had finished, the Master rose to suggest retiring to the adjoining room for coffee; as he did so, the portrait crashed to the ground, narrowly missing him. It was Alan's parting shot.

Works by A. J. P. Taylor

Unless otherwise indicated, the place of first publication is London. Volumes of essays are indicated by an asterisk.

The Italian Problem in European Diplomacy, 1847–1849 (Manchester University Press, 1934)

Germany's First Bid for Colonies, 1884–1885: A Move in Bismarck's European Policy (Macmillan, 1938)

The Habsburg Monarchy, 1815–1918 (Macmillan, 1941)

The Course of German History: A Survey of the Development of Germany since 1815 (Hamish Hamilton, 1945)

From Napoleon to Stalin* (Hamish Hamilton, 1950)

Rumours of Wars* (Hamish Hamilton, 1952)

The Struggle for Mastery in Europe, 1848–1918 (Oxford University Press, 1954)

Bismarck: The Man and the Statesman (Hamish Hamilton, 1955)

Englishmen and Others* (Hamish Hamilton, 1956)

The Troublemakers: Dissent over Foreign Policy, 1792–1939 (Hamish Hamilton, 1957)

The Origins of the Second World War (Hamish Hamilton, 1961)

The First World War: An Illustrated History (Hamish Hamilton, 1963)

Politics in Wartime: and Other Essays* (Hamish Hamilton, 1964)

English History, 1914–1945 (Oxford University Press, 1965)

From Napoleon to Lenin: Historical Essays* (Harper and Row, New York, 1966)

From Sarajevo to Potsdam (Thames and Hudson, 1966)

Europe: Grandeur and Decline* (Penguin, Harmondsworth, 1967)

War by Time-Table: How the First World War Began (Macdonald, 1969)

Beaverbrook (Hamish Hamilton, 1972)

The Second World War: An Illustrated History (Hamish Hamilton, 1975)

Essays in English History* (Penguin, Harmondsworth, 1976)

The War Lords (Hamish Hamilton, 1977)

How Wars Begin (Hamish Hamilton, 1978)

Revolutions and Revolutionaries (Hamish Hamilton, 1979)
Politicians, Socialism and Historians* (Hamish Hamilton, 1980)
A Personal History (Hamish Hamilton, 1983)
An Old Man's Diary (Hamish Hamilton, 1984)
From Napoleon to the Second International: Essays on the Nineteenth Century* (Hamish Hamilton, 1993)
Eva Haraszti Taylor (ed.): *Letters to Eva, 1969–1983* (Century, 1991)

Sources

A.J.P. Taylor's pupils were sometimes surprised or even slightly shocked to see him crumple a letter and drop it in the waste-paper basket. Documents are the raw material of history, cherished and even revered by historians. Taylor discarded every letter he received, even love-letters; he did not retain copies of letters he sent, nor even copies of his typescripts. As a young man (1919–1926) he had kept diaries, but he destroyed these after Henry Sara informed him that they were being read by his mother. Much later he also destroyed his archaeology 'diaries', seven large volumes containing detailed observations on the churches he visited since his schooldays at Bootham.

The result of all this destruction is that Taylor left no comprehensive archive. The only correspondence of his which was systematically preserved dates from the late 1960s and 1970s, when as Honorary Director of the Beaverbrook Library he employed a secretary. Some of this correspondence, together with a few earlier documents, was sold to the Harry Ransom Humanities Research Center in the University of Texas at Austin [HRC]. Also included in this collection is the original typescript of Taylor's *Beaverbrook*. He was in the habit of reusing the back of discarded typescripts for drafts of new works, and a few pages of autobiography appear on the back of this and other typescripts.

The biographer looking for Taylor's letters therefore has to search the archives of the recipients. As might be expected, the most substantial holdings are in institutions. Taylor's letters to three successive editors – W.P. Crozier, A.P. Wadsworth and Alastair Hetherington – are to be found in the *Manchester Guardian* collection held in the John Rylands University Library at Manchester; which also has Crozier's correspondence with Muggeridge and some material relating to the employment of Eve Crosland. Taylor's letters to Muggeridge are preserved in Wheaton College Special Collections, Wheaton, Illinois; a few letters to Betjeman survive in the Betjeman archive in the University of Victoria, British Columbia. The BBC Written Archives Centre at Caversham has plenty of letters to various producers and radio and television executives from 1942 until 1961, after which date records are not yet available. Even more interesting are the relevant parts of the Beaverbrook papers kept at the House of Lords Record Office [HoL]. As well as letters to Beaverbrook himself from both Taylor and his then wife Eve, there are copies of Taylor's letters while he was was Honorary Director of the Beaverbrook Library, and some other, as yet unsorted correspondence deposited there after his death by his widow Eva. There are also important holdings of Taylor correspondence in the Kingsley Martin papers at the University of Sussex; in the Liddell Hart Centre, King's College, London; and in the Sir George Clark papers in the Bodleian Library.

Sadly, very little of Taylor's correspondence with Sir Lewis Namier seems to have survived, but I was able to unearth a handful of letters in the unsorted boxes of correspondence in the History of Parliament [HoP]. The same archive also has some letters from Namier to Hugh Trevor-Roper. Namier's letters to Macmillan are taken from the Macmillan Collection in the British Library, which also has some early Taylor letters. There is a more substantial collection of Taylor's letters to Macmillan in the publishers' private archive in Basingstoke. Hamish Hamilton's archives are kept in the University of Bristol Library; and the OUP archives in the Press' Walton Street headquarters.

The papers of Taylor's brother-in-law Anthony Crosland, kept in the Library of the London School of Economics [LSE], include two letters from Taylor, and a letter to Crosland from the then Prime Minister, Harold Wilson, about him. Crosland's diaries contain references to Taylor and his works.

Taylor's letters to Eva Haraszti, later his wife, are published in edited form in *Letters to Eva*: all letters to her referred to in the notes come from this volume. I have not seen the originals of these. Other letters to individuals can be taken to come from private holdings unless indicated otherwise.

Dr Anne Whiteman was kind enough to allow me to examine the papers of Dame Lucy Sutherland in the Bodleian Library, which gave a sense of her working relationship with Namier, as well as casting a faint gleam of light on to the appointment of the Regius Professor in 1957. Dr Chris Cook lent me his file on the fund-raising appeal to buy June Mendoza's portrait. Richard Ingrams showed me Malcolm Muggeridge's typescript diaries, only parts of which have been published. I am particularly grateful to Eva Taylor for allowing me to see her unpublished autobiography *The English Husband*. Professor Ian R. Christie lent me his file on the Blunt affair. I have also used the press cuttings files at the *Observer*, the *Guardian*, Express Newspapers and the Oxford and Counties Newspaper Group, which incorporates the *Oxford Times* and the *Oxford Mail*.

The main printed source is, of course, A.J.P. Taylor's own autobiography *A Personal History*, published in 1983. The last two chapters of my book discuss the provenance of this work and some of the influences on Taylor when he wrote it. Though *A Personal History* is characteristically entertaining and well-written, I have discovered many small mistakes, too petty to be worth detailing, and I suspect that it is not completely reliable in larger matters, too. The very least one can say is that Taylor did not always verify his references – if references existed.

The other indispensable printed source is Chris Wrigley's *A.J.P. Taylor: A Bibliography*. This impressive work is daunting in size and scale; as Professor Wrigley writes in his Preface, the sheer volume of Taylor's writings is staggering. His magnificent labour has made my task much easier, and I heartily thank him for it. Other secondary sources are too miscellaneous to be worth listing separately and are given in the endnotes.

Notes

References are numbered separately for each chapter. The first British publisher is given whenever possible; the place of publication is London unless otherwise indicated. For full references to A.J.P. Taylor's own works, please refer to the separate list on pp. 407–408. Many of his essays, book reviews and other shorter pieces have been anthologised more than once; in such cases I have thought best to refer to the first publication in volume form. I have abbreviated the titles of some of Taylor's own works frequently cited, as *Origins*, *Struggle*, etc.

The note on sources (pp. 409-411) should reveal the location of most of the letters listed below. Where this is not immediately obvious, I have provided the name of the source in square brackets, using the abbreviations given alongside the sources. All letters to Eva Haraszti, later Eva Taylor, are taken from the book *Letters to Eva*. Other letters can be taken to come from private holdings.

Chapter 1: Home Alone (pp. 5–19)

1. *A Personal History*, p. 14.
2. ibid., p. 7.
3. Eva Haraszti Taylor: *A Life with Alan: The Diary of A.J.P. Taylor's Wife* (Hamish Hamilton, 1987), p. 111.
4. *A Personal History*, p. 16.
5. 'I Remember, I Remember', *Times Literary Supplement*, 6 December 1974.
6. 'Accident Prone', *Journal of Modern History*, March 1977; reprinted in *Politicians, Socialism and Historians*, p. 4.
7. 'Prince of Storytellers', a review of Guy Arnold: *Hold Fast for England: G.A. Henty, Imperialist Boys' Writer*, *Observer*, 13 April 1980.
8. John Keegan: 'Uncle Harry's Socks', a review of *A Personal History*, *New York Review of Books*, 13 October 1983.
9. *A Personal History*, p. 17.

10. *The Troublemakers*, p. 137.
11. *A Personal History*, pp. 21–2
12. David Boulton: *Objection Overruled* (Macgibbon and Kee, 1967).

Chapter 2: Badger (pp. 20–31)

1. S.W. Brown: *Leighton Park: A History of the School* (privately published, 1952), p. 97.
2. *A Personal History*, p. 32.
3. E.J. Brown: *The First Five: The Story of a School* (privately published, 1987), p. 5.
4. *A Personal History*, p. 33.
5. ibid., p. 36.
6. *English History, 1914–1945*, p. 143.
7. *A Personal History*, p. 37.
8. ibid., p. 34.
9. H.W. Jones: 'The Downs During the War', *The Badger*, Spring 1938, p. 12.
10. H.W. Jones: 'Our Last Years at The Downs', *The Badger*, Autumn 1938, pp. 12–13.
11. G.H. (Geoffrey Hoyland): 'Downs in Times Past', *The Badger*, Spring 1942, p. 24.
12. *A Personal History*, p. 40.

Chapter 3: 'The seed-time of life' (pp. 32–50)

1. *Preston Herald*, obituary of Percy Taylor, 1 March 1940.
2. *Manchester Guardian*, 2 September 1955.
3. *The Communist*, 27 May and 3 June 1922.
4. *A Personal History*, p. 47.
5. Francis E. Pollard (ed.): *Bootham School, 1823–1923* (Dent, 1926), p. 169.
6. *A Personal History*, p. 61.
7. *Bootham School, 1823–1923*, p. 172.
8. *A Personal History*, p. 62.
9. ibid., p. 63.

Chapter 4: 'Blow it up after I have gone down' (pp. 51–67)

1. *English History*, p. 171n.
2. J.I.M. Stewart: *Myself and Michael Innes* (Gollancz, 1987), p. 56.
3. Harold Hobson: *Indirect Journey* (Weidenfeld, 1978), pp. 158–9.
4. *A Personal History*, pp. 78–9, 83; 'Accident Prone', p. 6.

5. Quoted in Jan Morris (ed.): *The Oxford Book of Oxford* (Oxford University Press, 1978), p. 355.
6. *Indirect Journey*, pp. 134–5.
7. *Myself and Michael Innes*, p. 59.
8. *English History*, p. 260.
9. *The Strings are False: An Unfinished Autobiography* (Faber, 1965), p. 103.
10. *A Personal History*, pp. 74, 78–9.
11. *The Badger*, Spring 1938, p. 13.
12. *The Plebs*, March 1925, p. 124.
13. *A Personal History*, p. 78.
14. M.P. Ashley and C.T. Saunders, *Red Oxford* (Oxford University Labour Club, 2nd ed. 1933), p. 41.
15. *Red Oxford*, pp. 36–9.
16. 'Preston Revisited', *Spectator*, 11 October 1980.
17. 'Class War 1926', *New Statesman*, 30 April 1976.
18. *English History*, p. 250.
19. *Bootham*, December 1926, pp. 96–8.
20. *English History*, p. 244.
21. David Ayerst to his mother, 19 May 1926.
22. ibid., 24 October 1926.
23. *English History*, p. 250.
24. AJPT to Brian Pearce, 10 December 1979.

Chapter 5: 'An uncouth fellow' (pp. 68–82)

1. *Myself and Michael Innes*, p. 66.
2. Autobiographical draft [HRC].
3. *A Personal History*, p. 85.
4. ibid., pp. 85–6.
5. L.R. Phelps to David Ayerst, 19 August 1927.
6. *Myself and Michael Innes*, p. 67.
7. *Saturday Review*, 16 June 1928, p. 774. Years later AJPT wrote to Kathleen Tillotson, enclosing a copy of this review and disassociating himself from many of the opinions in it.
8. AJPT to Robert Gittings, 25 January 1983 [Brotherton Library, Leeds].
9. 'Diary', *London Review of Books*, 3–17 March 1983; reprinted in *An Old Man's Diary*, pp. 114–15.
10. *A Life with Alan*, p. 176.
11. *A Personal History*, p. 57.
12. AJPT to Eva Haraszti, 9 and 28 November 1975.
13. *A Personal History*, p. 8.
14. AJPT to Eva Haraszti, 8 November 1974.
15. AJPT to Charles Gott, 8 July 1928.

16. 'The Judgement of the Diplomat', *Saturday Review of Literature*, 11 December 1954; reprinted as 'Democracy and Diplomacy', in *Englishmen and Others*, p. 188.
17. AJPT and Innes Stewart to Charles Gott, 14 November 1928.
18. ibid.
19. *A Personal History*, pp. 90–1.
20. 'Accident Prone', p. 8.
21. *A Personal History*, p. 95.
22. ibid., p. 94.
23. ibid., p. 93.
24. ibid., p. 105.
25. ibid., p. 97.
26. Peter Gay: *Freud: A Life for our Time* (Dent, 1988), p. 173.
27. *A Personal History*, p. 96.
28. ibid., p. 98.
29. ibid., p. 98.

Chapter 6: 'Who whom?' (pp. 83–106)

1. 'The Manchester History School' in F.M. Powicke: *Modern Historians and the Study of History* (Odhams, 1955); W.A. Pantin: 'Ernest Fraser Jacob, 1894–1971', *Proceedings of the British Academy*, lviii (1972), pp. 447–474.
2. *Times* obituary, 8 October 1971.
3. *A Personal History*, p. 99; see also *The Troublemakers*, p. 178. In 'Munich Ten Years After', *New Statesman and Nation*, 2 October 1948, reprinted in *From Napoleon to Stalin*, p. 132, Alan wrote that he 'looked back with shame' to these lectures.
4. *Modern Historians and The Study of History*, pp.28–9.
5. *A Personal History*, p. 132.
6. *Myself and Michael Innes*, p. 67.
7. *Preston Herald*, 21 February 1936.
8. *A Personal History*, p. 65.
9. AJPT to Kingsley Martin, 25 November 1944.
10. *A Personal History*, p. 107.
11. See Robert Jungk: *Brighter Than a Thousand Suns: A Personal History of the Atomic Scientists* (Gollancz and Hart-Davis, 1958).
12. *A Personal History*, p. 107.
13. ibid., p. 37.
14. Malcolm Muggeridge: *Chronicles of Wasted Time, 1: The Green Stick* (Collins, 1972), p. 181.
15. ibid., p. 201; see also Richard Ingrams's introduction to the 1987 reissue of *Picture Palace*, pp. xii–xiii.
16. *Picture Palace* (second edition, Weidenfeld & Nicolson, 1987), p. 50.

17. AJPT to Eva Haraszti, 24 November 1972.
18. 'Extreme Views Weakly Held', a review of *A Personal History* in the *Sunday Times*, 29 May 1983.
19. 'Lewis Namier: A Personal Impression' in Martin Gilbert (ed.): *A Century of Conflict 1850–1950: Essays for A.J.P. Taylor* (Hamish Hamilton, 1966), pp. 220–1.
20. 'Symmetry and Repetition', *Manchester Guardian*, 1 January 1940.
21. 'Personal Impression', p. 218.
22. The review, by G.M. Trevelyan, appeared in *The Nation* on 15 November 1930. See Linda Colley: *Namier* (Weidenfeld, 1989), p. 13.
23. *A Personal History*, pp. 105, 112.
24. Norman Rose: *Lewis Namier and Zionism* (Oxford University Press, 1980), p. 59n.
25. 'Personal Impression', p. 215.
26. ibid., pp. 217, 218.
27. *A Personal History*, p. 113.
28. ibid., pp. 112–13; *Chronicles of Wasted Time* 1, p. 180; *Namier*, p. 46.
29. 'Personal Impression', p. 227.
30. John Cannon: Radio 3 broadcast, date unknown.
31. *A Life with Alan*, p. 53.
32. *A Personal History*, p. 112; 'Habeas Cadaver', *Listener*, 3 October 1968.
33. Cannon: Radio 3 broadcast.
34. L.B. Namier to Harold Macmillan, 31 October 1937.
35. Harold Macmillan to L.B. Namier, 12 August 1932; Namier to Macmillan, 20 February, 1 and 23 March, 19 May; AJPT to Macmillan, 1 March, 10 and 17 May; Macmillan to AJPT, 4 May 1933.
36. L.B. Namier to A.P. Wadsworth, 25 March 1946.
37. *The Italian Problem in European Diplomacy, 1847–1849*, pp. 1, 8.
38. *Bootham*, April 1935, pp. 105–6.
39. *The Italian Problem*, p. viii.
40. *A Personal History*, p. 60.
41. *Times* obituary by James Joll, January 1962; revised by Martin Gilbert, May 1969.
42. 'The Judgement of the Diplomat', *Saturday Review of Literature*, 11 December 1954; reprinted as 'Democracy and Diplomacy', *Englishmen and Others*, p. 185.
43. *A Personal History*, p. 113; AJPT to John Erickson, 20 May 1975. He continued: 'I expect I rely on these fingers overmuch'.
44. *Namier*, pp. 75, 82.
45. *A Personal History*, p. 126.
46. *A Life with Alan*, p. 50.

47. *A Personal History*, p. 110; W.P. Crozier to Malcolm Muggeridge, 10 May 1932.
48. Quoted in Malcolm Muggeridge: *The Thirties* (Hamish Hamilton, 1940), p. 64.
49. Margaret Cole: *The Life of G.D.H. Cole* (Macmillan, 1971), p. 159.
50. Michael Foot: *Debts of Honour* (Poyntor, 1980), p. 139.
51. Malcolm Muggeridge to W.P. Crozier, 6 September 1932.
52. *The Thirties*, p. 67.
53. *A Personal History*, p. 111.
54. Malcolm Muggeridge to W.P. Crozier, 16 December 1932.
55. ibid., 8 March 1933.
56. Cited by AJPT in 'The Traditions of British Foreign Policy', Third Programme, 6 January 1951; reprinted in *Rumours of Wars*, p. 79.
57. W.P. Crozier to Malcolm Muggeridge, 8 March 1933.
58. Malcolm Muggeridge to W.P. Crozier, 22 and 23 March, 3 April 1933.
59. AJPT to Malcolm Muggeridge, 13 February 1933.
60. *English History*, p. 348n.
61. Malcolm Muggeridge: *Winter in Moscow* (Eyre and Spottiswoode, 1934), p. vi.
62. David Ayerst: *Guardian : Biography of a Newspaper* (Collins, 1971), p. 511–13
63. AJPT to Malcolm Muggeridge, 16 June 1933.
64. 'He accepted the guilt of those accused; he was right and the sceptics wrong.' 'Intourism', a review of Joseph E. Davies: *Mission to Moscow, Time and Tide*, 6 June 1942. Davies had been American Ambassador; he attended the Radek Treason Trial in January 1937, and satisfied himself that the accused were guilty. See pp. 31–40 and 175–9.
65. *Manchester Guardian*, 14 January 1936.
66. 'Dreyfus', a review of Pierre Dreyfus: *Dreyfus: His Life and Letters, Manchester Guardian*, 7 May 1937.
67. *English History*, pp. 143–4, 274.
68. *Manchester Guardian*, 22 October 1934.

Chapter 7: Top of the World (pp. 107–122)

1. *A Personal History*, p. 117.
2. Unpublished diary entry, 25 October 1934.
3. *Picture Palace*, p. 69.
4. *Manchester Guardian*, 31 October 1956.
5. *Dictionary of National Biography, 1951–60* (Oxford University Press, 1971), pp. 1016–17.
6. 'Accident Prone', p. 10.
7. *A Personal History*, p. 130.

8. Quoted in Ben Pimlott: *Hugh Dalton* (Cape, 1985), p. 584.
9. AJPT to Kingsley Martin, undated but most likely 1965.
10. *Memoranda de Parliamento* (1893), pp. lxxxiii–iv.
11. *English History*, p. 385.
12. *Manchester Guardian*, 18 December 1935.
13. *English History*, p. 395.
14. 'Marxist Thriller', a review of H. Fagan: *Nine Days that Shook England, Manchester Guardian*, 23 August and 19 July 1938.
15. Richard Pares in the *Oxford Magazine*, 19 May; *Times Literary Supplement*, 19 March; E.L. Woodward in *The Spectator*, 26 March; L.G. Robinson in *International Affairs*, July–August 1938; *A Personal History*, p. 123.
16. e.g. *The Origins of the Second World War*, p. 140.
17. *Germany's First Bid for Colonies*, p. 14.
18. *Jewish Chronicle*, 27 February 1938.
19. 'The Naval Race', a review of E.L. Woodward: *Great Britain and the German Navy* (Oxford University Press, 1935), *Manchester Guardian*, 6 November 1935.
20. E.L. Woodward: *Short Journey* (Faber, 1942), pp. 234–46.
21. *The Italian Problem*, p. 8.
22. '1939 Revisited' (German Historical Institute, 1981), p. 8.
23. 'Personal Impression', pp. 219–20.
24. e.g. *Manchester Guardian*, 17 December 1938.
25. AJPT to Duff Cooper, 1 October 1938.
26. AJPT to Martin Gilbert, 2 May 1962.

Chapter 8: The War of the Words (pp. 123–158)

1. 'The French in Morocco', *Manchester Guardian*, 15 May 1939.
2. AJPT to Hamish Hamilton, 17 January 1947; *A Personal History*, p. 145.
3. AJPT to Harold Macmillan 17 April, 8 and 10 May, and 2 June; Macmillan to AJPT, 2 and 9 May, 1 June; L.B. Namier to Macmillan, 20 April and 9 June 1939. Despite what AJPT writes in his autobiography (p. 145), there is no evidence that Macmillan originally suggested this idea to Namier and that he passed it on. On the contrary, AJPT refers more than once during the correspondence to an approach from another publisher 'not on my initiative, with a request for such a work'. In one of his letters to Macmillan, Namier speculates that the other publisher may be Duckworth.
4. AJPT to Malcolm Muggeridge, 17 July 1939.
5. The second edition, published in 1948, has a slightly different title: *The Habsburg Monarchy, 1809–1918*.
6. *The Habsburg Monarchy*, pp. vii–viii.

7. *Journal of Modern History*, 4 December 1942.
8. *American Historical Review*, 2 January 1943.
9. *Manchester Guardian*, 28 March 1941.
10. *The Historical Review*, date unknown.
11. 'Accident Prone', p. 21.
12. Review of *The Diplomacy of Imperialism, 1890–1902, International Affairs*, November 1936.
13. *A Personal History*, p. 124.
14. 'History and Biography', *Manchester Guardian*, 4 December 1936.
15. *A Personal History*, p. 161.
16. 'History and Politics', *Manchester Guardian*, 1 December 1939.
17. 'The Historian', *Manchester Guardian*, 5 August 1938.
18. Robert Kee: 'Fighting Off the Boche', *London Review of Books*, 11 October 1990.
19. AJPT to Malcolm Muggeridge, 1 May 1939.
20. *A Personal History*, p. 146.
21. 'Fighting Off the Boche', op. cit.
22. *Preston Herald*, 1 March 1940.
23. Stanley Parker: 'Drawn and Quoted', *Oxford Mail*, 17 June 1943.
24. *A Personal History*, p. 150.
25. ibid., p. 156.
26. ibid., p. 147.
27. Magdalen College: 'Summary of Events for October 1940–October 1943'.
28. *A Personal History*, p. 151.
29. See 'Journey to the Centre' by Paul Addison, in Alan Sked and Chris Cook (ed.): *Crisis and Controversy: Essays in Honour of A.J.P. Taylor* (Macmillan, 1976), esp. pp. 176–7.
30. 'The War of Words', a review of Michael Balfour: *Propaganda in War, Observer*, 28 October 1979.
31. *Oxford Times*, 27 September, 4 and 11 October.
32. House of Commons Debates, volume 365, 1143–1145. See 'Journey to the Centre', p. 176.
33. AJPT to Paul Addison, 21 April 1970; *A Personal History*, p. 153.
34. *A Personal History*, p. 154.
35. *The Course of German History*, p. 223.
36. *Manchester Guardian*, 3 September 1943.
37. 'Drawn and Quoted', op. cit.
38. AJPT to Trevor Blewitt, 4 September 1942.
39. 'A Europe of Beautiful Wishes', *Time and Tide*, 31 October 1942.
40. *Picture Post*, 1 April 1944.
41. 'A Europe of Beautiful Wishes', op. cit.
42. Autobiographical draft [HRC].
43. *A Personal History*, p. 160.

44. 'Alarm in High Places', a review of Ian McLaine: *Ministry of Morale, Observer*, 8 April 1979; reprinted in *Politicians, Socialism and Historians*, p. 222.
45. *A Personal History*, p. 159.
46. *Oxford Times*, 12 February 1943.
47. 'Drawn and Quoted', op. cit.
48. Gerald Berners: *Far From The Madding War* (Constable, 1941), p. 141.
49. *A Personal History*, p. 155.
50. *English History*, p. 516.
51. *A Personal History*, p. 158.
52. *Time and Tide*, 13 March 1943, 2 May 1942.
53. 'Czechoslovakia's 25 Years', *Manchester Guardian*, 27 October 1943.
54. *Manchester Guardian*, 29 April 1940.
55. *Time and Tide*, 13 March 1943. In 1950 AJPT wrote a piece to commemorate the anniversary of Masaryk's birth. 'The essential condition which Masaryk laid down, though perhaps now unattainable, remains true; only co-operation between Russia and the Anglo-Saxon Powers can give Europe peace and security.' 'Thomas Garrigue Masaryk', *Manchester Guardian*, 7 March 1950; reprinted in *Rumours of Wars*, p. 74.
56. *New Statesman and Nation*, 9 December 1944.
57. AJPT to Trevor Blewitt, 12 April 1945.
58. C.H. Rolph: *Kingsley: The Life, Letters and Diaries of Kingsley Martin* (Gollancz, 1973), p. 163.
59. 'Standard-Bearer of the Left', a review of *Editor*, by Kingsley Martin, *Observer*, 31 March 1967.
60. AJPT to Trevor Blewitt, 22 August 1944.
61. ibid., 11 October 1944.
62. Published in *The Listener* as 'What Shall we do With Germany?', 19 and 26 October, and 7 December 1944.
63. AJPT to A.P. Wadsworth, 5 October 1944.
64. ibid., 4 November 1944.
65. *New Statesman and Nation*: correspondence headed 'What Can we do With Germany?', 21 and 28 October, 4, 11 and 18 November 1944.
66. AJPT to Kingsley Martin, 18 November 1944.
67. Kingsley Martin to AJPT, 21 and 22 November 1944.
68. AJPT to Kingsley Martin, 25 November 1944.
69. 'German Unity', *Manchester Guardian*, 29 and 30 March 1944.
70. AJPT to Hamish Hamilton, 11 March 1944.
71. AJPT to Trevor Blewitt, 22 August 1944.
72. Hamish Hamilton to AJPT, 26 September 1944.
73. AJPT to Daniel Macmillan, 20 October 1944.
74. From the Preface to the New (1951) Edition, p. 7.

75. *The Course of German History*, pp. 13, 14, 223, 146. Page references here and elsewhere are to the 1951 edition, which incorporates a new preface and two extra paragraphs at the end of the book.
76. *Spectator*, 28 February 1941, and *Time and Tide*, 17 May 1941; reprinted in *Conflicts: Studies in Contemporary History* (Macmillan, 1942).
77. *Times Literary Supplement*, 29 September 1945.
78. Colley: *Namier*, p. 14.
79. *The Course of German History*, pp. 68, 116, 138, 165, 208; *American Historical Review*, 4 July 1947.
80. AJPT to Eva Haraszti, 4 December 1970.
81. ibid., 4 December 1970 and 4 June 1975.
82. AJPT to Mr King (an employee of Hamish Hamilton), 21 November, almost certainly 1945.
83. *A Personal History*, p. 164; 'Fighting Off the Boche', op. cit.
84. A.P. Wadsworth to AJPT, 15 April 1944.
85. AJPT to A.P. Wadsworth, 19 May 1944.
86. 'British Policy', *Manchester Guardian*, 4 June 1945.
87. AJPT to A.P. Wadsworth, 24 September 1944.
88. 'Drawn and Quoted', op. cit.
89. *A Personal History*, pp. 169–70.

Chapter 9: 'The ideal life for a man' (pp. 159–198)

1. *A Personal History*, p. 177.
2. ibid., p. 189.
3. AJPT to A.P. Wadsworth, 29 November and undated postcard, presumably December, 1945.
4. Preface to Daniela Mrazkova, and Vladimir Remes (ed.): *The Russian War 1941–1945* (Cape, 1978), p. 11; *A Personal History*, p. 181.
5. 'War of Nerves', a review of André Fontaine: *History of the Cold War, 1917–1950*, *Observer*, 17 November 1968.
6. AJPT to A.P. Wadsworth, 30 May 1945.
7. ibid., 9 September 1945; Wadsworth to AJPT, 13 September 1945.
8. *A Personal History*, p. 182.
9. 'A.J.P. Taylor and Me', *Sunday Telegraph*, 16 September 1990.
10. Dylan Thomas to Margaret Taylor, 5 August 1949; in Paul Ferris (ed.): *Collected Letters of Dylan Thomas* (Dent, 1985), pp. 715–16.
11. Caitlin Thomas and George Tremlett: *Caitlin: A Warring Absence* (Secker, 1986), p. 130.
12. ibid.
13. *Closing Times* (Oxford University Press, 1975), p. 134.
14. Constantine Fitzgibbon: *The Life of Dylan Thomas* (Dent, 1965), p. 298.

15. Dylan Thomas to Caitlin Thomas, 2 December 1946, *Collected Letters*, pp. 607–8.
16. *A Personal History*, p. 185.
17. ibid., p. 186.
18. AJPT to A.P. Wadsworth, 4 May 1947
19. Quoted in A.P. Wadsworth to AJPT, 13 May; AJPT to A.P. Wadsworth, 15 May 1947.
20. ibid., 4 July 1948.
21. 'Tito and Stalin: "The Revolt From Within" ', Third Programme, printed in *The Listener*, 20 January 1949; reprinted in *From Napoleon to Stalin*, p. 216.
22. AJPT to A.P. Wadsworth, 9 September 1945.
23. Controller (Talks) to Assistant Controller (Talks), 24 September 1945; AC(T) to C(T), 2 October 1945.
24. Memorandum by C(T), 30 October 1945.
25. AJPT to BBC Copyright Department, 15 March 1946.
26. Trevor Blewitt to AC(T), 9 May 1946.
27. AJPT to Trevor Blewitt, 27 September 1946.
28. 'The Need for Controversy', 'Britain's Relations with the United States', 'British Policy towards Russia' and 'Great Britain and Europe', Third Programme, printed in *The Listener*, 12, 19 and 26 December 1946, and 2 January 1947.
29. House of Commons Debates, volume 431, 1237–40, 1285. The MP was Henry Strauss, Member of Parliament for the Combined English Universities.
30. 'Difficulties of Modern Diplomacy', printed in *The Listener*, 9 January 1947. A letter published in *The Listener* on 30 January suggested that Ensor should apologise to Alan.
31. AJPT to Harman Grisewood, 4 and 22 January; Grisewood to AJPT, 9 January 1947.
32. AJPT to Trevor Blewitt, 28 January 1947.
33. 'Lord Salisbury', Third Programme, spring 1947 [exact date unknown]; reprinted in *From Napoleon to Stalin*, pp. 121, 120.
34. AJPT to Harman Grisewood, 10 May 1947.
35. AJPT to George Barnes, 10 May; Barnes to AJPT, 16 May; Barnes to Harman Grisewood, Grisewood to Barnes, 12 March 1947.
36. AJPT to Peter Laslett, 15 December 1947.
37. AJPT to Anna Kallin, 9 August 1949.
38. 'The Earnest Age', a review of *Ideas and Beliefs of the Victorians*, *New Statesman and Nation*, 16 April 1949.
39. Dylan Thomas to Margaret Taylor, 12 April, 20 May, 2 and 4 June 1947, *Collected Letters*, pp. 625, 630–1, 634.
40. This is what AJPT says in his autobiography. Against this is a letter Margaret wrote to Stuart Thomas, solicitor for Dylan's estate,

undated but soon after Dylan's death in 1953; and a letter written by AJPT himself to Professor Bill Read, again undated but probably in 1962 or 1963 – both of which assert that Margaret bought South Leigh. However, there are other inaccuracies in AJPT's letter, and it is easy to see why both Alan and Margaret might have then preferred not to reveal that it was Alan who bought South Leigh. It is impossible to be certain, but on balance I think it more likely that AJPT bought South Leigh in an attempt to remove the threat that Dylan presented to their marriage.

41. Paul Ferris: *Dylan Thomas* (Hodder, 1977), p. 216.
42. ibid., p. 21.
43. Dylan Thomas to John Davenport, 17 November 1948, *Collected Letters*, p. 692.
44. Undated letter from Dylan Thomas to Caitlin, *Collected Letters*, p. 678.
45. *Caitlin: A Warring Absence*, p. 99. It should be born in mind that this source was written many years after the events described.
46. ibid., p. 103.
47. *A Personal History*, pp. 188–9.
48. Mary Lutyens: *Edwin Lutyens* (Murray, 1980).
49. *A Personal History*, p. 164. I have been unable to discover where Alan might have read about the personal life of Sir Edwin Lutyens at the time of his first marriage. Conceivably he was told about it by Lutyens's daughter Elisabeth, who was a friend of Dylan Thomas and who, as a distinguished composer, shared an interest in music with Margaret. Mary Lutyens's biography of her father, Sir Edwin Lutyens, was published in 1980, three years before the publication of Alan's own autobiography.
50. AJPT to A.P. Wadsworth, 14 March 1948.
51. AJPT to Hamish Hamilton, 20 December 1945, 25 February 1948.
52. ibid., 3 November 1949, *A Personal History*, p. 172.
53. *History*, October 1950, pp. 273–4.
54. AJPT to Hamish Hamilton, 16 February 1949.
55. 'Mr Taylor's Masterpiece', a review of *The Origins of the Second World War*, *Observer*, 16 April 1961.
56. AJPT to Roger Machell, 1 September 1948.
57. ibid., 2 August 1949.
58. *Spectator*, 16 June 1950; *Manchester Guardian*, 18 July 1950.
59. AJPT to Hamish Hamilton, 30 July 1946, 20 December 1945.
60. 'Pre-War', a review of Ima Barlow: *The Agadir Crisis*, *Time and Tide*, 28 November 1942.
61. AJPT to Hamish Hamilton, 9 October 1946 and 13 December 1947.
62. Preface to the New Edition (1951) of *The Course of German History*, pp. 10–11.

63. 'The Secrets of Diplomacy', *Times Literary Supplement*, 12 April 1947.

64. 'The Springs of Soviet Diplomacy', *New Statesman and Nation*, 22 May 1948; reprinted in *From Napoleon to Stalin*, p. 167.

65. 'How the War Began', *Manchester Guardian*, 10 January 1948.

66. AJPT to Harman Grisewood, 21 October 1946.

67. 'History in England', *Times Literary Supplement*, 25 August 1950. In this anonymous survey, AJPT mentioned his own books on Germany and Austria-Hungary among those works by English historians – Brogan on France, Sumner on Russia, Barraclough on Germany, Hugh Seton-Watson on Eastern Europe – which had contributed something 'to the history of the country concerned which might have escaped a native historian'. This was 'to conceal his identity' (AJPT to Chris Wrigley, 10 October 1977). When the survey was reprinted in his collection *Rumours of Wars*, AJPT omitted his books from the list.

68. *Europe in Decay: A Study in Disintegration, 1936–1940* (Macmillan, 1950), p. 147–8; 'The Traditions of British Foreign Policy', a review of James Joll (ed.): *Britain and Europe: Pitt to Churchill, 1793–1940*, BBC Third Programme, 6 January 1951; reprinted in *Rumours of Wars*, p. 77.

69. 'An Exercise in Contemporary History', BBC Home Service Broadcast, 13 January 1948.

70. 'Appeasement: German Version', a review of *Documents on German Foreign Policy, 1918–45*, Series D, volume I, 1937–8, *New Statesman and Nation*, 17 December 1949.

71. *New Statesman and Nation*, 2 October 1948; reprinted in *From Napoleon to Stalin*, pp. 131–2, 133.

72. 'Les Derniers Jours de Hitler', *Critique*, 20 January 1948.

73. See, for example, *New Statesman and Nation*, 8 July 1950; 'Hitler at Sea', a review of Anthony Martienssen: *Hitler and his Admirals, New Statesman and Nation*, 3 November 1948.

74. 'The Twilight of the God', *Times Literary Supplement*, 6 August 1954; reprinted in *Englishmen and Others*, pp. 179–183.

75. Review of Herbert Butterfield: *History and Human Relations, New Statesman and Nation*, 24 November 1951.

76. 'The Failure of the Habsburg Monarchy', a review of Robert A. Kann: *The Multinational Empire, Times Literary Supplement*, 27 April 1951; reprinted in *Rumours of Wars*, p. 68.

77. 'German History', a review of S.H. Steinberg: *A Short History of Germany, Manchester Guardian*, 18 October 1944.

78. e.g. *International Affairs*, November–December 1938; *Oxford Magazine*, 25 November 1943.

79. 'Vagaries of British Diplomacy', *New Statesman and Nation*, 18 December 1948.
80. 'The Balance of Power', a review of Nicholas Mansergh: *The Coming of the First World War, New Statesman and Nation*, 16 July 1949.
81. 'Munich Once More', a review of *Documents on German Foreign Policy, 1918–45*, Series D, volume II, 1937–8, *New Statesman and Nation*, 15 April 1950.
82. AJPT to Noel Fieldhouse, 31 May 1972.
83. Review of Hugh Seton-Watson: *Eastern Europe between the Wars, 1918–1941, Oxford Magazine*, 15 November 1945.
84. John Wain, in Stephen Schofield (ed.): *In Search of C.S. Lewis* (Bridge Publishing, 1983), p. 183.
85. Quoted in an interview with Norman Bradshaw, *In Search of C.S. Lewis*, p. 22.
86. *English History*, p. 538.
87. 'Graham Greene at Eighty', an interview with Martin Amis, *Observer*, 23 September 1984.
88. 'Heroes of '48', a review of Arnold Whitridge Burnham: *Men in Crisis, New Statesman and Nation*, 4 November 1950.
89. Cited in Hugh Thomas: *Armed Truce: The Beginnings of the Cold War 1945–6* (Hamish Hamilton, 1986), pp. 319–20.
90. 'Problems of the Peace-makers', Home Service broadcast, printed in *The Listener*, 10 January 1946. See also 'The Way to Agreement', Home Service broadcast, printed in *The Listener*, 16 May 1946; and elsewhere.
91. AJPT to Trevor Blewitt, 11 October 1944.
92. 'Vagaries of British Diplomacy', op. cit.
93. AJPT to Trevor Blewitt, 14 February 1946.
94. 'British Affairs – Political Scene', Overseas Service broadcast, 25 November 1947.
95. 'Problems of the Peace-makers', op. cit.
96. AJPT to Peter Laslett, 22 February 1948.
97. AJPT to A.P. Wadsworth, 12 May 1948.
98. *Like It Was – A Selection from the Diaries of Malcolm Muggeridge* (Collins, 1981), p. 267.
99. 'Intellectuals at Wroclaw: A Strange Congress', *Manchester Guardian*, 2 September 1948; reprinted as 'The Wroclaw Congress of Intellectuals', in *From Napoleon to Stalin*, p. 222.
100. 'Hyenas and Other Reptiles', op. cit. *New Statesman and Nation*, 4 September 1948.
101. Elvira Powell, formerly Lainyi-Littnova, to AJPT, 12 June 1982.
102. 'Hyenas and Other Reptiles', op. cit.
103. *New York Times*, 26 and 28 August 1948.
104. *Daily Telegraph*, 27 August 1948; *Like It Was*, p. 295.

105. 'Hyenas and Other Reptiles', op. cit.
106. AJPT to Roger Machell, 8 April 1948.
107. 'Hyenas and Other Reptiles', op. cit.
108. Susan Crosland: *Tony Crosland* (Cape, 1982).
109. John Beavan to A.P. Wadsworth, undated March 1974.
110. AJPT to Kingsley Martin, 3 October 1948.
111. AJPT to Malcolm Muggeridge, 27 November 1948.
112. AJPT to A.P. Wadsworth, 18 and 26 January 1949; AJPT to John Betjeman, 19 January 1949.
113. Unpublished diary entry, 21 December 1949.
114. AJPT to Malcolm Muggeridge, 27 November 1948.
115. Entry for 20–21 December 1949, *Like It Was*, p. 366.
116. *Critique*, January 1949.
117. 'Tito and Stalin', op. cit.
118. Introduction to Reginald Reynolds (ed.): *British Pamphleteers, Volume Two: From the French Revolution to the Nineteen-Thirties* (Wingate, 1951), p. 14.
119. 'Rational Marxism', a review of E.H. Carr: *Studies in Revolution, Manchester Guardian*, 13 June 1950.
120. 'Anti-Bolshevik Primer', a review of Julian Steinberg: *Verdict of Three Decades, New Republic*, 16 October 1950.
121. AJPT to A.P. Wadsworth, 29 July 1950.
122. 'Can We Agree With the Russians?', op. cit.
123. *British Pamphleteers*, op. cit., p. 13.
124. 'Benjamin Constant: the Liberal Intellectual', Third Programme, 17 August 1949.
125. 'No Illusions: And No Ideas', a review of Hans J. Morgenthau: *In Defense of the National Interest, The Nation*, 8 September 1951.
126. *Unprincipled and Unjust Accusations against the Yugoslav Communist Party*, cited in 'Tito and Stalin', op. cit.
127. 'Tito and Stalin'. This broadcast, the script of which was printed in *The Listener*, provoked several letters of criticism to the magazine from Communist sympathisers, including one from E.J. Hobsbawm. *The Listener*, 20 and 27 January 1949.
128. 'The Man of Blood', *New Statesman and Nation*, 29 January 1949.
129. 'Books in General', *New Statesman and Nation*, 27 November 1949.
130. AJPT to Mary Adams, Head of Television Talks, 13 December 1949.
131. Grace Wyndham Goldie: *Facing the Nation* (Bodley Head, 1977), p. 70.
132. Memorandum by George Barnes, 25 September 1953.
133. George Gretton, BBC European Talks to Miss Alexander, Copyright Department, 26 July 1950. AJPT was not 'struck off', as he maintains in his autobiography (p. 182). The memorandum cited above stresses that 'Mr Tayor is a frequent contributor whom we wish to retain,

and this is the first time we have had to reject a script from him'. He gave a further six talks on the European Service in 1950, and 20 more the following year.

134. AJPT to BBC Copyright Department, 8 August 1950.
135. *Tony Crosland*, pp. 57–8.

Chapter 10: *In the News (pp. 199–252)*

1. AJPT to Anna Kallin, 27 July 1951.
2. Dylan Thomas to John Davenport, 12 April 1951, *Collected Letters*, p. 793.
3. Dylan Thomas to Ruth Witt-Diamant, 10 October 1951, *Collected Letters*, pp. 811–12.
4. Margaret Taylor to the Dylan Thomas Trustees, 1 December 1953.
5. Caitlin Thomas to Oscar Williams and Gene Derwood, 9 February 1953, *Collected Letters*, pp. 865–6.
6. AJPT to Kingsley Martin, 22 August 1951.
7. 'An Exercise in Contemporary History', op. cit.
8. AJPT to Kingsley Martin, 2 March 1951.
9. AJPT to Roger Machell, 21 September 1952.
10. AJPT to Kingsley Martin, 17 August 1952.
11. 'TV's No Menace – And No Fun!', *Daily Herald*, 17 January 1953.
12. AJPT to George Barnes, 13 May and 9 October 1952, 2 May 1953.
13. 'Harold Laski', a review of Kingsley Martin: *Harold Laski, New Statesman and Nation*, 17 January 1953.
14. Much of what follows is based on the obituary notice 'K.B. McFarlane, 1903–1966' by Karl Leyser in *Proceedings of the British Academy*, lxii (1976), pp. 485–506.
15. *Times* obituary by James Joll.
16. Review of M.L. Pearl: *A Bibliography of William Cobbett's Writings, New Statesman and Nation*, 29 August 1953. When this review was reprinted in *Essays in English History*, AJPT mentioned that he believed this to be the first use of the term 'The Establishment'. In fact he had used it himself two years earlier in *British Pamphleteers*, op. cit.
17. Edmund Wilson: *The Fifties* (Farrar, Straus & Giroux, 1986), p. 138.
18. AJPT to A.P. Wadsworth, October 1949.
19. AJPT to Christopher Rowland, Producer, Overseas Talks, 24 April 1956.
20. AJPT to A.P. Wadsworth, 14 January and 4 March 1952.
21. ibid., 26 January 1952.
22. 'A New Voice for Culture', *The Listener*, 8 October 1953.
23. 'John Bright and the Crimean War', reprinted in *Englishmen and Others*, p. 64.

24. AJPT to Anna Kallin, 5 February; AJPT to A.P. Wadsworth, 9 March and Wadsworth to AJPT, 15 March 1954.

25. A.P. Wadsworth to AJPT, 18 November 1953; undated reply from AJPT.

26. 'French History in Dispute', *Times Literary Supplement*, 26 March 1954.

27. 'The Europe of 1848: A Congress of Historians in Paris', *Manchester Guardian*, 17 April 1948; reprinted in *From Napoleon to Stalin*, p. 218.

28. *A Personal History*, pp. 200–201.

29. AJPT to Hamish Hamilton, 20 November 1949.

30. *A Personal History*, p. 188.

31. D.M. Davin to The Secretary [Norrington], 8 April and 12 November 1947; 2 June and 11 November 1948; AJPT to Davin, 16 October 1949.

32. D.M. Davin to AJPT, 14 November 1949; Davin to F.W. Deakin, 21 October 1949.

33. Arthur Norrington to D.M. Davin, 30 May; Davin to F.W. Deakin, 14 June 1950; Davin to Norrington, 21 June 1950.

34. D.M. Davin to A.L. Poole, 21 October 1953; Davin to The Secretary (C.H. Roberts), 15 December 1955.

35. D.M. Davin to The Secretary, 14 June 1957.

36. AJPT to Hamish Hamilton, 1 September 1954.

37. AJPT to G.W.S. Hopkins, 27 September 1954.

38. *The Struggle for Mastery in Europe*, p. xxin.

39. He had anticipated this view four years earlier in 'The Failure of the Habsburg Monarchy', op. cit.

40. *Struggle*, pp. xx, 568.

41. ibid., p. 518.

42. ibid., pp. xxvi, xxiiin, and elsewhere.

43. ibid., pp. 17, 34n, 357, 61, 283, 420.

44. W.E. Mosse, *English Historical Review*, lxx, p. 297.

45. *Struggle*, pp. 4, 573.

46. ibid., pp. 569–71.

47. 'Accident Prone', p. 13.

48. Llewellyn Woodward to C.H. Roberts, 30 October 1954.

49. AJPT to D.M. Davin, undated but stamped '6 November 1954'.

50. Llewellyn Woodward to C.H. Roberts, 9 November 1954.

51. AJPT to D.M. Davin, undated but stamped '17 November 1957'.

52. *The Troublemakers*, p. 127.

53. 'War to End War', Third Programme, 4 August 1954; published as 'Could the War of 1914–18 have been Averted?', *The Listener*, 12 August 1954; reprinted as 'The Outbreak of the First World War' in *Englishmen and Others*, pp. 119, 121, 123.

54. 'Karl Marx', a review of L. Schwarzchild: *The Red Prussian*, *Manchester Guardian*, 16 January 1948.

55. Blanche Knopf to AJPT, 1 June 1948.

56. 'Another Version of the Same', a review of Michael Foot: *The Pen and the Sword*, *New Statesman*, 30 November 1957.

57. *Bismarck*, p. 178; 'Bismarck's Morality', a review of Erich Eyck: *Bismarck and the German Empire*, *New Statesman and Nation*, 19 August 1950; reprinted in *Rumours of Wars*, p. 44.

58. *Bismarck*, p. 79. Compare this passage from 'Bismarck's Morality', cited above: 'Bismarck fought "necessary" wars and killed thousands; the idealists of the twentieth century fight "just" wars and kill millions.'

59. *Bismarck*, pp. 79, 178, 265, 227; *The Struggle for Mastery in Europe*, p. 143; 'Bismarck's Morality', op. cit.; 'Bismarck: The Man of German Destiny', *Manchester Guardian*, 30 July 1948; reprinted in *From Napoleon to Stalin*, p. 74.

60. *Bismarck*, pp. 260–1, 70, 139.

61. ibid., pp. 13, 55, 11–12, 21.

62. *Observer*, 3 July; *New Statesman and Nation*, 9 July 1955.

63. *A Personal History*, p. 191.

64. 'Hitler's Seizure of Power', in *The Third Reich* (Weidenfeld, 1955); reprinted in *Englishmen and Others*, pp. 139–153.

65. Asa Briggs: *The History of Broadcasting in the United Kingdom IV: Sound and Vision* (Oxford University Press, 1979), p. 223.

66. ibid., p. 913.

67. 'And I Said I Wouldn't Laugh at the BBC . . .', *Daily Herald*, 23 February 1955.

68. George Barnes to AJPT, 18 April 1956.

69. Leonard Miall to Cecil McGivern, 10 and 11 February 1958.

70. AJPT to A.P. Wadsworth, 28 July, Wadsworth to AJPT, 29 July 1955.

71. AJPT to A.P. Wadsworth, 22 November; Wadsworth to AJPT, 24 November 1954.

72. AJPT to Hugh Trevor-Roper, 3 July 1955.

73. 'The Rise and Fall of "Pure" Diplomatic History', *Times Literary Supplement*, 6 January 1956; reprinted in *Englishmen and Others*, pp. 81–7.

74. 'Taylor's Law Confirmed', a review of Georges Bonnin: *Bismarck and the Hohenzollern Candidate for the Spanish Throne*, *Observer*, 19 January 1958. Here, Taylor's Law appears in its earlier form: 'the Foreign Office does not know any secrets'. See also Namier's preface to *Diplomatic Prelude*, p.v: 'a great many profound secrets are somewhere in print'.

75. AJPT to Anna Kallin, 9 March 1955.

76. 'The Seventh Veil', *New Statesman*, 28 September 1957.
77. *The Troublemakers*, pp. 11–13.
78. ibid., pp. 9, 185, 189, 167.
79. ibid., pp. 22–3, 40.
80. Hamish Hamilton to AJPT, 9 April; AJPT to Hamilton, 11 April 1956.
81. *Englishmen and Others*, p. vii.
82. 'Progress has been the great casualty of our age.' 'Hope no More', a review of G.D.H. Cole: *The Second International, New Statesman and Nation*, 14 April 1956.
83. 'J.A. Hobson's Imperialism', *New Statesman and Nation*, 26 March 1955; reprinted as 'Economic Imperialism' in *Englishmen and Others*, p. 80.
84. AJPT to A.P. Wadsworth, 13 July 1956.
85. *A Personal History*, p. 211.
86. *Manchester Guardian*, 26 November 1943. In another letter responding to this one on 30 November Quintin Hogg describes Alan's remarks as 'extraordinarily misleading and ill-informed'.
87. *A Personal History*, p. 212.
88. *Kingsley*, pp. 322–3.
89. 'Accident Prone', p. 14.
90. AJPT to A.P. Wadsworth, 4 August 1956.
91. *Tribune*, 21 August 1956. Cited in Keith Kyle: *Suez* (Weidenfeld, 1991), p. 190.
92. *A Personal History*, p. 213.
93. 'The Traditions of British Foreign Policy', op. cit.
94. *Bismarck*, p. 187.
95. *The Troublemakers*, pp. 23, 24.
96. *Manchester Guardian*, 31 October 1956.
97. L.B. Namier to Harold Macmillan, 8 December 1932.
98. AJPT to D.M. Davin, 30 November 1956.
99. D.M. Davin to The President, St John's [Poole], 4 December; President to Davin, 5 December 1956.
100. D.M. Davin to The President, St John's, 6 March; Davin to The Provost, Oriel [Clark], 11 March; The Provost to Davin, 24 March; The Secretary [Roberts] to the Delegates, 26 April 1957.
101. AJPT to Hamish Hamilton, 28 November 1956.
102. AJPT to Malcolm Muggeridge, 7 October 1957.
103. *New Statesman and Nation*, 8 June; *Spectator*, 28 June; *Times Literary Supplement*, 21 June 1957.
104. AJPT to Roger Machell, 26 July, 17 June 1957.
105. 'Personal Impression', p. 226.
106. ibid., p. 227. The volume was probably *Europe in Decay*, which AJPT reviewed in the *Manchester Guardian* on 7 March 1950.

'However much we admire Mr Namier as a journalist and a contemporary historian, we cannot forget that these works distract him from the great work on the history of eighteenth-century England which he alone is qualified to write. So long as his Ford Lectures of fifteen years ago remain unpublished we shall regret his preoccupation with Stalin and Hitler and such small fry.'

107. AJPT to A.P. Wadsworth, 14 March 1948.
108. 'The Namier View of History', *Times Literary Supplement*, 28 August 1953.
109. AJPT to Sir Lewis Namier, 14 April 1954.
110. ibid., 13 February 1956.
111. C.N. Ward-Perkins to Sir Lewis Namier, 14 January; Namier to Ward-Perkins, 18 January 1957.
112. 'Personal Impression', p. 228.
113. AJPT to Sir Lewis Namier, 4 April, Namier to AJPT, 10 April 1957.
114. AJPT to Hugh Trevor-Roper, 3 July 1955.
115. AJPT to Hamish Hamilton, 28 September 1956, 29 January 1957.
116. *Observer*, 20 January; *Oxford Mail*, 29 January 1957.
117. Noel Annan: *Our Age: Portrait of a Generation* (Weidenfeld, 1990), p. 5. 'Our Age' is defined as those who went up to Oxford or Cambridge (or the London School of Economics) between 1919 and 1951.
118. Hugh Trevor-Roper to Sir Lewis Namier, 19 January; Namier to Trevor-Roper, undated 1957.
119. AJPT to Hamish Hamilton, 23 May 1957.
120. J.C. Masterman: *On the Chariot Wheel: An Autobiography* (Oxford University Press, 1975), pp. 295–6; Anne Whiteman: 'Lucy Stuart Sutherland, 1903–1980', *Proceedings of the British Academy*, lxix (1983), pp. 611–30.
121. *A Personal History*, p. 216.
122. AJPT to Hugh Trevor-Roper, 4 June 1957.
123. Sir Lewis Namier to Hugh Trevor-Roper, 6 June; Trevor-Roper to Namier, 8 June 1957.
124. *Observer*, 30 April; AJPT to Machell, 1 May 1961.
125. Richard Brain to AJPT, 18 July; AJPT to Brain, 21 July 1957.
126. AJPT to Sir George Clark, 11 June 1957.
127. *The Troublemakers*, pp. 14, 76, and 100.
128. AJPT to Hamish Hamilton, 6 August 1960.
129. 'A Corner in Rationality', a review of Hugh Trevor-Roper: *Historical Essays, New Statesman and Nation*, 19 October 1957; AJPT to Trevor-Roper, 18 October 1957. I have assumed that Trevor-Roper was able to see AJPT's review before the official publication date, as copies of the *New Statesman*, like those of other subscription magazines, were despatched a few days early.

Chapter 11: In the Presence of the Lord (pp. 253–302)

1. AJPT to Sir George Clark, 31 May and 11 June 1957.
2. *A Personal History*, p. 237.
3. Hugh Trevor-Roper to Janet Adam Smith, 30 July 1958.
4. Anne Chisolm and Michael Davie: *Beaverbrook: A Life* (Hutchinson, 1992), pp. 480–3.
5. 'Sound and Fury', a review of Tom Driberg: *Beaverbrook: A Study in Power and Frustration*, *Observer*, 26 February 1956.
6. Lord Beaverbrook to AJPT, 2 March 1955; AJPT to Beaverbrook, 5 March 1955.
7. 'Lord Beaverbrook as Historian', a review of *Men and Power, 1917–1918*, *Observer*, 28 October 1956.
8. 'Robin Badfellow', a review of A.J.P. Taylor: *Beaverbrook*, *Observer*, 25 June 1972.
9. AJPT to Beaverbrook, 20 May: 27 May, 2 July; Beaverbrook to AJPT, 21 May, 13 June 1957. In fact Beaverbrook first sent Alan *Men and Power*; then *Politicians and the War* afterwards when he realised his mistake. The lunch is marked in Beaverbrook's appointment diary as being on 28 June.
10. *A Personal History*, p. 112.
11. AJPT to Beaverbrook, 25 November 1960.
12. 'Robin Badfellow', op. cit.
13. Beaverbrook to AJPT, 30 November 1960.
14. *Beaverbrook*, p. 96.
15. See C.M. Vines: *A Little Nut-Brown Man* (Leslie Frewin, 1968), p. 210.
16. AJPT to Beaverbrook, 13 March 1961.
17. Michael Foot: 'The Case for Beelzebub' in *Debts of Honour*, p. 81.
18. 'The Case for Beelzebub', p. 79.
19. AJPT to Malcolm Muggeridge, 7 October 1957.
20. 'Why Must We Soft-Soap the Germans?' *Sunday Express*, 27 October; 'London Diary', *New Statesman*, 3 August; 'Angry Proponents of Unification,' *The Times*, 7 November 1957.
21. 'The Chief', a review of Reginald Pound and Geoffrey Harmsworth: *Northcliffe*, *New Statesman*, 27 June 1959.
22. *A Personal History*, p. 214; Beaverbrook to AJPT, 29 June and 2 July 1957.
23. '(Un) Quiet Flows the Don: Alan Taylor Starts a "Revolution" on TV', *TV Times*, 9 August 1957.
24. *New Statesman*, 5 July 1963.
25. Joan Bakewell, *Radio Times*, week ending 22 July 1977.
26. '(Un) Quiet Flows the Don', op. cit.
27. Memorandum to Lord Beaverbrook, 14 September 1961. These

memoranda were summaries of newspaper reports prepared by Beaverbrook's staff.

28. AJPT to Stuart Hood, Controller of Programmes (Television), 1 February 1962.
29. AJPT to Kenneth Adam, 30 January 1961.
30. 'The Seventh Veil', *New Statesman*, 28 September; AJPT to Kingsley Martin, 29 September 1957.
31. AJPT to Kingsley Martin, 13 September, no year given but probably 1957.
32. ibid., 14 January 1958.
33. Ann Fleming to Evelyn Waugh, 29 March 1958; in Mark Amory (ed): *Letters of Ann Fleming* (Collins Harvill, 1985), p. 216.
34. 'Kennedy or Nixon: Does it Matter to us in Britain?', *Sunday Express*, 26 June 1960.
35. *Oxford Mail*, 18 January 1958.
36. AJPT to Beaverbrook, 16 October; Beaverbrook to AJPT, 21 October 1958.
37. This and other material about Alan as a teacher is taken from 'Recollections of A.J.P. Taylor' by W.E.S. Thomas.
38. *Observer*, 30 April 1961.
39. 'Recollections', op. cit.
40. Quoted in the Preface to Louis' *Great Britain and Germany's Lost Colonies, 1914–1919* (Oxford University Press, 1967), p. xi.
41. Paul Addison, 'The Wizard of Ox', *London Review of Books*, 8 November 1990.
42. Norman Dombey and Eric Grove: 'Britain's Thermonuclear Bluff', *London Review of Books*, 22 October 1992.
43. *Daily Herald*, 14 November 1960.
44. Alan's argument is a précis of his two CND pamphlets, which overlap; *Oxford Mail*, 22 February 1958.
45. Chris Wrigley (ed.): *A.J.P. Taylor: A Complete Annotated Bibliography and Guide to his Historical and other Writings* (Harvester, Brighton, 1980), p. 34.
46. Presidential Address to the joint meeting of The Mount Old Scholars' Association and the Old York Scholars' Association, 6 June 1960, in *Leslie Howard Gilbert: An Appreciation* (privately published, 1988), p. 35.
47. 'The Rogue Elephant', a review of Robert Speaight: *The Life of Hilaire Belloc, Observer*, 27 January 1957; reprinted in *Politicians, Socialism and Historians*, p. 150.
48. *Guardian*, 17 January 1961.
49. AJPT to Beaverbrook, 25 March 1959.
50. AJPT to Captain (Basil) Liddell Hart, 21 June 1957.

51. *The Times*, 7 March 1958; 'London Diary', *New Statesman*, 3 August 1957.
52. 'London Diary', *New Statesman*, 15 November 1958; 'Is this £90 million being spent the right way?', *Sunday Express*, 7 October 1962.
53. AJPT to Beaverbrook, 2 August 1958.
54. Alfred Gollin to Chris Wrigley, 4 February 1977, quoted in *A.J.P. Taylor: A Complete Annotated Bibliography*, op. cit., pp. 49–50.
55. 'Here's to You, Men I Never Met', a review of four books about Ireland, *New Statesman*, 6 May 1966.
56. Stephen Koss: 'Asquith versus Lloyd George: The Last Phase and Beyond', in *Crisis and Controversy*, pp. 68–9.
57. 'Too Good to be True?', *New Statesman*, 30 April 1960.
58. *New Statesman*, 2 January 1960; 'The Second Munich', a review of Josef Korbel: *The Communist Subversion of Czechoslovakia, 1938–1948*, *New Statesman*, 20 February 1960.
59. *A Personal History*, pp. 213–4; interview with Duncan Fallowell in the *Irish Times*, 21 June 1983.
60. 'Namier the Historian', *Observer*, 28 August 1960.
61. AJPT to Kingsley Martin, 11 November 1960.
62. 'Who Burnt the Reichstag?', *History Today*, 8 August 1960; reprinted in *Politics in Wartime*, p. 179.
63. AJPT to Basil Liddell Hart, 19 and 27 June, 6 August 1957.
64. AJPT to Hamish Hamilton, 19 April, 13 May, 30 October and 9 December 1958.
65. *The Origins of the Second World War*, p. 141. Page references are to the Penguin edition (1964), which includes the Foreword 'Second Thoughts'.
66. 'Hitler's Secret', a review of *Documents on German Foreign Policy, 1918–45*, Series C, volume III, 1934–5, *New Statesman*, 14 November 1959.
67. AJPT to Basil Liddell Hart, 1 October; Liddell Hart to AJPT, 5 October 1959.
68. *Origins*, p. 40.
69. 'Campaign Report', *New Statesman*, 29 March 1958.
70. *Origins*, p. 36.
71. ibid., pp. 31, 40.
72. *Guardian*, 1 February 1961.
73. *Origins*, pp. 135–6.
74. ibid., pp. 282–3.
75. ibid., pp. 234, 335–6.
76. ibid., p. 97.
77. ibid., p. 100.
78. 'The Other Dictator', a review of Paolo Monelli: *Mussolini: An Intimate Life*, *Observer*, 23 August 1953.

79. *Origins*, pp. 304, 172, 314.
80. ibid., p. 235.
81. ibid., pp. 284, 285, 318.
82. AJPT to Hamish Hamilton, 6 August 1960.
83. AJPT to Roger Machell, 5 April 1961.
84. AJPT to Sir George Clark, 20 May 1961.
85. H.R. Trevor-Roper: 'A.J.P. Taylor, Hitler, and the War', *Encounter*, July 1961; A.J.P. Taylor: 'How to Quote: Exercises for Beginners', and Trevor-Roper: 'A Reply', *Encounter*, September 1961; reprinted in Wm. Roger Louis (ed.): *The Origins of the Second World War: A.J.P. Taylor and his Critics* (Wiley, New York and Toronto, 1972). Page references given below are to Louis.
86. *Reynolds News*, 4 June 1961.
87. *Oxford Mail*, 10 July 1961.
88. Beaverbrook to AJPT, 10 July; AJPT to Beaverbrook, 12 July 1961.
89. 'Preface for the American Reader', *Origins* (Atheneum, New York, 1962).
90. AJPT to Kingsley Martin, 19 January 1958.
91. Ved Mehta: *Fly and the Fly-Bottle: Encounters with British Intellectuals* (Weidenfeld, 1963), pp. 144–5; this book is based on articles which appeared in the *New Yorker* in 1961 and 1962. 'A.J.P. Taylor, Hitler, and the War', op. cit., p. 50.
92. *Hampstead and Highgate Express*, 22 June 1964.
93. AJPT to Martin Gilbert, 16 May 1961.
94. AJPT to Edward B. Segel, 21 November 1964; quoted in *The Origins of the Second World War: A.J.P. Taylor and his Critics*, pp. 26–7, 2; see also 'Preface for the American Reader'.
95. *Origins*, pp. 20–22, 23.
96. ibid., pp. 25–7.
97. 'A.J.P. Taylor, Hitler, and the War', op. cit., p. 57.
98. *Namier*, pp. 99–100.
99. *Fly and the Fly-Bottle*, pp. 180–81.
100. *Facing East* (Macmillan, 1947), p. 25; 'The Missing Generation', *Conflicts*, op. cit., p. 81; 'Prophet and Pedant', *New Statesman*, 25 June 1955. Cited in Colley: *Namier*, pp. 38, 30, 43.
101. 'No Good Germans after all?', a review of Fritz Fischer: *Germany's Aims in the First World War*, *Observer*, 3 December 1967.
102. Geoffrey Barraclough: 'Did Hitler Intend War in 1939?', a review of *Origins*, *Guardian*, 13 April 1961.
103. Esmonde M. Robertson (ed.): *The Origins of the Second World War* (Macmillan, 1971); Louis, op. cit.; Gordon Martel (ed.): *The Origins of the Second World War Reconsidered* (Allen & Unwin, 1986).
104. Donald Watt: 'The Historiography of Appeasement', in *Crisis and Controversy*, pp. 110. See also p. 126.

105. 'History', *Avenues of History* (Hamish Hamilton, 1952).
106. *Origins*, p. 64.
107. 'The Historiography of Appeasment', p. 112.
108. See David Marquand: 'The Taylor Doctrine', a review of *Origins*, *New Statesman*, 21 April 1961. Namier's likening of history to psychoanalysis appears in his essay 'History', op. cit.
109. *Our Age*, p. 190.

Chapter 12: 'What an opportunity!' (pp. 303–328)

1. AJPT to Sir George Clark, 11 October 1960, 20 May 1961.
2. D.M. Davin to Sir George Clark, 14 June 1961.
3. *Evening Standard*, 25 April 1961.
4. AJPT to Beaverbrook, 20 and 26 April; Beaverbrook to AJPT, 24 April 1961.
5. AJPT to Sir George Clark, 11 October 1960, 1 February 1961.
6. *Sunday Times*, 12 March 1961.
7. *Daily Mail*, 15 July 1961.
8. Basil Liddell Hart to AJPT, 28 February and 20 March; AJPT to Liddell Hart, 2 and 27 March 1961.
9. AJPT to David Higham, 24 April 1961 and 23 March 1963; AJPT to Roger Machell, 8 September 1962 and 24 January 1963; AJPT to Hamish Hamilton, 6 February 1963.
10. AJPT to Basil Liddell Hart, 13 and 27 February, 16 and 29 May; Liddell Hart to AJPT, 2 March and 25 May 1962.
11. Robert Kee: 'History's Camera', *Observer*, 10 November 1963.
12. *The First World War: An Illustrated History*, pp. 38, 160, 13.
13. ibid., p. 277.
14. ibid., p. 16.
15. 'War by Time-Table: European Crisis July-August 1914', *History of the Twentieth Century* (Purnell, 1968–70), volume 1, pp. 443–8.
16. *The First World War*, pp. 17, 20. AJPT had anticipated this argument in an *Observer* series, 'How a World War Began', 16, 23 and 30 November 1958, which was reprinted in *Politics in Wartime*, p. 65–92.
17. 'Campaign Report' by AJPT, *New Statesman*, 21 June 1958.
18. In 'Backwards to Utopia', a *New Statesman* review of the 1950s (2 January 1960), AJPT identified this as the strongest popular argument against unilateral nuclear disarmament.
19. AJPT to Michael Howard, 17 January 1975.
20. 'Poor Old Muse', a review of E.H. Dance: *History the Betrayer*, *New Statesman*, 24 September 1960.
21. *New Statesman*, 5 December 1959; 'Moving with the Times', a review

of *What is History?*, *Observer*, 22 October 1961, reprinted in
Politicians, Socialism and Historians, pp. 53–5.

22. 'Requiescat in Pace', a review of J.H. Plumb: *The Death of the Past*, *Observer*, 28 December 1969.
23. AJPT to Beaverbrook, 26 January 1961.
24. 'Whatever Happened to the Whigs?', a review of Donald Southgate: *The Passing of the Whigs, 1832–1886*, *Observer*, 12 July 1962.
25. Beaverbrook to Harold Macmillan, 7 March 1962; quoted in *Beaverbrook*, p. 648.
26. Beaverbrook to AJPT, 9 December 1961; 'Why Do We Stir up Trouble in the Family?', *Sunday Express*, 3 December 1961.
27. *Sunday Express*, 19 January 1964.
28. AJPT to Beaverbrook, 20 May, Beaverbrook to AJPT, 22 May 1957; *Beaverbrook*, p. 630; *The First World War*, p. 181.
29. 'How to Seize Power', a review of Lord Beaverbrook: *Politicians and the War, 1914–1916*, *Observer*, 21 August 1960.
30. *Beaverbrook*, pp. 629–30. It must have been this review which Beaverbrook read in Michael Foot's presence and which, according to Foot, changed the whole course of Beaverbrook's life, by encouraging Beaverbrook to consider himself a serious historian. Foot refers to a comparison with Tacitus. Both AJPT's biography and the more recent one by Chisolm and Davie assume that he was reacting to AJPT's earlier review of *Men and Power*; but the latter contains no mention of Tacitus – nor is it flattering enough to produce the reaction described. The misattribution is also in AJPT's autobiography (p. 221): 'My praise was quite uncalculated. It did not occur to me that I should ever set eyes on Beaverbrook.'
31. *Beaverbrook: A Life*, p. 360.
32. Beaverbrook to AJPT, 1 and 7 June 1962, 17 March 1963; AJPT to Beaverbrook, 5 and 12 June 1962; 'Big Beast at Bay', a review of Lord Beaverbrook: *The Decline and Fall of Lloyd George*, *New Statesman*, 8 March 1963.
33. AJPT to Beaverbrook, 9 December 1961. In his Oxford history, Alan described Empire Free Trade as 'never much of a cause'; *English History*, pp. 282–3.
34. *Beaverbrook: A Life*, p. 511.
35. Paul Einzig to Martin Gilbert, 24 April and 9 May 1962.
36. AJPT to Martin Gilbert, 8 and 13 March, 28 May, 7 December 1962.
37. AJPT to Sir George Clark, 25 August 1962.
38. 'The nineteenth century was the best time for historians. In those days a historian was a man who wrote works of history . . . No nonsense about the historian teaching young students – that was done by hacks who were not qualified to do anything else.' 'Diary', *London Review*

of Books, 18 May–2 June 1983; reprinted in *An Old Man's Diary*, p. 129.

39. AJPT to Alastair Hetherington, 12 October 1962.
40. Paddy Monkhouse to AJPT, 26 November 1962.
41. Noel Annan to AJPT, 26 November 1965.
42. *A Personal History*, p. 217.
43. AJPT to Sir George Clark, 6 and 28 November, 7 December 1962.
44. *Daily Telegraph*, 8 December 1962.
45. *Oxford Mail*, 31 May 1963.
46. 'On Satan's Side', *New Statesman*, 31 May 1963.
47. 'My Farewell to Oxford', *Daily Express*, 31 May 1963.
48. 'Literature in a Vacuum', a review of J.I.M. Stewart: *Eight Modern Writers, Observer*, 28 July 1963.
49. Introduction to *Ten Days that Shook the World* (Penguin, Harmondsworth, 1977), p.vii; and manuscript draft [HRC].
50. AJPT to Beaverbrook, 1 and 5 June 1962.
51. ibid., 21 December 1962, 22 and 26 March 1963, 7 April 1963; AJPT to A. G. Millar, 10 April 1963.
52. AJPT to Beaverbrook, 25 April, 24 May 1963.
53. 'The Man Who Likes to Stir Things Up', *Sunday Express*, 21 October 1963; AJPT to Beaverbrook, 21 October 1963.
54. Beaverbrook to AJPT, 11 December 1963; AJPT to Beaverbrook, 27 December 1963, 28 March 1964.
55. Eve Crosland to Beaverbrook, 26 May 1961, 25 June 1962, 14 and 28 March 1963, 26 May 1964.
56. 'The Man Who Deals in Sunshine', *Sunday Express*, 24 May 1964.
57. AJPT to David Higham, 11 June 1964.
58. AJPT to Lady Beaverbrook, 24 June (two letters), 29 June and 22 July; Sir Max Aitken to Lady Beaverbrook, 26 June; Lady Beaverbrook to AJPT, 25 June 1964.
59. AJPT to Lady Beaverbrook, 18 September 1964.

Chapter 13: *Little England (pp. 329–373)*

1. AJPT to Sir George Clark, 18 July 1964.
2. Hugh Cudlipp: 'The Rage', in Logan Gourlay (ed.): *The Beaverbrook I Knew* (Quartet, 1984), p. 16; *Beaverbrook*, p. 674; *Beaverbrook: A Life*, p. 549.
3. AJPT to Basil Liddell Hart, 8 February; AJPT to Sir George Clark, 31 December, 8 February 1964.
4. AJPT to Sir George Clark, 12 June 1964.
5. *English History*, p. 600. 'The Second World War, socially speaking, was the best thing that ever happened to this country and THEY (the upper classes) are only just recovering from it.' 'Greatness and After',

a review of E.J. Hobsbawm: *Industry and Empire, Observer*, 5 May 1968.

6. *English History*, pp. 181, 368, 372.
7. ibid., p. 2n, 286n.
8. 'Langham Diary', *The Listener*, 29 October 1981.
9. *English History*, p. 4n, 483, 488.
10. ibid., pp. 440, 319, 293, 325, 319, 414.
11. ibid., pp. 517–20, 571n.
12. ibid., p. 317.
13. 'Acton Eclipsed', a review of Jacob Burckhardt: *Judgements on History and Historians, Observer*, 21 June 1959.
14. *English History*, pp. 170, 305–6.
15. ibid., p. 166, 62n.
16. ibid., pp. 156n, 233; C.H. Roberts to D.M. Davin, 2 April 1965.
17. Maurice Shock: 'England in Our Time', *Oxford Mail*, 21 October 1965.
18. 'England in Transition', *Government and Opposition*, volume I, no. 3 (1965), p. 413.
19. *English History*, p. 264.
20. AJPT to Sir George Clark, 6 October 1964 and 18 April 1965.
21. AJPT to C.H. Roberts, 26 September; Roberts to AJPT, 27 September 1965.
22. 'England from Asquith to Attlee', *Observer*, 24 October; 'Historian of the People', *New York Review of Books*, 9 December 1965; *American Historical Review*, July 1966; 'England in Transition', op. cit.; 'History Taylor-made', *Times Literary Supplement*, 16 December 1965; *English Historical Review*, October 1967.
23. AJPT to Noel Annan, undated November 1965 – the *New York Review of Books* sent Alan a proof of the review before publication; AJPT to the reviewer (via Arthur Crook), 18 December 1965.
24. Evelyn Waugh to AJPT, 28 October 1965.
25. Henry Pelling, *New Statesman* competition, 17 December 1965.
26. 'Some Like it Hot', a review of *The Last Battle, Observer*, 8 May 1966.
27. Some of what follows is inspired by Paul Addison's 'The Wizard of Ox' (op. cit.), a tribute to AJPT written on his death.
28. 'The Tools and the Job', *Times Literary Supplement*, 7 April 1966.
29. 'A Sceptic at Large', a review of Raymond Aron: *The Opium of the Intellectuals, New Statesman*, 31 August 1957.
30. 'Europe on Top of the World', a review of Charles Morazé: *The Triumph of the Middle Classes, Observer*, 2 October 1966.
31. AJPT to Sir George Clark, 19 December 1967.
32. AJPT to D.M. Davin, 24 July 1972.
33. AJPT to Robin Denniston, 22 July 1979.

34. 'Spanish Quadrille', a review of Raymond Carr: *Spain, 1808–1939, Observer*, 3 July 1966;

35. AJPT to David Higham, 23 September 1967 and undated (probably late July/early August) 1964.

36. ibid., 23 March 1963, 26 November 1968, 13 and 31 March 1970.

37. *Times Literary Supplement*, 15 December 1966.

38. AJPT to Keith Robbins, 21 April 1969.

39. AJPT to Roger Eatwell, 3 August 1972.

40. AJPT to Roger Machell, 15 November 1966; 'Received with Thanks', *Observer*, 20 November 1966; Paul Einzig to Martin Gilbert, 21 November 1966.

41. AJPT to Sir Isaiah Berlin, 10 May 1967.

42. David Higham to AJPT, 22 March 1967.

43. AJPT to Hamish Hamilton, 8 March 1956.

44. AJPT to David Higham, 23 March 1967.

45. AJPT to Sir Isaiah Berlin, 24 March, 10 May 1967.

46. AJPT to Margaret Lampard, 1 December 1969.

47. AJPT to W.E.S. Thomas, 6 October 1967.

48. 'A Little Knowledge . . .', a review of David Rees: *The Age of Containment: the Cold War; Observer*, 26 February 1967; Introduction to *The Communist Manifesto* (Penguin, Harmondsworth, 1967), p. 27; 'Flat Earth Man', a review of Isaac Deutscher: *Ironies of History: Essays on Contemporary Communism, Observer*, 4 December 1966; 'Lenin: October and After', *History of the Twentieth Century*, volume 3, p. 1030.

49. AJPT to Cameron Hazlehurst, 27 June, Hazlehurst to AJPT, 3 July 1972.

50. 'This Nonsense of Making Us All Go Slow', *Sunday Express*, 27 August; Basil Liddell Hart to AJPT, 31 August; AJPT to Liddell Hart, 1 September 1967.

51. AJPT to Karin Wood, 16 December 1968.

52. ibid., 21 December 1967.

53. John Betjeman to AJPT, 13 September 1968.

54. *English History*, p. 192; 'Lloyd George's Hour', *Observer*, 20 September 1964.

55. AJPT to Paul Addison, 12 August 1966.

56. *Daily Mail*, 25 September 1968.

57. AJPT to Karin Wood, 16 December 1968.

58. Cameron Hazlehurst to AJPT, 21 August; AJPT to Hazlehurst, 27 August 1968.

59. *Times*, 21 May 1971.

60. Miss E. Blackburn to AJPT, 21 April 1969.

61. AJPT to Eva Haraszti, 24 November 1969.

62. ibid., 2 November 1970.

63. 'The Wizard of Ox', op. cit.
64. AJPT to Kenneth O. Morgan, 12 January 1981.
65. AJPT to Stephen Koss, 15 January 1973. The review was in *Political Science Quarterly*, volume 87 (1972), pp. 678–80.
66. Stephen Koss to AJPT, 13 March; AJPT to Koss, 23 March 1971.
67. *Churchill: Four Faces and the Man* (Allen Lane, 1968). The other contributors were Robert Rhodes James, J. H. Plumb, Basil Liddell Hart and Anthony Storr.
68. AJPT to Dial Press, 22 April 1969.
69. AJPT to Robert Rhodes James, 27 February 1972.
70. 'The Historian as a Biographer', *Wiener Beitrage*, 1980; Anthony Storr to the author, 24 August 1991.
71. AJPT to Eva Haraszti, 3 March 1970.
72. *Guardian*, 24 February and 3 March; AJPT to Alastair Hetherington, 27 February 1970.
73. AJPT to Roger Machell, 22 December 1970.
74. ibid., 30 December 1970, 11 January 1971; Machell to AJPT, 23 December 1970; Hamish Hamilton to Macmillan, 1 January; Tim Farmiloe to Hamilton, 5 January 1971.
75. C.M. Woodhouse to Roger Louis, 4 February 1973.
76. AJPT to Roger Machell, 19 April 1972.
77. *Beaverbrook*, p. 46; *A Personal History*, p. 112.
78. *Beaverbrook*, p. 155; 'Crosstalk', *Listener*, 1 February 1973.
79. *Beaverbrook*, p. xv.
80. ibid., p. 448–9.
81. ibid., p. 24.
82. AJPT to Paul Addison, 15 October 1967; *Beaverbrook*, p. 408.
83. AJPT to Tom Driberg, 18 May 1971.
84. *Beaverbrook*, pp. 141–2.
85. 'Crosstalk', op. cit.
86. *Beaverbrook*, p. x.
87. Cameron Hazlehurst in *The Times*, 26 June 1972; *The Economist*, 1 July 1972; 'The Great Fixer', *Times Literary Supplement*, 30 June 1972; *History*, October 1973; Robert Blake in the *Sunday Times*, Richard Crossman in the *Sunday Telegraph* and Malcolm Muggeridge: 'Robin Badfellow', op. cit.
88. AJPT to Sir Charles Snow, 10 May 1971; AJPT to Tom Driberg, 18 May 1971.
89. *Beaverbrook*, pp. xiii, 381.
90. AJPT to Captain Stephen Roskill, 4 August 1972.
91. *Beaverbrook*, pp. 387–88.
92. 'Accident Prone', p. 18.
93. AJPT to Eva Haraszti, 9 October 1970, 28 May 1972, 28 April 1974, 21 February 1976.

94. AJPT to Roger Machell, 21 October 1974.
95. 'Accident Prone', p. 19.
96. AJPT to Eva Haraszti, 14 October 1972, 4 December 1970.
97. ibid., 4 August 1973, 28 April 1974.
98. 'Political Grandmaster', a review of Peter Marsh: *The Discipline of Popular Government: Lord Salisbury's Domestic Statecraft*, *Observer*, 24 December 1978.
99. AJPT to Eva Haraszti, 28 December 1971.
100. Addressee unknown, 12 December 1972 [HRC].
101. AJPT to Eva Haraszti, 24 November 1972.
102. *The Second World War – The Creighton Lecture in History, 1973* (Athlone Press, 1974), p. 11.
103. *The Second World War: An Illustrated History*, pp. 11, 30.
104. ibid., pp. 23, 30, 98.
105. ibid., pp. 172, 79, 130, 179.
106. ibid., pp. 186, 219, 223.
107. ibid., p. 21.
108. 'World War II in Perspective', *Observer*, 13 April 1975; *Listener*, 24 April 1975.
109. 'Crimes Beyond Punishment', a review of Eugene Davidson: *The Trial of the Germans, New York Review of Books*, 23 February 1967; *The Second World War*, p. 233.
110. 'On the Wings of a Dove', a review of Lord James Douglas-Hamilton: *Motive for a Mission, Observer*, 28 March 1971; 'Must This Man Stay in Prison for Ever?', 'The Strange Silence of the "Freedom" Brigade', 'Why Can't Wilson Speak out for this Lonely Man?', 'This Lonely Prisoner Shames the World', 'The Old Man who will again Spend Christmas Alone', *Sunday Express*, 23 December 1962, 22 October 1967, 27 April 1969, 7 April 1974, and 18 December 1977; *Times*, 17 September 1985; 'Hess as Film Prop', *Observer*, 12 May 1974.
111. *English History*, pp. 285–6.
112. *Beaverbrook*, p. 551.
113. 'The Leader who Got Lost', a review of Sir Oswald Mosley: *My Life*, *Observer*, 20 October 1968.
114. AJPT to Eva Haraszti, 2 November 1970.
115. 'Mosley's Mis-spent Talents', a review of Robert Skidelsky: *Oswald Mosley, Observer*, 6 April 1975; AJPT to Eva Haraszti, 22 April and 6 May 1975.
116. 'The Eternal Scapegoats', a review of Gisela C. Lebzelter: *Political Anti-Semitism in England, 1918–1939, Observer*, 11 March 1979; R. Stanton to AJPT, 11 March 1979 [HoL].
117. 'Thoughts in Solitude', 27 July 1981, *Letters to Eva*, p. 435.
118. AJPT to Eva Haraszti, 4 March 1972.

119. ibid., 11 November 1972.
120. ibid., 17 February 1974.
121. ibid., 2 February 1974.
122. ibid., 20 January 1973.
123. *The Times*, 22 February 1972.
124. AJPT to Eva Haraszti, 16 March 1973.
125. ibid., 28 November and 2 December 1973.
126. AJPT to Roger Ainscough, 16 April 1974 [HRC].
127. AJPT to Eva Haraszti, 12 May and 12 July 1974, 28 November 1973.
128. AJPT to Professor Noel Fieldhouse, 4 September 1974.
129. AJPT to Eva Haraszti, 31 August 1974.
130. ibid., 7 August 1974.
131. ibid., 31 August 1974.
132. ibid., 13 December, 25 May 1974.
133. ibid., 12 July, 28 October 1974.
134. ibid., 22 June 1974.
135. ibid., 17 January 1975 and 12 July 1974.
136. ibid., 5 October 1974.
137. ibid., 4 August 1973.
138. Interview with Matthew Levin, *Express and News*, 19 December 1975.
139. AJPT to Eva Haraszti, 9 June 1974, 20 February 1972.
140. AJPT to Bill Rodgers, 18 June 1974.
141. AJPT to Karin Wood, 5 December 1974.
142. AJPT to Christopher Seton-Watson, 31 January 1975.
143. AJPT to Eva Haraszti, 3 and 8 November 1974.
144. ibid., 30 March 1975.
145. ibid., 8 April 1975.
146. ibid., 6 May 1975.
147. ibid., 24 May 1975.
148. ibid., 20 January 1976.
149. ibid., 17 October 1975.

Chapter 14: His Last Bow (pp. 374–406)

1. AJPT to Eva Haraszti, 6 May 1975.
2. ibid., 16 June 1975.
3. AJPT to Ivan Sutton, 21 July; *Evening Standard*, 26 August 1975.
4. AJPT to Eva Haraszti, 11 November 1975.
5. *A Personal History*, p. 263.
6. AJPT to Eva Haraszti, 1 August 1975.
7. 'Accident Prone', p. 20.
8. Manuscript note [HRC].

9. William H. McNeill to the author, 19 November 1991.
10. AJPT to Malcolm Muggeridge, 8 April 1976.
11. 'Protestant Expulsion from Ulster by Irish Nationalists Would be the Best Solution', *The Times*, 12 April; 'Mr Taylor's Garden Path' and 'Bloodshed of the Innocents', *Guardian*, 13 and 14 April 1976.
12. AJPT to Eva Haraszti, 9 and 21 July 1976.
13. *Evening Standard*, 24 November 1976; *Daily Mail*, 12 April 1976.
14. 'Funeral in Berlin', a review of Lev Bezymenski: *The Death of Adolf Hitler, Observer*, 29 September 1968.
15. 'The Road to War', a review of John Rohl (ed.): *1914: Delusion or Design?, Observer*, 29 July 1973.
16. Hugh Trevor-Roper to AJPT, 28 October; AJPT to Trevor-Roper, 1 November 1976 [HRC].
17. AJPT to John Gross, 30 March 1976 [HRC].
18. 'Langham Diary', *Listener*, 27 November 1980; reprinted in *An Old Man's Diary*, p. 5.
19. AJPT to Karin Wood, 30 November 1977.
20. Geoffrey Wheatcroft in *The Spectator*, 26 November 1977; *The Economist*, 30 June 1979; Denys Blakeway in the *New Statesman*, 28 September 1979; Jonathan Sumption in the *Sunday Telegraph*, 1 July 1979.
21. Christopher Dowling to Bruce Hunter, 21 August and 21 September 1978.
22. AJPT to Eva Haraszti, 14 January 1977, 17 December 1976.
23. ibid., 4 February 1977.
24. ibid., 31 March and 2 April 1977.
25. ibid., 17 September 1977.
26. ibid., 30 December 1977.
27. 'It's that Man Again', a review of Robert G.L. Waite: *The Psychopathic God, Observer*, 17 July 1977.
28. 'The Fuhrer as Mohican', a review of David Irving: *Hitler's War, Observer*, 12 June 1977; 'Hitler the Opportunist', a review of David Irving: *The War Path: Hitler's Germany, Observer*, 18 June 1978.
29. *Times Literary Supplement*, 30 January 1977.
30. *Journal of Modern History*, 4 December 1975.
31. Lord Bradwell to AJPT, 13 February 1976 [HRC].
32. Harold Wilson to Anthony Crosland, 4 September 1975 [LSE].
33. *Daily Express*, 28 September 1977.
34. 'Bottom of the Class', a review of Sir Harold Wilson: *A Prime Minister on Prime Ministers, Observer*, 6 November 1977.
35. AJPT to Eva Taylor, 18 November and 12 December 1977.
36. Entry for 22 February 1981, *A Life with Alan*, p. 145.
37. AJPT to Bruce Hunter, David Higham Ltd., 8 July 1983.
38. AJPT to Eva Taylor, 20 January 1978.

39. *A.J.P. Taylor: A Complete Annotated Bibliography and Guide to his Historical and Other Writings*, op. cit.
40. AJPT to Eva Haraszti, 24 November 1979.
41. Much of what follows is derived from an autobiographical manuscript which Sir Kenneth Dover was kind enough to show me. I am grateful too to Professor Ian R. Christie for showing me his file on the 'Blunt affair'.
42. *The Times*, 24 and 26 June 1980.
43. *Sunday Express*, 29 June 1980.
44. *Daily Telegraph*, 4 July 1980.
45. AJPT to Chris Wrigley, 11 July 1980.
46. AJPT to Sir Kenneth Dover, 19 August 1980.
47. Ian R. Christie: 'A Confusion of Fellows' and Kenneth Dover: 'The Blunt Affair Again', *Encounter*, October and November 1980; Norman Gash: 'Blunt and the British Academy', *Policy Review*, Winter 1981; George Steiner: 'The Cleric of Treason', *New Yorker*, 8 December 1980.
48 'Did He Jump or Was He Pushed?', *Guardian*, 21 August 1980.
49 AJPT to Eva Haraszti, 21 July 1980.
50. 'Thoughts in Solitude', 26 and 30 July 1981, *Letters to Eva*, pp. 435, 437.
51. Entry for 26 February 1982, *A Life with Alan*, p. 173.
52. ibid., entry for 8 September 1980, p. 121.
53. AJPT to Eva Haraszti, 10 February 1978, 'Thoughts in Solitude', 31 July 1981, *Letters to Eva*, pp. 383, 438–9.
54. 'Diary', *London Review of Books*, 17–31 March 1983, reprinted in *An Old Man's Diary*, p. 119; Bruce Kent to AJPT, 7 April 1983 [HoL].
55. AJPT to Roger Machell, 29 June 1982.
56. Roger Machell to Eve Crosland, 31 August; Crosland to Machell, 4 September 1982.
57. Preface to *A Personal History*, pp. ix–x.
58. *A Personal History*, p. 57. (both)
59. AJPT to Eva Haraszti, 16 March 1974.
60. *A Personal History*, p. 260.
61. 'Langham Diary', *Listener*, 5 February 1981, reprinted in *An Old Man's Diary*, p. 15.
62. *A Personal History*, pp. 58, 59, 70, 90, 113.
63. ibid., pp. 63, 84, 122, 217 (excised from the final manuscript), 242.
64. John Gross: 'Media Star and Major Historian', *New York Times Book Review*, 25 September 1983.
65. 'Odd Historian Out', *Daily Telegraph*, 26 May; Byron Rogers: 'Histories Make Men Wise?', *The Times*, 2 June 1983.
66. *A Personal History*, p. 137, 140, 178.

67. AJPT to Roger Machell, 6 August 1982.
68. AJPT to Eva Haraszti, 6 January 1973.
69. Entry for 20 April 1978, *A Life with Alan*, p. 2.
70. The Vice-President to Christopher Cook, 8 February 1984.
71. 'Diary', *London Review of Books*, 18–31 August 1983, reprinted in *An Old Man's Diary*, pp. 143–4.
72. AJPT to Karl Miller, 14 October 1985.
73. Entries for 4 October, 18 December 1985, *A Life with Alan*, p. 231, 239.
74. *Warfare, Diplomacy and Politics: Essays in Honour of A.J.P. Taylor* (Hamish Hamilton, 1986).
75. AJPT to Muggeridge, 11 October 1981.
76. 'St Mugg of Manchester', *Guardian*, 15 November 1990.

Index

NOTE: Ranks and titles are generally the highest mentioned in the text